Social History, Popular Cu
Geoff Eley, Series Editor

Growing Up Female in Nazi Germany, Dagmar Reese
Justice Imperiled: The Anti-Nazi Lawyer Max Hirschberg in Weimar Germany,
    Douglas G. Morris
The Heimat Abroad: The Boundaries of Germanness, edited by Krista O'Donnell,
    Renate Bridenthal, and Nancy Reagin
*Modern German Art for Thirties Paris, Prague, and London: Resistance and
    Acquiescence in a Democratic Public Sphere,* Keith Holz
*The War against Catholicism: Liberalism and the Anti-Catholic Imagination in
    Nineteenth-Century Germany,* Michael B. Gross
German Pop Culture: How "American" Is It? edited by Agnes C. Mueller
Character Is Destiny: The Autobiography of Alice Salomon, edited by Andrew
    Lees
*Other Germans: Black Germans and the Politics of Race, Gender, and Memory in
    the Third Reich,* Tina M. Campt
*State of Virginity: Gender, Religion, and Politics in an Early Modern Catholic
    State,* Ulrike Strasser
Worldly Provincialism: German Anthropology in the Age of Empire,
    H. Glenn Penny and Matti Bunzl, editors
Ethnic Drag: Performing Race, Nation, Sexuality in West Germany, Katrin Sieg
Projecting History: German Nonfiction Cinema, 1967–2000, Nora M. Alter
Cities, Sin, and Social Reform in Imperial Germany, Andrew Lees
The Challenge of Modernity: German Social and Cultural Studies, 1890–1960,
    Adelheid von Saldern
Exclusionary Violence: Antisemitic Riots in Modern German History,
    Christhard Hoffman, Werner Bergmann, and Helmut Walser Smith, editors
Languages of Labor and Gender: Female Factory Work in Germany, 1850–1914,
    Kathleen Canning
That Was the Wild East: Film Culture, Unification and the "New" Germany,
    Leonie Naughton
Anna Seghers: The Mythic Dimension, Helen Fehervary
*Staging Philanthropy: Patriotic Women and the National Imagination in Dynastic
    Germany, 1813–1916,* Jean H. Quataert
Truth to Tell: German Women's Autobiographies and Turn-of-the-Century Culture,
    Katharina Gerstenberger
The "Goldhagen Effect": History, Memory, Nazism—Facing the German Past,
    Geoff Eley, editor
Shifting Memories: The Nazi Past in the New Germany, Klaus Neumann
Saxony in German History: Culture, Society, and Politics, 1830–1933,
    James Retallack, editor
*Little Tools of Knowledge: Historical Essays on Academic and Bureaucratic
    Practices,* Peter Becker and William Clark, editors

Social History, Popular Culture, and Politics in Germany
Geoff Eley, Series Editor
(Continued)

Growing Up Female
in Nazi Germany

Dagmar Reese

Translated by William Templer

The University of Michigan Press   *Ann Arbor*

English translation copyright © by the University of Michigan 2006
All rights reserved
Originally published in German as *"Straff, aber nicht stramm—
Herb, aber nicht derb"* in 1989 by Beltz
Published in the United States of America by
The University of Michigan Press
Manufactured in the United States of America
♾ Printed on acid-free paper

2009   2008   2007   2006   4   3   2   1

A CIP catalog record for this book is available from the British Library.

Library of Congress Cataloging-in-Publication Data

Reese, Dagmar, 1952–
    [Straff, aber nicht stramm—herb, aber nicht derb. English]
    Growing up female in Nazi Germany / Dagmar Reese ; translated by
William Templer.
        p.   cm. — (Social history, popular culture, and politics in
Germany)
    Includes bibliographical references.
    ISBN-13: 978-0-472-09938-2 (cloth : alk. paper)
    ISBN-10: 0-472-09938-8 (cloth : alk. paper)
    ISBN-13: 978-0-472-06938-5 (pbk. : alk. paper)
    ISBN-10: 0-472-06938-1 (pbk. : alk. paper)
        1. Women—Socialization—Germany—History.   2. Bund Deutscher
Mädel—History.   3. National socialism.   I. Title.   II. Series.
    HQ1210.R4713   2006
    305.235'2094309043—dc22   2006006236

The full citation for the original German language edition is *"Straff, aber nicht stramm—
Herb, aber nicht derb": Zur Vergesellschaftung von Mädchen durch den Bund Deutscher Mädel
im sozialkulturellen Vergleich zweier Milieus.* Weinheim and Basel, 1989.

WELTENDE

Es ist ein Weinen in der Welt,
Als ob der liebe Gott gestorben wär,
Und der bleierne Schatten, der niederfällt,
Lastet grabesschwer.

Komm, wir wollen uns näher verbergen . . .
Das Leben liegt in aller Herzen
Wie in Särgen.

Du! wir wollen uns tief küssen—
Es pocht eine Sehnsucht an die Welt,
An der wir sterben müssen.

—Else Lasker-Schüler

[WORLD'S END

There's a sobbing in the world
As if God were dead
And the leaden shadow that falls
is ponderous as the grave
Come, let's hide closer together . . .
Life lies stretched in all hearts
as in coffins.
O let us kiss now, deep deep—
A longing is knocking on the world
It knolls our time to die.]

Contents

Acknowledgments

The publication of this study in English goes back in particular to the interest of Geoff Eley in seeing this project come to fruition. I would like to express my great gratitude for his unflagging support in its realization. I also owe a debt of gratitude to the generous financial support provided by three institutions: the Goethe-Institute Inter Nationes; the Zentraleinheit zur Förderung von Frauen- und Geschlechterforschung at the Free University Berlin, in whose publication series this book first appeared in Germany; and the Henry M. Jackson School of International Studies at the University of Washington in Seattle, where I worked as a visiting DAAD (German Academic Exchange Service) professor from 1997 to 2002. Bill Templer has prepared an excellent translation of this study. I am very grateful for his work and for our good cooperation in its completion.

Introduction

Beginning in the mid-1930s, the Hitler Youth emerged as the largest single formation of the National Socialist Party. It claimed to embrace all of German youth.[1] The organization was headed by Baldur von Schirach, who was appointed *Reichsjugendführer* (Reich youth leader) of the NSDAP in 1931 and *Jugendführer des Deutschen Reiches* (youth leader of the German Reich) in 1933.[2] It was structured by both age and gender. The first bracket comprised young people ages ten to fourteen: *Pimpfe* (young boys) were organized in the Deutsches Jungvolk

---

1. Data on the quantitative development of Hitler Youth membership after 1933 all stem from National Socialist sources and must be viewed critically. Michael Buddrus gives a figure of 3.4 million members at the end of 1934 and 7.7 million at the beginning of 1939. Michael Buddrus, *Totale Erziehung für den totalen Krieg. Hitlerjugend und nationalsozialistische Jugendpolitik,* vol. 1 and 2 (Munich, 2003), 288f. For a critical discussion of National Socialist membership figures, see also chap. 2, section "The Development of the League of German Girls, 1933–1945," this study.

2. Baldur von Schirach, born in 1907, was the son of a famous Weimar theater director and his American wife. He had earlier contact with National Socialism; initially was active in the Nationalsozialistischer Deutscher Studentenbund (National Socialist German Students' League, or NSDStB), which he led from 1928 to 1931; and was then involved in the Hitler Youth. Schirach was appointed *Reichsstatthalter* (Reich governor) and *Gauleiter* (regional NSDAP leader) of Vienna in 1940 but also remained *Reichsleiter* of youth education of the NSDAP. Artur Axmann took over his functions as Reichsjugendführer and Jugendführer des Deutschen Reiches, remaining in those posts until 1945. Schirach was responsible for the deportation of the Jews of Vienna. At the Nuremberg Tribunal, his defense was that he had protested unsuccessfully against the "inhuman" treatment of the Jews at the hands of the National Socialists. He was sentenced to twenty years in prison and was released in 1966. Schirach died in 1974. As Reichsjugendführer, Schirach directed the work of the party formation Hitler Youth; as youth leader his power extended in principle to all of German youth. On this topic, see Martin Broszat, *Der Staat Hitlers. Grundlagen und Entwicklung seiner inneren Verfassung* (Munich, 1969), 334ff. On Baldur von Schirach, see Jochen von Lang, *Der Hitler-Junge. Baldur von Schirach. Der Mann, der Deutschlands Jugend erzog* (Hamburg, 1988); Michael Wortmann, *Baldur von Schirach, Hitlers Jugendführer* (Cologne, 1982); the following books by former leading Nazis must be considered part of the literature of justification: Artur Axmann, *"Das kann doch nicht das Ende sein." Hitlers letzter Reichsjugendführer erinnert sich* (Dortmund, 1995); Günter Kaufmann, *Baldur von Schirach. Ein Jugendführer in Deutschland. Richtigstellung und Vermächtnis* (Selbstverlag, 1993); and Baldur von Schirach, *Ich glaubte an Hitler* (Hamburg, 1967).

(German Young Folk, or DJ), while *Jungmädel* (young girls) were organized in the ranks of the formation by the same name, the Jung-mädel (JM). *Jungen* ages fourteen to eighteen were organized in the HJ, while *Mädel* in the same bracket were organized in the BDM.[3] The BDM-Werk "Glaube und Schönheit" (BDM section "Faith and Beauty") had a special position in this configuration of youth formations. Established in 1938, it included young women between the ages of seventeen and twenty-one. The three sections for girls—JM, BDM, and BDM-Werk "Glaube und Schönheit"—together constituted the Bund Deutscher Mädel or Mädelbund (League of German Girls). It had a female leader, the *Reichsreferentin des Bundes Deutscher Mädel* (Reich representative of the League of German Girls). Overall in the command structure, she was subordinate to the Reich youth leader. Nonetheless, the league was autonomous in that its leaders were bound from above only in regard to decrees and instructions incumbent on all German youth. In matters pertaining solely to girls, they had full authority to issue orders and instructions.[4] Such a comprehensive youth organization was unparalleled in German history. Even though both boys and girls were included, public discourse on the National Socialist dictatorship and its consequences has tended to ascribe only a secondary importance to the organization of females. In the English-speaking world, there is generally very little literature on the National Socialist youth organization as a whole and almost nothing on the League of German Girls.[5] Yet the changes that the league brought for

3. For the sake of clarity in this book, the term "Hitler Youth" is used for the entire organization with all its subformations. The term "League of German Girls" (Bund Deutscher Mädel) signifies the totality of all subformations for girls. By contrast, the abbreviations HJ and BDM are used here to refer solely to the formations for the older male and female youth ages fourteen to eighteen.

4. According to this, decrees and ordinances pertaining to youth as a whole were issued by the Reich youth leader and were obligatory for all subformations. Orders and instructions meant solely for the girls came from the Reich representative of the League of German Girls. On this matter, see remarks by the former Reich representative Jutta Rüdiger, *Die Hitler-Jugend und ihr Selbstverständnis im Spiegel ihrer Aufgabengebiete. Studienausgabe* (Lindhorst, 1983), 41.

5. Literature on the League of German Girls can be found in the English and German scholarship both in the context of studies on National Socialist youth policy as well as on family and women's policy. The oldest publications in English include the works by Clifford Kirkpatrick, Erika Mann, and Howard Becker. While Mann draws a hermetic picture of National Socialist indoctrination in *School for Barbarians: Education under the Nazis* (New York, 1938), Becker gives a more differentiated view, taking into account the history of the German youth movement, in *German Youth: Bond or Free* (New York, 1946). An important study in English published in the 1970s is Peter Loewenberg, "The Psychohistorical Origins of the Nazi Cohort," *American Historical Review* 76 (1971): 248–58. Also stemming from this

the history of women in Germany in the twentieth century were substantial, reaching in their consequences far past 1945 into the postwar period in the two German states.[6] Why are these not adequately perceived?

The explanation for this neglect is complex. For one, there are the difficulties inherent in properly grasping and evaluating the political character of the extramural National Socialist education of girls. Down to the present, the organization is associated with a kind of homespun apolitical conventionality, a sort of girls' auxiliary. The league is seen as the site where the German "Gretchen" was recruited

---

period is the work by Peter Stachura on the history of the Hitler Youth in the Weimar Republic: *Nazi Youth in the Weimar Republic* (Santa Barbara and Oxford, 1975). Daniel Horn published on youth resistance: "Youth Resistence in the Third Reich: A Social Portrait," *Journal of Social History* 7 (1973): 26–50. Among the more recent publications is Detlev Peukert's survey article on the history of everyday life: "Youth in the Third Reich," in Richard Bessel, ed., *Life in the Third Reich* (Oxford and New York, 1987), 25–40, and Michael H. Kater, *Hitler Youth* (Cambridge, Mass., 2004; published in German as *Hitler-Jugend* [2005]). The documentation volumes by Jeffrey Noakes and Geoffrey Pridham also contain material on the Hitler Youth, especially vol. 2 (*State, Economy, and Society*) and vol. 4 (*The German Homefront in World War II*): *Nazism, 1914–1945*, vols. 1–4 (Exeter, 1995; reprint, 1998). More specialized but highly instructive is the autobiography of Jost Hermand, who describes his experiences with evacuation camps for schoolchildren during the war: *A Hitler Youth in Poland: The Nazi Children's Evacuation Program during World War II* (Evanston, 1998). A contemporary study on women and the family in Nazi Germany is Clifford Kirkpatrick, *Nazi Germany: Its Women and Family Life* (Indianapolis and New York, 1938). Among the earliest works in English in the postwar period on women in National Socialism are those by the British historian Jill Stephenson, *Women in Nazi Society* (London, 1975) and *The Nazi Organization of Women* (London, 1981). They also touch on the history of the League of German Girls as well as the female Labor Service. The same is true for Leila Rupp, *Mobilizing Women for War: German and American War Propaganda, 1939–1945* (Princeton, 1978). Louise Willmot completed an excellent, but unpublished, PhD dissertation on the League of German Girls: "National Socialist Youth Organizations for Girls: A Contribution to the Social and Political History of the Third Reich," PhD diss., Oxford, 1980. Alison Owings published a book containing interviews with women of various ages and from diverse social backgrounds, including women who had to fulfill a youth service obligation: *Frauen: German Women Recall the Third Reich* (New Brunswick, 1993). Lisa Pine deals with the League of German Girls in the context of a study on National Socialist women's and family policy: *Nazi Family Policy, 1933–1945* (Oxford and New York, 1997). Elizabeth Heinemann, in her study on single women in Germany in the 1930s and 1940s, deals with the female Labor Service and the deployment of young women for service during the war effort: *What Difference Does a Husband Make? Women and Marital Status in Nazi and Postwar Germany* (Berkeley, 1999). Elizabeth Harvey has recently published a study on the deployment of women and female youth in the occupied territories of Poland and the Soviet Union: *Women and the Nazi East: Agents and Witnesses of Germanization* (New Haven and London, 2003).

6. Dagmar Reese, "The BDM-Generation: A Female Generation in Transition from Dictatorship to Democracy," in Mark Roseman, ed., *Generations in Conflict: Youth Revolt and Generation Formation in Germany, 1770–1968* (Cambridge, 1995), 227–46.

into service to the Reich—a blue-eyed, naive, braided young female whose main goal in life was supposedly limited to procreation: the mothering of a goodly number of "racially impeccable" offspring. Yet this image is not corroborated by the narratives of the women involved, nor is it reflected in the sources. Consider the history of their uniform: before 1933, girls in the League of German Girls wore a brown dress. With this uniform, the generally older female youth expressed their basic orientation to the Sturmabteilung (Storm Division, or SA) and saw themselves as part of that brown army committed to the goal of the "German revolution."[7] In 1933, the Hitler Youth declared this brown dress henceforth illegal, forbidding its wearing. This was a concession to convention, necessary if the organization was to grow to encompass, as the rulers now envisioned, all of the female German youth between the ages of ten and twenty-one.

The literature also systematically neglects the fact that in the early 1930s girls were often drilled to march in formation and trained in field exercises and sometimes marksmanship with air rifles—against the later development, which has been dubbed the "feminization" of the league. According to Arno Klönne, the organization did not evolve into its final form until the end of the 1930s, then stressing the inculcation of skills as a homemaker.[8] Evidence for this turn were the establishment of BDM schools for home economics (*BDM-Haushaltsschulen*), the introduction of required training in domestic service in 1936 (*hauswirtschaftliche Ertüchtigungspflicht*), and the obligatory year of service in 1937 (*Pflichtjahr*).[9] Further support for this thesis was the establishment of a separate organization for older female youth within the BDM-Werk "Glaube und Schönheit" in 1938.[10] Yet this interpretation is at best just one reading. It can be replaced and supplemented

7. A nice contemporary quotation showing the attraction of this uniform resembling the SA can be found in Johanna Gehmacher, *Jugend ohne Zukunft. Hitler-Jugend und Bund Deutscher Mädel in Österreich vor 1938* (Vienna, 1994), 236.

8. Arno Klönne, *Jugend im Dritten Reich. Die Hitler-Jugend und ihre Gegner* (Cologne, 1984), 32. Martin Klaus has the same view. Taking a tack different from that of Klönne, he emphasizes the internal party differences surrounding the image of femininity and the woman in the Mädelbund: Martin Klaus, *Mädchenerziehung zur Zeit faschistischer Herrschaft in Deutschland—Der Bund Deutscher Mädel,* 2 vols. (Frankfurt a.M., 1983), 238. The book was reprinted, most recently by Pahl Rugenstein in 1998.

9. Angela Vogel, *Das Pflichtjahr für Mädchen. Nationalsozialistische Arbeitseinsatzpolitk im Zeichen der Kriegswirtschaft* (Frankfurt a.M., 1997).

10. Sabine Hering and Klaus Schilde, *Das BDM-Werk "Glaube und Schönheit." Die Organisation junger Frauen im Nationalsozialismus* (Opladen, 1994). The book was reprinted in 2004.

by others that view these measures as preparation for the coming war, here related to girls, who were the last great reservoir of reserve labor—which the National Socialists subsequently made systematic use of for the first time in modern German history.[11] These measures would only be successful in this venture if the German girls were prepared to respect cultural boundaries and be duly considerate of the social consensus within the country.

So, on the one hand, the political character of organizing girls in the League of German Girls tends to be underestimated, by placing it within the continuity of bourgeois middle-class conceptions of femininity, with which National Socialist policy was no longer compatible.[12] On the other hand, this view is based on the behavior of the women involved: when it comes to childhood and youth in National Socialism, there are more publications by male than female authors.[13] Particularly in the aftermath of 1945, women appear to have grown silent, withdrawing into the private sphere. The reasons for that are not exclusively traditional.[14] There is strong evidence that male discourse was initially moored in the consciousness of having been sent as young

    11. Dagmar Reese, "Mädchen im Bund Deutscher Mädel," in Elke Kleinau and Claudia Opitz, eds., *Geschichte der Mädchen- und Frauenbildung*, vol. 2: *Vom Vormärz bis zur Gegenwart* (Frankfurt a.M., 1996), 271–82.

    12. See chap. 3, this study. See also Gabriele Czarnowski, *Das kontrollierte Paar. Ehe- und Sexualpolitk im Nationalsozialismus* (Ergebnisse der Frauenforschung, Bd. 24) (Weinheim, 1981); Jill Stephenson, "Modernization, Emancipation, Mobilization: Nazi Society Reconsidered," in Larry Jones and James Retallack, ed., *Elections, Mass Politics, and Political Change in Germany, 1880–1945* (Washington, DC, 1992), 223–43; Ann Taylor Allen, "The Holocaust and the Modernization of Gender: A Historiographical Essay," *Central European History* 30 (1997): 349–64. For a broader historical view on women in German history, compare Ute Frevert, *Women in German History: From Bourgeois Emancipation to Sexual Liberation* (Oxford, Hamburg, and New York, 1981).

    13. In the extensive autobiographical literature, women also play a less prominent role than men. This may be due in part to the fact that several well-known male writers and scholars have published their autobiographies. Along with Hermand, *A Hitler Youth in Poland,* see also Ludwig Harig, *Weh dem, der aus der Reihe tanzt* (Munich, 1990); Erich Loest, *Durch die Erde ein Riß Ein Lebenslauf* (Munich, 1990); Martin Walser, *Ein springender Brunnen* (Frankfurt a.M., 1998); Dieter Wellershoff, *Der Ernstfall. Innenansichten des Krieges* (Cologne, 1997). Only few publications by women attain the literary quality of these works. One exception is Christa Wolf's *Kindheitsmuster* (Darmstadt and Neuwied, 1977), unsurpassed in its intellectual depth. On the other hand, only in connection with books by women do we find that a very good book—such as Sybil Gräfin Schönfeld's *Sonderappell. 1945—Ein Mädchen berichtet* (Munich, 1984)—being classified as a book for youth.

    14. On this issue, see Robert G. Moeller, *Protecting Motherhood: Women and the Family in the Politics of Postwar West Germany* (Berkeley, 1993); Carola Sachse, *Gerechtigkeit und Gleichberechtigung in Ost und West 1939–1994* (Göttingen, 2002).

soldiers to the slaughter.[15] A sense of victimhood made it easier for men to grasp their own guilt and entanglement. But that is only partially true in the case of girls and women. Like male youth, many girls were recruited into the war effort, at times directly as army assistants and ack-ack girls[16] but most especially for shoring up the home front. Girls were deployed as laborers in agriculture, for labor and war relief service, for travelers' aid at train stations, in collections, as assistants in kindergartens, and even as conductors on streetcars. The war, which for the first time claimed more civilian than military victims, went hand in hand with huge psychological duress.[17] This continued in the strains and tribulations of the immediate postwar period.[18] Nonetheless, more women than men tended to prevail and survive.

Also, the scope for action and the avenues that were open to women substantially expanded during the war. For example, there were more women than ever before studying at German universities in the early 1940s.[19] A growing number of young women rose to positions of leadership; they replaced men in the decimated ranks of the *Reichsjugend-führung* (Reich youth leadership) or were deployed as "colonizers" in the German-occupied Polish territories.[20] Service in the League of Ger-

15. Exemplary for that tendency in postwar German literature are the stories and plays of Wolfgang Borchert. In Wellershoff there is a powerful description of the impression made on him and his fellow students by the first broadcast of Borchert's radio play *Draussen vor der Tür* in February 1947. Interestingly, Wellershoff mentions the expression "war generation" in this connection about himself, the author, and the all-male fellow residents in an ex–army barracks, where they were quartered for the duration of manual labor in cleanup and reconstruction that was required of them as future students before beginning their studies. Though women are not expressly excluded, their experiences in this war are clearly different. Dieter Wellershoff, *Die Arbeit des Lebens. Autobiographische Texte* (Cologne 1985), 201ff.

16. One of the most recent publications collecting interviews with former Wehrmacht assistants is Rosemarie Killius, *Frauen für die Front. Erinnerungen von Wehrmachtshelferinnen* (Leipzig, 2003).

17. Gerhard L. Weinberg, *A World at Arms: A Global History of World War II* (Cambridge, 1994). See also the more recent publications on the bombing war in Germany and its impact on the population. There may be various reasons why the traumatic experience of the massive bombing of German cities was perceived only at such a late date. One reason may be that in doing so the aperture is widened to include the fate of women and children as war victims. Jörg Friedrich, *Der Brand. Deutschland im Bombenkrieg, 1940–1945* (Munich, 2002), and Stephan Burgdorff and Christian Habbe, eds., *Als Feuer vom Himmer fiel. Der Bombenkrieg in Deutschland* (Munich, 2003).

18. For one of many autobiographical accounts, see Christian Graf von Krockow, *Die Stunde der Frauen. Pommern 1944 bis 1947* (Stuttgart, 1988).

19. Michael Grüttner, *Studenten im Dritten Reich* (Paderborn, 1995), 120ff., 488.

20. Elizabeth Harvey, "'Die deutsche Frau im Osten': 'Rasse', Geschlecht und öffentlicher Raum im besetzten Polen 1940–1944," *Archiv für Sozialgeschichte* 38 (1998): 191–214.

man Girls helped to create the foundations for these developments. In its dynamic of socialization, girls had been separated from their families of origin and successfully adapted to a role within social institutions and hierarchies.[21] All this was accompanied by an enhanced sense of female self-esteem, inextricably bound up with the unjust National Socialist regime, as was a similar sense of self-identity among the male soldiers. But unlike the men, women lacked military experience and the experience of military defeat. For this reason among others, it appears more difficult for the generation of women involved to associate their experiences—frequently positive though by no means always so—with National Socialist injustices and brutalities. Many of these women have ambivalent feelings or feel at a loss when they reflect on the League of German Girls. Such sentiments make it all the more urgent to grapple with the political character of the National Socialist girls' organization and their own entanglement and responsibility.[22]

The League of German Girls can be approached and investigated on several levels:

through a history of the institution

by looking at the ideology espoused and propagated by the league

via exploration of the history of everyday life and the history of personal experiences at whose center these women were, that is, within the context of specific cultural and social milieus.

All these perspectives are included within the present study, but they have differential weighting. I proceed from the basic assumption of historical continuity: namely, that the historically evolved cultural and social local conditions remained a powerful force even under the dictatorship and changed, if at all, only at a slow rate. National Socialist

21. On National Socialist women in leading positions and their ideology, see Leonie Wagner, *Nationalsozialistische Frauenansichten. Vorstellungen von Weiblichkeit und Politik führender Frauen im Nationalsozialismus* (Frankfurt a.M., 1996). In an exciting interview by Sabine Hering and Klaus Schilde, Gertrud Wulf talks about her encounter as a teacher at a school in North-Rhine/Westphalia after 1945. Here, Wulf encountered many former leaders of the female Labor Service. Some were apolitical, but others were still ardent National Socialists. Hering and Schilde, *Das BDM-Werk "Glaube und Schönheit,"* 202.

22. On the connection between the degree of entanglement and the extent of responsibility among leaders of the League of German Girls, see Dagmar Reese, "Verstrickung und Verantwortung. Weibliche Jugendliche in der Führung des Bundes Deutscher Mädel," *Sozialwissenschaftliche Informationen* 2 (1991): 90–96. A revised version of this article appeared in Kirsten Heinsohn, Barbara Vogel, and Ulrike Weckel, eds., *Zwischen Karriere und Verfolgung. Handlungsspielräume von Frauen im nationalsozialistischen Deutschland* (Frankfurt a.M., 1997), 206–22.

policy was obliged to take them into account.[23] It follows from this that, despite an increasing regimentation and unifying of the organization (chap. 1), the League of German Girls enjoyed a differing degree of acceptance in various regions and cultural milieus and had a differential impact.

The objective of this study is to examine the link between social conditions and the subjective experiences of the generation of girls and female youth participating in the National Socialist youth organization. This is achieved by presenting two contrasting social milieus (chaps. 4 and 5): the small Protestant town of Minden in Westphalia and a proletarian neighborhood in the urban metropolis of Wedding in Berlin. By contrast, the history of institutions plays a subordinate role in this analysis (chap. 2).

I decided in the main not to evaluate the written material issued by the league, developing a critical analysis of its ideology.[24] There are several reasons for this. First, the ideological contents of schooling in the league were meager, controversial, and subject to various changes over the twelve years of National Socialist rule. Second, "doctrinal schooling" was the task of young female leaders, who mainly worked in a voluntary capacity, many of whom themselves had had little or no training in such matters.[25] These points tend to support the thesis that the teaching of ideology within the league was less important than was the ideological role played by public opinion, the print and electronic media, the schools, and the girls' own families.

Instead, chapter 3 seeks to show that the effort to integrate the girls within the National Socialist movement achieved success by means of offering them an equal degree of participation within German youth—notwithstanding an ever-present element of racial exclusion. These girls were influenced and shaped not by ideological content but by a *living practice* in the National Socialist organization. Attitudes internalizing the concept of achievement and thinking in terms of hierarchies were inculcated via sports[26] and a massive construction of careers

23. As in the dictum by Georg Simmel: "Valid everywhere for political parties: I'm their leader, so I have to follow them." Georg Simmel, *Philosophie des Geldes* [= Gesamtausgabe, vol. 6] (Frankfurt a.M., 1989), 59.

24. I have published such an analysis elsewhere: Dagmar Reese, ed., *Die BDM-Generation. Nationalsozialistische Herrschaft und weiblicher Lebenszusammenhang in Deutschland und Österreich* (Potsdam, forthcoming).

25. This view is supported by Rolf Schörken, "Singen und Marschieren. Erinnerungen an vier Jahre Jungvolk 1939–1943," *Geschichte in Wissenschaft und Unterricht (GWU)* 7 (1998): 453ff.

26. Dagmar Reese and Gertrud Pfister, "Gender, Body Culture, and Body Politics in National Socialism," *Sport Science Review* 4 (1995): 91–121.

as "leaders" within the league. By contrast, the loss of autonomy and self-determination as young people, the drastic reduction in their lives of free, unbound play for no purpose, appears only in their recollection. And their memory seems strangely vacated when talk turns to the League of German Girls.[27] Instead, their own enhanced self-importance and growth in social and leadership skills, and in power, are totally entwined with a regime in whose name millions of crimes were committed. This makes it difficult for many of these women, even today, to develop an objective attitude about their own (her)story.

For the English translation, this study has been reworked. Much has changed in recent years. Under the impact of the demands of feminist scholars and the findings of women's studies, we now are aware that to speak about youth means to talk about young men *and* women. It is of course obvious that youth is gendered. But the two genders are not in some sort of additive relation. Rather, they stand in a relational configuration that is by no means unambiguous and in many respects fractured. The example of National Socialism shows how a regime can successfully promote a political agenda utilizing social competition and rivalry between the sexes. The National Socialist practice of organizing girls in a compulsory youth movement demonstrates that there are rivalries between the genders that can be exploited with just as much success and effect as the rivalries between young and old, tradition and progress.

That emergent picture can be used to mediate in a debate that took place among historians in the 1990s on the responsibility of women for National Socialism and its crimes.[28] Its main protagonists were the historians Gisela Bock and Claudia Koonz.[29] Koonz argued that the guilt

27. See chaps. 3 and 4, this study.

28. On this, see the introduction in Heinsohn, Vogel, and Weckel, *Zwischen Karriere und Verfolgung;* Atina Grossmann, "Feminist Debates about Women and National Socialism," *Gender and History* 3 (1991): 350–58; Liliane Kandel, ed., *Feminismes et Nazisme* [= Cahiers des C. E.D.R.E.F.] (Paris, 1997); Birthe Kundrus, "Frauen und Nationalsozialismus," *Archiv für Sozialgeschichte* 36 (1996): 481–99; Dagmar Reese and Carola Sachse, "Frauenforschung und Nationalsozialismus—Eine Bilanz," in Lerke Gravenhorst and Carmen Tatschmurat, eds., *Töchter Fragen. NS-Frauen-Geschichte* [= Forum Frauenforschung, vol. 5] (Freiburg i.Br., 1990), 73–106, and the other articles in this volume; Adelheid von Saldern, "Victims or Perpetrators? Controversies about the Role of Women in the Nazi State," in David Crew, ed., *Nazism and German Society, 1933–1945* (London and New York, 1994), 141–65; Theresa Wobbe, "Das Dilemma der Überlieferung. Zu politischen und theroretischen Kontexten von Gedächniskonstruktionen über den Nationalsozialismus," in Wobbe, ed., *Nach Osten. Verdeckte Spuren nationalsozialistischer Verbrechen* (Frankfurt a.M., 1992), 13–43.

29. The debate began with Gisela Bock's review of Claudia Koonz's book *Mothers in the Fatherland: Women, the Family, and Nazi Politics* (London, 1987), in Gisela Bock, "Die Frauen und der Nationalsozialismus." Bemerkungen zu einem Buch von Claudia Koonz,"

of Nazi women lay in their conscious retreat to a gendered sphere separated from men and reserved exclusively for women, which they maintained in exchange for political abstinence in the spheres dominated by men.[30] Bock stressed that, in evaluating the guilt of women, what is important is not only differences between the sexes but likewise also similarities.[31]

The history of the league could help to differentiate these views and findings. It clearly shows that the attraction of the organization began to mount in the early 1930s, when it was incorporated into the broader youth group. The National Socialist women's associations, which traditionally had viewed work with girls as their exclusive bailiwick, then lost their girls' groups, while the Hitler Youth increased in significance and size. So initially it is impossible to maintain that there was a tacit agreement of some sort between National Socialist women and men regarding separate spheres for the sexes. On the contrary, there was vigorous competition[32] in which the male-dominated youth organization finally succeeded in gaining the upper hand. But it could do so only because it succeeded in taking advantage of the competition between younger and older women. The desire of the girls involved for equality and parity thereby was the decisive factor. Attractive in their eyes was the fact that the league, despite its formal subordination within the total organization under the Hitler Youth, remained independent. This meant that no local Hitler Youth or party leader was empowered to interfere in the work of the league, even though such instances naturally did occur in practice. On the other hand, the fact that the Hitler Youth was not coeducational but rather made a strict separation between the sexes was not some sort of fundamental decision. Nor was it meant to somehow show consideration for the interests of the older female party members. Decisive here were pragmatic

Geschichte und Gesellschaft 15 (1989): 563–79. Koonz responded to this review: Claudia Koonz, "Erwiderung auf Gisela Bocks Rezension von 'Mothers in the Fatherland'," *Geschichte und Gesellschaft* 18 (1992): 394–99, and was again commented by Gisela Bock, "Ein Historikerinnenstreit?" *Geschichte und Gesellschaft* 18 (1992): 400–404.

30. Koonz, *Mothers in the Fatherland,* 55. Koonz expanded this argument in the German translation of her book: *Mütter im Vaterland. Frauen im Dritten Reich* (Freiburg, 1991), 70.

31. Gisela Bock, "Ganz normale Frauen. Täter, Opfer, Mitläufer und Zuschauer im Nationalsozialismus," in Heinsohn, Vogel, and Weckel, *Zwischen Karriere und Verfolgung,* 266ff. See also Gisela Bock, "Antinatalism, Maternity and Paternity in National Socialist Racism," in Crew, *Nazism and German Society,* 110–40.

32. Claudia Koonz was the first to describe this competition of female party members before 1933. See Claudia Koonz, "Nazi Women before 1933: Rebels against Emancipation," *Social Science Quarterly* 56 (1976): 553–63, as well as Koonz, *Mothers in the Fatherland,* 125ff.

motives of the top party echelon, bound up with power politics: it simply would not have been politically possible to create and implement an organization encompassing all German youth in the 1930s had the structural basis chosen been coeducational.

As an organization solely for girls, the league in turn created a diverse array of career paths for females and in addition offered numerous opportunities for the inclusion of girls within National Socialist politics. Girls and young women had an interest in maintaining these new spheres of influence. And that interest grew in proportion to the power they themselves gained. Finally, work in the leadership ranks in a salaried capacity[33] was marked only by graduated differences in respect to the sexes. In the *Führerkorps* (leadership cadre) of the Hitler Youth, primary emphasis was on implementation of National Socialist policies. The young women here had to accommodate and find their place within the internal hierarchies, asserting themselves against competition, both from their own ranks and in the entire organization. Viewed from the perspective of the salaried leader echelon, the difference between the genders could thus be used as a tactical argument by the women involved. The aim of that argument would have been to achieve and maintain participation in power, while claiming to represent the girls in the league.

But if the perspective is shifted, from the female leaders to the rank and file, the picture changes. The youth groups opposing the state youth that came into being, especially during the war, differentiated themselves from the Hitler Youth by including both male and female members. Meanwhile, the Hitler Youth lost some of its attraction because it continued to separate the sexes.[34] Equality and difference must therefore be seen as a game both in which the subjects—boys and girls and men as well as women—are involved and to which they are subordinated. In this game, which basically concerns the distribution of social power, gender and age function as stakes, which divide up the field of social opportunities, perpetuating a continuing dynamic struggle over their distribution. Because that is the case, differentiation by gender should serve as a methodological instrument in the investigation of political generations: it can shed needed light on the internal dynamics of this youth.

---

33. Leaders were divided by discourse into two categories: those who were *hauptamtlich,* that is, on a salary, and who were thus part of the leadership corps of the Hitler Youth, and all the others, who worked *ehrenamtlich,* that is, on a voluntary basis.

34. Peukert, "Youth in the Third Reich," 32.

Methodological Preface

Selecting the Interviewees

For this study I conducted interviews in both Minden and Wedding. Some of these interviews (four in Minden and one in Wedding) can be classified as expert interviews; that is, they were with respondents who had privileged insight into the work of the League of German Girls as adults by dint of their activity or profession.[35] I located the other interviewees in various ways. Some contacted me in response to announcements or ads in the media (e.g., radio and newspapers), while others were found as a result of my contacting diverse social institutions, such as churches, political parties, and associations. Most of the interviews came about by personal word-of-mouth references, in a kind of snowball effect.

Conducting the Interviews

Two sessions were arranged for each interview. A few required three and some even four sessions. The expert interviews generally were completed in a single session. All interviews were conducted in the place of residence of the interviewees and recorded on audio cassette. As a rule, the interviewer was alone with the respondent; in rare cases, a family member, such as the husband or daughter of the interviewee, was also present. A session lasted ninety minutes. Between the first and second session, there was always an interval of at least a week; this allowed me to assume that the second session was a continuation in content, but at a certain remove from the first, and thus to some extent independent of it. In the interval between the first and second sessions, I reviewed the interview on tape to discover any inconsistencies or omissions; these were noted down, and an attempt was made to broach them during the second round. As the interviewer, I tried to leave the interviewee as much space and freedom as possible, endeavoring to disturb their open-ended narrative as little as possible. Nonetheless, for the sake of comparing data, some structuring of the interview was unavoidable. For that reason, a guide outline, based on a rough breakdown into nine areas, was prepared in advance and tested.[36] In order to

35. These were such professions as a welfare worker, an assistant in a parish, a salaried leader, or the head of a special troop (*Sonderschar*).
36. The nine areas included parents, living circumstances, prospects for the future, dreams, work, leisure time, friends, environment, and reflections.

make my own orientation clear, this guide was given to the interviewees before the interview, and they were asked to make note of it. I
then took the guide back so that the narrative would not be shaped too
strongly by its specified categories. Even under these restricting conditions, there were further limits to the free flow of narration, because the
interviewee often faltered or came to a prolonged pause and had to be
stimulated by questions. In order to maintain the smooth flow of narration, I tried to focus it on everyday events and to insert specific questions to generate images whose fuller visualization was able to provide
a picture of social conditions. For example, the question about eating
was followed by a description of preparing the meal, the division of
labor within the family, and shopping. This in turn helped illuminate
the family's social network. Photos were gathered as material but not
utilized as stimuli in the sense of a focused interview.

Evaluating the Interviews

All citations from interviews appear in the book with a letter that distinguishes between places (Minden = M, Berlin-Wedding = B) and a number that indicates the interview. The reader can find out more about the
interviewees—his or her social background, school and professional
education, political affiliation, and membership and career in the Hitler
Youth—at the end of the book. Working with qualitative interviews
makes it necessary for the researcher to carefully consider the implica-
tions of the subjective character of his or her materials This includes the
key question of how to check the credibility of each individual piece of
information. In the present study this was done by means of three com-
parative, interlocking procedures. First, the interview was listened to in
order to check its internal coherence. This was often done directly during the interview or at the latest during transcription or initial work on
the transcript. Ruptures and contradictions occurred in all interviews,
and it was important to reveal the trajectory of their internal logic. This
can be illustrated by the following example: in one of the Wedding interviews with a woman from a very poor family, I had trouble figuring out
exactly how many people were actually in the family. At the beginning of
the interview, she had mentioned six brothers and sisters, but at various
points she repeatedly mentioned the death of a sibling. Only through
later questioning was I able to determine that three of the seven children
had survived while four had died: Doris got "cramps," Dieter burned to
death as a result of scalding from hot cabbage, Günther had been torn
apart by bombs, and Wolfgang died of diphtheria. It at least seemed rea-

sonable to me that such a series of horrible shocks cannot simply be narrated in a sequential chain, as I (personally uninvolved) am quite able to recount in retrospect.

Compounding the harshness of proletarian life, which makes it a difficult experience to recall the past, was the fact that the miserable conditions frequently acted to disrupt any continuity. This is most impressively manifest in the huge number of changes of residence some subjects were forced to endure. Thus, ruptures in the flow of narrative are the mirror of the stark reality of proletarian life. But they can become so predominant in an interview that the interviewees close their mind to the interviewer. For this reason, I decided that this interview conducted in Wedding could not be included in the final corpus.

In contrast to being bogged down by breaks, ruptures, and contradictions, an interview can on the other hand be so slick, unfold so smoothly, that the information it contains is virtually worthless. One interview with a high-ranking leader met that description. Responding to the question of how many girls were in the Berlin section of the League of German Girls in January 1933, the interviewee answered:

B 24: Gee, well, here in Berlin in '33, I mean when they seized power, we were around 3,000.

I: In the entire city of Berlin?

B 24: In the whole city. That's a very small district, here in Steglitz we were, uh, I can't give any statistics, I don't know. But those I was aware of, the number was less than 50. That probably didn't change all that much down to '33, January '33. I joined the end of '31, when I was 15, and by '32, I'd already become a leader. And we were already 20 districts then [in all of Berlin], so you can figure it out more or less, 3,000. So there were certainly not more than 50 of us here.

I: And how was that distributed over the various districts? From which ones were you able to recruit the most girls?

B 24: I can't tell you when it comes to Berlin.

I: Didn't you have some general overview of that at the time?

B 24: You couldn't get a general picture, because at that time, well, you were in your own small circle. It wasn't possible to get any overall picture of the full dimensions. All I know is that when we met to celebrate the winter solstice, for example in '31, and then when we got together in '32 for sports festivals, actually it was the same then in all districts. Like in Schöneberg, it was exactly the same. For example, I went to school in Schöneberg district, and we had the same percentage there. I can't say that it was different from district to district. And then afterwards, in '33, then everything had increased by a factor of ten, of course. I think in '33 there were 30,000 of us here.

If you grant credibility to the personal experience of B 24 that in January 1933 in the Steglitz district of Berlin about fifty girls were members of the League of German Girls, and if, perhaps even with certain reservations, you also consider it correct that the number in the league there was similar to that in other districts in Berlin, then you can make a quite simple calculation: twenty districts in Berlin had a total membership of one thousand. So how does B 24 arrive at three thousand or thirty thousand girls at the end of 1933? In order to better understand that discrepancy, I would like to quote first from a brochure by the first Reich representative of the League of German Girls, Trude Bürkner, published in 1937, and then from an interview conducted by Martin Klaus with Ms. Bürkner in 1980: "Despite the period of the ban in the spring of 1932, on January 30, 1933 there were already more than 3,000 girls in Berlin organized under the banner of National Socialism."[37]

M.K.: About how many girls did the BDM have then?
T.B.: I can only tell you the official figures for the Obergau of Berlin. When Adolf Hitler became Reich Chancellor in 1933, I had about 3,000 girls and younger girls in the BDM in Berlin. By the end of 1933, it was already more than 30,000.[38]

What my interviewee had reproduced was a mixture of her own experiences on the one hand and the official statistics of the league on the other. These latter numbers had been produced and propagated in National Socialism and had become an integral component of personal memory.

While I excluded the first interview from Wedding I left this last one in. But I utilized it only in a limited way: in order to shed light on the perspective, intentions, and presentation of a person who had been a responsible high-ranking leader.

The first step was thus to check the internal coherence of the interview. The second was to compare information within the sample cor-

---

37. Trude Bürkner, *Der Bund Deutscher Mädel in der Hitler-Jugend* (Berlin 1937), 8.
38. Klaus, *Mädchenerziehung zur Zeit,* 14.

pus. As a rule, I tried to avoid using unique statements; that is, the quoted material in the study can almost always be replaced or supplemented by other similar quotes. If that was not possible, I checked on how representative the statements were in another way. For example, take the information of M 3, another high-ranking leader who, contrary to all expectations, tried in the summer of 1941 to set up a group of girls in the rural countryside. I was only able to include this quotation because it appeared to be sufficiently corroborated by the findings in a study by Klönne, who reported something similar for Bavaria.[39] This approach points to the third method, namely, examining interview statements by comparing them with other materials.

An exact knowledge of the social milieu as this emerged from the diverse sources used was absolutely essential for evaluating the statements made. This not only made it possible to clear up certain contradictions but also shed light on other statements. Let me give one example. In reply to my question about whether the residents on "red" Kösliner Straße were really only Communists, and not Social Democrats, B 7 replied: "No, we didn't have any SPD people where we lived, no, well, I can't rightly recall. Well, we did have an SPD guy, but he got shot, by accident. There probably were some SPD people there, but where we lived, fact is, there were only Communists."

What seems here at first to be nonsensical thoughts actually contains two precise pieces of information at differing levels. On the one hand, B 7 is reporting on the actual social composition of residents on Kösliner Straße, where Communists, Social Democrats, and people who were not politically involved or who had other political persuasions were all living together. On the other hand, she echoes the public formula essential for the street and its perception. According to the formula, Kösliner Straße was a "Communist street" in Wedding, just like in popular parlance the stretch known as Krücke, the back part of Kolonie Straße.[40]

The hardest thing to evaluate is what remains unstated. Because the memory causes pain or ill feeling, it is omitted. In Wedding, difficulties in remembrance were almost always associated with poverty. This apparently was not only the experience of suffering but something that

---

39. Arno Klönne, "Jugendprotest und Jugendopposition. Von der HJ-Erziehung zum Cliquenwesen der Kriegszeit," in Martin Broszat, Elke Fröhlich, and Anton Großmann, eds., *Bayern in der NS-Zeit,* vol. 4, *Herrschaft und Gesellschaft im Konflikt, Part C* [= Veröffentlichung im Rahmen des Projektes Widerstand und Verfolgung in Bayern 1933–1945] (Munich and Vienna, 1981), 545.

40. B1, B 13.

a person was still ashamed of in retrospect. This is made clear by the
following interview excerpt.

> I can still remember that I went off with my dad, and somehow we
> tried by, uh, well I can't remember what it was, but what we tried to
> do, uh, I don't know, just uh, maybe we just went around and were
> singing to get some money. He did something like that with me.
> Though that was just for a short time. But like I said, I have only a
> very vague memory of that. I must have been a real small kid back
> at the time, maybe three or four years old, five at the most. (B 2)

Yet I noticed very few difficulties in remembering when it came to the
specific history of National Socialism. B 15 talks about this but can
nonetheless recall her memory.[41] By contrast, I did encounter genuinely
repressed material in the case of victims—for example, a woman from a
Jewish background.[42] She had contacted me in response to a call in the
media, and I think it is reasonable to assume that her primary interest in
telling me her life history was to narrate something about the fate of a
non-Aryan woman in Wedding. The interview did not actually provide
much material of interest. But quite accidentally, it turned out that
another interviewee (B 9) was in the same class at the *Handelsschule*
(commercial school) as B 19.[43] B 19 described the teaching at the school
as having been "strongly influenced by National Socialism."[44] She narrated the following incident with her homeroom teacher.

> The girls were actually pretty good, they didn't let me feel anything,
> you understand. Once the teacher made a real stupid remark, and
> mentioned the word *Mischling* [someone of 'mixed' German-Jewish
> descent], but not in connection at all probably with other human
> races. Then she suddenly blurted out: "there's one sitting back over
> there." I found that a bit strange. (B 19)

Due to the way she told me this story (she was laughing as she narrated) and her choice of words, I was unable to properly comprehend
how painful this experience had actually been for her. I had a similar
experience at another point in the interview when she described how,

41. See chap. 3, section "Making Careers," this study.
42. One of the grandparents of B 19 was Jewish.
43. I was able to reconstruct that by the year of birth, location of the school, and the special teaching methods of a certain instructor there. Neither interviewee knew about the other.
44. Also B 19, B 10.

after 1945, one of her teachers had asked her for a de-Nazification certificate, which she then gave him. I had the clear impression that she was furious about this, but since she had described the teacher objectively in terms of his teaching methods, and did not go into his behavior toward her any further, I was not sure why she was upset. The interview with B 9 provided this narrative with certain new nuances, which immediately put the situation of B 19 in a more drastic light. Thus, I learned that the homeroom teacher was an ardent National Socialist, with her hair wound into an obligatory *Glaubensdutt* ("believer's bun") at the back of her neck and a party pin on her chest. When at another point I asked B 9 directly about Jewish girls in her class, she mentioned B 19 and then went on, visibly moved: "I recall we had this teacher, he must have been quite a Nazi, because he always used [to ask] M [name of B 19]: Are you a Jew? Or a Jewess? He was really hostile to her because of her Jewish background."

For B 19, the teacher's remark was not just a humiliation before the class; given the situation in the Third Reich, it was at the same time a very clear threat. But the fear, helplessness, rage, and sadness the comment had provoked in her was something B 19 was no longer able to reproduce. In a certain way, her story had gone on right by me: what I believe was her deeply hidden sadness had not risen to the surface even in the form of an intimation of what lay within.

Though the life histories were the most important single category of material, they were nonetheless only one source among others. For the period prior to 1933, further material was brought in based on the reading of local newspapers and periodicals. The detailed analysis of this material had the advantage of providing a vital picture of the world into which the concrete specific everyday life of the girls was then integrated. Similar sources reflecting everyday life were largely lacking for the period after 1933. Supplementary valuable sources were the Germany Reports of the Social Democratic Party issued between 1934 and 1940 under the auspices of the Executive Committee in Exile of the SPD,[45] as well as the secret reports of the Security Service known as the

45. *Deutschland-Berichte der Sozialdemokratischen Partei,* abbreviated as *Sopade.* A copy in the Archive of Social Democracy of the Friedrich Ebert Foundation was the basis for a facsimile reprint with a detailed index in the Verlag Petra Nettelbeck, Salzhausen, and Zweitausendeins, Frankfurt a.M. (1980). The *Sopade* reports were meant more as a description of the factual situation than as an assessment of the "mood" of the population. See *Sopade* 1 (1934): 79. The reliability of the *Sopade* is confirmed by many authors; see, for instance, Michael H. Kater, "Die Sozialgeschichte und das Dritte Reich. Überlegungen zu neuen Büchern," *Archiv für Sozialgeschichte* 22 (1982): 661–82; Detlev Peukert and Jürgen Reulecke, eds., *Die Reihen fast geschlossen. Beiträge zur Geschichte des Alltags unterm Nationalsozialismus* (Wuppertal, 1981), 17.

Reports from the Reich (Meldungen aus dem Reich).[46] But in the case of our investigation, these sources' utility is largely limited to Wedding, whose special political character was important both for the SPD and the National Socialists and which as a consequence is more frequently mentioned in these sources. That deficiency was partially compensated by material in the archives. It proved possible to integrate the local pictures thus assembled into the broader history of the League of German Girls, which has been reconstructed utilizing archival materials from the Federal Archive in Berlin and Koblenz, the Institute for Contemporary History in Munich, the Main Bavarian State Archives in Munich, the Munich State Archives, and an array of periodicals, published sources, and secondary literature. The German Central Archive in Potsdam is now integrated into the Federal Archives.[47]

The present study is divided into five chapters. It begins with an ideal-typical description of the path of the German girl, the National Socialist ideal of mobilization of young females. This is followed by a short survey of the history of the League of German Girls. The third chapter attempts to shed more precise light on several essential features of the National Socialist mobilization of young girls. This involves the ideology of femininity within the league, sports, and career leaders. In the last section of chapter 3, I examine the forms of remembrance of past membership in the league. The local historical studies in Minden and Wedding make up the fourth and fifth chapters, which in structure are almost identical. They begin with an overview of the history of the area and then proceed to place the essential structural elements worked out in this analysis in a context of family relations. The chapter on Wedding contains two sections on the importance of organizing young people and their leisure time behavior, a key prerequisite due to the special conditions prevailing in this metropolitan area. This lays the foundation for the last section in each chapter, which spotlights the work of the League of German Girls in Minden and Wedding.

46. Still basic here is Heinz Boberach, ed., *Meldungen aus dem Reich 1938–1945. Die geheimen Lageberichte der Sicherheitsdienstes der SS,* 17 vols. (Herrsching, 1984). Supplementary to this study, new collections of sources have been published in recent years centering on regional or thematic foci: Hermann-Josef Rupieper and Alexander Sperk, eds., *Die Lageberichte der Geheimen Staatspolizei zur Provinz Sachsen,* vol. 1: *Regierungsbezirk Madgeburg* (Halle [Saale], 2003); vol. 2: *Regierungsbezirk Merseburg* (Halle [Saale], 2004); vol. 3: *Regierungsbezirk Erfurt* (Halle [Saale], 2004); and Otto Dov Kulka and Eberhard Jackel, eds., *Die Juden in den geheimen NS-Stimmungsberichten 1933–1945* (Düsseldorf, 2004).

47. Archival material on the League of German Girls that had been located in the Potsdam archives and had not been accessible to me before 1989 has now become part of the Bundesarchiv. It is marginal and has been checked for this translation.

CHAPTER 1

"The Path of the German Girl"

Contrary to what one would expect, the "Aryan" required an unprecedented degree of "pedagogical" influence in order to unfold his or her "natural" superiority. The "members of the master race" were surrounded by an entire web of specially created organizations; these enveloped all their activities, shaping the phases of their lives. In the bosom of the League of German Girls, views about how to "educate"[1] a "German girl" and mold her into a proper "German woman" took on concrete, palpable form. External appearance was standardized: a navy blue skirt, fitted with buttons for girls ages ten to fourteen, and a white blouse, whose left sleeve sported a triangular emblem emblazoned with the name of the respective *Obergau* (area) of the league, topped by a black neckerchief fastened together by a brown leather knot. The outfit was complemented by white stockings, replaced in the cold winter months by long brown hoses, and laced shoes. In inclement weather, girls donned a brown vest, the so-called *Kletterweste* (climbing vest), or a black peasant costume jacket, the *Berchtesgadener Jäckchen* (Berchtesgaden jacket). Here was an image of girlhood both smart and sporty, devoid of any superfluous frippery. The uniform clothing underscored membership in a group and German folk community. Its unambiguous message: no one was to deviate from the prescribed norm.

The "path of education" of a "German girl" had to be as uniform as her external appearance. Next to the parental home and the school, the League of German Girls was considered the third educational institution in society.[2] It was responsible for "educating" "female German youth . . . in the spirit of National Socialism, dedicated to service to the

1. When I use the word *education* here, I refer to National Socialist discourse. However, since I do not consider the League of German Girls to be an effective pedagogical instrument in the framework of an ideological system—as I will elaborate on in chap. 3, section "Between Tradition and Progress," this study—I have left the term here in qualifying quotation marks.

2. Hitler Youth Law, Dec. 1, 1936, RGBl. I 1936, 993, § 2.

people and the folk community."[3] How this external National Socialist "education of girls" was to be organized and implemented within
the league closely geared to National Socialist conceptions and ideals
was set down in precise detail.

"The Path of the German Girl"

> We use the term "children" for those non-uniformed creatures of a
> younger age who have never taken part in a social evening, have
> never been on a march.[4]

The National Socialist state began to educate its wards at the age of
ten, which, as Baldur von Schirach phrased it, marked the end of childhood. The legal foundation for entry into the League of German Girls
was paragraph 9 of the Second Ordinance on Implementation of the
Hitler Youth Law (HJ-Law). Article 1 of that law stated: "All young
people must report to their local Hitler Youth leader by the 15th of
March at the latest in the calendar year in which they reach the age of
10, in order to enter the Hitler Youth."[5] Children were mobilized for
registration by means of public announcements, information passed
on in the classroom, and registry lists. Every April 20, Hitler's birthday, brought a special festive ceremony as new members of the Hitler
Youth were initiated. Young girls first joined the Jungmädelbund, the
female equivalent to the Deutsches Jungvolk of the male Hitler Youth.
After six months, the girls were expected to pass the *Jungmädelprobe*[6]
and were then given the leather knot, an ID card, and the emblem, thus
becoming full-fledged members of the organization. Once "graduated"
into the League of German Girls, they had to purchase the uniform,
which was obligatory when in service.

The regular round of service in the League of German Girls consisted of the *Heimabend* (social evening or afternoon get-together),
sports activities, and excursions. The Heimabend was a two-hour
affair that took place once a week. Jungmädel under the age of fourteen had their get-together in the afternoon, while the older girls gath-

3. Hitler Youth Law, Dec. 1, 1936, RGBl. I 1936, 993, § 3.
4. Baldur von Schirach, *Die Hitler-Jugend. Idee und Gestalt* (Leipzig, 1934), 87.
5. Second ordinance on implementation of the Hitler Youth Law from March 25, 1939.
RGBl. I 1939, 710.
6. The Jungmädelprobe was a test introduced in 1935. In order to pass it, girls had to
answer questions on ideological schooling, to do sport exercises, and to attend a night excursion. See Arno Klönne, *Hitlerjugend. Die Jugend und ihre Organisation im Dritten Reich*
(Hannover and Frankfurt a.M., 1955), 16.

ered in the evenings. Every Heimabend included ideological schooling (*weltanschauliche Schulung*), craftswork, and singing. Likewise once a week, the girls came together for sports. The overriding aim here was to train the body thoroughly but not to strive after individual achievements. Rhythmic gymnastics played a major role, especially in the BDM section "Faith and Beauty," which sought to develop the spiritual and physical graces of the older girls. Also obligatory was participation in short weekend excursions into the nearby countryside; these outings lasted from one to one and a half days and were generally organized in the summer months. The excursions had a double purpose: physical training and internal consolidation of the group.[7] In addition, service in the league was sometimes greatly augmented by additional activities, such as participation in festivals and public rallies, evenings for parents, and promotional evenings. The scope of service continued to be expanded, reaching a high point during the war. Members of the league were increasingly mobilized for assistance with collections to help the war effort, were put to work harvesting or helping in the neighborhood, or sent on visits to field hospitals. At first, such wartime activities were something extra, tied to the obligatory range of service, but ultimately they got the upper hand, becoming the dominant focus.[8]

Sondereinheiten (special units) akin to the Maritime Hitler Youth or the Equestrian Hitler Youth did not exist in the League of German Girls, but the girls did take part in *Sonderausbildungen* (special courses), such as training to be a medical assistant in the health services (*Gesundheitsdienstmädel*). In the Jungmädelbund, the training period for young girls was four years. When they reached the age of fourteen, they were officially graduated into the BDM, again in festivities scheduled to coincide with the Führer's birthday on April 20. This graduation into the BDM was accompanied by a special secular rite, the so-called Verpflichtung der Jugend (Ceremony of Commitment for Youth), which originally was intended to replace religious confirma-

7. The League of German Girls also organized camps and trips that went for several days or even weeks and covered greater distances. Participation in such trips was on a voluntary basis.

8. Already in December 1939, *Der Reichsbefehl der Reichsjugendführung der NSDAP,* a magazine for Hitler Youth leaders, published "Guidelines for Deployment of Young People in War-Related Service." On such wartime deployment activities in the League of German Girls, see Dagmar Reese, "Bund Deutscher Mädel—Zur Geschichte der weiblichen deutschen Jugend im Dritten Reich," in Frauengruppe Faschismusforschung, ed., *Mutterkreuz und Arbeitsbuch. Zur Geschichte der Frauen in der Weimarer Republik und im Nationalsozialismus* (Frankfurt a.M., 1981), 174ff.; Buddrus, *Totale Erziehung für den totalen Krieg,* chaps. 1, 7, and 8.

tion.[9] In the BDM, girls went through a further four-year period of training. When girls reached the age of seventeen, they were encouraged to serve their *Pflichtjahr* (obligatory year).[10] At the age of eighteen, the obligatory youth service was terminated. Participation in one of the study groups of the BDM section "Faith and Beauty" was an option following BDM membership. It was voluntary and could commence from the age of seventeen.

The BDM Section "Faith and Beauty"

The BDM section "Faith and Beauty," founded in 1938, was initially under the direction of Clementine zu Castell, who resigned after her marriage in the summer of 1939. Her successor was Annemarie Kaspar, who directed the enterprise until early May 1941, then likewise tendering her resignation after marrying. Following Kaspar, Martha Stöckl headed the section until, finally, in February 1942 the Reich representative of the League of German Girls put the section under her leadership.[11] The concept of the "Faith and Beauty" section took into consideration the limited free time of young women who were often themselves working women, busy on the job. Service involved two to three hours a week, divided on a monthly basis into one period of physical exercise, two periods with a study group, and one period at a social evening. The two fixed components of the service were physical training and ideological schooling. Besides those there were various areas of work, open for the girls to choose voluntarily. Writing in the journal *Mädelschaft* (Edition A, November 1938), Clementine zu Castell men-

9. See Klönne, *Hitlerjugend,* 174ff.

10. The "Anordnung des Beauftragten für den Vierjahresplan über den verstärkten Einsatz von weiblichen Arbeitskräften in der Land- und Hauswirtschaft" (Decree of the Delegate for the Four-Year Plan on the Intensified Utilization of Female Workers in Agriculture and as Domestic Workers), in short "Pflichtjahr" (obligatory year), was introduced on February 15, 1938, by Hermann Göring, then "Beauftragter für den Vierjahresplan" (Delegate for the Four-Year Plan). This decree made it compulsory for all single women under the age of twenty-five to prove they had put in a year of service working in agriculture or as a domestic in order to be employed in private or state factories or offices as a blue-collar or white-collar worker. The obligatory year of service was limited to certain professions, involving in the main the clothing, textile, and tobacco industries or work in commercial enterprises and offices. It can be viewed as a kind of preparation for war in that it was intended to help relieve the projected labor shortage in agriculture and the sphere of domestic workers. It was possible in general to complete the obligatory year between the ages of fourteen and twenty-five. See Reese, "Mädchen im Bund Deutscher Mädel"; Birgit Jürgens, *Zur Geschichte des BDM (Bund Deutscher Mädel) von 1923 bis 1939* (Frankfurt a.M., 1994), 186ff. For an extended discussion, see Vogel, *Das Pflichtjahr für Mädchen.*

11. Personal letter from Jutta Rüdiger, former Reich representative of the League of German Girls, to the author from Oct. 26, 1982.

tioned eleven such focus areas. But what looked like a broad and diverse array was in actuality a narrow selection: typically, no areas of the natural sciences or technical subjects were represented. Of the 30,082 study groups in 1943, about a third, some 11,000, dealt with questions of home economics (cooking, sewing, home living, and family culture); 1,726 were study groups for the health services; and 5,526 centered on physical exercise. The others pursued a variety of topics, such as music, national folk life, anti–air raid protection, and fashion design.[12] In general, membership in the "Faith and Beauty" section was voluntary, but once a girl joined it was obligatory for her to take part in the study groups. Girls remained in this section until they reached the age of twenty-one. If they had not joined the National Socialist Women's Association (NS-Frauenschaft) at the age of eighteen, they were then supposed to be graduated into its ranks at the age of twenty-one.

Leaders in the League of German Girls

As a mass organization that was constantly expanding, the League of German Girls had great need of leaders: given its impressive growth, many girls were given the opportunity of being appointed to leadership positions. The advancement of a girl to the function of leader unfolded in accordance with detailed specific guidelines. The first move was to be selected by the leader of the *Mädelschar* (girls' platoon). The girl handpicked for advancement completed a practical preparation regimen for leaders and was then installed as leader of a *Mädelschaft* (girls' squad), the bottom formation within the League of German Girls, usually containing some ten to fifteen members.[13] As a matter of principle, every leader in the league was commissioned by their local authority and went through a six-month probationary period, after which they were officially appointed or promoted. A leader of a squad could visit an advanced course for platoon leaders and was then given control of such a unit. Then she began the core training program for leaders of the League of German Girls, encompassing in particular participation in weekend courses once a month.[14] If she so chose, she could voluntarily attend courses at the Girls' Leadership Training Centers of the Hitler

12. *Das junge Deutschland* 37, no. 1 (1943): 38.
13. The smallest group was a Mädelschaft (squad), consisting of about ten to fifteen girls. Four squads made up a Mädelschar (platoon), and four platoons constituted a *Gruppe* (company); three to five such companies made a *Ring* or battalion. Four to six Ringe constituted an *Untergau* (district). Around twenty districts made up an *Obergau* (region) and around thirty-five regions constituted the Reichsjugendführung.
14. *Wir schaffen: Jahrbuch des BDM* (Munich, 1938).

Youth (Führerinnenschulungswerk der Hitlerjugend). Those girls who wished to advance to a higher level of leadership, such as the leader of a *Mädelgruppe* (girls' company), continued their training at the regional leaders' schools and then at the Reich School for Leaders of BDM battalions (Mädelring), or they attended a course for leaders at the Academy for Youth Leadership (Akademie der Jugendführung).[15]

The female leadership of the Hitler Youth was structured according to rank and position. Position was the concrete function a leader was assigned, while service rank marked the level she had reached in the leadership hierarchy. Up to the rank of *Hauptmädelführerin,* the girls worked in a voluntary capacity. Ranks above this were part of the "leaders' circle" (*Führerinnenring*), the echelon of official full-time paid leaders established by Baldur von Schirach in 1933.[16] The HJ-Law of December 1, 1936, specified the legal position, powers, and obligations of these leaders. Official special uniforms for leaders were obligatory from the level of *Untergau* (district) and above. The uniform was a dark blue jacket, white blouse, and dark blue hat and coat. In the summer, the blue jacket was replaced by a white linen blazer. For festive occasions, there was a special dark blue two-piece suit with a cape and hat. Leaders could be distinguished through badges indicating their rank and region as well as cords in different colors that they wore as a part of their uniform. Cords and badges played a similarly important role within the Hitler Youth as banners and pennants that identified the specific battalions, companies, districts, and regions.

Within the "Faith and Beauty" section, the leadership tasks were distributed along slightly different lines. There were educated leaders who supervised the specific study groups, along with one leader responsible for "political-ideological schooling," who headed a complex consisting of ten study groups. A participant member selected as coordinator by this group leader was responsible for the practical implementation of tasks and duties within the individual study groups. The sports supervisors and leaders of girls in health service had special leadership functions.

However, the League of German Girls did not start out with an exacting carefully spelled out conception of what a National Socialist girls' organization ought to be. Rather, that agenda and vision evolved as a result of its history and the augmented power enjoyed by the league especially after 1933.

15. On the selection of leaders, see Klaus, *Mädchenerziehung zur Zeit,* 172ff.
16. Klönne, *Hitlerjugend,* 57.

CHAPTER 2

A Thumbnail Sketch of the History of the League of German Girls

National Socialist Girls' Organizations before 1933

National Socialist organizations for girls came into being within the framework of the National Socialist youth organization, inside the women's associations, and later likewise as an alliance of National Socialist schoolgirls. The evident early lack of interest in the NSDAP to clarify the scope and nature of an organization for girls makes it clear just how little importance was attached to young female members and how minuscule the number of girls in organized groups must have been. There were, however, constant attempts to recruit girls to the cause, though for a long time with little or no success.

Within the National Socialist youth organization, there were already groups for girls operating in the early 1920s.[1] The first such group was set up by Adolf Lenk.[2] In the first central office for the Hitler Youth, established by Kurt Gruber in 1926, a special department was set up for girls, headed by Helene Kunold and Anna Bauer.[3] Beginning in 1927, there was an increased drive to recruit girls in various localities as members in so-called sororities or sisterhoods (*Schwesterschaften*) inside the Hitler Youth. The *Hitler-Jugend-Zeitung* carried a report in July 1927 on the first such sisterhood in Plauen.[4] Yet despite intensive recruitment propaganda, there was little real interest in joining these groups. A situation report by the police in Dresden (February 18, 1929) notes, for example, that the sisterhood in

1. Numerous details on the early history of the League of German Girls can be found in Jürgens, *Zur Geschichte des BDM.*
2. "Institut für Zeitgeschichte," Fa. 88, Fasc. 333. Adolf Lenk, "Das Werden der NS-Jugendbewegung." See also Stachura, *Nazi Youth in the Weimar Republic,* 9.
3. Stachura, *Nazi Youth in the Weimar Republic,* 24.
4. Hans-Christian Brandenburg, *The Geschichte der HJ. Wege und Irrwege einer Generation* (Cologne, 1968), 52.

27

Chemnitz headed by Martha Aßmann could boast a total membership of just fifteen girls.[5] Nonetheless, the first contours of a broader structure appeared in the spring of 1929 with the appointment of Martha Aßmann as the first Reich leader of sisterhoods.[6]

Just like the leaders of the youth organization, the National Socialist women's associations also attempted early on to establish groups for girls. In 1923, the German Women's Order "Red Swastika" (Deutscher Frauen Orden "Rotes Hakenkreuz," or DFO) set up the first groups for young girls.[7] The first NS-Jungmädel groups were set up by the Associations for National Socialist Women (Frauenarbeitsgemeinschaften).[8] Groups for girls were created in the framework of local associations of National Socialist women.[9] Some were not part of the narrower National Socialist camp but belonged within the broader ambit of folkish groups, such as the Völkischer Mädchenbund[10] or the Deutscher Mädel Ring, founded in 1927. This organization was initially limited locally to Bavaria and through the spring of 1932 was under the tutelage of the Freecorps commander Gerhard Roßbach. Only later, when its head, Hilde Königsbauer, was appointed leader of the BDM in Munich, was the organization incorporated into the League of German Girls.[11]

A characteristic feature of the large number of small National Socialist and folkish girls' groups before 1933 was the fierce competition and scramble between them for a limited potential membership. In this diverse landscape of groupings, the girls' organization within the Hitler Youth, renamed in 1930 the League of German Girls within the

5. StA München (State Archive Munich), Pol. Dir. 6840. Lina Martha Aßmann, salesgirl, born December 22, 1895. Michael Buddrus has collected the short biographies of several Hitler Youth and League of German Girls leaders in his latest work on the Hitler Youth during the war. Buddrus, *Totale Erziehung für den totalen Krieg,* 1111–230.

6. See report on her appointment in *Hitler-Jugend-Zeitung* 6, no. 4 (1929).

7. Bundesarchiv Koblenz (BA), Sammlung Schumacher Collection Schumacher, G VIII/251, Dec. 2, 1931.

8. Frauenarbeitsgemeinschaften came into being in 1929, first in Berlin; see Stephenson, *Nazi Organization of Women,* 39.

9. Stephenson, *Nazi Organization of Women,* 84f.

10. Founded on May 1, 1925. For the program of the founding ceremony, see StA München, Pol. Dir. 6841/17.

11. BA Koblenz, Sammlung Schumacher, G VIII/251. "Hilde Königsbauer am 23. Ostermonds 1933 an den NSDAP-Gau München Oberbayern." The Deutscher Mädel Ring organized National Socialist schoolgirls and was thus actually a precursor of the NS League of Schoolgirls (NS Schülerinnenbund), set up in 1929. See also Brandenburg, *Geschichte der HJ. Wege,* 49; Klönne, *Hitlerjugend,* 9.

HJ (Bund deutscher Mädel in der HJ),[12] stood out. Though it was by no means larger than the various girls' groups attached to the National Socialist women's organizations, it enjoyed an advantage as a result of its uniform organization and incorporation within the ever more powerful bureaucratic structures of the Hitler Youth. In the summer of 1931, the various local National Socialist women's groups, the Association of National Socialist Women (Frauenarbeitsgemeinschaften), and the DFO merged to form the National Socialist Women's Association (NS-Frauenschaft). Elsbeth Zander, the former head of the DFO and a "tried and tested" veteran National Socialist, took over the reins of leadership.[13] At the same time, this marked the inclusion of the girls' groups under the aegis of the organized National Socialist women within a single unified structure. The consequence was an intensification of the struggle and frictions between the Hitler Youth and the NS-Frauenschaft over influence on the girls. While the women insisted on traditional rights to educate the girls, the Hitler Youth took a progressive stance, demanding a certain separate life for young people, including the girls.[14] The conflict came to a head in late 1931 and early 1932, highlighting the urgency of finding a solution.[15] On July 7, 1932, Gregor Strasser and Baldur von Schirach issued a directive dissolving all girls' groups in the NS-Frauenschaft and ordered their immediate transfer into the League of German Girls.[16] In one fell swoop, the league was thus installed as the sole National Socialist organization for girls.

But the NS-Frauenschaft was not willing to quickly admit defeat. Since the league included girls ages ten to eighteen, in the fall of 1932 the women set up the NS-Mädchenschaften (NS Girls' Associations), whose brief was to organize girls between the ages of eighteen and twenty-one.[17] In a letter on February 23, 1933, Lydia Gottschewski,

12. See *Völkischer Beobachter*, June 1, 1930.
13. On Elsbeth Zander, see Wagner, *Nationalsozialistische Frauenansichten*, 187.
14. See Schirach's remarks in a paper (Feb. 1, 1932) on the reasons why National Socialist work with girls must be carried out "within the framework of the total program for youth of the Hitler Youth," StA München, Pol. Dir. 6845/548.
15. For example, in connection with the disbanding of the German Women's Order and its incorporation into the NS-Frauenschaft, the Gau leader of the German Women's Order in the Ostmark ordered the disbanding of the girls' groups in the Hitler Youth and their reincorporation into the group for young girls under the aegis of the NS-Frauenschaft; see letter dated August 14, 1931, BA Koblenz, NS 22/349.
16. BA Koblenz, Sammlung Schumacher, G VIII/251.
17. BA Koblenz, Sammlung Schumacher, G VIII/230; letter, Schirach to Strasser, Nov. 8, 1932.

then the national head of the League of German Girls, pointed out just how swiftly these NS-Mädchenschaften were spreading, underscoring the threat they posed to the league.[18] At the end of March, in a countermove, the age limit for the league was raised to twenty-one, thus dissolving the NS-Mädchenschaften. Lydia Gottschewski now replaced Elsbeth Zander as head of the NS-Frauenschaft, this in addition to her duties as leader of the League of German Girls.[19] That double function was meant to suggest the important role of the organized women for girls' education and, at least temporarily, to throw oil on the troubled waters.[20]

Yet even if the league obtained autonomy at the local level, as a whole it remained subject to the male-dominated Hitler Youth. In a speech given by Baldur von Schirach at a conference of regional (*Gau*) and district (*Untergau*) leaders of the league held on June 20–21, 1934, in Potsdam, he left no doubts as to what limits his audience, the higher leadership echelon of the League of German Girls, had to respect: "I would like to make it perfectly clear here that I don't think it's right for BDM units to be placed directly under the control of the Hitler Youth formations. Nonetheless, I want to demand here that the BDM unconditionally accept the leadership of the Hitler Youth leaders in regard to any and all political questions. It seems to me this is so self-evident that we don't have to waste much talk here about this matter."[21]

The Development of the League of German Girls, 1933–45

When the drums beat a tattoo for the great festival, then standing opposite the brown ordered rows of the boys, you will see the girls'

18. BA Koblenz, NS 22/342. Lydia Gottschewski, whose married name was Ganzer-Gottschewski, was appointed national leader (*Bundesführerin*) of the League of German Girls by Baldur von Schirach at the third conference of league leaders held February 1933 in Weimar (the first two had been in Braunschweig in 1931 and 1932); see *Der deutsche Sturmtrupp* 1, no. 4 (1933), and 2, no. 13 (1934). Between March 15, 1932, and December 1932, this office of federal leader (*Bundesführerin*)—or of "expert for questions pertaining to girls in the national office of the Hitler Youth," as the post was designated before the ban of the SA in 1932, which also affected Hitler Youth and League of German Girls as subordinated parts (*Gliederungen*) of the SA—had been held by Elisabeth Greiff-Walden. In December 1932, in the course of a "purge" within the Hitler Youth, Greiff-Walden was dismissed; see Klaus, *Mädchenerziehung zur Zeit,* 229f.

19. BA Koblenz, NS 26/345, letter by Ley, Apr. 25, 1933.

20. Stephenson, *Nazi Organization of Women,* 89, points out that the Gauleiter often backed the side of the NS-Frauenschaften in the confrontation between them and the League of German Girls.

21. *Der deutsche Sturmtrupp* 2, no. 13 (1934).

groups, arrayed in a uniform and disciplined formation. And above all their heads on high, the banners fluttering in the wind: the flags of Prussia, of socialism and of the German Idea [*deutsche Idee*].[22]

When on January 30, 1933, the "drums for the great festival" were triumphantly sounded as Hitler ascended to power, the Hitler Youth was one of the National Socialist organizations that had remained quite small after 1930, this despite the upsurge of members in the NSDAP and the SA.[23] It stayed a relatively small organization both within the Nazi Party and also inside the broader youth movement as a whole. Yet it was still large as compared with the League of German Girls. When it comes to the size of its membership on the eve of the seizure of power, even internal Nazi sources are contradictory. One source indicates that in January 1932 there were 1,669 BDM girls and 66 *Küken* (chicks), as the young girls ages ten to fourteen were then called.[24] The NS League of Schoolchildren (NS-Schülerbund, or NSS) gave different figures: in February 1932, a total membership of 3,691 BDM girls and 345 young girls, surging to 5,184 BDM girls and 750 young girls for the month of March.[25] According to other NSS figures on the strength of the Hitler Youth in individual regions, total membership in April 1932 included 2,465 BDM girls and 423 young girls.[26] In October 1931, the league officially listed its membership at 5,000 girls,[27] doubtless too high an estimate. It seems realistic to assume a total figure for the end of 1932 of between 10,000 and 15,000 girls.[28] Yet in contrast with the Hitler Youth, whose membership numbers were stagnating, the league showed a disproportionately large growth since the end of 1931, a fact even noted outside the ambit of the Hitler Youth.[29] Though it had fewer members than the Hitler Youth, the league was marked by a growing attraction for female youth, since it

22. Gotthart Ammerlahn, "Der Bund Deutscher Mädchen," *Angriff,* July 13, 1931.

23. At the end of 1932, the Hitler Youth numbered about fifty thousand members; see Peter Stachura, "The Ideology of the Hitler Youth in the Kampfzeit," *Journal of Contemporary History* 8, no. 3 (1973): 158f.; see also Brandenburg, *Geschichte der HJ. Wege,* 124.

24. BA Koblenz, Sammlung Schumacher, G VIII/239.

25. StA München, Pol. Dir. 6845/388.

26. StA München, Pol. Dir. 6845/389, Apr. 11, 1932.

27. Josepha Fischer, "Entwicklungen und Wandlungen in den Jugendverbänden im Jahre 1931," *Das junge Deutschland* 26, no. 2 (1932): 44.

28. This figure is based on extrapolating the growth of 66 percent between the numbers given for January 1932 (1,735 girls in toto) and the NSS data for April 1932 (2,888 girls in toto) down to the end of 1932, which yields an estimated total of 13,210 members.

29. See Josepha Fischer, "Entwicklungen und Wandlungen in den Jugendverbänden im Jahre 1932," *Das junge Deutschland* 27, no. 2 (1933): 52.

appeared to satisfy certain needs of an ever larger number of adolescent girls.

For both organizations, January 30, 1933, was a watershed. The gigantic influx of new members in the league from then on was based on various reasons.[30]

1. Much of the upsurge in numbers, specifically in the case of girls, was due to new members who joined voluntarily. The "militant youth" had now become the youth movement of an established party. Although it had retained much of its earlier militant impetus, membership in its ranks no longer posed any social disadvantages or even dangers for the girls. This not only made the league an attractive option in the eyes of many youngsters; it also impacted the attitude of numerous parents, who no longer had any objections to their daughters joining the League of German Girls. For the same reason, there was a dramatic jump in the number of girls under fourteen years of age, the Jungmädel, separately organized within the framework of the league. While there were few such younger girls in the organization before 1933, their number at the end of that year was some 20 percent higher than that of girls ages fourteen and older.[31]

2. At the same time, the Hitler Youth utilized various compulsory measures in order to lend emphatic force to its desires for power. The usurpation by force of the leadership of the Reich Committee of the German Youth Associations (Reichsausschluß deutscher Jugendverbände) on April 5, 1933, the umbrella organization for all youth organizations in Germany, with a total membership of between 5 and 6 million young people, marked the beginning of *Gleichschaltung* of the political, religious, and youth movement–oriented youth organizations, their disbanding or forced transfer into the Hitler Youth. This led to a significant increase in the Hitler Youth membership ranks and at the same

30. According to Günter Kaufmann, himself a high-ranking Hitler Youth leader and personal assistant of Baldur von Schirach during his time in Vienna, there were 243,750 BDM girls and 349,482 young girls (Jungmädel) in the membership ranks of the organization at the end of 1933. I regard those figures as a very high estimate, but we lack any others for comparison. Günter Kaufmann, *Das kommende Deutschland* (Berlin, 1940), 39.

31. This calculation is based on Kaufmann's figures, since we have no other data for the end of 1933. Yet figures from 1935 would appear to confirm this ratio of Jungmädel to older girls ages fourteen and over; see Kaufmann, *Das kommende Deutschland,* 39.

time augmented the ranks of the league.[32] The Hitler Youth continued to expand its sphere of power. For example, an agreement signed with the Reich sports leader (*Reichssportführer*) made it possible by 1936 to construct an organizational nexus, making any individual activity in sports dependent for all practical purposes on concomitant membership in the Hitler Youth.[33] Similar agreements existed with the Reich Ministry for Nutrition (Reichsnährstand), the organization of National Socialist female students (Arbeitsgemeinschaft nationalsozialistischer Studentinnen, or ANSt), the National Socialist Welfare Organization (NSV), and the National Socialist Labor Organization (DAF).[34] By binding more and more activities and interests to compulsory membership in the Hitler Youth, the net of inclusion became ever tighter and more closely meshed.

Most successful were compulsory measures implemented in cooperation with the schools. As early as June 1934, State Youth Day (Staatsjugendtag) was introduced: on Saturdays the classes normally held at school were now put at the disposal of the Hitler Youth for organizing various sports activities.[35] All children and teenagers not in the Hitler Youth had to attend school on this day, and the teachers—some of

---

32. The official statistics for membership in youth organizations in Prussia for the year 1928 for youth ages fourteen to twenty-one were calculated on the basis of figures supplied by the Local and District Committees for Youth Welfare. These data indicated that 34.1 percent of the girls (47 percent in Berlin, 33 percent in Minden) were members in organizations. Among the boys, the corresponding figures were 57.9 percent (52 percent in Berlin, 48.1 percent in Minden). The surprisingly high figures for organized youth can be partially explained by the fact that the data for the total number of young people these figures were based on were inaccurate; see *Das junge Deutschland* 23, no. 12 (1929): 580f. Robert Dinse arrived at other figures in his study of leisure-time activity among adolescents in large urban areas, published in 1932. According to his findings, only about one-third of the boys and one-fourth of the girls were members of youth organizations. Interestingly, among the boys in his data, it was mainly high schoolers in the upper grades who were in organizations (42 percent), while among the girls a contrasting picture emerged: only 22 percent of those in higher grades in high school were in youth organizations, with the figures much higher for female clerks; see Robert Dinse, *Das Freizeitleben der Großstadtjugend. 5.000 Jungen und Mädchen berichten* [= Schriftenreihe des Deutschen Archivs für Jugendwohlfahrt 10] (Eberswalde, 1932), 101f. The largest proportion of organized young people belonged to a gymnastics society, sports club, or team (53.7 percent overall; 63.4 percent in Berlin, 50.4 percent in Minden); see *Das junge Deutschland* 23, no. 12 (1929): 583.
33. Kaufmann, *Das kommende Deutschland*, 84f.
34. Klönne, *Hitlerjugend*, 15.
35. Klönne, *Hitlerjugend*, 16.

them in party uniform or with a party badge—were obliged to teach topics pertaining to National Socialism. This opened the door to putting the children under enormous internal pressure to conform, a pressure that increased with the number of children and youth who remained nonmembers and had to show up for Saturday classes in school declining. The connection between school and membership in the Hitler Youth becomes especially clear from a survey conducted in December 1935 on membership in National Socialist youth organizations among pupils at schools in the state of Hesse.[36] While in the state secondary high schools, the figures for boys and girls in National Socialist youth organizations were nearly equal (96 percent of the male pupils, 95.9 percent of the females),[37] in the elementary schools (*Volksschulen*), 91 percent of the boys but only 82.7 percent of the girls became members in National Socialist organizations. The degree of membership was even lower in the vocational schools (*Berufsschulen*). Here only 73.7 percent of the boys were organized in the Hitler Youth, while the corresponding figure for girls was 45.1 percent. Kater cites similar findings from a survey at thirty elementary schools in the Oldenburg district, which showed that only 53.3 percent of the boys and a mere 20.8 percent of the girls were part of the Hitler Youth.[38] All these data clearly indicate that pupils with less education were less willing to join the ranks of the Hitler Youth, a tendency more pronounced in the case of the girls. Based on this linkage, one might conclude that susceptibility to the activities of the Hitler Youth was correlated with social class and was more marked in higher social strata. Yet this does not explain the gender difference: why were girls clearly less willing to become members than boys? Instead, we must assume that the schools themselves played a central role here: teachers exerted substantial pressure on young people to join the Hitler Youth, so that their willingness to become a member was bound up with the importance of the role that schools and education played in the biography of a young person. Where school was little more than an onerous obligation, the demands it made were followed only reluctantly and with hesitation. But where

36. Bavarian Central State Archive Munich (BHSA), Sec. 1 MK 14.858. Kater points out that in Hesse membership in the Hitler Youth was disproportionately high; see Michael H. Kater, "Bürgerliche Jugendbewegung und Hitlerjugend in Deutschland von 1926 bis 1939," *Archiv für Sozialgeschichte* 17 (1977): 170.

37. By contrast, only 59 percent of the boys and girls in private schools were Hitler Youth members. Since there is express mention that in some private schools HJ membership reached 90 to even 100 percent, this means that in other such schools there was quite evidently no pressure exerted in this respect; see BHSA, Sec. 1 MK 14.858.

38. Kater, "Bürgerliche Jugendbewegung," 169.

personal and vocational advancement was dependent on the school, pupils adhered to the positive attitude demanded. In this manner, willy-nilly, the school and thus its teachers became important accessories in implementing the external pedagogical agenda of the Hitler Youth for all German youth.[39]

Nonetheless, by the end of 1935, not even half of those between the ages of ten and eighteen had joined the Hitler Youth.[40] According to internal membership statistics for the end of the year 1935, 829,261 boys were members in the HJ and 569,717 girls were in the BDM. Again, the lower numerical figure contrasted with the fact that the rate of growth in the BDM, both in absolute and relative terms, was far higher than that of the HJ.[41] A drop in membership, such as that recorded for the HJ in Berlin (28.3 percent),[42] occurred in the BDM only in the areas of Central Elbe and Munich–Upper Bavaria and was so small that it can be disregarded.[43] A graphic presentation of membership figures indicates that the tendency noted for the HJ and BDM was far more pronounced for the younger ones ages ten to fourteen, who were organized within Deutsches Jungvolk (DJ) and Jungmädel (JM). While the absolute increase in the DJ was a bit below that of the HJ, the relative increase was only half as large.[44] By contrast, the absolute increase in the case of the JM was double that in the BDM, while the relative increase hovered only slightly above that of the BDM.[45] Thus, we may hypothesize that the DJ had reached something like a saturation point and was hardly expanding. Its membership was almost twice that of the HJ or the JM. The differences in membership between the JM and the BDM were not as marked, but here too the organization of younger girls clearly had more members than the

39. This does not mean that teachers became willing accessories. Yet they were a "suitable tool," as we will see later. The difficult situation teachers faced at the time is graphically described by the writer and playwright Ödon von Horvath in *Jugend ohne Gott* (Frankfurt a.M., 1977).

40. Brandenburg, *Geschichte der HJ. Wege,* 123, gives a figure of 47.7 percent. Kater, "Bürgerliche Jugendbewegung," 170, cites a figure of 45.24 percent, which is a total of 3,943,421 young people.

41. BA Koblenz, NS 26/358. "Statistik der Jugend." Growth in the BDM was 20.7 percent (97,773 girls), contrasted with 5.5 percent for the HJ (43,361 boys).

42. This amounted to some 7,400 boys; see BA Koblenz, NS 26/358. "Statistik der Jugend."

43. It was around 1 percent; see BA Koblenz, NS 26/358. "Statistik der Jugend."

44. On this basis, the number of boys organized in the Deutsches Jungvolk in December 1935 can be estimated at roughly 1,600,000; see BA Koblenz, NS 26/358. "Statistik der Jugend."

45. BA Koblenz, NS 26/358. "Statistik der Jugend."

BDM. Yet in contrast with HJ and DJ, whose membership stagnated or grew only by a meager increment, growth in the two girls' organizations was significant, just under 20 percent. Nonetheless, as of December 1935, the actual numbers lagged far behind the targeted goal of 100 percent membership.

The year 1936 was named the "Year of the Deutsches Jungvolk," marked by an energetic campaign to recruit new members. The objective was to enroll all from the cohort of 1926 in its ranks. For the first time, recruitment lists were put together and parents were sent letters instructing them to register their children.[46] By April 19, 1936, the eve of Hitler's birthday, some 90 percent of those born in 1926 had been recruited as members. A "stop on new members" ordered a short time later[47] was designed to put pressure on the remaining 10 percent of the ten year olds—and also on all those older children and teenagers who until that point had refused to join. Nonetheless, despite intensive campaigning, the Hitler Youth managed only to reach and recruit some 60 percent of all young people between the ages of ten and eighteen.[48]

Yet Baldur von Schirach remained confident: "And I was totally convinced that the remaining 40 percent would come on in of their own accord."[49] Be that as it may, von Schirach nevertheless chose to provide that confidence with a legislative boost. On December 1, 1936, the HJ-Law was promulgated, cementing the Hitler Youth as the official state youth organization. Paragraph 2 of the law stated: "In addition to the parental home and the school, the Hitler Youth must educate and mold all of German youth, physically, mentally and morally, in the spirit of National Socialism, for service to the people and the folk community."[50]

So the Hitler Youth was now installed as the third educational institution in the Reich, alongside family and school. Yet what appeared at first glance as augmented power turned out on closer inspection to be a Pyrrhic victory. This is borne out by remarks by a senior leader in the League of German Girls:

I: Yes, and then you already mentioned, 1933 was, at least for the BDM, the great turning point.

46. Brandenburg, *Geschichte der HJ. Wege,* 178.
47. This happened on May 26, 1936.
48. Klaus, *Mädchenerziehung zur Zeit,* 236, cites a Bavarian source that reports that they had successfully recruited the boys but not the girls. Kater, "Bürgerliche Jugendbewegung," 169ff., has a similar argument,.
49. Schirach, *Ich glaubte an Hitler,* 232.
50. "HJ-Gesetz," Dec. 1, 1936, RGBl. I 1936, 993.

B 22: Right, it sure was, then everything started to flow.

I: How pleased or unhappy were you with this influx of new kids?

B 22: Well, in the beginning very pleased. Like in the beginning, well, it was usually the case that some kind of bond was still there between the individual girls who got together at a social evening. But it became worse afterwards, see, when the state youth came in, in '36. When everybody came on in, including those who weren't interested at all. You know, before it had been on a voluntary basis, and then of course you get much more enthusiasm. I mean the pleasure in taking part in a social evening is a lot greater for the kids than when *every*body's in there, including lots who don't feel like even being there.

New problems arose after 1936, generated directly by the new compulsory character of the Hitler Youth. The tendency distinctive to National Socialism of trying to implement socially desired ends by means of organizational and technocratic measures had not reckoned with the possible consequences: a huge wave of disinterest swept over the ranks of new recruits, blocking the primary purpose of the Hitler Youth—namely, to inculcate young people with National Socialist ideology.[51] In his regional study of the development of the Hitler Youth in Bavaria, Klönne concludes: "Seen overall, the ambition to organize youth in its entirety through the HJ and to socialize it in the image and thought of the NS turned out, pedagogically speaking, to be quite unrealistic."[52]

The lack of possibilities to integrate Hitler Youth allowed the smoldering disputes between the NS-Frauenschaft and the League of German Girls to flare anew.[53] Klönne points out that one response to the waning attractiveness of the organization was the "development of a whole system of competitions and contests between young people" and "in the case of the boys . . . offering options involving military-like activities for youth, generally fused with technical interests."[54] Bespeaking a total lack of imagination, it had been decided that the girls should be given training in domestic science,[55] forging a closer bridge in content to the work of the NS-Frauenschaft. As a result, a

51. Beginning in 1936–37, social evening folders with study guidelines and materials were issued so as to make them more uniform, forestalling any deviations in presentation of the required content; see "Wir schaffen," *Jahrbuch des BDM* (1938).

52. Klönne, "Jugendprotest und Jugendopposition," 546.

53. See Stephenson, *Nazi Organization of Women,* 90f.

54. Klönne, "Jugendprotest und Jugendopposition," 550.

55. See Klönne, *Hitlerjugend,* 19; Klaus, *Mädchenerziehung zur Zeit,* 238.

new dispute erupted over what should be done with the girls between the ages of eighteen and twenty-one. One of the first measures introduced by the newly installed Reich representative of the League of German Girls, Jutta Rüdiger, who replaced Trude Mohr-Bürkner on January 24, 1937,[56] was her order establishing special groups of the BDM (*Sonderscharen*), a directive spelled out in her public New Year's address in 1938. After the creation of the BDM section "Faith and Beauty" on January 19, 1938, these were renamed working groups (*Arbeitsgemeinschaften*).[57] These working groups replaced the customary service in the BDM and were interest focused. Their creation was an attempt to take the needs of young women into greater account, making the organization more attractive and thus helping to bring in more members. Nonetheless, the rivalry with the NS-Frauenschaft continued.[58] Its external frame was the elaboration of the regulations on implementation of the HJ-Law. Those regulations were ready in March 1939, marking a clear defeat of the leadership of the Hitler Youth (*Reichsjugendführung*). Just as for the boys, obligatory service for the girls was now from the age of ten to eighteen, excluding BDM members ages seventeen to twenty-one from any special consideration in this connection. In August 1937, Bormann had still emphasized that girls should not be transferred to the NS-Frauenschaft until they reached the age of twenty-one.[59] But the balance of power had shifted so substantially by October 1939 that von Schirach believed it was necessary to come to an understanding with Gertrud Scholtz-Klink, leader of the National Socialist Women's Organization.[60] This agreement specified that it was left to the personal decision of the individual girl whether to remain in the league after finishing her obligatory service or to become a member of the NS-Frauenschaft.[61]

56. Lydia Gottschewski served as national leader of the League of German Girls until the summer of 1933. The organization was then run for a year by the five heads of the BDM regional Gau associations (East, West, North, Central, and South), until Trude Mohr (later Mohr-Bürkner) was appointed leader. See Klaus, *Mädchenerziehung zur Zeit,* 232; Jürgens, *Zur Geschichte des BDM,* 58, 74ff.

57. Personal communication, Jutta Rüdiger, Oct. 26, 1982.

58. A letter by Baldur von Schirach dated July 6, 1938, suggests that it was Rudolf Heß in particular who tried to have the older girls placed under the aegis of the NS-Frauenschaft; see BA Koblenz, R, 43 II/525a.

59. Martin Bormann (1900–1945), party member since 1927, served as Reichsleiter and Stabsleiter for Rudolf Hess beginning in 1933. In 1941 he became head of the party chancellery and in 1942 Hitler's secretary. During the end of the war, he was Hitler's closest collaborator.

60. Gertrud Scholtz-Klink (1902–99), party member since 1929. From 1934 onward, she was leader of the National Socialist Women's Association. On Scholtz-Klink see Böltken, *Führerinnen im Führerstaat,* chap. 2; Koonz, *Mothers in the Fatherland,* 17ff; Anna Maria Sigmund. *Die Frauen der Nazis I* (Vienna, 1998); Wagner, *Nationalsozialistische Frauenansichten.*

61. Stephenson, *Nazi Organization of Women,* 91.

The decomposition of this huge and inflated bureaucracy, quite obvious after 1936, continued to exacerbate during the war. The service aspect dissolved more and more and was revamped to meet the demands of the war. War-related jobs and activities of all kinds dominated everyday life in the league.[62] Along with the economic utility that accrued,[63] there was the enhanced sense of certainty that young people's hands were in fact busy and under proper control. The problem of leadership, in any case always latent, now became acute. The consequence was a series of rationalizations and the increased use of female leaders, even in the Hitler Youth.[64] In 1941, the separation between the DJ and the HJ and between the JM and the BDM, long since obsolete, was abandoned,[65] and in early 1943, the leadership echelons of the Hitler Youth and the League of German Girls were then combined.[66] From 1943 on, the heavier bombing raids prevented any kind of continuous service. As a result of evacuations, the destruction of houses and apartments by bombing, and the resulting frequent moves by families to new quarters, control was rendered extremely difficult, if not virtually impossible, in the large urban areas. Free spaces were generated, uncontrolled, which young people seized on for their own purposes.[67] This provided fertile soil for lawlessness, in particular for the gangs and cliques that began to proliferate.[68] The Hitler Youth fought

62. See Reese, "Mädchen im Bund Deutscher Mädel," 174ff.

63. For instance, between November 1941 and August 1942, the War Service of the League of German Girls (Hilfseinsatz des Bundes Deutscher Mädel) relieved the Berlin Transportation Service (BVG) by providing 6,601 working hours; see BA Koblenz, NS 26/358. "Kriegseinsätze der Hitlerjugend," 91.

64. See Reese, "Mädchen im Bund Deutscher Mädel," 183; Klaus, *Mädchenerziehung zur Zeit,* 245.

65. *Der Reichsbefehl,* Jan. 2, 1941, 19f.

66. *Der Reichsbefehl,* Feb. 10, 1943, 79.

67. There was, however, also an element of increased control during the war insofar as children, especially in large metropolitan areas, were sent to "Kinderlandverschickungslager" (KLV-Lager), evacuation camps for children, to avoid being exposed to air raids. Here they were supervised by a teacher and a member of the Hitler Youth. An excellent account of this experience is given by Hermand, *A Hitler Youth in Poland.*

68. Lothar Gruchmann, "Jugendopposition und Justiz im Dritte Reich. Die Probleme bei der Verfolgung der 'Leipziger Meuten' durch die Gerichte," in Wolfgang Benz, ed., *Miscellanea. Festschrift für Helmut Krausnick* (Stuttgart, 1980), 103–30; Matthias von Hellfeld, *Edelweißpiraten in Köln. Jugendrebellion gegen das 3. Reich. Das Beispiel Köln-Ehrenfeld* (Cologne, 1981); Horn, "Youth Resistance in the Third Reich"; Arno Klönne, *Gegen den Strom. Ein Bericht über die Jugendopposition im Dritten Reich* (Hanover and Frankfurt a.M., 1957); Klönne, "Jugendprotest und Jugendopposition"; Detlev Peukert, "Die Edelweißpiraten. Protestbewegungen jugendlicher Arbeiter im Dritten Reich," in Richard Löwenthal and Patrick von zur Mühlen, eds., *Widerstand und Verweigerung in Deutschland 1933 bis 1945* (Berlin and Bonn, 1982), 177–201.

bitterly against these groupings, and they were pursued without mercy by the state authorities.

In summary, we can delineate three periods in the history of the League of German Girls. Before 1933, membership in the organization was voluntary. The organization remained small but from mid-1931 began to grow. Between 1933 and 1936, the league went through a huge cycle of expansion. From the tiny and dedicated "militant cadre community" a mighty organization developed that came to encompass nearly one-half of all German girls between the ages of ten and eighteen. This enormous spurt in its ranks was the result of an alternating policy of voluntary membership and compulsion. Compulsory measures were concealed, perceptible primarily as internal pressure. Beginning in 1936, however, the compulsory character of the Hitler Youth was evident to all. The state youth now had an increasingly more sophisticated organizational and legal apparatus at its disposal in order to implement its claims to power.[69] But the zenith of external power spelled at the same time the onset of internal decomposition as the organization unraveled within. The factor of compulsion led to a lack of interest, boredom, and useless busywork. This was a tendency that only increased in direct proportion to the more rigidly preplanned external framework, intensifying as the scope became more circumscribed for more freely chosen involvement and activity. An inescapable circle arose between an ever more perfected control over young people and an ever greater readiness on their part to resist and refuse to cooperate. That tendency spread during the course of the war as service in the Hitler Youth was gutted of its meaning and the external situation became ever more confused.

---

69. Kater, "Bürgerliche Jugendbewegung," 169, correctly stresses that membership in the Hitler Youth could only be implemented by force after 1939, that is, after the promulgation of the regulations on implementation of the HJ-Law. Michael Buddrus, *Totale Erziehung für den totalen Krieg,* 289, even argues that it took as long as 1941–42, actually until 1944, to force every young person into the Hitler Youth and to talk about a state youth, as only then did the authorities have a realistic overview over those who had to be drawn to service in the Hitler Youth. Nonetheless, for a ten-year-old it was often virtually impossible after 1936 to avoid being recruited into the ranks of the Hitler Youth, while the older boys and girls might manage to avoid being recruited.

CHAPTER 3

Ideology and Practice of Organizing Girls in the League of German Girls

Between Tradition and Progress: The League's Ideology of Femininity

> Where human beings are nothing but a function, they have to be young.[1]

Writing in 1937 in a key publication that was to influence the ideology of the League of German Girls, Trude Bürkner, Reich representative of the league, summarized the guiding ideals of National Socialist "education for girls."

> The work of the BDM is framed by two pedagogical slogans given to us by the Führer himself and the leader of German youth, Baldur v. Schirach. Speaking at the youth rally in Berlin on May 1, 1936, the Führer handed us our brief: "And you in the BDM, educate the girls—make them for me into strong and brave women!" And at the beginning of our work, our Reich youth leader once formulated the task before us in these words: "In the BDM, the girls should be molded into champions of the National Socialist world view." These two sentences, so simple in formulation, summarize our entire educational work with all of German girlhood.[2]

The programmatic pronouncements on the pedagogical goals of the League of German Girls rarely contain anything profound. Rather, their distinguishing mark is a rhetorical pathos behind which the con-

1. Karl Jaspers, *Die geistige Situation der Zeit* (Berlin and New York, 1979), 44.
2. Bürkner, *Der Bund Deutscher Mädel*, 7.

41

tours of a pedagogical concept can be dimly discerned. The only concrete element that repeatedly reoccurs in the pedagogical postulates is the self-evident character of motherhood as an integral component of female existence. The scientific proof commonly mustered for the importance of motherhood in National Socialist education for girls is Hitler's famous dictum: "The unshakable aim of female education must be the coming mother."[3] It would seem only natural to seek the educational goals of the league in these articulated ideals.[4]

National Socialist emphasis on motherhood as the meaning of female existence is quite evident, as are the measures for promoting marriage and the family. But can we assume this exhausts the National Socialist conception of the woman? There are two objections to any such conclusion. First, empirical studies show that women, generally speaking, were not nudged out of the job market and ushered back into the bosom of the reproductive family.[5] Second, within the concept of motherhood, side by side with its being a natural given fact, there is always a secondary substantive interpretation: here anthropological dimensions are necessarily supplemented by historical and cultural aspects. The notion that motherhood should be an essential part of a woman's life was widespread: National Socialism shared the view not just with other political groups but also with many girls and women themselves. We should thus try to pinpoint the content in the National Socialist concept of motherhood that is distinctive.

More recent research indicates that there was no wish for children "at any price"; rather, the paragon of an ideal mother was bound to the

3. Adolf Hitler, *Mein Kampf. The First Complete and Unexpurgated Edition Published in the English Language* (New York, 1939), 401.
4. See Hans-Jochen Gamm, *Führung und Verführung. Pädagogik im Nationalsozialismus* (Munich, 1964), 38 ff.; Margret Lück, *Die Frau im Männerstaat. Die gesellschaftliche Stellung der Frau im Nationalsozialismus. Eine Analyse aus pädagogischer Sicht* (Frankfurt a.M., 1979), 86; Dorothee Klinksiek, *Die Frau im NS-Staat* [= Schriftenreihe der Vierteljahreshefte für Zeitgeschichte, No. 44] (Stuttgart, 1982), 50; Pine, *Nazi Family Policy,* 49; Michael H. Kater, *Hitler Youth* (Cambridge, Mass., 2004; published in German as *Hitler-Jugend* [Darmstadt, 2005]; citations are to the German translation), 67.
5. Space here precludes any detailed examination of female employment under National Socialism. See Stefan Bajohr, *Die Hälfte der Fabrik. Geschichte der Frauenarbeit in Deutschland 1914–1945* (Marburg, 1979); Timothy Mason, "Zur Lage der Frauen in Deutschland 1930–1940. Wohlfahrt, Arbeit und Familie," in *Gesellschaft. Beiträge zur Marxschen Theorie,* vol. 6 (Frankfurt a.M., 1976), 118–93; Rupp, *Mobilizing Women for War;* Carola Sachse, *Siemens, der Nationalsozialismus und die moderne Familie. Eine Untersuchung zur sozialen Rationalisierung in Deutschland im 20. Jahrhundert* (Hamburg, 1990); Stephenson, *Women in Nazi Society;* Annemarie Tröger, "Die Frau im wesensgemäßen Einsatz," in Frauengruppe Faschismusforschung, ed., *Mutterkreus und Arbeitsbuch,* 246; Dörte Winkler, *Frauenarbeit im "Dritten Reich"* (Hamburg, 1977).

fulfillment of specific behavioral norms—cleanliness, order, punctuality, efficiency. Attempts were made to realize these norms via a dual policy of "selection and eradication."[6] So to assert that the primary pedagogical aim of the league was to prepare the girls for their future roles as housewives and mothers requires further substantive clarification. If we take a closer look at the program and programmatic statements of the league, what is striking is that, aside from a couple of global pronouncements, there is hardly any reference to motherhood and its content. The former Reich representative of the League of German Girls, Jutta Rüdiger, commented on this candidly in retrospect.

In the period right after the government takeover, there were a couple of men, not authorized in any way to do so, who expressed their own ideas on what they thought the role of the woman should be, talking about "noble womanhood." Or asserting that the woman's place is in the home, etc. This didn't phase us in the slightest—I mean female youth at the time. Sure, we were convinced that the degrading way women had been treated in the past, both as housewives and mothers, was leading to a dissolution of the family, and thus to the destruction of the primary cell of what constitutes a people. So we quite agreed with the view that a woman's life, biologically in a physical and mental sense, could be most happily fulfilled if she were a shaping force for the family, both morally and in the sphere of culture. But that wasn't supposed to mean that a woman should only "stay home" and stick to the kid's bedroom or the kitchen pots. No, she should also be active in the job world or in political life, educated or trained in her way. In the education of girls—and that was an area where we had more autonomy than any generation that had gone before us!—we rarely spoke about "motherhood." Rather, we educated the girls in their own interest and that of the nation, preparing them to lead healthy wholesome lives, to take an active role in the world of work and in society. But first and

6. See Gisela Bock, *Zwangssterilisation im Nationalsoziaismus. Studien zur Rassenpolitik und zur Frauenpolitik* [= Schriften des Zentralinstituts für Sozialwissenschaftliche Forschung der Freien Universität Berlin, vol. 48] (Opladen, 1986); Gisela Bock, "'Zum Wohle des Volkskörpers . . .' Abtreibung und Sterilisation im Nationalsozialismus," *Journal für Geschichte* 2, no. 6 (1980): 58–65; Gisela Bock, "Antinatalism, Maternity, and Paternity in Nazism Socialist Racism," in David F. Crew, ed., *Nazism and German Society, 1933–1945* (London and New York, 1994): 110–40; Gabriele Czarnowski, "Frauen—Staat—Medizin. Aspekte der Körperpolitik im Nationalsozialismus," *Beiträge zur feministischen Theroie und Praxis* 8, no. 14 (1985): 79–98.

foremost, what we wanted was to educate them to have a bright and cheery life as young girls.[7]

This statement makes clear that the league did not seek in a one-sided way to orient girls to the obligations of the family.[8] It also indicates that direct reference to motherhood in the education of girls itself had little importance. Other criteria topped the list here: the "toughening" of the body, physical and mental health, a sense of duty, and—what seems most important—a separate life of their own as young girls.

The strict separation between an adult world and a world of youth—and the express inclusion of girls in that second category—points to a central element in National Socialist education for girls. It reoccurs in almost all of the programmatic books and pamphlets of the League of German Girls. Yet initially the view that girls were part of Jugend and should be reckoned with other young people, and not subsumed under some rubric together with women, derived from another source: namely, the desire for power of the male leadership echelon of the Hitler Youth. Salient here was their aim to expand the organization and enhance its importance, since, in the earlier phase, female membership in the Hitler Youth was quite controversial. At a special conference of the Hitler Youth held in Nuremberg in August 1929, F. Bucher from Hamburg put forward a proposal, its second section relating to female membership in the Hitler Youth.

In this connection, we should clarify whether the sisterhoods that have been operating up to now under the umbrella of "Gruber-Plauen" could affiliate with working groups of this Hitler organization. As far as I can judge, the women's movement is just as opposed to this readiness on the part of certain girls' groups for affiliation as

7. Personal communication, Jutta Rüdiger, Oct. 26, 1982.
8. Tröger cites Zimmermann-Eisel, who determined that the National Socialists "stuck far more resolutely . . . to the principle of specific female occupations than they did to the dogma of rejecting jobs for women outside the home"; see Tröger, "Die Frau im wesensgemäßen Einsatz," 250. Evidence suggests, however, that while it was considered a matter of course that a girl learned a profession and worked in a job, National Socialist labor policy tried to channel the girls to those jobs within domestic economy, agriculture, childcare, and nursing that—apart from being considered a female domain—had a serious labor shortage especially during the war. BA, NS 22/447 (Völkischer Beobachter, 12.10.1941); Reichsbefehl 24/41 K (29.5.1941): 4f. That the effort of girls within their profession was important especially during the war is confirmed by Buddrus, *Totale Erziehung für den totalen Krieg,* 558–59; Reese, "Mädchen im Bund Deutscher Mädel," 271–82.

is male youth itself. It's noteworthy that on the basis of my own personal inquiries, both Jungsturm and Jung Stahlhelm[9] are also adamantly opposed to allowing affiliation for young girls. On the other hand, a segment of the young girls organized within the women's movement have a complaint: they believe they are not receiving the proper stimulation and training to become active members of the German folk community in keeping with the purposes and aims of the German Women's Order. And right inside our own movement, we should not overlook what's happening. Now even patriotic organizations of the far right are starting to indoctrinate women and educate them to cooperate more closely with the men.[10]

There are two different stated positions regarding this proposal: one coming from the national central office of the NSDAP and the other from leadership of the Hitler Youth. The proposal suggests that it was mainly the girls themselves who wanted their groups to affiliate with the Hitler Youth,[11] an idea rejected both by the women and the young men. While the NSDAP considered "the formation of groups for young girls in our youth associations . . . questionable," initially recommending that the party "study the situation in connection with the upcoming Nuremberg workers' sports festival,"[12] the leadership of the Hitler Youth declared: "The existing girls' groups in the Hitler Youth, organized in the so-called sisterhoods of the Hitler Youth, should be welcomed as something positive, and we should promote their development."[13]

This indicates that the party, whose primary interest lay in boosting the party's image and achieving the greatest possible attraction for the masses, was far slower in abandoning traditionalist views than the power-hungry Hitler Youth. Yet its position was not fundamentally conservative but rather opportunistic, its leadership preferring to observe the course of the events. That was without a doubt possible for the party because, in its perception, the so-called girls' question was at best little more than a marginal problem. When the party decided to allow the girls to stay within von Schirach's Hitler Youth three years later, that indicated a strategic consideration: the inclusion of girls in

9. These are two youth groups on the political right.
10. BA Koblenz, NS 26/352.
11. Unfortunately, no additional evidence for this could be found.
12. BA Koblenz, NS 26/352.
13. BA Koblenz, NS 26/336.

the Hitler Youth was viewed as the basis for incorporating girls, voluntarily and in mass numbers, into the "movement."

An analysis of the arguments put forward during the dispute over authority that raged in 1931–32 between the NS-Frauenschaft and the Hitler Youth can shed useful light on certain aspects of the character of the League of German Girls. The differences, ultimately bound up with the jockeying for power of the two organizations, involved questions regarding the organization and substantive content of their work. While the women insisted on affiliating the girls' groups with the NS-Frauenschaft, even if they were prepared to grant them a certain autonomy within the organization, the Hitler Youth stuck to its principled guns: "Youth must be led by youth."[14] The following quotation shows that behind this principle lurked a pure and simple opportunism, not fundamental considerations.

> Germany went down to defeat not only due to the lack of political education of its soldiers, but also of a large segment of its women. What would be more appropriate then but to make use of the new uniform attitude towards youth, which quite evidently includes female youth? And, by extending it, to educate a new generation of women in accordance with our thinking. This will only be possible if the young people feel a certain contrast between themselves and the older generation of women. I think that psychological factor is of extraordinary importance. It needs to be taken into special consideration.[15]

So the Hitler Youth made pragmatic use of the politicization of female youth, their reserve and skepticism toward the older generation of women. These attitudes point to just how much that generation had been impacted by the broader youth movement, even if it had not necessarily been actively involved.[16] The girls who grew up in the 1920s

14. This slogan emerged within the German youth movement and was meant to suggest a certain independent life for young people. Although independency ceased to exist where youth had to subject themselves unquestionably to their respective group leaders within the Hitler Youth, there still remained a certain independence on the lower levels within the Hitler Youth and the League of German Girls.

15. From a letter dated February 2, 1932, in which von Renteln presents reasons why "N.S. work with girls must be carried out in the framework of a total program of work with youth in the HJ." BA Koblenz, Collection Schumacher, G VIII/251, 4.

16. See Lisbeth Franzen-Hellersberg, "Die Frau und die Jugendbewegung," in Richard Thurnwald, ed., *Die neue Jugend* [= Forschungen zur Völkerpsychologie und Soziologie, vol. 4] (Leipzig, 1927), 129–44; Irene Stoehr, "Neue Frau und alte Bewegung. Zum Generationenkonflikt in der Frauenbewegung der Weimarer Republik," in Jutta Dahlhoff, Uschi Frey,

were no longer shaped by the duality dominant before 1914: the image of a woman geared to the intimacy of the family versus women fulfilling themselves and being active outside the home. They had instead been influenced by the ideal of the self-confident and self-assertive "new woman" and the "female comrade" and her ideals.[17] Seen in this context, the political position of the NS-Frauenschaft seemed obsolete, outmoded in terms of the criterion of efficiency.

This is evident if one looks at their concrete substantive program, where there were evident differences between the girls' groups in the German Women's Order (DFO) and the League of German Girls. Though militancy was more pronounced in the groups associated with the DFO—the girls were encouraged to despise their oppressors—the actual "struggle" and political activism were pared down to quite conventional mundane activity: donkey work for the men in the party. By way of illustration, in the spring of 1931, girls were asked to volunteer in Berlin for laundry work, namely, to do the wash of the SA. Three weeks later, the regional National Socialist paper *Angriff* carried the following report:

"Group of Jungmädel reports for laundry duty Friday evening at 8!" They walk across the dark courtyard, descending into a dimly lit laundry room in the basement below. The girls arrive slowly, dribbling in. They've got a hard day's work behind them. They're worn out. Often theirs is a job they don't like: mechanical work, working for a Jewish boss, a nerve-shattering job in an office or factory. But now as they climb down the worn steps one by one and gradually assemble downstairs in the laundry room, every one of them is beaming, a smile on her face. Because the task that awaits them is but a small portion of the enormous work for Germany. It's labor for the SA.[18]

and Ingrid Schöll, eds., Frauenmacht in der Geschichte. Beiträge des Historikerinnentreffens 1985 zur Frauengeschichtsforschung (Düsseldorf, 1986), 390–400.

17. See Atina Grossmann, *Reforming Sex: The German Movement for Birth Control and Abortion Reform 1920–1950* (New York, 1995); Dagmar Reese-Nübel, "Kontinuitäten und Brüche in den Weiblichkeitskonstruktionen im Übergang von der Weimarer Republik zum Nationalsozialismus," in Hans-Uwe Otto and Heinz Sünker, eds., *Soziale Arbeit und Faschismus. Volkspflege und Pädagogik im Nationalsozialismus* (Bielefeld, 1986), 223–41; Cornelie Usborne, *The Politics of the Body in Weimar Germany: Women's Reproductive Rights and Duties* (Houndsmill, Basingstroke, and Hampshire, 1992).

18. *Angriff,* Apr. 2, 1931.

One can easily imagine the actual "enthusiasm" of these young female workers and the true "effectivity" of such propaganda and recruitment. After all, these were girls contemporaries often criticized for being bent on seeking diversion and the pleasures of consumption.[19] Moreover, the leisure time available to them was quite limited. The self-presentation of the League of German Girls, then, was very different: "Hey kids, that's right! Girls, let's get active in the HJ! Forget all the warnings of the philistines. Our message is loud and clear: come on over to us. We have to become a people! Everyone should be part of that! This is the most positive kind of activity, working with youth."[20]

Trude Mohr, later Reich representative of the League of German Girls, was unequivocal in expressing support for National Socialist youth and the primacy of the Hitler Youth in this article in *Angriff*, in which she called for setting up BDM groups in Brandenburg.[21] The activities in the league were patterned quite closely on those from the broader youth movement, involving trips and excursions, sports, and evening social meetings with hands-on handicraft activities and singing. This was not only important politically; it also had relevance for power politics. Trude Mohr, an experienced leader from the Bündische Jugend, was pursuing a successful trajectory: at the beginning of 1932, the "Gau Brandenburg" she headed had become the second largest BDM Gau in Germany, boasting a membership of 155 girls.[22] Her appointment in 1931 as BDM leader for the Berlin region should be seen against this backdrop. The subsequent decision in November 1932 in favor of the league as the sole National Socialist organization for girls also indicates that the league, with a program decidedly geared to the youth movement, had proven itself to be the more attractive and effective organization in terms of the NSDAP con-

19. See Lisbeth Franzen-Hellersberg, *Die jugendliche Arbeiterin, ihre Lebensweise und Lebensform. Versuch sozialpsychologischer Forschung zum Zweck der Umwertung proletarischer Tatbestände* (Tübigen, 1932); Hildegard Jüngst, *Die jugendliche Fabrikarbeiterin. Ein Beitrag zur Industriepädagogik* [= Neue Beiträge zur Erziehungswissenschaft 5] (Paderborn, 1929); Mathilde Kelchner, *Kummer und Trost jugendlicher Arbeiterinnen. Eine sozialpsychologische Untersuchung an Aufsätzen von Schülerinnen der Berufsschule* [= Forschungen zur Völkerpsychologie und Soziologie, vol. 6] (Leipzig, 1929).
20. *Angriff,* July 1, 1931.
21. Mohr had been a BDM leader there since the end of the 1920s; see the interview with Mohr-Bürkner in Klaus, *Mädchenerziehung zur Zeit,* 2:8–33.
22. In the forty-five Gau districts across Germany in January 1932, the BDM was represented in fourteen of them, with a membership of 1,735 girls; see BA Koblenz, Collection Schumacher, G VIII, 239.

ception of mass politics. Let us now turn to the question of the historical function of the concept of "youth" and its importance and fascination for the girls.

Philippe Ariès has shown that childhood is not just an anthropological given but has gone through a long historical development. And Norbert Elias has described how the gap between adults and children and adolescents widened in the "process of civilization."[23] That breach was filled in part by what we call education, and there can be no doubt that this sphere grew ever larger. It was given its most essential impetus by the process of urbanization in the eleventh century, whose complex economic forms necessitated a postponement of the age of "coming of age."[24]

There were three forms of youth in the Middle Ages: squires, students, and apprentices. They had three "symbolic declarations" of maturity:[25] bestowal of knighthood, graduation, and conclusion of apprenticeship. As Heinrich Feilzer showed in a study on youth in medieval feudal society, it was solely the factor of education that brought about a "decoupling between youth and the adult world."[26] In constituting youth as a developmental phase, a consciousness of youth arose by itself as a spin-off of the educative process. This was a process that, significantly promoted by the Renaissance and Reformation, culminated in the Enlightenment, in the pedagogical writings of Rousseau. If the existence of youth initially augmented the range of options for adults to influence adolescents, youth consciousness marked a caesura that allowed adolescents to step out of the constraints of tradition. The concept of youth was thus highly ambivalent.

In a small treatise published in 1947, Theodor Litt argued that the relation to history changed with the Enlightenment.[27] While the world of the fathers and forefathers had previously circumscribed the universe of past experience that adolescents were expected to internalize and orient themselves toward, now all hope centered on the future. Unburdened by the ballast of the past, youth gained a whole new

23. Philippe Ariès, *Centuries of Childhood: A Social History of Family Life,* trans. Robert Baldick (New York, 1962); Norbert Elias, *The Civilizing Process,* trans. Edmund Jephcott (New York, 1978).

24. Leopold Rosenmayr, "Jugend," in René König, ed., *Handbuch der empirischen Sozialforschung,* 2d rev. ed., vol. 6 (Stuttgart, 1976), 73.

25. Rosenmayr, "Jugend," 73.

26. Heinrich Feilzer, *Jugend in der mittelalterlichen Ständegesellschaft. Ein Beitrag zum Problem der Generationen* [= Wiener Beiträge zur Theologie, vol. 36] (Vienna, 1971), 272.

27. Theodor Litt, *Das Verhältnis der Generationen. Ehedem und heute* (Wiesbaden, 1947).

dimension. The "wheel of progress" now began to whirl ever faster, driven by them and in their name. While youth in the German Sturm und Drang still saw themselves in the limited sense of an intellectual current, toward the end of the nineteenth century the art deco movement (*Jugendstil*) and the free youth movement (*Jugendbewegung*) turned against society as a whole in the name of a biological category. To counter society's alienation and isolation, they held up the concept of a romantic feeling of group solidarity; to counter its technologization, they espoused a transfigured ideal of nature. The development can also be traced in the history of the term itself: its change from the *Jüngling* (young man) and *Jungfrau* (young woman) to *Jugendlicher* (youth) at the end of the nineteenth century. While the concepts of *Jüngling* and *Jungfrau* still implied clear social attribution, the concept of *Jugendlicher* embraced all social classes and both genders.[28] Youth thus became an abstract foil against whose backdrop adolescents dissociated themselves from their social roots. In the end, the abstract claims of the rebellion of middle-class youth within the youth movement culminated in a bureaucratic solution: the Reich Youth Welfare Act of 1922.[29]

Linked to the formation of bourgeois society, the concept of youth, understood as a developmental and educational phase between childhood and adulthood, embraced the notion of the bourgeois individual. Though this in principle encompassed both genders, de facto it was first mainly boys who were implied. Although we can also trace back the history of education for women and girls to its medieval beginnings, it was initially subject to parochial or private initiative, not becoming a public concern until the Reformation.[30] Yet right from the start, education for girls had contradictory aims. There were two reasons for this. As bourgeois society established itself, an essential feature was that it delegated activities of representation and the culture of sociability to its women. Literary salons became centers of intellectual discussion in the rising educated middle class (*Bildungsbürgertum*) in the late eighteenth and early nineteenth century in Germany, led by such preeminent women as Henriette Hertz, Bettina von Arnim, and

28. See Lutz Roth, *Die Erfindung des Jugendlichen* (Munich, 1983).

29. See Frank Trommler, "Mission ohne Ziel. Über den Kult der Jugend im modernen Deutschland," in Thomas Koebner, Rolf-Peter Janz, and Frank Trommler, eds., *"Mit uns zieht die neue Zeit." Der Mythos Jugend* (Frankfurt a.M., 1985), 14–49.

30. Helene Lange and Gertrud Bäumer, eds., *Handbuch der Frauenbewegung,* vol. 3: *Der Stand der Frauenbildung in den Kulturländern* (Berlin, 1902), 18.

Rahel Varnhagen.[31] Though this provided some direct basis for the necessity to provide education to middle-class women, such a pedagogical approach, geared primarily to external demands, easily ran the risk of atrophying into aestheticism. Furthermore, for women, the same transition from feudal to bourgeois society, which accorded education and thus youth such a central place in society, was marked by a key change: their labor was no longer contained in the frame of the economy of the "entire house." Rather, it was juxtaposed to the ever more common form of paid work outside the home—unpaid domestic labor now took on a private character.[32]

As the social character of the reproductive activity performed by women disappeared from consciousness, the social importance of the modern family grew, at its core the primacy of education.[33] This was in keeping with the sentimental revaluation of internal family space. In a world dominated ever more by objects, the family became a locus of feeling and "true humanity," with the woman as its caring custodian. Her work became stylized as activity imbued with "maternal love," and the backwardness inscribed in domestic labor bore the savor and aura of a past and better world. "The woman" (*die Frau*) appeared as the embodiment of "pure nature," surrounded by "animal warmth,"

31. See Barbara Hahn, "Die Salons der Rahel Levin Varnhagen," in Hannelore Gärtner and Annette Purfürst, eds., *Berliner Romantik. Orte, Spuren und Begenungen* (Berlin, 1992), 105–22: Deborah Hertz, *Jewish High Culture in Old Regime Berlin* (New Haven and London, 1988); Ulrike Weckel, "A Lost Paradise of a Female Culture? Some Critical Questions Regarding the Scholarship on Late Eighteenth- and Early Nineteenth-Century German Salons," in *German History* 18, no. 3 (2000): 310–36.

32. See Gisela Bock and Barbara Duden, "Arbeit aus Liebe—Liebe als Arbeit. Zur Entstehung der Hausarbeit im Kapitalismus," in *Frauen und Wissenschaft. Beiträge zur Berliner Sommeruniversität für Frauen im Juli 1976,* Berliner Dozentinnen, eds. (Berlin, 1977), 118–99; Barbara Duden, "Das schöne Eigentum. Zur Herausbildung des bürgerlichen Frauenbildes an der Wende vom 18. zum 19. Jahrhundert," *Kursbuch* 74 (1977): 125–40; Karin Hausen, "Die Polarisierung der 'Geschlechtscharaktere'.—Eine Dissoziation von Erwerbs- und Familienleben," in Werner Conze, ed., *Sozialgeschichte der Familie in der Neuzeit Europas. Neue Forschungen* (Stuttgart, 1977), 363–93.

33. An excellent book in this respect is Rebekka Habermas, *Frauen und Männer des Bürgertums: eine Familiengeschichte* (Göttingen, 2000). See also Anne-Charlott Trepp, *Sanfte Männlichkeit und selbständige Weiblichkeit. Frauen und Männer im Hamburger Bürgertum zwischen 1779 und 1840* (Göttingen); Karin Hausen, "'. . . eine Ulme für das schwache Efeu'. Ehepaare im deutschen Bildungsbürgertum. Ideale und Wirklichkeiten im späten 18. Jahrhundert und 19. Jahrhundert," in Ute Frevert, ed., *Bürgerinnen und Bürger* (Göttingen, 1988), 85–117, as well as Ulrike Weckel's remarks concerning this text: "Was kann und zu welchem Zweck dient das Efeu?" in Barbara Duden, Karen Hagemann, Regina Schulte, and Ulrike Weckel, eds., *Geschichte in Geschichten. Ein historisches Lesebuch* (Frankfurt a.M., 2003), 78–83.

driven by "primal instinct," and holding out hope and an intimation of utopia. As such she was modulated as an antipode of a technological society.

Yet it was precisely this change that necessitated (despite or perhaps specifically for this reason) a regimen of careful instruction and education for the girls. In a study on girls' education in the nineteenth century, Monika Simmel notes: "ever since human education ex ovo began to attract the attention of educators, education for mothers . . . has also been a focus for pedagogical theory."[34] In keeping with the distinctively contradictory situation of women, we find diverse educational institutions in the eighteenth century with different sets of goals: the *Töchterschule, Gynäzeum, Realschule,* and *Philanthropin.*[35] Of these, only the Töchterschule succeeded in spreading: it recruited its pupils exclusively from the higher social classes and contained a pedagogical program concentrated on aesthetic education.[36] During the second half of the nineteenth century, the claim to education for girls became more general and inclusive. On the one hand, a basis of livelihood had to be created for those middle-class women who, themselves unmarried, had been forced out of their families of origin. On the other hand, philanthropic programs increasingly promoted the foundation of families, especially among the lower classes, thereby aiming at relieving want and securing social peace. This in turn necessitated a general increase in the level of education for females and was realized with the introduction of compulsory elementary education.[37] It also led to expanding the system of secondary schools for girls, which in turn helped spark the struggle in the women's movement for the right of girls to a high school diploma, or *Abitur* (from 1896), as well as the right to enter universities (in Germany from 1908 onward). At the same time, domestic science instruction for girls from all social strata became a recognized desideratum, which ultimately was taken into consideration in the establishment of home economics as an integral part of the female curriculum under National Socialism.[38]

34. Monika Simmel, *Erziehung zum Weibe. Mädchenbildung im 19. Jahrhundert* (Frankfurt a.M. and New York, 1980), 11.
35. This last school was founded by Johann Bernhard Badedow (1723–90), who related his own ideas to those of Jean Jacques Rousseau.
36. See Gerda Tornieporth, *Studien zur Frauenbildung. Ein Beitrag zur historichen Analyse lebensweltorientierter Bildungskonzeptionen* (Weinheim and Basel, 1977), 79.
37. There had been efforts starting in the seventeenth century to introduce compulsory elementary education in various German states and territories.
38. From 1939, home economics became obligatory for pupils in the final grade at all elementary schools; see Tornieporth, *Studien zur Frauenbildung,* 285.

The gender-specific education of girls appeared to be in keeping with the blueprint for the bourgeois family as a counterimage to society, but such appearances are deceptive. The shifting of household education from the intimate ambit of the family into the public sphere harbored a contradiction at its core. This and more: right from the outset, the criteria of social production were transposed to the management of the household. This is already evident in a statement of the educator Campe in 1791: "Home economy is dexterity raised to the level of the skill of administering and utilizing your acquisitions in such a manner that you may have the greatest utility and comfort with the least possible expenditure."[39]

Paradoxically, it was precisely those social forces that had a positive interest in a carefully thought out and planned organization of the running of the household that were also centrally concerned about the fate of women in society and their social betterment. As a consequence, the women's movement in particular lent its support to the teaching of home economics in the schools, a curriculum designed to impart practical knowledge for appropriate household management. This tendency toward rationalizing the household continued more intensively after World War I, abetted by the comprehensive measures to rationalize industrial production in the mid-1920s, the greater number of women employed in the job market, and the increasing spread of the mass media.[40] At the end of the eighteenth century, education for girls was diverse and hardly unified, thus in keeping with the differing aims of female education. Following World War I, there was increased application of the criteria of efficiency and rationality in all domains of society. Now the family no longer functioned as a counterimage and counterweight to society. Rather, society seeped, ever more relentlessly, into the intimate sphere of the family. There it acted to forcibly impose the same views and skills required in the workaday world outside the home. How did that impact the crystallizing concept of youth among the girls?

First, youth as a phase of development and education emerged

39. J. H. Campe, *Väterlicher Rath für meine Tochter. Ein Gegenstück zum Theophron. Der erwachsenen weiblichen Jugend gewidmet* (Braunschweig, 1791), quoted in Tornieporth, *Studien zur Frauenbildung*, 65.

40. Space here precludes going into this problem in greater detail. See, for example, Karen Hagemann, "Of 'Old' Men and 'New' Housewives: Everyday Housework and the Limits of Household Rationalization in the Urban Working-Class Milieu of the Weimar Republic," in *International Review of Social History* 41 (1996): 305–30; Mary Nolan, *Imagining America, Modernizing Germany: Fordism and Economic Reform in the Weimar Republic* (New York, 1994).

among girls at the same historical juncture as among boys, yet it only impacted a small segment of the girls. One reason for that was the subordinate status of girls' education. But the primary factor was that the aim of bourgeois-female education split and ramified into educating girls to be housewives, mothers, and wives. Only after the tasks of representation receded into the background—duties delegated to the bourgeois woman in the transition from feudal to bourgeois society— and the bourgeois image of the family in society more generally was permeated by the same rational criteria did the necessity for a new type of education arise. This new education not only would embrace both sexes but became increasingly identical, even if applied to different spheres. The upshot of all this was that the reality of youth for girls did not begin to gain traction more generally until the end of the nineteenth and beginning of the twentieth century.

Second, as a consequence, the consciousness of youth emerged slowly among girls at the beginning of the twentieth century in Germany, remaining confined initially to the upper social classes. Developments in the youth movement can serve to illustrate this trend. According to Harri Pross, the first groups of girls, like those of boys, organized around the turn of the century.[41] But while the groups of young boys quickly consolidated their organization, thus augmenting their circle of influence, the girls lacked sufficient self-confidence for independent action, and they initially sought modes and modalities of affiliation with the existing boys groups. It was not until around 1910, when the existence of girls in the youth movement began to take on the character of a self-evident fact, that there was a marked rise in the number of female members.[42] But being counted among youth included at the same time the abstraction of gender. Insistence on the

41. Harri Pross, *Jugend, Eros, Politik. Die Geschichte der deutschen Jugendverbände* (Bern, Munich, and Vienna, 1964), 121.
42. Not long thereafter, the first independent league of girls, the Deutscher Mädchen-Wanderbund, was set up in the town of Hattingen; see Magdalena Musial, "Jugendbewegung und Emanzipation der Frau. Ein Beitrag zur Rolle der weiblichen Jugend in der Jugendbewegung bis 1933," PhD diss., Essen, 1982, 69. For women and girls in the youth movement, also see Sabine Andresen, *Mädchen und Frauen in der bürgerlichen Jugendbewegung. Soziale Konstruktion von Mädchenjugend* (Stuttgart, 2003); Irmgard Klönne, "*Ich spring in diesem Ringe.*" *Mädchen und Frauen in der deutschen Jugendbewegung* (Pfaffenweiler, 1990); Marion de Ras, *Körper, Eros und weibliche Kultur. Mädchen im Wandervogel und in der Bundischen Jugend 1900–1933* (Pfaffenweiler, 1988); Rosemarie Schade, *Ein weibliches Utopia. Organisation und Ideologien der Mädchen und Frauen in der bürgerlichen Jugendbewegung 1905–1933* (Witzenhausen, 1996).

ideal of comradeship[43]—as Busse-Wilson has aptly described it for the girls in the youth movement and as Weber has done so for the first female students[44]—was due in part to a concession to bourgeois morals. Yet ultimately it was based on the conception of a life within a framework of formal equality, structured solely along the track of time.[45] By contrast, the concept of gender always has an associated social connotation that points to an underlying (hi)story. Girls' insistence on the primacy of youth aimed at individual freedom. It went hand in hand with the negation of a special female history and a distinctive female fate, as expressed in the rejection of the world of the mothers and their political organization, the women's movement. Ultimately it led to isolation and alienation. Rephrasing a quotation from Horkheimer on the process of individualization at the beginning of the modern period, one might say:

In reality, liberation for the majority of women [those affected] initially meant that they were exposed to and at the mercy of the terrible mechanism of exploitation of society [factory production]. Women [individuals] left to fend for themselves found themselves confronted with an alien power that they had to acquiesce to. In theory, they were not supposed to regard the judgment of any human institution as binding for themselves without first checking, according to the criteria of reason. Yet now they were all alone in the world, and compelled to conform if they wished to survive.[46]

After this historic excursion, let us turn once more to the program of the League of German Girls, comparing it with that of the DFO. A

43. The tradition of the concept of comradeship points far beyond the rise of the youth movement. Dagmar Reese, "Jenseits der 'Ordnung der Geschlechter': Gefährten, Kameraden, Partner," in Christof Klotter, ed., *Liebesvorstellungen im 20. Jahrhundert. Die Individualisierung der Liebe* (Giessen, 1999): 293–309.

44. Elisabeth Busse-Wilson, "Liebe und Kameradschaft," in Werner Kindt, ed., *Grundschriften der Deutschen Jugendbewegung* [= Gemeinschaftswerk Dokumentation der Jugendbewegung] (Cologne and Düsseldorf, 1963), 327–34; Marianne Weber, "Vom Typenwandel der studierenden Frau," in Weber, *Frauenfragen und Frauengedanken. Gesammelte Aufsätze* (Tübingen, 1919), 179–201. Irmgard Klönne, *"Ich spring in diesem Ringe,"* chap. 6.

45. See Martin Kohli, "Die Institutionalisierung des Lebenslaufs. Historische Befunde und theoretische Argumente," *Kölner Zeitschrift für Soziologie und Sozialpsychologie* 37, no. 1 (1985): 1–29.

46. Max Horkheimer, "Allgemeiner Teil," in *Studien über Autorität und Familie. Forschungsberichte aus dem Institut für Sozialforschung,* ed. Erich Fromm, Max Horkheimer, Hans Meyer, and Herbert Marcuse (Paris, 1936), vol. 1, 31.

self-description of the substantive work of the groups of young girls affiliated with the DFO states:

> Thus, the work of these young girls touched on the entire array of female duties. Together with the women, they organized German cultural evenings in a very refined manner, they cultivated German high culture, especially art and literature. They pursued German traditional culture, especially song, games and dance. But at the same time, they attended medical courses to gain a basic grounding in medical care. Or they did handicraft work for the brown shirts.[47]

It was precisely this substantive conception of their work that the Hitler Youth criticized.

> On the basis of a knowledge of the women's groups, though not comprehensive, I feel it necessary to express my serious reservations about whether the women, who are often older, will be in any position to carry out a uniform and comprehensive program of rigorous thoroughgoing education for female youth, since that presupposes a corresponding understanding of what is needed. Anyone who has any intensive experience with youth work knows it's not anywhere near enough to just darn socks, cook soup for the SA and sing a few songs, as important and urgent as those things may be.[48]

In contrast with a program based on the nineteenth-century notion of the polarity of the sexes, and thus adhering to a "traditionally female" array of duties, the phrase "rigorous thoroughgoing education" (*Durchbildung*) indicates what the alternative represented by the Hitler Youth consisted of: namely, a heavy emphasis on sports, which was to make up a full two-thirds of work with the girls. Over against gender-specific education, the Hitler Youth advocated a physical training regimen that was obligatory for both sexes. If the ideological program of the National Socialist girls "education" within the League of German Girls, as pointed out in the beginning, lacked any evident content, the reason was that it was no longer possible to define any independent and distinctive notion of femininity. The broad spectrum of National Socialist images of femininity, in part in themselves quite contradictory, was in keeping with this pluralistic quandary. Corre-

47. BA Koblenz, Collection Schumacher, G VIII/251, 3, Dec. 2, 1931.
48. BA Koblenz, Collection Schumacher, G VIII/251, v. Renteln, Feb. 2, 1932, 2.

sponding with the arbitrary nature of the ideologies formulated, there was a social practice totally dominated by the desire to retain smooth functioning at all costs. In this practice, elements of diversity and tension were dysfunctional and subject to sanction.

It is not my intention here to conjure up a static picture of the League of German Girls. There is no doubt that the Hitler Youth was forced to make concessions to traditional female models, especially toward the end of the 1930s, when the Hitler Youth also forfeited some of its strength of integration for female youth. A striking emblem of this was the change in uniform in 1933: the brown dress of the period of struggle, reminiscent of the SA uniform, was now replaced by the blue skirt and white blouse.[49] At the end of 1933, von Schirach made the following remarks on small-caliber sports guns, which later were prohibited for use by girls:

I'd like to offer an answer here to a question that isn't directly connected with this. Some are saying that marksmanship courses have been organized here and there inside the BDM. And that this is unfeminine. I disagree. My view is that small-caliber weapons are a sport like any other. And I just can't understand that there are people in Germany today who regard such exercise by girls as activity unbefitting the distaff side. Marksmanship trains people to have a steady hand, to quietly weigh their next move, to wait for the right moment. It schools the nerves. We should not allow ourselves to be confused by old men, or by old women, who now come a-running, eager to tell us a tale: that actually mothers ought to be the sole educators of the young girls.[50]

Thus, the image of the National Socialist girl as presented by the League of German Girls was subject to the dialectic between the wishes and needs of the girls themselves, the wishes and needs of the Hitler Youth leadership, and the ideas of the Nazi Party—even into the late 1930s, as pointed up by the creation of the BDM section "Faith and Beauty." On the occasion of a dispute between the Hitler Youth and the NS-Frauenschaft regarding where it was best to place girls ages eighteen to twenty-one, von Schirach laid it out to the party: "The aim of the women's organization to prepare the 18-year-old and 19-year-old girls for their future tasks as mothers may seem tempting to the the-

49. Already in August 1933, a ruling was issued that the brown skirt was only to be worn on trips; see *Verordnungsblatt der Reichsjugendführung* 1, no. 49 (October 1933).

50. BA Koblenz, NS 26/336, Nov. 30, 1933, 6.

oretician. But the man of practice will always consider it better to toughen up girls of this age by a regimen of healthy physical exercise."[51]

Even if von Schirach was defeated in this confrontation, and even if the creation of the "Faith and Beauty" section has to be understood as a concession to the women's organization through the work of the League of German Girls, a female generation came into being, which a conservative critic of the times, Ursula von Kardorff, described as follows:

> This is yet another sign that the times are becoming more and more inhumane. Women are no longer considered by nature the weaker sex. Is it any surprise then that male chivalry is also ever more on the wane? Just look at this person who extinguishes incendiary bombs, dousing them dressed in trousers like a fireman. Or who, spade in hand, digs escape holes in buried basements. Or with a steel helmet on her head, keeps a fire-watch up on the roof. Who drags furniture from burning rooms. Who, like a trained artillery gunner, knows how to estimate flak explosions and bomb impacts. This person without a sex, brave and highly capable—is she still actually a woman? Does she still need protection? Women no longer faint, they don't have migraine headaches any more, nor get capricious thoughts. They're no longer creatures of luxury, but just beasts of burden. And OK, why *should* anything change in that? After all, it's precisely in keeping with the trend of the times toward mass society, mass man.[52]

Thus, the substantive conception as formulated by the League of German Girls provides very little grist for the actual analysis of the ideology and practice of National Socialist education for girls. Rather, what was characteristic for this type of education was a praxis that sprang pragmatically from changing interests and that, by appealing to youth, assured itself the interest of the girls and their involvement. By subsuming girls under the category of youth, National Socialism subordinated their desire and efforts for emancipation under party control, though this did not go hand in hand with any implicit emancipation in their lives. Although their organization within the League of German Girls entailed, as we will see later in detail, a dissociation from

51. BA Koblenz, R 43 II, Schirach to Lammers, July 6, 1938, 2.
52. Ursula von Kardorff, *Berliner Aufzeichnungen aus den Jahren 1942 bis 1945* (Munich, 1962), 127.

the traditional bonds of the family, parental authority was supplanted solely by that of the state. So National Socialist education for girls led perforce to isolation and alienation, ultimately cementing a situation where women and girls were more amenable to greater social control. To that extent, and accompanied by appeals to the abstract concept of youth, for the greater masses of women this marked the culmination of the process of individualization that men had experienced at the genesis of bourgeois society. Just as the concept of the free and equal individual had initially entailed nothing but the pitiless and ruthless exploitation of man by man, this formal equality between young men and women mediated via the concept of youth boiled down to one thing: the spaces for autonomy that had sprung as a necessary consequence from the polarity between the sexes ceased to exist. Seizing on the concept of "intellectual motherhood" (*geistige Mütterlichkeit*), the women's movement had reconfigured the special situation of women into a weapon against the encroachments of technology.[53] By contrast, the Nazis now tried their best to effect just the opposite: namely, to make motherhood subordinate to technology. Thus, education in and through the League of German Girls did not mean education for femininity and motherhood, not gendered education geared to a polar conception of the sexes. Rather, it sought to develop an education aimed at fungibility. Moored on isolation, there stood at its core, both for boys and girls, control of the body and discipline, rationality and efficiency. This will be explored in greater depth in the next section.

Disciplined Bodies: Sports in the League of German Girls

In each and every individual, our relation
to our own inner nature can stand for our
relation with nature as a whole.[54]

In the memories of women, looking back in critical retrospect, their membership in the League of German Girls is rarely connected with

53. On the history of the concept of "intellectual motherhood," see Ann Taylor Allen, *Feminism and Motherhood in Germany, 1800–1914* (New Brunswick, 1991); Irene Stoehr, "Organisierte Mütterlichkeit. Zur Politik der deutschen Frauenbewegung um 1900," in Karin Hausen, ed., *Frauen suchen ihre Geschichte. Historische Studien zum 19. und 20. Jahrhundert,* 2d ed. (Munich, 1983), 225–53; Irene Stoehr, "Das Jahrhundert der Mütter? Politik der Mütterlichkeit in der deutschen Frauenbewegung 1900–1950," in Meike Baader, Juliane Jacobi, and Sabine Andresen, eds., *Ellen Keys reformpädagogische Vision. Das Jahrhundert des Kindes und seine Wirkung* (Weinheim, 2000), 81–104.

54. Rudolf zur Lippe, *Naturbeherrschung am Menschen I. Körpererfahrung und Entfaltung von Sinnen und Beziehungen in der Ära des italienischen Kaufmannskapitals* (Frankfurt a.M., 1974), 27.

any recollections of the conscious inculcation of an ideology. Rather, what they recall is participating in an array of activities, such as singing, handicrafts, and sports. The unpolitical nature of such activity is quite evident and also emphasized: "Well, I joined up voluntarily, 'cause we just, well, we used to do a lot of stuff back then in the BDM. Like games and singing, and I really enjoyed that a lot. Quite honestly, I thought that was really marvelous" (M 12).

Of central importance was sports.[55] The former national head of the League of German Girls, Jutta Rüdiger, has written about its key role in the curriculum of the Hitler Youth in a book that can be classified as part of the growing "literature of justification" on the organization and that describes the structure and identity of the Hitler Youth:[56]

In the framework of its educative function for German youth outside the parental home and school, physical education, right from the outset—and almost down to the bitter end—played a decisive role in work in the Hitler Youth. Unlike in any other sphere of activity, options opened up here for youth leadership in two main areas:

it proved easy to reach all of female and male youth, and to infuse most of them with enthusiasm. This began by tapping the impulse for play among young people, in a natural way, by measuring a person's strength, training the body by improving physical skills and capacities, until a top performance level is achieved;

it was possible to exercise a broad impact on the development of character and attitude of the individual and of the group, as well as of the individual within the group.[57]

55. In this section I will deal exclusively with sports as practiced in the smaller groups (squads and platoons) of the Jungmädel and in the BDM. I will not touch on the entire complex of rhythmical gymnastics inspired by Hinrich Medau and practiced in the BDM section "Faith and Beauty." Though that form of gymnastics is often identified with the league, it only involved a small number of girls. For example, only two of my interviewees were members of "Faith and Beauty." Yet the "mass ornamentations" (*Kracauer*) that were effectively staged by utilizing rhythmic gymnastics did not fail to leave a deep and lasting impression on the girls.

56. A few high-ranking leaders within the Hitler Youth have published their memories recently, all of them with this implication to justify their role and the role of the organization. See Kaufmann, *Baldur von Schirach;* Axmann *"Das kann doch nicht das Ende sein."* Jutta Rüdiger published two more books, the last one is her autobiography with the telling title *Ein Leben für die Jugend. Mädelführerin im Dritten Reich* (Preußisch Oldendorf, 1999).

57. Rüdiger, *Die Hitler-Jugend,* 71. The initial plan right from the start was to place all sports activities in the BDM under the direction of sports supervisors; see *Verordnungsblatt der Reichsjugendführung* 1, no. 67 (1933). From 1935 on, the League of German Girls introduced full-time sports supervisors (*Sportwartinnen*), who then were given a regular course of training in keeping with their level of responsibility and rank.

This quotation points up two salient aspects. First, the organization was successful in generating interest and enthusiasm among both boys and girls through its sports program, and it did this "easily," that is, without the need for any greater expenditure in terms of personnel or funds. Second, the girls too were very positive about the program, relishing physical activity, games, and competitions. At times, that might even have been the main reason for deciding to concentrate on sports: "So, then I said, well, I usually asked 'em first: 'What's on the agenda for today, what do you prefer? Weather's nice—should we go into class, read, do some handicrafts? Or how about sports?' Naturally then, well, most of the girls opted for sports" (M 21).

Another important reason why sports in the League of German Girls had such a magnetic attraction was that, given the age and training of the league leaders, it was less regimented than the physical education (PE) offered at school. Moreover, the interests of most of the young leaders were quite similar to those of the girls.

M 19: Well, it was simply different, because with sports at school, well, we had our PE teacher, a real old fogey, let me tell you. Why, she used to stand there shaking her raised index finger at us, stuff like that. But here it was just something else, I mean like more relaxed. And then we used to get together again with girls from other villages, for sports, whatever. Sometimes they'd arrange that, bring us together, say for a whole afternoon. Or we'd get together for new competitions, like when we'd compete with others, they'd organize some of that.

I: Let's get back to this PE teacher at school, did she do any other kind of sports with you kids?

M 19: Right, she did, gymnastics. We always had that. We called it *Turnübungen* [gymnastic exercises], *Freiübungen* [free exercises], that kind of thing.[58] And then, well, when we wanted to play some game, we'd have to kind of beg a little, like when we wanted to play *Völkerball,* for example.[59]

---

58. The German term *Turnen* was coined by Friedrich Jahn, the *"Turnvater"* Jahn (1778–1852). Jahn derived the term from *Turniere* (tournaments in the Middle Ages), a term he identified as German. In 1811, Jahn set up the first *Turnplatz* (athletic grounds) on Berlin's Hasenheide. Since the mid-nineteenth century, physical education was integrated into school curricula, first in boys' schools and since around the turn of the twentieth century also in girls' schools. German immigrants brought *deutsches Turnen* to North America, and the terms *turner* for gymnast and *turnverein* for athletic club entered American English in the mid-1850s.

59. This is a field game for two teams where the object is to hit an opponent with the ball and put him or her out of the game.

I: And in the BDM, you'd have games?

M 19: Right, lots of games. Competitions, you know. We'd get together in a few small groups, and then see who were the best. You really could let loose, play wild.[60]

Sports were a main focus in the league's educational program because they were very popular with the girls and were low resourced, not requiring much material or special personnel. A third factor in favor of sports becomes clear from the remarks by Rüdiger, namely, their educational function, the substantive content. The rigorous education (*Durchbildung*) in and through athletics became the means to create a new "type of girl." At the same time, participation in sports was the criterion distinguishing one generation of girls from another.

You know, this seven years' difference between me and my sis, we often talk about it. See, like my sister can't swim, she can't do gymnastics. Even though they had that then too. I think, well, some of it is because of the type of person she is. But it's also on account of the whole attitude people had, the way things were back then. So she grew up, wearing her hair in a bun in the back, and very pointed, high-heeled shoes and stuff. And even today I still remark, when she's wearing something like that, I say: "Well, you know, you're a lady and me, guess I'm just not." See, so somehow that's the difference. That's how they all were, not just . . . That was life then, things were still that way, let's say, you know, a little like a stick held at your back and a bit more constricted. Yeah, and as I got older, things loosened up. And maybe you could even say that perhaps the big change then, it played a role too. You know, then there were also these . . . uh, sports were pushed more, right . . . that was more actively promoted. And so naturally you could see this in everything. Everything became more athletic; people wore flat heels, for example, and you went swimming. Like for my sister, let's say, that would have been impossible. Pretty much impossible. And then she started in a bit too, you understand, but for her to . . . Like for her to go swimming with a mixed group of guys, and stuff, she didn't do that. In my case, though, well I did. (M 20)

Athletics as it crystallized in this form—that is, in the creation of a distinctive "type of girl or woman"—actively promoted by National

---

60. See also the descriptions by Marie-Elisabeth Lüders and Valeska Gert in Gertrud Pfister, *Frau und Sport. Frühe Texte* (Frankfurt a.M., 1980), 83f.

Socialism, was also encompassed by people who certainly had their political differences but liked the new look.

> M 4: The special type of woman which National Socialism was developing, I really liked that. Like keeping your hair neat, a bun. Me too, well I also wore my hair in a bun for a long time, 'cause I thought that was nice. And they were always dressed in an athletic-looking way, I liked that a lot too. And no make-up, that was very good too. . . .
> I: What did you associate with all these things?
> M 4: A natural way of living.

If members of the league recall their activities in the association—due to the centrality of sports in those activities—as being in retrospect unpolitical, this also reappears in the broad level of acceptance the National Socialist image of the woman enjoyed among women and girls. Behind an external appearance marked by simplicity and practicality, whose symbolic expression was the uniform, there was an internal attitude toward life that had older roots, reaching back both politically and in time to a world before National Socialism.

> 6.30 a.m. Gilgi's up, out of bed. She stands in the freezing room, stretches and rubs the sleep from her expressionless eyes. Does some exercises before the wide open widow. Forward bend: up, down, up, down. Her finger tips touch the floor, her knees are stretched. That's the right position. Up, down, up, down.[61]

In her famous character Gilgi, Irmgard Keun described the image of the "new woman" of the 1920s. The young woman's attitude toward life was rational, and it slowly dawned on her that maybe everything she was doing was nothing but an attempt to escape her own desires.[62] She understood it was a kind of challenge she had to take up anew every day. Her objective, sober attitude encompassed not only all her actions but also her own relation to herself: "A mirror like that, there's something nice and friendly about it, when you're 20, with a face that's clear, no wrinkles. A face that's taken care of. Taken care of is more than pretty, it's your own merit, what you do for yourself."[63]

61. Irmgard Keun, *Gilgi—eine von uns* (Berlin, 1931; reprint, BergischGladbach, 1981), 5.
62. Keun, *Gilgi—eine von uns,* 144.
63. Keun, *Gilgi—eine von uns,* 6.

But the phenomenon of the "new woman"—of which Keun created a kind of emblem for the 1920s in the figure of Gilgi—had a predecessor: the "new woman" in imperial Germany.[64] Yet while she had developed closely embedded in the context of a political, social, and cultural milieu, a composite of either the women's, youth, and/or reform movement, the new woman of the 1920s appeared to be disencumbered of all political and social attributions, and the meaning of her life was moored on her own self. This was mirrored in her relation to her body, whose "liberation" through sports was not the expression of political rebellion, as it had been in the *Kaiserreich.* Now that body was an instrument, preserved and maintained as part of the struggle for survival. Congruent with this shift in meaning was a new popularity: what formerly had been restricted to a political avant-garde and an artistic bohemian milieu now became a mass phenomenon.

Physical exercises, as planned sequences of movement that have a meaning and aim external to the activity itself,[65] became part of a general educational system in Germany promoted by the Philanthropa schools influenced by the Enlightenment. In the programs of Guts Muths, Pestalozzi, Campe, and Vieth,[66] the human being was seen as a creature whose full development can only be achieved in harmony between intellectual nurture and physical sustenance.[67] When Friedrich Jahn appeared on the pedagogical scene, he added a tone of nationalism to school gymnastics. *Vaterländisches Turnen* (patriotic gymnastics) was not limited to the mastery of physical exercises but also implied a "way of life and intellectual attitude at which you arrive beginning with the body, traveling down the path of the educating of the living, breathing individual."[68]

Even though Philanthropa syllabi concentrated mainly on the young boy, these schools, in line with the tenets of their own educa-

64. Space does not permit any further discussion of this issue. See Dietlinde Peters, *Mütterlichkeit im Kaiserreich* (Bielefeld, 1984); Susanna Dammer, *Mütterlichkeit und Frauendienstpflicht. Versuche der Vergesellschaftung "weiblicher Fähigkeiten" durch eine Dienstverpflichtung* (Weinheim, 1988).

65. Ulrich Popplow believes their earliest manifestation can be seen in dance; see Horst Ueberhorst, "Ursprungstheorien," in Ueberhorst, ed., *Geschichte der Leibesübungen,* vol. 1 (Berlin, Munich, and Frankfurt a.M., 1972), 11–38.

66. Like Friedrich Jahn, Johann Christoph Friedrich Guts Muths (1759–1839) was an educator who was convinced that physical instruction was a central part of school education. The same is true for Joachim Heinrich Campe (1746–1818) and Gerhard Ulrich Anton Vieth (1763–1836).

67. See Gerhard Lukas, *Geschichte der Körperkultur in Deutschland,* vol. 1 (Berlin, 1969), 170f.

68. Bruno Saurbier, *Geschichte der Leibesübungen* (Frankfurt a.M., 1955), 124.

tional philosophy, also had to focus and reflect on the physical education of the girls. Starting with Rousseau, there was an intimation of what later ultimately returns in the sports activity of the League of German Girls as the slogan "firm but not strapping, strict but not coarse."[69]

Women must be so strong that everything they do is done gracefully. . . . Women mustn't be robust *like* men. But they should be firm and sturdy *for* men, so that those they give birth to can be strong.[70]

Physical activity by women was caught up in the ambivalence of an educational program that on the one hand emphasized the functional and aesthetic aspects of the woman, while on the other held out the possibility of liberating physical self-realization. From this it drew both its lasting power of attraction for the women themselves and magnetic pull for those who wanted to control and have power over them.

In the sign of a time of new departures, enlightenment, the women's movement, and reform movements more generally, physical exercise began to spread among women.[71] Although numerically but a minuscule minority,[72] women by the time of World War I were present in almost all areas of gymnastics and sports, and although they had no voting rights in the associations run by the men,[73] they increasingly succeeded in articulating their needs.[74] World War I was the turning point: women not only were granted the right to vote and political

69. "Straff, aber nicht stramm, herb, aber nicht derb"; the slogan goes back to Trude Bürkner, first Reich representative of the League of German Girls, who described the aims of the sports program of the League of German Girls. See Bürkner, *Der Bund Deutscher Mädel,* 13.

70. Quoted in Angelika Tschap-Bock, *Frauensport und Gesellschaft. Der Frauensport in seinen historischen und gegenwärtigen Formen. Eine historische und empirische Untersuchung* [= Sportwissenschaftliche Dissertationen, vol. 20] (Ahrensburg, 1983), 78.

71. For example, Louise Otto-Peters (1819–95), writer, journalist, founder of the Frauenzeitung (1849), and cofounder of the Allgemeiner deutscher Frauenverein (1865), campaigned for including gymnastics in the school curriculum for girls; see Pfister, *Frau und Sport,* 19.

72. Pfister gives a figure of fifty thousand women and girls in sports associations and clubs at the turn of the century, with some twenty-seven thousand of these in the Deutsche Turnerschaft; see Pfister, *Frau und Sport,* 22.

73. Until 1908, when the old restrictions were lifted, women could not become a member in an association or a political party in Prussia.

74. Gertrud Pfister, "Körperkultur und Weiblichkeit. Ein historischer Beitrag zur Entwicklung des modernen Sports in Deutschland bis zur Zeit der Weimarer Republik," in Michael Klein, ed., *Sport und Geschlecht* (Reinbek bei Hamburg, 1983), 53.

equality but also found themselves with more latitude for action as many old traditions lost their meaning. Female physical activity in sports did not become a widespread phenomenon until the 1920s, such that many historians regard this point as the actual beginning of women's sports.[75] For the "modern woman," the "new woman," who was trying to combine a household, family, and occupation, but most especially for the young girl, sports became the unquestioned "*on dit*" and at the same time an external proactive demonstration of one's own attitude toward life.

> If the magic of images assails the masses from without, then sport—indeed the whole culture of the body, which has led also to the custom of the weekend—is the primary form of their existence. The systematic training of the body no doubt fulfils the mission of producing a vitally necessary counterweight to the increased demands of the modern economy. The question, however, is whether the contemporary sports industry is concerned only with this admittedly indispensable training. Or whether sports is not ultimately assigned so eminent a place in the hierarchy of collective values today because it offers the masses the welcome opportunity for distraction—which they exploit to the full.[76]

Among young people, the magnetism of sports was manifested in the high membership figures in the associations for physical exercise, which among the associations for young people were the largest single grouping.[77] In 1929 in Berlin, for example, 63.4 percent of all young people who were members in an organization were in a sports club or association.[78] An empirical study by Dinse in the early 1930s on the leisure time behavior of urban youth indicates that 84 percent of the boys and 74 percent of the girls engaged in physical exercise of some kind.[79] While girls generally remained a minority in the youth associations and youth leagues, their participation in sports organizations and athletic activities was high, nearly rivaling that of the boys. Thus, in the

75. See Tschap-Bock, *Frauensport und Gesellschaft,* 105.
76. Siegfried Kracauer, "Shelter for the Homeless," in Kracauer, *The Salaried Masses: Duty and Distraction in Weimar Germany* (London and New York, 1998), 94.
77. Deutsches Archiv für Jugendwohlfahrt, ed., *Kleines Handbuch der Jugendverbände* (Berlin, 1931), 21.
78. Whereas 15.3 percent were members in associations for intellectual and moral betterment of youth that had no actual physical exercise activity, 21.1 percent were in associations with an athletics component; see *Das junge Deutschland* 23, no. 12 (1929): 583.
79. Dinse, *Das Freizeitleben der Großstadtjugend,* 85.

Arbeiter-Turn-und Sportbund (Workers' League for Gymnastics and Sports) alone, more than 130,000 of its approximately 400,000 young members were female, some 32.5 percent.[80] So the sports magnet overcame class barriers on the one hand and gender barriers on the other: "Indeed, Marx might well have been nearer the mark had he referred to sport rather than religion as the opium of the masses."[81]

There were several reasons for the enhanced importance that sports took on in the late nineteenth and early twentieth century in the industrializing world. To counter the one-sided heavy work load, there was need for some kind of physical exercise to offset it. Second, labor was going through a process of intensification along with reduced working hours, creating something new, time for leisure. Initially, the workers spent that free time according to the old custom, namely, dancing and drinking.[82] Not unexpectedly, churches, business firms, and factories were the first to successfully organize sports activities in response to emerging patterns of living that threatened to undermine morale on the job and the moral order.

In 1893, the Freier Arbeiter-Turnbund Deutschland (Free Workers' Association for Gymnastics) was founded.[83] The Social Democrats initially viewed it with some suspicion as an "unpolitical organization," but they did a gradual about-face and by 1908 finally began to further its work.[84] The aim of this gymnastic association was to circumvent the dominant power of the ever more militarized middle-class associations in imperial Germany by creating autonomous workers' associations that were politically independent and open to all. Their program gave priority to noncompetitive activities, gymnastics, bicycling, hiking, and swimming,[85] trying to shape their own distinctive approach to the advance of sports in the society. In contrast with the health regimen of gymnastics, and the system of *Deutsches Turnen* (German gymnastics) going back to Turnvater Jahn (Friedrich Jahn) and closely bound up

80. Deutsches Archiv für Jugendwohlfahrt, ed., *Kleines Handbuch der Jugendverbände*, 54.

81. Robert F. Wheeler, "Organized Sport and Organized Labour: The Workers' Sports Movement," *Journal of Contemporary History* 13 (1978): 193.

82. Wheeler, "Organized Sport and Organized Labour," 192; on alcoholism in the male workforce and the discussion of this problem in the workers' movement, see Martin Soder, *Hausarbeit und Stammtischsozialismus. Arbeiterfamilie und Alltag im Deutschen Kaiserreich* (Gießen, 1980), 54ff.

83. Heinz Timmermann, "Geschichte und Struktur der Arbeitersportbewegung 1883–1933," PhD diss., Marburg/Lahn, 1969, 14.

84. Timmermann, "Geschichte und Struktur," 16f.

85. Wheeler, "Organized Sport and Organized Labour," 196.

with the German *Kleinbürgertum* (petty bourgeoisie), sports had a totally different origin and character. In "patronized sport," the English nobility had appropriated exercises and competitions of the people,[86] developing them, dissociated from their old social and ritual context, into a separate practice of their own.[87] In Britain, "gentlemen's sport" percolated into the public schools around 1800 via the sons.[88] The attractiveness of sports, especially for young men, was rooted in this social history. As an activity with a bourgeois origin, sports remained a means for social distinction: indeed, horseback riding, rowing, and tennis retained some of this "exclusive" social character for a long period within the twentieth century.[89] At the same time, heavier emphasis on the competitive nature of sports meshed with advanced industrialization, as athletic activity was seen as a corresponding counterweight to a labor process oriented ever more to the yardstick of increased output.[90] Radiating from England, the twentieth century, especially during the 1920s, witnessed an unbroken triumphal march of sports across Central Europe. As Saurbier stresses, it is striking "that in England, physical exercises were not incorporated into the curriculum as a means of education by the teachers, but rather implanted themselves from below into the advanced educational institutions of the country, often against the will of the educators."[91] If the workers' parties before 1914 had consciously looked for an alternative to patriotic gymnastics for workers' sports, now, just like all other associations, they offered the entire spectrum of bourgeois middle-class types of sports.[92] They put on competitions and, by according ever more space to sports reporting in their newspapers, helped contribute to an emerging market shaped not by workers' solidarity but by

86. Saurbier, *Geschichte der Leibesübungen,* 155.

87. See Pierre Bourdieu, "Historische und soziale Voraussetzungen modernen Sports," *Merkur* 39, no. 7 (1985): 575–90.

88. Saurbier, *Geschichte der Leibesübungen,* 146.

89. Bourdieu, "Historische und soziale Voraussetzungen," 581.

90. Tschap-Bock, *Frauensport und Gesellschaft,* 93. Elias and Dunning have demonstrated an increasing tendency to reduce violence through rules of the game, the prerequisite that turned unregulated conflict into ordered "fair play." See Norbert Elias and Eric Dunning, "Zur Dynamik von Sportgruppen," in Günther Lüschen, ed., *Kleingruppenforschung und Gruppe im Sport* [= Kölner Zeitschrift für Soziologie und Sozialpsychologie, Special Issue no. 10] (Opladen, 1966), 124ff.; see also Norbert Elias and Eric Dunning, *Sport im Zivilisationsprozeß. Studien zur Figurationssoziologie,* ed. W. Hopf (Münster, n.d. [1985]).

91. Saurbier, *Geschichte der Leibesübungen,* 156.

92. Wheeler, "Organized Sport and Organized Labour," 198; Timmermann, "Geschichte und Struktur," 43.

rivalry, performance, and victory.[93] At the same time, there was a huge upsurge in the number of members.[94] Not until the 1930s, in connection with the rise of National Socialism, did people in the workers' movement begin to become aware of the *political* importance of modern sports. In Austria, a survey showed that the members of a local National Socialist group were young workers who all belonged to middle-class (i.e., *bürgerliche*) sports associations.[95] Thus, even before 1933, the National Socialists were skillful in utilizing the felt need among the young for sports activity and chalked up successes in this area. After 1933, this blossomed into a general trend and also impacted across gender lines, specifically helping to recruit young girls into the ranks.

Right from the start, the National Socialists assigned sports a major role in educational work with the girls. Early on, in 1934, Baldur von Schirach formulated a working rule of thumb: two-thirds of the work in the League of German Girls should be dedicated to sports.[96] The goal was the "rigorous training" through sports of an entire generation of girls in the framework of a program based on racialist ideology: "The eternal stream of blood can only be kept pure within a human being whose genetic material is healthy [*erbgesund*]. So it is all the more urgent now to strengthen maternal and racial awareness of the body which is genetically healthy, strong and beautiful."[97] These sentences contain the programmatic themes of a state founded on racism, though this ideological armature was not directly reflected in the girls' orientation and intentions. For them, sports was a pleasurable activity devoid of politics, to be relished in and of itself.

As already mentioned, sports was especially suited as a pedagogical medium initially by dint of its "unproblematic" nature, that is, the fact that it was low cost for the National Socialists to implement and it held

93. Wheeler, "Organized Sport and Organized Labour," 196, 206.

94. Figures here are contradictory. Wheeler mentions 1.2 million members for the Arbeiter Turn- und Sportbund (ATUS) in 1929, while Timmermann gives a figure of 750,000 for 1928. In any event, both point to the enormous increase in membership ranks; see Wheeler, "Organized Sport and Organized Labour," 197; Timmermann, "Geschichte und Struktur," 56.

95. Wheeler, "Organized Sport and Organized Labour," 205.

96. Schirach, *Die Hitler-Jugend,* 99.

97. Hans Möckelman, *Die Leibeserziehung der Mädel in den Entwicklungsstufen* (Berlin, 1943), 24, quoted in Hajo Bernett, *Nationalsozialistische Leibeserziehung. Eine Dokumentation ihrer Theorie und Organisation* [= Theorie der Leibeserziehung—Texte—Quellen—Dokumente, no. 1] (Schorndorf, 1966), 76.

out the promise of solid success. If they were to follow the principle of "youth leads youth"—a principle that seemed an expedient necessity if alone due to the large number of leaders required in such a mass organization—they had to find a modality in youth work that guaranteed a high degree of consensus with the goals of National Socialist policy even without intensive indoctrination of the youth leaders. Sports appeared to be an ideal candidate, especially since it met many of the young people's needs. At the same time, it guaranteed that the young would be kept busy and thus under control. Arno Klönne comments on the continuing distraction that resulted from the constant situation of tension in which the young people were kept as a result of repeated sports competitions.[98] But especially for the girls, sports had an even greater importance. A speech given by von Schirach in November 1933 develops some thoughts on the meaning and function of sport activities in the League of German Girls.

> Inside an organization of boys, educating them to serve the community is a simple matter. That's because within the organization, and inside each and every boy, there is a hereditary consciousness present, a genetic awareness of discipline and subordination to the community which his male forebears have practiced for centuries, for more than a thousand years. Unconsciously, every boy always associates himself with the military tradition of his forefathers that has been passed on down to him in his blood. But girls have no ancestors who were skilled in organization, no forebears who were oriented to the military. They have no unconscious memory of a sense of incorporation every German woman might well have experienced in earlier centuries had it existed, but it didn't. We are the first to address the task of building such an organization for women and girls within the German people. And the first who thus could create such a center of memory for the generations to come.[99]

What von Schirach stressed here is that, in contrast with the male population, the female population lacked a tradition of discipline, and it was the task of National Socialism to inculcate and consolidate this discipline in the ranks of German womanhood. The chosen instrument for this was athletics and sport in the League of German Girls.

Wherever we found the BDM lacking in discipline we simultane-

98. Klönne, "Jugendprotest und Jugendopposition," 538.
99. BA Koblenz, NS 26/336, Nov. 30, 1933, 5.

ously noted they were not involved enough in active sports. And wherever the BDM appears as a disciplined organization, training in sport is closely intertwined with the total educational program.[100]

Yet the lack of discipline among women that von Schirach mentioned, and wished to remedy by a vigorous diet of sports, was not simply a lack of self-control and order. The Latin etymon of "discipline" means "teaching" and is linked with schooling and reason. So women lacked reason, their actions were unpredictable, and their guiding criteria differed from those of technical rationality in an industrial society. Women had to be educated, that is, disciplined (in its root sense) by and through sports.

But we will not grasp the real importance of sports in National Socialism if we dwell on the dimension of domination and control, its implementation, and maintenance. Sports meant above all else the enjoyment, the organized fun, which the girls were so keen to participate in. It was that relish in sports that made National Socialist girls policy such a success. Of course, we have been talking here about "sports in National Socialism," and the idea of sports did gain huge impetus through National Socialist youth work. It is true that an old pedagogical dimension was manifest in the priority accorded the rigorous athletic "training" of an entire generation over the systematic promotion of individual achievement in the arena of sports and gymnastics.[101] And in the polemical attack on the professionalization and marketing of sports, there was the audible echo of a tradition that linked up with the heritage of Deutsches Turnen.[102] Yet there were endless athletic competitions under National Socialism, and even if this rivalry was mainly in the form of teams competing against other teams, the fighting spirit tended to be intensified rather than lessened by subordinating the goals of the individual to those of the group. The special test for the younger girls (*Jungmädelprobe*) was a similar means of enhancing group morale, since it was a demonstration of physical training that was obligatory for every candidate for the Jungmädelbund.[103]

100. BA Koblenz, NS 26/336, Nov. 30, 1933, 5.

101. Thus, in a speech given in November 1933 on sports in the League of German Girls, von Schirach stressed: "Sports in Germany will be community sports. It will be a form of sports that necessarily encompasses the entire BDM, with each and every member, not only individuals who have a desire to participate in athletics." See BA Koblenz, NS 26/336, Nov. 30, 1933, 5f.

102. See Kurt Richter, "Die Leibesübungen im neuen Staat," *Die Jugendpflege* 10, no. 9 (1933): 205–8. Richter notes: "In certain associations for physical exercise, there was more and more stress on specialists and breaking records, and competition in sports was often degraded into a good source of income" (206).

103. See chap. 1, section "The Path of the German Girl," this study.

The demands were not excessive, and every girl was supposed to be able to meet them. Yet this also meant that ultimately every young girl was "put to the test," that all were subjected to the same yardstick for physical achievement.[104] In and through athletic activity, therefore, the bodies of the women were inscribed with the laws of struggle and achievement, of integration into a common group and the subordination to a common goal. And by internalizing these statutes and rules of an industrial society, the women simultaneously earned the right to participate in it.

Concretely, that can be seen in two aspects. First, membership in the League of German Girls opened the door to exclusive categories of sport, such as rowing, thus facilitating a certain kind of social advancement, however limited. Second and more important, athletic activity in itself, even in critical retrospect, is viewed by participants as something liberating. There is a consensus, apparently uninterrogated, that what is "unpretentious and practical," "healthy and natural" deserves to have priority over the "irrationality" of tradition. By creating a framework in which these tendencies were able to gain the upper hand, by representing and promoting the concerns of the daughters over against their parents, National Socialism seemingly helped to promote a kind of historical "progress." This is true even for people who otherwise may be quite critical of National Socialism.

Yet what is perceived subjectively here to have been some sort of emancipation turns out on closer scrutiny to be an illusion. That can be shown by examining the concept of "not athletic" (*unsportlich*). In the reconstruction of the life history of former Hitler Youth members, Claudia Gather describes the relation of a BDM member named Gisela to her brother: "In her eyes, he was not athletic. And on top of it, he was not as much of a supporter of National Socialism as she was."[105] Very openly here, the concept of being "not athletic" is used as a metaphor for those who are "different," who do not (or don't want to) belong or fit in. In this discourse, Jews, pious Germans, and intellectuals from the opposition were stigmatized as "unathletic." The binarism of "athletic/unathletic" was utilized to transpose political and social differences onto the plane of the physical. Then, appealing to what was considered "natural," these differences were rendered imper-

104. See later section "Diffuse Memories," this chapter.

105. Gabriele Rosenthal, et al., *1945—Ende oder Neuanfang? Lebenslaufrekonstruktionen von Angehörigen der "Hitlerjugendgeneration"* [= Institut für Soziologie, Freie Universität Berlin, Mitteilungen aus dem Schwerpunktbereich Methodenlehre, no. 10] (Berlin, 1984), 131.

vious to interrogation. Seen from this vantage, the desire among women for athletic activity was driven in part by an element of rebellion against the social exclusion of their gender—an exclusion they sought to elude by more intensive adaptation to society. But inscribed in their desire for social advancement was an implicit acknowledgment of the laws of a sexist society. An inescapable vicious circle arose, at whose end lay alienation and subjugation.

I: Now if you look back and think about the fact that for 12 years, you were in a decisive position. And so you had a definite influence on the female generation—what . . . where do you think . . . what did you achieve? And how was this generation influenced by it?

B 22: I can't really say.

I: A short while ago you mentioned *Trümmerfrauen* [the women removing the ruins in postwar Berlin] . . .

B 22: Well, of course, that was a very tough generation. And sure, that's the way it was trained to be, through our sports.

Making Careers: Leaders in the League of German Girls

The Reich Youth Leader Baldur von Schirach distinguished between two kinds of leadership for youth: one that was laid down and channeled, delegated from above, and then independent leadership. The former was the standing practice in many youth organizations around the world: to place young people under the guidance of adults (teachers, officers) equipped with a set program. The experience these leaders had gained derived from another time, from the past. That was their weakness. At best, this type of youth leadership could result in a well-functioning organization. But it could never lead to a youth movement. The other path was the more difficult of the two, yet more productive: namely youth in charge, leading itself. This was the path that the Hitler Youth had chosen to tread.[106]

The National Socialists repeatedly stressed the principle of self-leadership by youth. The reasons are evident. Where "youth leads youth," even in retrospect one cannot speak about a "totalitarian state" or a "state youth." Instead, this principle emphasized the right of young people to exercise autonomy. In actual fact, the leaders in the Hitler Youth were quite young. In clear contrast with the German youth movement or youth leagues, they were as a rule only a few years older

106. Rüdiger, *Die Hitler-Jugend.*

than the boys and girls in their charge. Measured in terms of the authority they enjoyed, the top leadership of the Hitler Youth was also unusually young. When Baldur von Schirach was installed in 1931 as Reich youth leader of the NSDAP, he was only twenty-four years old. Jutta Rüdiger became Reich representative of the League of German Girls at the age of twenty-seven. The youthfulness of the Hitler Youth served a double purpose: it was an attractive allure for young people and at the same time was functional in terms of power politics. Yet, above all, it offered a solution to the constant shortage of leaders.

If we assume that at the end of 1935 some 4 million young people were Hitler Youth members and the size of a squad (*Schaft*)[107]—its smallest units—was between ten and fifteen persons, then the organization required on average between 266,000 and 400,000 leaders.[108] The BDM alone, with 569,717 girls numerically the smallest organization,[109] needed between 38,000 and 57,000 leaders. In 1936, with the promulgation of the HJ-Law and the consequent growth of the movement, especially in the ranks of Jungvolk and Jungmädel, that need for leadership personnel was significantly increased. It is obvious that such a large number of leaders could not be paid for their services. Most had to serve voluntarily and without any recompense. Yet this meant that, right from the start, there would be a large turnover in the leadership ranks and a lowering of the criteria for selection. It also necessitated having to mobilize girls as leaders who were younger as well as to rely on institutions that—within the *Gemeinschaft der deutschen Jugend* (folk community of German Youth)—reinvigorated via the leadership the traditional social elites.

As the youth movement of a totalitarian state, the Hitler Youth, from its inception, was not a voluntary association. Nonetheless, it is impossible to explain its establishment and maintenance solely on the basis of legal constraints and the application of political force. There was a constituent element of voluntary participation and commitment on the part of members, which was considerable and should not be underestimated. Through this engaged voluntary participation, the Hitler Youth was able to sustain and stabilize itself. Of crucial importance in this process were the leaders. They were at the critical seam, so to speak, determining whether membership in the league would be per-

107. While the boys were organized in Jungenschaften for those ages ten to fourteen and Kameradschaften for the older ones, the equivalent for the girls were Jungmädel and Mädelschaften.

108. Michael Buddrus estimates around 403,000 paid and unpaid leaders at the end of 1935 and 765,584 in mid-1939. Buddrus, *Totale Erziehung für den totalen Krieg*, 323.

109. BA Koblenz, NS 26/358, Statistik der Jugend.

ceived as compulsion or as a pleasurable experience, a source of fun. The key function of the leaders was most evident where there was no social network into which the Hitler Youth was integrated, no social ambient that sustained and stabilized it. That was true in the first phase of the construction of the organization and in regional and social conditions that acted to impede the establishment of the Hitler Youth. The two following interview excerpts can serve to point up this circumstance.

> B 14: Well, it must've been the summer of '33 when I joined the BDM . . . but I didn't much like it. Anyhow, I must've been a member until '34. . . . And in 1934, we took another one of those school excursions, and by then I guess I quit the organization, because when I finished school, I was no longer in the BDM. Because the leaders, they were younger than us. The whole thing was so chaotic, such a mess, there was no organization at all. . . . Like we would come together once a week, and sometimes the leader didn't show up. Or someone came from another group to sub for her. And let me tell, you could just resign, quit the thing, nobody gave a damn!
>
> I: How did you explain resigning from the organization?
>
> B 14: Well, in our group, see, our leader, I mean, she didn't care at all. So our whole group, we simply stopped going. And nobody said anything at all about that, nothing.
>
> I: The whole group just stopped going?
>
> B 14: Yes, the thing just kind of fell apart. Some went over into another group, 'cause we didn't have a real *Heim* [center], we just had a kind of room here where we'd meet. And than that was no good. I mean, there was no organization to it.
>
> I: You mean, here on this street?
>
> B 14: Right, we'd taken a room, a little store. And this leader, well, at some point she just lost interest. I don't know what it was. And then she had this guy, her boyfriend, see. The whole thing just fell apart.
>
> I: And at that point, you no longer had anything to do with it?
>
> B 14: No, nothing.
>
> I: And none of the leaders tried to . . .
>
> B 14: None of them reported that we'd quit, or something, nothing at all was said.
>
> I: And along with you there were a lot of other girls who quit too, is that right?

B 14:   Like we were 12 girls in the group, see, and the whole thing just fell apart.

M 3:   I remember that when I took over the *Bann* (district), I went on out there, in that certain area, where they were a little bit behind. And I went to the school. I can recall that I rode out there in the morning. And then I walked from village to village, 'cause I didn't have a bike. We didn't have cars then. So anyhow, I spoke with the teacher and asked him to name some girl who could . . . I just set up the service, the whole thing right from the start.

I: You just set it up then, in 1941?

M 3:   Well, of course, it had already existed. But it was at some distance from Minden, it was a remote little place. . . . it couldn't be properly serviced from here, we had too few people for that. Once it had existed, but then it stopped. Like when the leader left, or didn't want to continue, or whatever. So then you had to start all over again from scratch.

In these two situations, there were plenty of girls wanting to join the League of German Girls. What was lacking were the leaders and a social environment favorable and beneficial for the process of organizing the young people. Moreover, it is clear that the legal framework did not guarantee the smooth functioning of the organization either. On the contrary, it tended to point up the problem of a perennial shortage of leaders.

There was no legal lever to force the girls to . . . well, one could resort to police action to compel them to join, but that was never done. And basically this group of girls was ruined by the way it was selected. There were all sorts and types now in the organization. Some who'd joined out of a sense of enthusiasm. And then you got the dregs of society, too, those who were really, I mean, they used to disturb the meetings, they didn't make, uh, didn't make trouble exactly, but they were a nuisance . . . so that first I wanted to get my bearings in this place, find my way around. And if I didn't know any leader who was from the place or whom I had on tap, well, then I just started from scratch all over again. (M 3)

Even though you could force a girl by a court order to join the league, in fact the organization was only viable on the basis of the voluntary work of innumerable leaders. So the success or failure of

National Socialist youth work hinged on one key factor: the extent to which leaders could be found and motivated to participate.

If one looks at the way the league presented itself, then the criteria of selection were strict yet simultaneously diffuse: in choosing a leader, it was not only specific requirements and qualifications that mattered but the whole personality of the girl.

The personalities of the leaders should be distinguished by character, achievement. Not dry knowledge but solid education, and an exemplary attitude.[110]

Demanding requirements were formulated, yet they remained strangely vague, thereby offering scope for a broad practical interpretation and application. On the one hand, it becomes very clear that what was sought after and deemed desirable was by no means limited exclusively to doctrine and political conviction. What was required was at the same time both more and less: the decisive factor was a candidate's personality, her character, whether she belonged to a certain "type of girl." On the other hand, what precisely was meant by such "personality" or "character" or "type of girl" was left ill-defined. Consequently, the young people were largely given a free hand. Yet this was in keeping with the dominant material constraint: namely, the permanent shortage of leaders.

And then, I can recall, naturally they were always looking for some kind of group leader. Such a group leader always was in charge of eight or ten girls, she had to take care of them. And she would determine the topics to be discussed. I can still remember, once she [her leader] said to me: "Listen here, after all, you're attending a *Lyzeum,* a good high school, you can do a lot better than the others. And you're a bit more intelligent too." I can't remember whether there was any extra training, I'm sorry but I really can't say now, don't recall. "So just do it," she said, "I'm gonna recommend you. You can handle it." Naturally I felt horrified. "I can't, I'm too busy at school."—"Oh c'mon, it's not much work, you can handle that, I'm sure!" So then I kind of wiggled out of it, see. My health is not the best. Anyhow I found some possibility to get out of it. And I told her: "Look, I'm not well, I can't do it."—"Oh c'mon," she said, "it

110. Rüdiger, *Die Hitler-Jugend,* 50.

won't be all that hard!" But then I flat refused. I didn't do it. And I'm glad I didn't too. (B 10)

The girl who was recommended in this case was not some enthusiastic member of the League of German Girls, not an ardent National Socialist. Before 1933, her father had been an active member of the Social Democratic Party (SPD). As a result, after 1933, he had come under mounting pressure from the National Socialists. Finally, at the request of her father, this girl joined the league as a kind of tribute to the "new times" and its "new leaders." In contrast with other girls whose fathers were not Nazis or were even opposed to them, she did not like becoming a league member. She was just doing her duty—reluctantly but without any thought of rebellion. Yet, what was the significance of the fact that, despite all this, one was prepared to recommend her for a leadership role? Apparently, the lack of commitment and ideological conviction and the background of a Social Democratic parental home were no impediment for becoming a leader. The topics for discussion and program could be imposed from above and were largely set in advance through the introduction and spread of *Heimabendmappen,* magazines that provided material for organizing a home evening.[111] Really key here was another factor. This girl lived in Wedding and was one of the few girls there attending a high school. That was what distinguished her from the other girls in her group. Most were working-class kids with little education and limited in their intellectual capacities. Though many of these girls were enthusiastic and loyal members of the league, that was not enough to qualify them as potential leaders of a group. Requisite for that were the ability to plan, a determination to get things done, and a willingness to assume responsibility. On the one hand, these were skills acquired at school, through scholastic training. On the other hand, they were closely bound up with a certain kind of family background.

An excursion was planned. And we were supposed to present a kind of skit to the parents about the excursion: like what they shouldn't do, what they should give the girls to take along. How it should be organized. So we put on this sketch, see, and I was given the role of the leader. And I guess I was so terrific in this role that afterward, well, the others all said: wow, she's a perfect leader, really qualified.

111. The magazines were called *Kameradschaft, Jungenschaft, Mädelschaft,* and *Jung-mädelschaft.* See Klönne, *Hitlerjugend,* 31; Rüdiger, *Die Hitler-Jugend,* 109.

I was 10 years old, I'd just joined up. And so I was sent to a training course for leaders. But I was a lot taller than other girls my age, so people always thought I was older. (B 15)

This girl also lived in Wedding, came from a well-educated middle-class family, and attended a high school. This made her so clearly superior to the other girls in her group that she was recommended for leadership training at the age of ten. Once again, the decisive factor was not her ideological conviction but her very pragmatic ways of dealing with problems. Her leadership qualification was based on an objective competence. But since the National Socialists were dependent on such abilities, they were forced to give some consideration to the old established elites. Especially in the small towns, it was amply evident that the social differences within the "community of youth" were reconstituted via the group of leaders. Those who became leaders were largely high schoolers. That was painfully palpable for all those girls who did not want to climb that ladder or were unable to. A woman from Minden with a Jewish grandparent recalls:

So I also spent those first two years in the Jungmädchen, though not with any exaggerated enthusiasm for the thing. Especially since back then if you were at a high school, or what they called a *Lyzeum,* you were a bit more gifted than the average kids. So the special groups, and then the craft group, I was in both and liked it. . . . And I wasn't discriminated against in any way. On the contrary: if something turned out especially nice, the objects I made were displayed too. But then I noticed that all those from my class, see, they were tapped to become leaders. Yet when it came to me, of course, I was left out. That wonderful selection process just passed me by. (M 6)

As a rule, the girls were recommended for the task of leader when they were still in the Jungmädel, between the ages of ten and fourteen. This had extensive consequences in that the girls then stayed on in the Jungmädel as leaders without having been promoted to the BDM. The upshot was that, not only did the BDM lose members in this way,[112] but it also took on a different social makeup from the Jungmädel, which again led to a further decline in its potential attractiveness. This

112. According to data that Michael Buddrus, who uses the official National Socialist figures, presents, the proportion of Jungmädel in the overall membership in the league was 59 percent in 1933, 65 percent in 1935, 62 percent in 1937, and 56 percent in 1939. Buddrus, *Totale Erziehung für den totalen Krieg,* 1:289.

development was hard to counter, because as a result of meetings held in the afternoon in the Jungmädelbund, they were dependent on high school girls, who, because of their free afternoons, were the only ones able to take on leadership positions for the girls in the ten to fourteen age bracket. The old social elites were thus reinstituted by this echelon of leaders, which also stamped the social character of the organization. One woman described the atmosphere at a gathering of leaders in the very class-conscious town of Minden.

> I never felt comfortable there. I mean, there were a lot of these, uh, there were some daughters, like of lawyers, and then a few girls whose dads were senior government officials. And they really showed their origins, kind of paraded it for all to see. And the rest of us were more or less second class, made to feel like trash or something. And they weren't friendly the way it should have been, you know what I mean? No, not at all. But the leader of the *Untergau* [district], she was very nice. I'd be lying if I didn't say that she was OK. Yet when it came to some of the others, well, it was pretty bad. This had nothing to do with Hitler at all. Like it was the way they, uh, let me explain how it was. The leaders all had this special cord they wore,[113] and then the tie. And then you had this brown knot. And they had this, either it was green and white or green, I can't recall the color combo for the group leader, when they started that. Anyhow, as soon as they had this cord and were a bit better than the rest, well then it just kind of went to their heads, they were never the same, something like that. (M 21)

Nonetheless, this recourse to the old elites bore a new note and was intricately bound up with the political system of National Socialism. Since this social differentiation within the membership of the league was based on objective criteria and a priori hardly had any social connotations, it offered an instrument for exclusion on the one hand and opportunities for social advancement on the other. Although still far removed from a "community of youth," social transparency was nonetheless enhanced. This is clear from the following statement, where a girl from Minden describes her relation as a leader to the male leadership.

113. Cords marked the rank of a leader by their colors. Schaft leaders had red and white cords, Schar leaders green ones, Gruppen leaders green and white cords, and Ring leaders white ones. Untergau leaders were distinguished by red cords, Gau leaders by red and black ones. Obergau leaders wore black cords.

I knew a few, and sometimes I even see them today. They were from another social class. But most of those you had contact with and who were also active as leaders naturally came from similar social backgrounds. They were students at the Gymnasium, the local high school for boys, and would go to dancing lessons with us. (M 9)

The old social hierarchies were thus revived via the Hitler Youth leadership, but not completely, and they bore a different note. One needed more than social privileges to reach a position of leader. The unconditional prerequisite was an active commitment and engagement. So although they were in large part identical, the new elites differed from the old by their consciousness of personal achievement: people were making careers. Nonetheless, there were significant social differences in the manner in which the ladder was climbed. The Jungmädelbund became the preferred playing field for the ambitions of upper-class youth—not just as a result of external conditions, such as the fact that activities within the Jungmädelbund took place in the afternoon, but also because sports and games were foregrounded, while political content tended to be largely relegated to a secondary role. In the BDM leadership ranks and in salaried leadership positions in the Hitler Youth, the situation was different.[114] A teacher from Minden, who worked closely together with the Hitler Youth, described its top echelon.

OK, well, the Hitler Youth *Bann* Minden,[115] as I experienced it, was like this. There was the *Bann* leader, usually a Hitler youth who was dedicated and had risen in the ranks. Those were generally people we didn't have much to do with. Who in some cases were socially beneath us. I mean, they were primitive, right? Like today, someone who has a good party record gets ahead. Well it was the same back then. So those were people we teachers felt were not on our level, we were generally superior to them, I mean in our mental attitude and educational background. (M 5)

Only in the case of a very small number of boys or girls did party work become an actual career. In almost all such instances, these were not people who stemmed from the upper classes. Rather, they were individuals for whom the pathway to another career in keeping with

114. See Reese, "Verstrickung und Verantwortung."
115. See appendix A, "The Structure of the Hitler Youth."

their levels of ambition and intelligence was not open. Excerpts from interviews with two top-echelon league leaders can illuminate this situation.

> I stayed at home for a time and took care of the housework because my mom was sick. And then I worked for a few years in a library, but only half days, because I still had to manage the household. And then one day the BDM showed up and asked me if I wanted to work for them. In the BDM section "Faith and Beauty." They asked whether I could take over these study groups. And I told them that I had to take care of the household, and was also working half days in the library. So that I probably had no time. And then they made me an offer, said I should quit the library and work for them, in the BDM. So then I took over the study groups for "Faith and Beauty." (M 2)

> I was an office worker. Then I went to work on a salary at the BDM. And that was really very nice for me, I liked it a lot. Though I enjoyed working with the girls more than the paper work, which also was part of it as a salaried staff member. So I always used to neglect the office stuff, I was a bit negligent, sloppy. Working with the young people, though, that was a lot of fun and satisfaction. Apart from the politics. But politics didn't play much of a role when it came to these young people. (M 3)

So the lack of prospects for the future, or insufficient options, was here the precondition for taking on a salaried job in the League of German Girls. But the situation was different for girls from the upper classes. Given the circumstance of compulsion, a more or less forced total recruitment of German youth, those girls had joined the league out of necessity. They had done so either voluntarily or perhaps with some reluctance. Many had seized on the chance to become a leader, which expanded their options for possible activity and appealed to their sense of self: an opportunity to test their strength, to prove themselves. In addition, in this way they could avoid boring indoctrination sessions and the imposition of group interests far removed from their own personal ones. So the career of a leader became a terrain for motives that were very much in their own self-interest. The girls accommodated, seeking to capitalize on the political circumstances for their own benefit. But that also meant avoiding to compromise oneself by a mode of identification that went too far: in the upper social classes, involvement in the league had a very carefully calculated scope and limit.

> M 3: I told you about Ms. —— already. She had actually wanted to work on a salary in the league, but her father had laid down conditions. He said: OK, first you learn a vocation. And that was a very good idea, it made good sense. And then somewhere she or her dad had heard things, rumors, well, he didn't want her to continue. Anyhow, the longer the war went on, people started whispering.
>
> I: What are you alluding to?
>
> M 3: Well, the concentration camps, of course. Things, one didn't like, or said "oh, my God." Or thought at first it was some kind of lie, or enemy propaganda. Yes, and plenty of people maybe also sensed how uncertain this whole thing was. They let their kids go, saying: OK, let them go, no harm in that. But I can imagine that there were responsible parents back at that time who said: no way, you're not working on a salaried basis for them, that's out of the question.

As previously discussed, the selection of a girl as a leader in the league was based mainly on their social and educational abilities to lead a group independently. Given the perennial pressing problem of a shortage of leaders, ideological conviction receded more and more into the background compared with these requirements—especially since the actual topics discussed in study groups could readily be imposed from above. In addition, such a choice was in keeping with the specific quality of working with girls, shaped more by specific activities than a National Socialist ideology. Dependent on locating qualities of leadership, the National Socialists were forced to appeal to the youth from the upper and middle classes, their educational and social background. Their participation was a sine qua non, especially beyond the age of fourteen, when a job or apprenticeship slashed the free time available to most of the other girls substantially, reducing it to a few hours in the evening. Social differentiation in the community of the League of German Girls was thus reproduced via the leadership echelon. The option of a leadership role also specifically took into account the interests of girls from the middle and upper strata. It was congruent with their level of intelligence and scholastic training, their need for some arena of activity. It also meshed with the fact that they sometimes stayed on as members in the league far longer than the other girls. Once they had begun a job or an apprenticeship, working-class teens were generally neither able nor willing to full their obligation for youth service; by contrast, the school left ample scope for this. Moreover, it also provided a framework for monitoring the girls' activity. Thus, engagement as a leader became for many a welcome opportunity to combine the unavoidable with utility. Yet the participation on the part of girls from these better social strata was carefully calibrated, concentrated in particular on the Jungmädelbund and less on the BDM. And there were very few recruited into salaried work on the staff. Other girls were active in those ranks, ones whose social background closed the door on an occupation that conformed with their mix of ambition and intelligence. In the case of most girls, there was a clearly discernible personal choice behind their decision to become a league leader. Only a small number were "true idealists" who lived by their convictions. But the tighter their interests meshed with those of the state, the ever more they were integrated into National Socialism. Nonetheless, in many instances selfish motives continued to predominate. The girls neither internalized nor spurned the concerns of the state. Instead, they accommodated to the prevailing winds, utilizing the situation to their own advantage. Once again, this raises the question of the content of the work a leader was assigned to watch over.

> I never noticed this had anything to do with Hitler at all. What was it like? Well, we made things by hand, and for what used to be called the Winterhilfswerk [Winter Relief Program], like we'd knit those little baby panties. And we read the old classic writers a lot, I told you already, Rosegger, Storm, Löns. And then we did a lot of sports. The leader was the daughter of our principal, and then another one became our leader. She too did the same things. And guess what, when I was 15, well, I took over the group . . . and I did just the same things too. A lot of that same kind of activity. And we used to sing loads of folk songs. (M 21)

As leader of a Schaft, a girl assumed responsibility for organizing the program of the home evening. First she had to arrive on time. Punctuality was something she also expected from the other girls. And whether she wanted to sing, do handicrafts, read some book together, or play some sport, it was necessary for her to successfully plan at least one afternoon or evening in advance. Once the group was assembled, it was her job to see that the plan was carried out. That required silence, discipline, and proper order; the girls' attention; and their active participation. The picture was something like this: ten or fifteen girls sitting together, initially enthusiastic but later increasingly bored by a compulsory service. In front of them stood their leader, hardly much older than they were themselves. She tried, more or less honestly, to do justice to the task before her. Of course, there were "born leaders," those who had the spark to spur enthusiasm in their group. But naturally there were others whose groups were bored to death or who frightened and intimidated the girls. The leaders could not proceed about their tasks freely but rather were compelled to teach the contents required and to maintain discipline. The two following excerpts give a vivid picture of this scenario.

> I remember, I think I mentioned it already, well, I was supposed to give a lecture in —— about Hitler. But I never did. I don't know why, but somehow I could never muster the enthusiasm to do it. And you have to understand it was, uh. No, let me go on with this first. This girl [a higher-ranking leader] stood behind the door, I think back then they called it a *Ringführerin* [battalion leader]. Well, this girl suddenly burst into the room and started to criticize me something awful, see. Because I hadn't read everything that was written down there. And she wanted to report me, and then I would be removed from the leadership of the Jungmädel group. (M 21)

> You know the old story, people never believe the big shots, the guys who did terrible things, when they say they don't remember. Now I can understand that. Because I've totally forgotten a whole lot of things from that time, completely gone from memory. But I have these fleeting images, like isolated recollections. I recall that once I had to have the group assembled in formation. We had this home [center], very near to our own apartment, but we only went there rarely, like when a bigger group got together. So my task was to get the whole group to stand in formation. And that meant to shout commands, like with soldiers: "Assemble now in three ranks! March, on the double!" And I said this very softly now, see. And I blushed and had a red face. And I knew that the fruit seller and his wife were standing over on the other side with a big grin on their faces, because they knew about my parents' political views.[116] And then, oops, my parents came along. It was really awful. I had to stand there at attention and bark something like: "Group leader

116. Her parents actively opposed the NSDAP.

reporting, group 12 assembled in three ranks and ready." Or something like that. The whole block knew what my parents thought, and I had to make a strong impression there. I had to look like the big leader. And I remember once that I made the group do some punishment drill, because they hadn't obeyed my orders. Why? Because I used to get as red as a beet every time I had to give an order. And I would start to stutter. So they just didn't obey me. I can't recall what they did, if they were noisy or something. So then I had to get tough. I shouted: "On the double! This whole group, down on your bellies! Crawl over to the ditch! Get a move on! Faster! . . ." And I had to imitate what I'd heard or seen in the weekly newsreels at the cinema, the way men, soldiers, would do it. Let me tell you, it was awful. (B 15)

These were "feats of achievement" performed by children and teens. Their activity was devoid of anything playful and anticipated the world of adults. It was these girls' job to plan, organize, get things done, take responsibility, decide, and render judgment where necessary. They had to conform and find their place in a hierarchy of ranks and powers. And the abstract aspect of their activity became all the more pronounced the higher they climbed, very consciously, up the career ladder. The reports of two women illuminate this dimension.

> B 11: Then I became *Ringsportwartin* [supervisor for the sports in one battalion], for the entire *Ring,* there were already some 300 girls.
> I: So what did you do with these 300?
> B 11: Well, personally that was it for me, I didn't do anything more. Because the other *Gruppensportwartinnen* [sport supervisors for a group] were all there, and we would . . . OK, I put together and organized competitions, that was the leading function, up on top, see. And what you can delegate to others below, you pass that on to them.

> I: How did your activity change then?
> M 9: Oh, I really can't tell you now. In the *Ring,* naturally, on the State Youth Day, you had to organize a lot more stuff. And it became much more theoretical. And while earlier on my work had concentrated on the individual simple member, I got away from that position very fast. Then, for all practical purposes, my job involved only other leaders. A select few.

I: *Schaftführerinnen* [squad leaders]?

M 9: Right, *Schaftführerinnen*. Because as a *Gruppenführerin* [group leader] you had to make sure everything was organized in the individual squads, and what was done in the group. And as a *Ringführerin* [battalion leader], you were above that level, and had discussions with the leaders. You were out of touch, a notch above, no longer had direct contact with the others, the more simple members.

The fruit of such efforts were power and prestige. The girls were, as a matter of course, integrated into a system in which relations between children and youth were structured in terms of commands and subordination. And with a modicum of desire and ability they themselves were soon an integral small wheel in the machinery. All too quickly, their dreams departed the fields of fantasy and took on a more mundane form and the guise of blue, red, and green cords, emblems of rank within the Hitler Youth. The ambition awakened at an early stage knew only itself, developed without inhibitions, and was devoid of any and all morality. Participating in power, these girls helped to cement and maintain it. Few perceived the burden placed upon them, the suffocating seriousness that smothered their joy in life and channeled them into rigidly preset tracks. Anxieties and nightmares such as in the following excerpt were rarely recalled.

For example, I had a terrible fear that I would have to go on a trip alone with these little girls. And then what I told you last time. I got up out of bed and checked and thought, my calculation wasn't right, the account was wrong. And some time or other, I still recall very well, my ID was missing. I mean, I was dreaming. I woke up and said to myself, tomorrow you'll need your ID, so where is the thing? And I was incredibly disorganized, and didn't know where I'd put it. So the upshot was that my mom also woke up and the both of us went looking for this ID at night. Nightmares, real nightmares. Maybe I've forgotten a lot because of these fears. Some time or other I once said to someone, that was what ended my childhood: choosing me to become a leader. (B 15)

Most girls probably just slid unaware into a world shaped and dominated by power, achievement, and social hierarchy. Here they accommodated themselves, preparing for a life that could only be imagined as an arena of struggle—one in which they wanted to emerge as the victors.

I wasn't even particularly interested in becoming a leader. I simply had an interest in educating kids. Or more precisely, afterwards teenagers too. And that's what interested me. And I think I also integrated that interest into my profession. I never wanted to remain just some insignificant little kindergarten teacher. I wanted more. So by means of further education, I slowly worked my way up the ladder. (B 11)

The woman reporting here seems to have little interest in the content of what she did. Just as she didn't become a leader for the sake of the persons she educated, her efforts to gain more knowledge was not meant to benefit the children in her kindergarten classes. At the core of her action is preoccupation with her own ego: to become someone who has accomplished something in life. The lack of conscience and morality evident here is not some personal problem or failing. Rather, it is the consistent product of a system of "education" in an authoritarian and racist state that also imposed its laws mercilessly on children—a state adept at turning them into young accomplices. The price was a piece of their childhood happiness. Hardly conscious of the fact, these children became cogs in an inhuman machinery that functioned smoothly but left the soul withered.

Sure, OK, I have to say that maybe a lot of what people did back then was bad. But there was something special too about it. . . . I mean, you had another kind of sense of duty, another kind of discipline. And you can still notice that in the behavior of fellow workers around you from that time. (B 11)

Diffuse Memories

I: OK, so what was the main thing you used to do on *Heimabende* with the girls?

B 2: There were games, we sang, learned songs. What else? Let's see. Oh, then there were the big assembly formations, where you'd have to stand someplace with your group. And we used to have excursions too. Let's see, so what else did we do? I think I really didn't go often enough to remember real well.[117]

I: What kind of girls came to your group?

117. This woman was in the Jungmädelbund for four years, from 1938 to 1942.

M 9: I can't remember any of them. Can you imagine that?! I mean, no memory left of them at all! It's a blank, nothing whatsoever!

I: But in general, then, you really don't have much of a recollection of the Jungmädelbund, do you?

M 16: Nope, just that I was somewhere or other. And that all our free time was organized by doing some kind of activity. More than that I can't recall. But I do remember that it was very nice. That we could do things, we were among ourselves, I mean, among kids our own age.

If you insert these remarks on the League of German Girls into the broader discursive context of the individual life histories of these women, it is striking how colorless these descriptions are, how little graphic, how devoid of detail. There is a short enumeration of activities—"singing, handicrafts, lots of sports"—to describe a whole span in a person's life, often at the same time termed "beautiful" or "something you shouldn't miss out on."

The contrast stands out in high relief when these narratives are counterposed to stories about growing up with other kids, the games and fun the girls remember when they were smaller.

It always sounds so strange when people say: "oh, back then, in the old days, well, it used to be different," like "we used to have a real summer, a real winter then." But when I think back, it really was that way! During the winter, when I was a kid, why we'd go tobogganing for weeks on end. Without ever even thinking that the snow might vanish. There was snow all over and in the afternoon, when school let out, we'd go tobogganing til it got dark. And in the summer it was exactly the same. But then we had the river. Like after school, and after I started working, there wasn't a single evening when I didn't go down to the river, the Weser. And then there still used to be a few, not many, just a few of the steamboats with their big wheels, yeah, and the boats, the big barges. And we used to grab hold and hang on down the river all the way to Porta [next little town]. In back there were these little lifeboats, out in back. And we'd swim alongside, right, and sometimes it was pretty dangerous. But we'd swim alongside and get close, and then climb on into the boats. And then we just sort of let ourselves be pulled along, almost all the way to Porta. And then we'd come back down again, to Minden. You hardly needed to swim at all, like just being pulled along by these boats. Those are my most beautiful memories. It was wonderful. (M 20)

One may of course object that this contrast is due to repression—that the women do not want to remember a chapter in their lives that they regard in retrospect with quite mixed feelings. But a precondition for the genesis of such a conflict is the feeling that you had a choice. Yet that dimension existed only with a certain segment of the girls, namely, those who joined up voluntarily and others who made a career there, who, for personal reasons, went further than what was demanded of them. For all the others another explanation must be sought. This raises the question of the content of service. What did the girls find so appealing?

Joining the organization began on an elevating note, a "grand ritual" of sorts. Accompanied by her mother, the following ten-year-old girl went to the local league office and registered. She filled out an application form and put her signature to this declaration: "I am of German extraction and hereby promise, as signed by me below, to promote the movement to the best of my ability and energy in keeping with the National Socialist world view."[118] The girl then learned that her circle of activities and tasks would now be expanded beyond just home and school to include service as a Jungmädel. She became part of the "movement," the "great German community." Her mother stood at her side. "If you sign this now, then you won't belong just to me alone any more, you'll belong to the Führer too. Do you understand?"—"How much do I belong to the Führer, is it much more than to you? And is that bad? But, OK, I'll sign, I really want to be in the Jungmädel."[119]

After the new member had been informed of the date, place, and time of her first *Heimnachmittag* (afternoon meeting), the everyday life of the organization began. Initially there was an element of excitement because it involved getting prepared for the Jungmädelprobe. A woman from Berlin comments on that test:

> B 15: It was a test of courage and proof that you were a real German girl. You had to run in the forest, there was a paper chase, a bunch of questions they'd ask. And our neighbor, her daughter,

118. *Das deutsche Mädel* 3, no. 4 (1937): 18.
119. *Das deutsche Mädel* 3, no. 4 (1937): 18.

who was a leader herself, she let on what it was and told us all the answers. And if she hadn't, then I'd have blown the thing, I'd have failed miserably. I didn't know anything. And then, in the paper chase, you had to find your way through the woods to some meeting place.

I: All by yourself?

B 15: Well, right, or maybe two of you, three, possibly four kids together. And then you had to do some athletics. The exercises weren't so hard, I mean, I wasn't good at gymnastics, but I did all of them. Though I practiced beforehand to get ready. Our neighbor had told us about that too. Then there was also a nighttime hike. With those famous rhymes—"Grip tight your umbrella, stick and hat / A person may not know where she's at" and "Trees to the left, trees to the right / Between them spaces, all in sight"[120]—that you'd shout as you walked to drown out your own feelings of fear.

Only after the candidate had passed her test was she really a full-fledged member of the Jungmädel, and in a festive ceremony she was presented with her kerchief and knot, symbolizing her membership.

And then it would take a while until you got the kerchief and the knot. So initially you're just on probation. I can't remember how long that lasted. . . . Naturally, if you . . . of course you wanted to be a regular full member, 'cause just to run around in a skirt and blouse without the kerchief and knot, well, that was nothing. You didn't feel like you really belonged. (B 2)

After this promising beginning, then you were in the real thick of the action: excursions, sports, games outside in the summer, handicrafts for the Winter Relief, collecting for charity, and singing in the winter.

You know, like it wasn't always summer when we could go out into the park and stuff. We had the winter too. Then we'd have handicrafts, the older girls would knit something for the soldiers. I can't remember everything we did there. We pasted some kind of stars and were singing songs. Naturally the traditional Christmas songs.

120. "Ein Hut, ein Stock, ein Schirm, der Mensch, der kann sich irrn"; "Links sind Bäume, rechts sind Bäume, in der Mitte Zwischenräume."

But their songs too, like *"Hohe Nacht der klaren Sterne"*[121] [High Night of Clear Stars], if you've ever heard this song. (B 21)

There were many reasons why the girls found these activities so appealing.

What I liked was that you were allowed to do lots of stuff that otherwise as a girl was always forbidden. Like marching, climbing trees, stuff like that. Like hikes across the fields with knapsacks, and then there were excursions too. That really struck a chord with me, I really liked it, see, 'cause I had brothers, and there was always this rivalry between us. But other girls felt the same too, I'm sure. (B15)

The League of Girls opened up new, uncustomary options for girls, but ones they found were fun. Especially those girls who had brothers felt at a disadvantage. It wasn't only that the parents would often use two yardsticks, a kind of double standard. In many cases, the boys would also vie with the girls.

My mom allowed us to shoot with the air gun, at old hangers that were hung up somewhere as targets. But many times, the boys didn't let us play. For example, they wouldn't let us come into the dugout they'd built. And we were much smaller; I was four years younger. So when the boys'd play together, who lived in our building or who were friends, then you had to kind of earn the right to play with them. Now my brother will deny this to his dying day, but they used to make me lie down in my bathing suit in the nettles, and then I'd be allowed to play with them. And once they made me eat a rain worm first as a condition. (B 15)

In the league the girls became part of the "national community," part of "German youth." They were equal to the Hitler Youth on a plane that was perceptible, local, and real. The symbol of their belong-

121. *"Hohe Nacht der klaren Sterne"* was a song by Hans Baumann (1914–88), a popular song composer in Nazi Germany and especially within the Hitler Youth. The song avoids all allusions to the birth of Christ and Christmas and praises with great pathos the winter solstice and a holy motherhood. *"Hohe Nacht der klaren Sterne"* was the only nonreligious Christmas song that became popular. There are many well-known Hans Baumann songs, some of them unpolitical, such as *"Es geht eine helle Flöte"*; some closely linked with National Socialism, as in the case of *"Es zittern die morschen Knochen."* Baumann was a member of the Reichsjugendführung but also wrote the songbook for German soldiers *"Morgen marschieren wir."*

ing was the uniform, especially the kerchief and knot. And the fact that to preserve these they had to do something in return only heightened their sense of satisfaction. But that feeling was short lived; it soon faded into habit, not just in the life of the individual member but also more generally in the course of the twelve years of National Socialist rule. The uniforms were passed on from sister to sister, cousin to cousin; the rituals became familiar, old hat; the content of the service lost the charm of novelty and was pressed more and more into the mold of a prescribed scheme. An end was put to the thrill girls had felt earlier on in the organization, the lure of being able to enter previously closed male domains. The female character of the service was re-emphasized, bringing back the old barriers and restrictions of the "second sex." The girls sensed this element of reversal, responding with declining interest and élan. "And then we knitted little wristlets for the soldiers at the front. I guess it was crucial for the war effort for them to have these wristlets" (M 10).

Again and again we encounter the statement from the girls that they were looking for the group, for a community of peers. At first glance, this appears understandable. But from narratives about growing up as smaller kids with their friends, we know that the girls were not alone.[122] And initially it was characteristic for league recruitment to find entire groups of children from the same street or village joining up together. A voluntary but solid group of kids bonded together; living only for its own interests, became a group in the service of the "movement." This upward transformation toward a kind of supra-individual significance for the group went hand in hand with restrictions on the freedom of movement, on imagination and sovereignty—before young people had *lived their youth,* oriented to their own interests and remote from the adult world of duties and obligations. Now young people began to feel that they *were youth,* consciously belonging to a group. This was an act of self-demarcation, drawing a line around one's own identity. That was often directed first against one's own parents.

> For me, when I look back now and think about it, membership in the BDM was on a kind of par with going against the wishes of my parents. Like when I attended the children's services at the church. They made just as many nasty remarks about that. (B 15)

---

122. However, the drop in the number of children even in working-class or rural areas during the 1920s also led to a new situation for them in that it was more difficult to create a community for them.

In resistance against one's own parents, a subjective consciousness formed, the feeling of one's own personality crystallized. Nonetheless, the more girls who joined the ranks of the league, the greater was the sense of loneliness of those who didn't become members. Was the feeling here one of isolation? Or was it rather a sense of having been excluded? As a rule, service in the league required two hours one afternoon a week, sometimes two. Then there was a weekend trip once a month during the summer. Naturally, activities in the organization were flexible, could be stretched to whatever length desired, and leaders in particular were often constantly busy. But most of the girls who were members still had a lot of free time at their disposal, which they used as they had in the past. So the quest for the group was not an attempt to find people but rather a feeling of belonging not available through the existing structures of tradition, that is, parents and a process of integration into the social, religious, and sexual codes they represented. Rather, that sense of belonging was mediated by two abstract concepts: age and nation. To belong now meant to be a part of "German youth," a kind of imagined community.[123]

Many women mention that the league shaped and organized their free time. There was always something going on, some activity, something to do. What does that mean? As we saw, children and youth even outside the ambit of the league always had things to do. And if we compare the spectrum of activities, what they organized themselves tended to be more diverse, more imaginative, more fun. Moreover, since it came from their own initiative, it was far more emotionally laden for them than were the group activities organized by the League of German Girls. So what specifically attracted them?

> Well, for a while I took up rowing. That was a special deal I was able to get cheaper through the Hitler Youth. You could take part in a special study group for rowing in the rowing club. I mean, that's a group I would never have been able to get into otherwise. It was a closed circle, see, there was no access for us. Wasn't our social milieu. That would be just like if I'd gotten some grand notion that I wanted to start playing tennis or something. That's simply the way things were, we were not accepted in those select circles. (M 18)

123. Benedict Anderson, *Imagined Communities: Reflections on the Origin and Spread of Nationalism* (London and New York, 1996).

The attraction here is obvious. The Hitler Youth facilitated access to activities that were otherwise reserved for a higher social stratum.[124] Through the league, girls learned how to swim; they could visit drama performances in open-air theaters, take hikes through the nearby countryside, which often was not familiar to them. They met girls from other villages and towns and maybe even had the special experience of "seeing the Führer." Asked what she found attractive about membership in the league, this woman from a poor family living on the outskirts of Minden answers:

> M 12: Participating whenever I could, in my free time. Because as a kid, and at home, well, we never went anywhere. So we just had to join in something like that.
> I: And then you had the feeling that you're were getting out a bit, having a chance to see something?
> M 12: Right, like we took trips on bikes, they'd lend us a bike to take . . . or we'd hike, like up into the mountains, and that was wonderful, so beautiful.

So through the league a girl had the chance to peek a bit out over her own narrow social horizon and saw and experienced things that otherwise would have remained closed to her—for financial reasons, because of the existence of social barriers, or simply because of a lack of initiative. The pleasure a girl derived from these activities, the relish she felt, did not spring just from the activities themselves. To an appreciable extent, it also derived from the fact that, in this way, girls were able to step out beyond the perimeter of their own social framework.

> So back then we thought that was very important. The thing was, well, it kind of filled your free time a little. After all, back then we didn't have all the stuff in the media you have today. So we had to think for ourselves: OK, what are you gonna do in your free time today? Like when you were done with homework. Now in my case, well I had things really planned out in advance. A full schedule from Monday to Friday. And then on Saturdays, Sundays, my parents would organize something if I wasn't out on an excursion. (B 11)

---

124. But the Hitler Youth also attracted young people by offering discounts, for instance, on clothing and free passes for movie shows, as M 18 and B 12 remembered.

Although she emphasizes that she had to think about her free time and how to fill it up, the characteristic feature of her everyday life was precisely the fact that it was so planned in advance that she hardly ever had a chance to wonder about what she should do. There was no tedium, no terrible boredom that might give birth to an idea, let's say, for a new game. You didn't have to look for other kids to create a community. It was all there, ready at hand, just waiting—the community of the "like-minded," with prescribed content, the same repeated activities. It was rare for something unexpected to occur. On the other hand, it was all very convenient. And it was attractive for youngsters: lots of new playgrounds were built,[125] the Hitler Youth had plenty of equipment,[126] youth had its assigned place in the large political parades, and their ceremonies were put on with style. Who would not want to be a part of that?

> No, I didn't have the feeling that everyone was. . . . Only I was always sad that the ones who couldn't participate were standing there at the side and just watching, and were sad about it. Because we really had a lot of activities offered for our free time, there was a lot to do. So that young people were not out on the street. I mean, I won't mince words here, just say what I think: that was something I thought was very positive, a good thing, at the time. (B 11)

The communities of young people and children were groups that crystallized outside the perimeters of the home. The apartments they lived in were far too small to provide space for the children's need to be active. Even the larger apartments generally had no more than one living room or den, and that had to satisfy the needs of all family members, which meant that children were not free to engage in much movement of any kind there.

---

125. M 25 worked as a youth department head for the Minden municipality. Her job was in particular to set up sports fields: "And we were also . . . we were so wonderfully free. Like we used to get, we got money, a certain amount for every child, so we had funds we could spend. . . . For example, like the biggest thing I accomplished, I was able to arrange in Bad Oeynhausen for them to get a wonderful big soccer field or sports field. That was something funny, maybe, but it was really the case, I could do everything, I mean, I had money!"

126. They confiscated this equipment from the youth organizations that were dissolved! For example, in the Protestant community center in Hille, there was sports equipment that the Eichenkreuz Association, which had been prohibited from working with young people in sports, finally was forced to sell at bargain-basement prices. The municipality in Hille, which bought the equipment, then put it at the disposal of the local Hitler Youth; see St. A. Detmold, M 2 Minden C 150.

As I told you, at home there were lots of things that were forbidden for me. I wasn't allowed even to go into the living room. We had the sofa there; I was never permitted to sit on it, that was an absolute no-no. And mom was very neat and orderly, everything was in its place, and I simply had to accept that, no choice. (B 1)

As soon as the children started to walk, they would be sent outside, often accompanied by an older sister or brother. "Outside" in Wedding-Berlin was mainly the streets and pavements. In Minden, that meant the gardens, the Glacis slope, the Weser River, and a lot of still unspoiled nature. The forms of play such groups of kids in Wedding engaged in, even under the conditions of a crowded urban neighborhood, could be quite varied.

Gee, we used to have so much free time. Not only did we play out in the street. We used to go off, singing and playing music, a group of 10 or 20 kids, and walk along the canal all the way over to Tegel, the whole canal, all the way down. We were always a big gang of kids. Then there were the street fights, and it used to be the Transvaal Terrors against the Cameroon Kids against the guys from Reinick-endorf. (B 6)[127]

This quote underscores how little was necessary for the children to organize their free time in a satisfying and pleasurable way. It also shows that one sine qua non for free play was sufficient space. But the freedom of movement of the children was already significantly curtailed, in Wedding more than in Minden. Traffic here had already come to dominate the streets, the children were chased from the courtyards by the doormen, and in the parks guards with clubs made sure that children stayed off the grass. The few areas of unspoiled nature were converted into lots for construction. The huge sand dunes in the north of Wedding were transformed into green parks. But what the adult world celebrated as progress was a loss for the children. Instead of a huge area that invited kids to seek new adventure, now they had a few standard playgrounds and sports fields, all of the same form, with the same facilities. This new restriction was often not even perceived as such, because these new facilities came in the guise of a special donation to explicitly address the needs of the young. That alone bore a certain attraction: this was the right place for children to be. Hand in hand

127. These are all names of streets and districts.

with the reduction of free space for free play, the street was decried as a proper space for children. Traditionally, community had evolved in and through the agency of the street and its spaces. The stores were the communicational nodes for the women, the *Kneipen* (beer halls) the same for the men. The children had their fixed place in the web of communication and interaction that the street represented and embodied.

Even before 1933, it was the unchallenged premise of youth policy that it was necessary to get youth off the streets. The street was blamed for all manner of negative behavior: immoral, politically rebellious, wild, and uncontrollable. The gangs were children of the street. Organizing as a means to discipline youth extended into the working-class neighborhoods. A woman in Wedding gave her rationale for joining the Falcons: "Look, I was supposed to, like I was a little wild, see, I was like five jocks. I was supposed to take a back seat a bit when there was these gang fights, 'cause I was sort of always right in there with 'em" (B 14).

By trying to bring in all young people under their umbrella, the National Socialists continued this process. It went hand in hand with a mounting moral discrediting of those youngsters who were still out on the pavement. These "street kids" were considered neglected children; the girls in particular were put under growing pressure to avoid the street as the customary place for flirting[128] and meeting young men.

> B 18: In these two apartments that faced the courtyard, well, there were a lot of, you know, a big crowd of kids. Like and you didn't know where they all were from. Yeah, and the girls, the older girls there, they also looked as if they were already hitting the streets, you know, prostitutes. You'd hear people talking bad about them at our house, like "hey, what are they up to down there again? They're always standing out in front of the entrance. Don't they have some job to keep 'em busy, wouldn't that be better? Their mother works her fingers to the bone for them, and these bimbos just don't do a damn thing." Talk like that.
>
> I: And you, you didn't play with those kids?
>
> B 18: Oh, sure we did, sure. Like when we had the harvest celebration, they also came round, all the goldbrickers down there, or

---

128. For example, Dinse quotes a young worker: "I usually pick up my girlfriend from the shop where she works. After we get home we go stand out in front of the door, watching the passersby. If it gets too boring, then the two of us go for a little stroll"; Dinse, *Das Freizeitleben der Großstadtjugend*, 76.

the whores. I don't really know, but it sort of seemed like that, going hawking on the street. I mean, I really had no idea.

After 1933, the streets of Wedding emptied out. The statement by a woman from Wedding "when I was a kid, why, there was another kind of life on the streets" (B 17) is not an isolated observation. The traders on the street, the beggars, were driven off, the groups of young unemployed youth playing cards disbanded. The Jewish ice cream parlors at Gesundbrunnen had to close down, just like many other shops, especially during the war. The power of the street had created itself through conversation; it was generated discursively. As anxiety and terror now spread, conversation was choked off, silenced. Now the street was generally deemed a space to be avoided. It was a place where there were too many unpredictable dangers and frightening events you could be compelled to witness. And you felt less and less courage to oppose them, the more you had the feeling that you stood alone. The power of the street was smashed. Finally, the children who played with their tops or balls on its pavements were organized into the Hitler Youth. And off they went to the newly created areas designated "appropriate for children," the playgrounds and sports fields built by the regime. Long ago the city had begun to restrict their latitude for movement, to pen them in. Now, with the loss of space, they also were forced to forfeit a portion of their autonomy. Consciously, that is barely experienced as a perceptible loss. It is only preserved in discourse as a memory that narrates in animated color about the games and free play, while speaking vaguely, with an interest that quickly turns tepid, about the activities of the League of German Girls.

Summing Up

The racial state can also carry on the education of the girl on the same principles as that of the boy. Here too the main emphasis must be placed above all on physical culture, secondly on the development of spiritual, and lastly on intellectual, values. The unshakable aim of female education must be the coming mother.[129]

This quotation is generally trotted out as proof of the conservative, backward-looking orientation of education in the League of German Girls. The reference to motherhood seems to clinch that reading. Yet

129. Hitler, *Mein Kampf,* 401.

the quotation in its fuller context begins differently, namely, by noting an analogy between male and female education, assigning the highest priority to the disciplining of the body. Was this supposed to lead for men to the "bliss" of independent employment, for girls to the "slavery" of motherhood?

In a 1947 essay on authority and the family, Max Horkheimer noted:

> The ideal modern mother plans the education of her children almost in a scientific way, from a balanced diet to an equally as balanced relation between praise and criticism, just as the literature in popular psychology recommends. Her entire attitude toward children becomes rational: even love is handled like a component of pedagogical hygiene.[130]

This development Horkheimer describes was furthered in Germany by National Socialism and especially by the organizing of female youth in the League of German Girls. The primacy of the family for the education of girls was limited by conscripting them into service outside the home through the league. The education of girls under National Socialism became public to a far greater degree than ever before. Yet as girls participated in external society, they also subordinated themselves to its constraints. In sports, they inscribed their bodies with the laws of a competitive, achievement-oriented society. In the groups of girls, they learned how to conform socially; in the career trajectory of the leader, they got early training in negotiating the paths of social advancement. Yet in this takeover of the behavioral patterns of a technological-rational world, the "education" of girls was subject to the same premises as that of the boys. Paradoxically, the National Socialists, bent on organizing youth, discovered that the girls were their strongest potential allies. Born into a world that denigrated what was feminine to something second class and inferior, the most spirited among the girls sought ways and means to elude the social fate of their gender. Precisely because the League of German Girls did not embody "traditional female values," but rather, under the banner of the concept of youth, entailed a process of socialization, it had a special appeal for the girls. Not only was the League of German Girls as an institu-

---

130. Max Horkheimer, "Autorität und Familie in der Gegenwart," in Horkheimer, *Zur Kritik der instrumentellen Vernunft. Aus den Vorträgen und Aufzeichnungen seit Kriegsende,* ed. Alfred Schmidt (Frankfurt a.M., 1967), 277; first appeared under the title *Eclipse of Reason* (New York, 1947).

tion comparable with and equal to the Hitler Youth, it also offered the girls new and unfamiliar arenas and spaces for action. Because girls considered the social connotations that clamp down onto the living reality of the existence of two genders as something real and had long since internalized them, all their energy was invested into adapting and conforming to the external world, imagined as a male universe.

> I always wanted to be a boy. . . . Although today, well, actually I can't understand why, 'cause we were allowed to do so many of the same things the boys were. Just not to wear trousers. Which just, well, that came then a lot later. As a small kid, I always wanted to wear my brother's leather pants. I was only allowed to secretly though, in the morning, when my parents were still asleep. Then our maid would let me put on my brother's trousers, with a little bow in my hair. See, like I wasn't allowed to do that either, mom also didn't like that much. (B 15)

As the quotation graphically shows, the desire of the girl to be a boy had nothing to do with genuine sexuality: she had no problem combining the trousers with a bow in her hair. Instead, the yearnings of the second sex contained an element of social rebellion, were permeated by the wish for social distinction and personal social advancement. The fact that the reality of a class society is replicated in the duality of male/female[131] is at the same time also the precondition for maintenance of a sexist society. But only when the strangeness and lack of transparency of the other sex in the bourgeois capitalist world had disengaged from the framework of rite and ritual, seemingly dissolving totally into economic categories, did the boundless rivalry between the sexes unfold. This was a struggle at whose endpoint women face(d) a total alienation from their own gender—which they nonetheless continue(d) to embody.

131. See Pierre Bourdieu, *Entwurf einer Theorie der Praxis* (Frankfurt a.M., 1976), esp. 48–65; translated as *Outline of a Theory of Practice* (Cambridge: Cambridge University Press, 1977).

CHAPTER 4

A Study in Local History: Minden in Westphalia

Minden, a Prussian, Protestant Town of Civil Servants and Soldiers

Those likable Westphalians
I always loved them dearly:
So firm, so sure, so loyal, without
Pride or hypocrisy—nearly.

How fine they looked in the fencing hall:
Like lions and just as fierce!
How true their blows and so well meant
Each quarter and every tierce.

They fence so well, they drink so well,
They shake hands with you like oaks
When they want to make friends, and they always weep.
They're sentimental old soaks.

May Heaven preserve you, doughty folk,
And bless your crops and your seeds,
And keep you from war and things like fame
And free from heroic deeds.

May Heaven provide an easy exam
To all your sons in common
And bring your daughters in good time
Safe to the altar—Amen!

—Heinrich Heine

On his trip through Germany in 1844, later immortalized in his book *Germany: A Winter's Tale,* the poet Heinrich Heine paid a visit to Minden. Then still ringed by moats and bastions, this small Westphalian town symbolized for Heine the narrowness and lack of liberalism of the Prussian state.[1] In the period of our historical focus, the fortifications had long since been dismantled, save for a sole reminder of their former construction, the remaining green belt around the city, the so-called *Glacis.* But Minden had continued to be a narrow and stifling town, with rigid social barriers and an irrevocable moral code.

I only know, I thought Minden was incredibly narrow and restricting. And I thought to myself: OK, once you got your high school diploma, the first thing will be to get out of the place. It's a God awful place, you just can't live here, it's suffocating. (M 10)

Minden's location directly on the Weser River was a determinant factor, especially in the town's early history. The presence of a ford here led early on to the formation of trade routes. Pottery finds date back to 500 BCE, and there was continuous settlement documented from the eighth century. The first reference to the town in writing is from 775, when Charlemagne crossed the Weser using the ford at Minda. In 803, Minden became a bishopric, and construction was started on a cathedral that was fortified with palisades and moats. Between 800 and 1100, a trade settlement called the "Wik" sprang up around this bishopric, and by 1230 the Wik had become an actual town with its own laws, municipal seal, and city council. In the thirteenth century, work was begun on a town hall. It emerged as an autonomous urban community vis-à-vis the bishop, and Minden's importance grew in proportion to the economic dependence of the financially strapped bishops on the town. The bishops' financial problems were due in large measure to expenses for maintaining a court and footing the bills for knightly ostentation. In 1306, the bishop left the town, relocating to Petershagen.

Eighty years prior to this, in 1226, Minden together with two other Westphalian towns, Münster and Osnabrück, had established the Landsberg Alliance, the first Westphalian urban league. Minden became a member of the Rhenish-Westphalian League of Towns and the "Hanse," the Hanseatic League. The leading social stratum in the

1. Heinrich Heine, *Germany: A Winter's Tale,* trans. Herman Salinger (New York, 1944), 46f.; originally published in German, 1844.

city was merchants. There were fierce political struggles for local political power between the artisans and merchants in the early fifteenth century. One result was that the guilds were granted the right to be elected in the Committee of the Forty, a kind of municipal council.

The Reformation arrived in Minden early, between 1525 and 1530. In 1529, a dispute erupted between the Protestant guilds and the Catholic city council. A short time later a ban in the emperor's name, the so-called *Reichsacht,* was placed on Minden, and the Swedes occupied the town in 1634 during the Thirty Years' War. The Peace of Westphalia in 1648 awarded the princely bishopric of Minden to the prince-elector of Brandenburg: against its will, the town came under the thumb of Prussia.[2]

With the change in political rule, Minden not only lost its political freedom, but it also forfeited its economic importance. In the eyes of the Brandenburg prince-elector, the town was a "bridgehead on the Weser" and solely of military interest. This was reflected in the town's demographics; though its population in 1550 had numbered between 4,000 and 5,000 residents, by 1722 it had declined to only 2,959.[3] The fortifications of the town prevented any kind of economic growth, and in any event, the dominating social strata were uninterested in such prospects. These political priorities did not change until under Frederick the Great. In 1763, the fortifications were dismantled, and a year later a sugar refinery was founded, a business for which Minden was granted a monopoly in the western Prussian provinces.[4] But the political situation ensured that these first proto-industrial attempts were short lived: in 1816, in the wake of the German-French war, the town was refortified once more.[5]

Minden remained what it was: a Prussian town with a strong military presence and a sizeable number of civil servants. Its confines,

2. Both Kaeller and Engel report that the town resisted its incorporation into Prussia, resistance that was only broken by armed intervention by the Brandenburg authority. See Gustav Engel, *Politische Geschichte Westfalens* (Cologne and Berlin, 1968), 184; Reinhard Kaeller, *Die konservative Partei in Minden Ravensberg, ihre Grundlagen, Entstehung und Entwicklung bis zum Jahre 1866* [= 26. Jahresbericht des Historischen Vereins für die Grafschaft Ravensberg in Bielefeld] (Bielefeld, 1912), 19.

3. Martin Krieg, "Einwohnerzahlen der Stadt Minden. Über die Bevölkerungsbewegung in Minden seit 700 Jahren," *Mindener Tageblatt,* Dec. 1, 1949.

4. See Stephanie Reekers, "Beiträge zur stat. Darstellung der gewerblichen Wirtschaft Westfalens um 1800. Teil 2: Minden-Ravensberg," *Westfälische Forschungen* [= Mitteilungen des Provinzialinstitutes für westf. Landes- und Volkskunde, vol. 18] (Münster, 1965), 89.

5. Reekers points out that in any event there were only very few workers employed in the industrial enterprises; Reekers, "Beiträge zur stat."

emblematic of its intellectual lack of tolerance, both created and buttressed its spatial constriction.

In this "most Prussian town in Westphalia,"[6] there was little manifest sign of the social tensions that marked the period down to 1848. This was only to be expected. Even though Minden had also been hit by poverty and starvation,[7] and even though here, too, as elsewhere throughout Westphalia, people suffered from the arrogance and self-importance of the military and civil servants,[8] the dominance of precisely this social group hampered any and all liberal political development within its ramparts.

These special conditions imbued the revolts of March 1848 with their own distinctive physiognomy and character. In Minden, there were but a small number of the "less well-off,"[9] artisans and workers who took part in disturbances. Rather, it was largely the burghers who joined in the rebellion, many of whom belonged to the town's educated class, especially the Jewish intelligentsia.[10] The military quickly dispersed the crowds, and the spirit of democracy that had briefly stirred was soon totally defeated. Its champions were forced to withdraw from public life or even emigrate.

Though at first glance its social configuration thus appeared to be a kind of perpetuation of feudal relations into modern times, a perceptible social change was under way, visible, for example, in the growth in population. Between 1818 and 1858, the town nearly doubled, and it almost quadrupled in the nine decades between 1818 and 1905.[11] This meant an increase in the working-class population, since almost nothing had changed in the status of the town as a military and administrative center. Economic development was again spurred by the second dismantling of fortifications, completed in 1879. Now nothing stood in the way of the town's expansion, the arrival of new industries, and growth in the population. Despite this, industrial development was

6. Wilhelm Schulte, *Volk und Staat. Westfalen im Vormärz und in der Revolution 1848/49* (Münster, 1954), 247.

7. See Arno Herzig, *"In unseren Herzen glüht der Freiheit Schein." Die Entstehungsphase der bürgerlichen und sozialen Demokratie in Minden (1848–1878)* [= Mindener Beiträge 19] (Minden, 1981), 84; Hellmuth Assmann, "Beiträge zur Geschichte des Kreises Minden von 1816 bis 1945," *Mitteilungen des Mindener Geschichts- und Museumvereins* 40 (1968): 92.

8. Schulte, *Volk und Staat,* 51.

9. Schulte, *Volk und Staat,* 171.

10. See Herzig, *"In unseren Herzen glüht der Freiheit Schein,"* 11ff.

11. See Stephanie Reekers, *Westfalens Bevölkerung 1818–1955. Die Bevölkerungsentwicklung der Gemeinden und Kreise im Zahlenbild* [= Veröffentlichungen des Provinzialinstitutes für westfälische Landes- und Volkskunde, ed. 1, no. 9] (Münster, 1956), 71.

slow, because the dominant social classes in the town continued to do little to encourage or foster it. Yet a drop in the number of emigrants leaving Minden between 1884 and 1914 points to rising economic prosperity.[12] It also evidences the political consensus that the city had apparently been able to preserve between all social strata and interests groups. We turn now to an examination of the historical origins and political consequences of this small-town idyll—where even those who differed politically shared similar ideals of God, folk, and fatherland.

Even contemporaries in the nineteenth century considered Minden-Ravensberg the "Prussian Vendée,"[13] a "conservative small model state."[14] A conservative element continued to dominate the district unchallenged, and Stoecker's brand of anti-Semitism had considerable appeal.[15] There were two reasons for the comparatively high level of stability in conservative electoral behavior: the economic structure of the district and the presence of a political Protestantism that had crystallized in the nineteenth century and remained a factor down into the twentieth century.[16]

The district of Minden-Ravensberg was surrounded by three bishoprics: Paderborn, Münster, and Osnabrück, as well as two secular territories, Lippe and Rheda. This helps explain the typical sense of separation or difference felt in the district. People distinguished themselves from the surrounding territories both in religious affiliation and in eco-

12. See Leopold Kulke, "Die wirtschaftliche Entwicklung der Stadt Minden nach der Entfestigung 1873," *Mitteilungen des Mindener Geschichts- und Museumvereins* 45 (1973): 42, 75.

13. Karl Friedrich Watermann, "Politischer Konservatismus und Antisemitismus in Minden-Ravensberg 1879–1914." Hausarbeit zur ersten Staatsprüfung für das Lehramt an Gymnasien, Teil 1 und 2. (Münster, 1979), 59. The *Frankfurter Zeitung* coined this expression for the conservatives in Minden-Ravensberg, see 177.

14. Watermann, "Politischer Konservatismus," 7.

15. See Arno Herzig, *Judentum und Emanzipation in Westfalen* [= Veröffentlichungen des Provinzialinstitutes für westfälische Landes- und Volkskunde, ed. 1, no. 17] (Münster, 1973), 82. Adolf Stoecker (1835–1909), a Protestant pastor and *"Hofprediger,"* founded the Christlich Soziale Arbeiterpartei in 1878 in an attempt to reconcile workers with a conservative Christian philosophy. Stoecker was a staunch advocate of anti-Semitism since 1879, when it became evident that his party failed to reach workers and he increasingly turned to artisans and the lower middle classes instead. Stoecker's anti-Semitism was motivated politically, since he considered Judaism as a supporter of liberalism, which, in turn, he regarded both as a danger to Christianity and as a political threat to Germany. He was elected as an avowed champion of these views to the Prussian diet in 1879, serving until 1898, and was also a member of the Reichstag from 1880 to 1893, reelected in 1898. Thomas Nipperday, *Deutsche Geschichte, 1866–1918, Band 1: Arbeitswelt und Bürgergeist* (Munich, 1990), 497–504.

16. Watermann, "Politischer Konservatismus," 21.

nomic and historical development.[17] The county of Ravensberg had been taken over by Brandenburg-Prussia at an early juncture, on the eve of the Thirty Years' War in 1614, while Minden had come under their tutelage subsequent to the Peace of Westphalia in 1648. When Prussia incorporated the rest of Westphalia after 1815, there was a feeling of being a Protestant island in a sea of Westphalian Roman Catholicism.[18] The economic development here was also totally different from that in the surrounding areas. Minden-Ravensberg was a traditional region for growing flax,[19] with a legacy of linen production going back centuries. This manufacture began to take on proto-industrial features from the second quarter of the eighteenth century.[20] The consequence of this economic development was an above-average increase in the population unparalleled anywhere else in Prussia and indeed quite rare in Europe.[21] However, this growth was not urban but, typical of Minden-Ravensberg, concentrated in the rural countryside and meant an expansion of the system of hired hands. Agricultural hired hands were a "rural working class," the veritable "serfs" (*coloni, Hintersassen*) of the farmers.[22]

The formation of the system of tenant farming goes back to the sixteenth century and even earlier:[23] "Once population growth had exceeded a certain level in mesh with medieval agricultural conditions, there was an inevitable formation of a stratum of tenant farmers who owned no land yet were rooted in the land, and largely dependent on secondary sources of income."[24]

The system of farmhands was given added impetus by the prevailing

17. Kaeller, *Die konservative Partei,* 8f.

18. Watermann, "Politischer Konservatismus," 7; Schulte, *Volk und Staat,* 13.

19. Due to the quality of the local soil, flax had been cultivated there since the twelfth century; see Kaeller, *Die konservative Partei,* 30f.; Kulke, "Die wirtschaftliche Entwicklung," 15.

20. See Wolfgang Mager, "Haushalt und Familie in protoindustrieller Gesellschaft: Sprenge (Ravensberg) während der ersten Hälfte des 19. Jahrhunderts. Eine Fallstudie," in Neidhard Bulst, Joseph Goy, and Jochen Hoock, eds., *Familie zwischen Tradition und Moderne* [= Kritische Studien zur Geschichtswissenschaft 48] (Göttingen, 1981), 142.

21. According to Kaeller, the principality Minden had 38,500 residents in 1722, soaring to 68,000 in 1792; see Kaeller, *Die konservative Partei,* 33.

22. Wilhelm Wilms, *Großbauerntum und Kleingrundbesitz in Minden-Ravensberg* [= 27. Jahresbericht des Historischen Vereins für die Grafschaft Ravensberg zu Bielefeld] (Bielefeld, 1913), 53.

23. Kaeller, *Die konservative Partei,* 25; Mager, "Haushalt und Familie," 144; Hans-Jürgen Seraphim, *Das Heuerlingswesen in Nordwestdeutschland* [= Veröffentlichungen des Provinzialinstitutes für westfälische Landes- und Volkskunde, ed. 1, no. 5] (Münster, 1948).

24. Seraphim, *Das Heuerlingswesen in Nordwestdeutschland,* 16.

inheritance law common in Minden-Ravensberg[25] and was the way labor was typically organized on the single farm.[26] This was expanded in the seventeenth and eighteenth centuries,[27] in part on the basis of the evolving linen industry, because the farmhands needed a second job to make ends meet.[28] Another reason for the expansion was the system of land parceling known as *Markenaufteilung:*[29] farmers received land sometimes a considerable distance from their own farmsteads and found it more advantageous for them to rent out these fields in a hereditary leasehold or to lease them in tenancy to hired hands. The dominance of medium-sized and smaller farms and the general absence of large estates led early on to an intensification of agriculture, fueling an agricultural boom in parallel with the upturn in linen manufacture and trade.[30] This upsurge in economic development was abruptly interrupted by industrialization, which initially had a particular impact on textile production. "In the heart-rending pictures of misery some men have given as they describe the distress of the weavers and spinners in Silesia, we can find a very faithful description of the pressures being faced by numerous families right here."[31]

Distress and misery were especially grave "where industry had affected conditions in agriculture as well."[32] In the main, this involved hired hands, who had been robbed of their options for extra income as a result of the decline in traditional linen manufacture. That distress was exacerbated by the many failed harvests after 1830. So the dramatis personae on the streets in Minden-Ravensberg during the March 1848 revolution were principally small farmers and hired hands, up in arms against the land-owning agricultural class. But their uprisings

25. A characteristic feature of this law was that the farm could only be inherited by one heir, either a son or daughter, while all the other children were given a financial settlement.

26. Seraphim, *Das Heuerlingswesen in Nordwestdeutschland,* 16; Kaeller, *Die konservative Partei,* 25.

27. Seraphim, *Das Heuerlingswesen in Nordwestdeutschland,* 11.

28. Spinning and weaving flax was the most important second occupation, but not the only one. Other sources of extra income were making wooden shoes and working in Holland. Particularly in Minden and Lübbecke, it was quite common to go as a migrant laborer to dig peat in Holland, where the system of hired farmhands also developed at a later historical date; see Seraphim, *Das Heuerlingswesen in Nordwestdeutschland,* 16; Wilms, *Großbauerntum und Kleingrundbesitz,* 54.

29. This system was operative from 1770 into the nineteenth century; see Wilms, *Großbauerntum und Kleingrundbesitz,* 20.

30. See Mager, "Haushalt und Familie," 142.

31. *Öffentlicher Anzeiger für die Grafschaft Ravensberg,* quoted in Schulte, *Volk und Staat,* 130.

32. *Öffentlicher Anzeiger für die Grafschaft Ravensberg,* quoted in Schulte, *Volk und Staat,* 122.

were quickly quelled. That was due in part to the heavy military presence in the district as well as to the fact, as Mager demonstrates in the
case of Sprenge, that the "structural antagonisms continued to remain
significantly shaped by paternalism."[33] This points up another salient
factor: the great influence that Pietism enjoyed in this region.

This conservative influence of Pietism, rejecting any revolution, is
especially important to consider in looking at the oppressive hardship afflicting the weavers. Because here, where distress was greatest
and the democrats and socialists were passionately involved, . . . an
uprising would have been the most likely turn of events. Yet no area
in Westphalia was more opposed to an overthrow than the Ravensberg district.[34]

Since the Reformation, the population of Minden-Ravensberg had
been largely Protestant.[35] However, down into the eighteenth century
the residents remained basically indifferent when it came to religion.
As a popular religious movement, Pietism was an answer of German
Protestantism to the rationalistic theology of the time, historically
rooted in the Enlightenment.[36] Pietism reached Minden-Ravensberg
through two movements of religious awakening in the eighteenth and
nineteenth centuries. The first proved less successful,[37] since the lay
communities were persecuted by the Prussian government.[38] The second evangelical movement, in the 1830s and 1840s, was linked with the
conjuncture of the wars for freedom and the change of the throne in
1840.[39] Its preeminent representative was Johann Heinrich Volkening
(1796–1877). A hallmark of this movement was that the missionary festivals were conducted by laypersons. Laypersons prayed at graves or
on the threshing floors of farmsteads, speaking in the local Low German vernacular, and trombone bands were formed. This "populariz-
ing" of religion was associated with the "great willingness to sacrifice
for the mission's sake, an upsurge in church-related associations, a
practical Christianity that provided assistance where needed, here pre-

33. Mager, "Haushalt und Familie," 160.
34. Schulte, *Volk und Staat,* 213.
35. In 1858, 82.6 percent of the inhabitants in Minden were Protestant; in 1950 that figure
was 79.6 percent, virtually unchanged; see Reekers, *Westfalens Bevölkerung 1818–1955,* 72.
36. See William O. Shanahan, *Der deutsche Protestantismus vor der sozialen Frage
1815–1871* (Munich, 1962), 10f.
37. Kaeller, *Die konservative Partei,* 43.
38. Schulte, *Volk und Staat,* 212.
39. Kaeller, *Die konservative Partei,* 44.

dating social legislation, and a powerful movement for abstinence."[40] Volkening was opposed to dancing, card playing, brandy, and spinning rooms.[41] Pietistic ideas and young German patriotism converged in religious awakening. There was a conjoined restructuring of the concept of God into a "lord of fates," and from this a "German God" was derived, along with a "German Chosen People."[42]

> The awakening is especially important as a factor in German history, because it united church orthodoxy with political conservatism. In Germany, and most especially in Prussia, it forged the intellectual foundations for that emphatic interest in the validity of Christian principles in society, a feature typical of the Restoration.[43]

It was the pastors, most particularly Volkening and Huchzermeyer, who were active in championing the old political system and its ideals. In the countryside, the influence of the pastors was enhanced by the simple fact alone of their preeminent social position; in town, especially in Minden, they worked hand in hand with the bureaucracy and the military.[44] These structures were bolstered by the church societies and the web of associations more generally. In the 1840s, Christian rigorism in Minden led to a pogrom.[45] Anti-Semitism in Westphalia was strongest among the farmers in Minden-Ravensberg, and though it was not actively supported by the pastors, it was fondly condoned. Significantly, it was a pastor who brought Adolf Stoecker to Minden-Ravensberg and assisted him there in his success at the polls.[46] In the 1848 revolution, the special wrath of the democrats was reserved for the pastors, but it soon became evident who wielded greater influence. The Socialist associations had failed in part precisely because of the fierce anticlerical hostility smoldering among their leading personalities.[47] The influence of Pietism in all this was evident. One reason was the lack of an aristocracy and the fact that, despite strict class boundaries, farmers and their hired hands were fairly close, both socially and

40. Kaeller, *Die konservative Partei,* 47.
41. Schulte, *Volk und Staat,* 212.
42. See Klaus Scholder, "Neuere deutsche Geschichte und protestantische Theologie," *Evangelische Theologie* 23 (1963): 527f.
43. Shanahan, *Der deutsche Protestantismus,* 70.
44. Kaeller, *Die konservative Partei,* 60.
45. Herzig, *Judentum und Emanzipation in Westfalen,* 83–86.
46. Pastor Dietz was called the "little Stoecker"; see Herzig, *Judentum und Emanzipation in Westfalen,* 89.
47. Schulte, *Volk und Staat,* 240.

in spatial propinquity.[48] Conjunct with the mild contours of the class barriers, there was also a gentle gradient between town and countryside. A characteristic feature of Minden-Ravensberg was its working class, whose social composition had a decided and abiding rural quality. That also held true after the decline of traditional linen manufacture and long down into the twentieth century, when the cigar manufacture that had sprung up in the area in the 1840s allowed hired hands to continue to make ends meet.[49] Under the impact of tobacco manufacture, two tendencies emerged in the Minden-Ravensberg area in the second half of the nineteenth century. In the industrialized districts such as Minden, Herford, and Bielefeld, the number of farms with less than a half hectare (one-half hectare = 1.24 acres) increased, while in the more agriculturally dominated areas, the number of farms increased that had between one-half and two hectares of farmland. So while in the latter areas the observable tendency was to make dependent farms more independent, in the former land was reduced to the size of a garden that could be easily worked in addition to a job elsewhere.[50] The hired hands thus became industrial workers,[51] whose quite favorable financial situation allowed them to acquire their own home and to keep one to two goats, some chickens, and often a pig as well.[52]

If this marked the economic basis for the specific influence of Pietism, other roots point to Protestantism itself. The special susceptibility of German Protestantism for conservatism is generally derived from Lutheran theology, especially the doctrine of the two realms, which teaches that the state and the church are both institutions established by God. Other explanations refer to the close link that Protestantism developed in the nineteenth century with the ruling family, manifested in Westphalia in the fact that, according to the Westphalian ecclesiastical constitution of 1835, the king was at the same time the

48. Kaeller, *Die konservative Partei,* 25, mentions that marriages between hired hands and farmers were rare; see also Josef Mooser, "Heirat und Berufswahl. Zur Verfassung der ländlichen Gesellschaft im 19. Jahrhundert," in Heinz Reif, ed., *Die Familie in der Geschichte* (Göttingen, 1982), 137–62.

49. In 1889, there were 6,869 persons employed in the tobacco industry in the Minden, Herford, and Halle districts; by 1895, that number had climbed to 12,218, rising again to 20,989 by 1907, some half of whom were women. Just in Minden alone, at the time there were 3,735 women in the branch; see Watermann, "Politischer Konservatismus," 15f.

50. Wilms, *Großbauerntum und Kleingrundbesitz,* 45.

51. See Seraphim, *Das Heuerlingswesen in Nordwestdeutschland,* 23ff. In 1946, 78 percent of all positions as hired labor in the Minden district were in industry, 63.

52. Wilms, *Großbauerntum und Kleingrundbesitz,* 63.

highest bishop in the Prussian state church.[53] In addition, Jacobs points to reasons that lay in internal Protestant thinking itself.[54] In contrast with Roman Catholicism, the evidence for faith does not lie for Protestants in dogma and the church but in the act of faith itself. While dogma in Catholicism constructs a solid worldview, Protestantism ultimately always points back to the individual. This leads in Protestantism to distinctive emancipatory impulses, but it also generates its special inner affinity for reactionary currents. Adolf Stoecker knew quite well that the attraction of his political program lay in the fact that "we proclaim Christianity not merely as a creed, but as a worldview."[55] In the Christian Protestant and at the same time national "German" community, so passionately invoked by pastors in their sermons,[56] all the contrasts and rifts and fissures in modern industrial society wondrously dissolved.

This attitude is one of the important strains that finally led to the raucous patriotism that accompanied Germany's entry into World War I. In his *Reflections of a Nonpolitical Man,* Thomas Mann observed:

> In my opinion, then, there has been the most complete unanimity from the first moment that the intellectual roots of this war, "the German war," as it is called with every possible justification, lie in Germany's inborn and historical "protestantism." . . . So there was general unanimity, I think, right from the first moment, that the intellectual roots of this war, which with all possible right may be termed the "German war," lay in the indigenous and historical Protestantism on German soil.[57]

The grand binge in national feeling between 1914 and 1918 was followed by a profound and extended phase of stocktaking. For a town like Minden, the year 1918 was as drastic a historical caesura as 1648, which marked the end of its existence as an independent commercial city and the beginning of Prussian sovereignty. With the defeat and its disillusionment, the twin buttresses of political identity in the city—the

53. Schulte, *Volk und Staat,* 81.
54. Manfred Jacobs, "Weltanschauung, Politik. Die evangelischen Kirchen und die Option zwischen dem zweiten und dritten Reich," *Vierteljahreshefte für Zeitgeschichte* 31, no. 1 (1983): 108–35.
55. Jacobs, "Weltanschauung, Politik," 113.
56. Jacobs, "Weltanschauung, Politik," 116.
57. Thomas Mann, *Reflections of a Nonpolitical Man,* trans. with an introduction by Walter D. Morris (New York, 1983), 29.

Prussian monarchy on the one hand and Protestantism on the other, the latter bearing Pietism's distinctive imprint and being elevated to *Weltanschauung* (worldview)—were weakened: "The war is over: undefeated by arms and nonetheless conquered, Germany had agreed to a cease-fire."[58]

Self-righteous blindness and a powerful sense of rejection characterized attitudes among the dominant social strata in Minden toward the Weimar Republic. Decisive in their view was the fact that stability could not be achieved in the short-lived republic. Thus, on the heels of the incomprehensible defeat on the battlefield came the November 1918 revolution. In Minden, that was an event still totally imbued with the mentality of the small-town idyll. It was an "overthrow" of the government in which, in the proud reminiscences recorded in 1932 by the head of the Social Democrats in Minden, not a single window pane was smashed and the revolutionaries had marched through the city to the rousing tones of a military band, the correct song for the occasion on their lips. "As far as we were able to pass on the word and let the guys know, the workers' council and the organized workers also showed up."[59]

The image, which viewed from outside has a certain comical streak, appeared to contemporary Minden citizens perhaps precisely so unbelievable because of a stark fact: in actuality only the actors had been replaced, but the contents—God, folk, and fatherland—had remained the same. This barely understandable political change was soon followed by the existential anguish of inflation, and after a short upturn in prosperity the economy descended into the vortex of the Great Depression. All this was a source of profound insecurity for a society accustomed to stability, relying on the iron anchor of a firm worldview to maintain social order and solve social contradictions. Moreover, there was nothing to serve as a pinpoint of light, a source of inspiration and excitement. Government affairs turned out to be dull hack work in the service of a society that could only be grasped in terms of figures and their crunching. The military no longer symbolized Prussia's "splendor and glory," and the lieutenants in their white gloves not only broke the hearts of the local maidens but—as was evident from the

58. Katharina Krickau, *Die Geschichte des Mindener Oberlyzeums 1826–1926. Zum 100jährigen Gründungstage* (Minden, 1926), 85.

59. Willi Michel, "Aus den Novembertagen (Erinnerungen)," manuscript, Sept. 1, 1932. The band he mentions was that of the Fifteenth Infantry, the traditional "Minden main regiment." According to a report carried on November 18, 1918, in the *Minden-LübbeckerKreisblatt,* some four hundred persons took part.

experience of the war—dabbled in banal and bloody trafficking. Everything became very trite, mundane, ordinary. The *Butjers,* the poorest of the poor, now even had a political party of their own; their kids went to the same schools as their more well-to-do counterparts. Nonetheless, the restrictions and hardship suffered had their limit. This became clear during the Great Depression years. Between 1930 and 1932, tax revenues in the city plummeted, while municipal expenses skyrocketed.[60] Nonetheless, even if people found the going rough, they could still walk. The Great Depression was a palpable and heavy burden for all, yet many did not find themselves totally down and out.[61] This can be explained quite logically by the socioeconomic situation in the town, namely, the high percentage of civil servants and the military: though they faced serious economic hardship as a result of the emergency decrees, they had permanent positions. Grinding poverty of the kind endemic in Berlin's Wedding neighborhood was rare here because most families had some sort of vegetable garden to help tide them over. Yet it was precisely this more general absence of grave existential privation coupled with the loss of all the prewar privileges for the social elites of the city that made the Great Depression appear so menacing.

> Well, I always think, and that was also what my dad used to say: if Germany hadn't been so deep down in the muck back then, then he wouldn't have been able to get anywhere. Hitler, I mean. But this, this terrible poverty, the lack of money, and then if you had a lot of kids on top of it, just think. And all of us here, I mean, we really can't say anything, 'cause we have gardens. See, and we could get everything we needed from the gardens. But those people now, like the ones in Berlin, for example, some of them had seven or eight kids, and then living in those apartments they had. (M 21)

60. See Marianne Nordsiek, *"Fackelzüge überall . . ." Das Jahr 1933 in den Kreisen Minden und Lübbecke* (Bielefeld, Dortmund, and Münster, 1983), 9.

61. Nordsiek notes that as of October 15, 1930, the labor office in Minden had 2,929 unemployed (including those on special Depression welfare) on the books in the Minden and Lübbecke districts. The number of unemployed in the town of Minden was 498, some 17 percent of the jobless in these two districts. The number of those out of work in the two districts peaked in January 1932 at 13,760 and then declined. If one keeps the same proportion and the figure of 17 percent for the Minden municipality, then the town itself had some 2,339 unemployed when the jobless figures reached their maximum in January 1932, nearly five times the number on the dole in mid-October 1930; see Nordsiek, *"Fackelzüge überall . . . ,"* 9.

The style of life, as it had developed during centuries in this Prussian military and administration city, had lost its political and social moorings. Nonetheless, it was still alive in many ways, had its essential core in the family, and, in that matrix, via the organization of everyday life, repeatedly confirmed itself.

The Protestant Family

The families in which my interviewees had been brought up were largely Protestant. Protestantism left its stamp on everyday life in the family and their views of family. How was that manifested in concrete terms in their lives?

Inseparable from Luther's Reformation was a new value placed on marriage and the family. There were two reasons for this. Firmly anchored in the tradition of the medieval church, Luther assumed that man was sinful and regarded chastity as the highest religious virtue. But while the Roman Catholic Church had offered an option for a godly life in the trajectory of the monk and the nun, Luther rejected this as mere *"Werkerei"* (doing good deeds), the arrogant sanctimonious bid for a self-elected holiness. Instead, he championed marriage, which seemed in his eyes a concession to human nature, enclosing desire within a framework and thus putting an end to lust. This view led Luther to make marriage into a kind of duty. For women, that was a mixed blessing. On the one hand, it elevated the status of the married woman; on the other hand, it shut the door for Protestant women on life as a single woman outside marriage, because from now on the path into a monastery was forever closed.[62] A new affirmative and accepting attitude toward human nature evolved, springing from this different Protestant relation to God, from whom grace could not be demanded without forfeiting it. Though that attitude contained a kernel of emancipation, its basic prerequisite was the admission of earthly sinfulness. This served to validate the institution of marriage as the proper road for the believing Protestant. But what was the reason behind the prime importance ascribed now to the family?

In medieval Christianity, the church had been the mediator between God and the individual. In Protestantism, this relation was reconfigured as immediate and direct, mediated only by belief in the

---

62. See Marianne Weber, *Ehefrau und Mutter in der Rechtsentwicklung. Eine Einführung* (Tübingen, 1907), 284.

Word. Individuals were now on their own, in a sense alone with God, and the family became the locus where a life pleasing in the sight of God had to be created. This engendered the central importance ascribed in Protestant faith to everyday life on the one hand and the socializing function of the family on the other. That value is reflected in the books on domestic discipline in the Protestant context[63] or in the special value accorded the individual biography, as pointed out by Scharfe and Mitterauer in their work on Pietism.[64] The central importance of the family as a supreme moral relation is inscribed in Luther's interpretation of the fourth commandment as it was codified in the Great Catechism and inculcated in Protestant hearts and minds through church services and religious education. The first three commandments dealt with the relation of the individual to God; the following seven regulated relations with one's fellow men and women. Among them, the commandment to "honor Thy father and mother" was the highest and most important.

As Luther notes: "God has placed a special value on fatherhood and motherhood for all classes that are under Him. He does not simply command to love one's parents but to honor them. While for brothers, sisters and neighbors he generally commands nothing higher than that you love them. But he differentiates for father and mother, separating them from all others on this earth, and placing them next to Himself."[65] For Luther, the highest authority was not the church but the parents, who had to be respected in God's stead. In Luther's view, the commandment to love and honor them was not simply a duty for children—it was a component and prerequisite of religious service. He writes:

> It would have been impossible to establish monastic life or the clergy if each child were to stick resolutely to this commandment, directing its conscience to God and saying: If I am to do good and holy works, I know no better means than to show my parents all the honor and obedience possible, because God Himself has thus commanded. Because what God orders must be far more noble than anything we ourselves may think.[66]

63. Tornieporth, *Studien zur Frauenbildung,* 12.
64. Martin Scharfe, *Die Religion des Volkes. Kleine Kultur- und Sozialgeschichte des Pietismus* (Gütersloh, 1980), 36, 54 ff.; Michael Mitterauer, *Sozialgeschichte der Jugend* (Frankfurt a.M., 1986), 36.
65. Martin Luther, *Werke. Kritische Gesamtausgabe (Weimarer Ausgabe),* vol. 30 (Weimar, 1910; reprint, Weimar, 1964), 147.
66. Luther, *Werke,* 148.

Though the commandment was directed to all believers, it was addressed in particular to the children and thus was accorded a definite pedagogical character.

So let us learn for the sake of God that young people should look aside from all other things and focus their attention first upon this commandment if they wish to serve God with the correct good works, doing what their father and mother, or those in their place to whom they are subservient, find pleasing.[67]

As the children learned to subordinate themselves "lovingly" to parental authority, they underwent a socially significant process of learning: integration into the family prepared the path for integration into the wider society, because, as Luther notes, "all other things flow and spread from the authority of the parents."[68] The relation between the authority of the father and social authority, which Luther consciously stresses, has to be viewed as mutual. This meant that, when necessary, social authorities would stand at the father's side; contrariwise, social authorities were invested with power by dint of their appearing as paternal authorities: "Thus, all those called 'lord' or 'master' are in the stead of the parents. They must take from them the power and might to govern."[69] From this meld of paternal and social authority and the supreme position of the father in the family, not limited by an earthly or spiritual institution, there sprang the feature of patriarchy so characteristic of Protestantism.[70] Let us look at this more closely. Previously, the church had attempted to contribute to a moral marriage as a mediator between the man and the woman.[71] But now in Protestant marriage, the two partners faced each other as individuals responsible for themselves, without any assistant at their side. This by no means implied that the woman was subordinate to her husband.

67. Luther, *Werke*, 149.
68. Luther, *Werke*, 152.
69. Luther, *Werke*, 162.
70. See Weber, *Ehefrau und Mutter*, 284; Horkheimer, *Allgemeiner Teil*, 51; Heide Lauterer-Pirner, "Vom 'Frauenspiegel' zu Luthers Schrift 'Vom ehelichen Leben'. Das Bild der Ehefrau im Spiegel einiger Schriften des 15. und 16. Jahrhunderts," in Annette Kuhn and Jörn Rüsen, eds., *Frauen in der Geschichte III* (Düsseldorf, 1983), 63–85.
71. Doris Kaufmann points out that women in the Weimar Republic had a special bond with the Roman Catholic Church because, when faced with marital problems, they were able to seek pastoral advice and consolation; see Doris Kaufmann, "Vom Vaterland zum Mutterland. Frauen im katholischen Milieu der Weimarer Republik," in Hausen, *Frauen suchen ihre Geschichte*, 250–75. At the same time, of course, the church was able in this way to consolidate its control over the family.

Rather, the personal relationship between the spouses was infused with the moderate influence of the church as a moral demand.

In his *Traubüchlein für den einfältigen Pfarrherrn,* Luther provided the pastor with a text for the wedding pair. It began: "Men, love your wives!" This was followed by the demand that all women should adhere to: "Women are subordinate to men as their lord."[72] Both spouses were in a bond of mutual obligations, which regulated their web of relations. The power of a husband over his wife was mitigated by the demand for an emotional tie in the relationship, lessening the scope of subjection required of her. The obligations were defined in religious terms and thus independent of each other. A person was obliged to fulfill them as a duty to God, not to one's spouse. Levin Schücking has described this process of a relation that has become reflexive in its structures of power.

Because the obligation on the part of one party most certainly does not yet imply the right of the other. Rogers clarifies this principle, still ardently espoused by Richardson in the 18th century, using the hilarious example of a couple trying to select a dress for the wife. If she has set her heart on the green dress and her spouse prefers the red one, then the missus has to give in. This is part of the concept of subjection. But it is not very nice of the man to insist on having his will done, because in matters of female dress, he should have to accommodate to the heartfelt desires of his spouse. That is integral to the special obligations of the husband toward his wife. Even if in such a case we find that the competing obligations are not of the same status, they are nonetheless obligations all the same. In such a way, the biblical principle of the absolute subjection of the wife to the will of her husband is totally hollowed out from within, no matter how unshakeable it may appear externally, and the path is laid in practical terms for a new development.[73]

Already in the thinking of Luther, where this process was only barely developed and fell together with the emphatic commandment to the husband to love his espoused partner,[74] there is an indication of the

72. Martin Luther, *Ein Traubüchlein für den einfältigen Pfarrherrn* (1529), in *Luther Deutsch. Die Werke Martin Luthers in neuerer Auswahl für die Gegenwart,* vol. 6, ed. Kurt Aland (Stuttgart, 1966), 168.

73. Levin L. Schücking, *Die Familie im Puritanismus. Studien über Familie und Literatur in England im 16., 17. und 18. Jahrhundert* (Leipzig and Berlin, 1929), 48.

74. Martin Luther, *Vom ehelichen Leben* (1522), in *Luther Deutsch,* vol. 7 (Stuttgart, 1967), 296.

mechanism that was later employed to place limits on the liberatory element this development harbors, namely, via a gender-specific division of labor and the associated process of the "polarizing of sexual stereotypes."[75]

For Luther, it was clear that "women are created for the household, men for dealing with public affairs, matters of war and the law," and he elaborated:

> My wife can persuade me as often as she desires, because she holds all power in her hand. I am happy to grant her full power in running the household, but I also wish to have my full right, unlimited and uncurtailed, and women's rule has never resulted in anything positive.[76]

By a distribution of the spaces for power and work, which assigned the woman power within the household while her husband was given the task of representing the home externally in social and political terms, any possibilities for reflection in the gendered symmetries of power were drastically restricted, defusing the emancipatory potential inherent in Luther's conception. Moreover, by means of this strict separation of the spheres of life between the sexes, the actual power of the man over the woman was not only left unimpaired but even consolidated. Through this gender-specific ascription of different spheres of life, demonstrably negotiated as equal in value, the Protestant conception of marriage provided a misleading illusion of equality between man and woman.[77] This and more: it transformed the openly displayed relation of power into a condition that was deemed quasi-natural and given, a state of gendered affairs whose constraints none believed able to escape.[78]

According to Marianne Weber, a "patriarchalism worthy of the Old Testament" was the shaping force behind Luther's conceptions of the relation between the sexes in marriage.[79] And indeed, in early Protestantism, emphasis on the subjection of the wife to the will of the hus-

---

75. A term coined by Karin Hausen. See Hausen, "Die Polarisierung der 'Geschlechtscharaktere.'"

76. Martin Luther, *Der Christ in der Welt. Tischreden,* in *Luther Deutsch,* vol. 9 (Stuttgart, 1983), 278.

77. Within the right-wing and National Socialist discourse of the twentieth century this is contained in the expression "Gleichwertig aber nicht gleichartig" (of equal value but not of the same kind).

78. Hausen, "Die Polarisierung der 'Geschlechtscharaktere'"; Duden, "Das schöne Eigentum."

79. Weber, *Ehefrau und Mutter,* 284.

band appeared to be but little mitigated by the obligation of the husband to love his wife. Yet there was a clear improvement of the status of the women within the various Protestant sects, among the Puritans, Baptists, and Pietists.[80] It came about, as intimated by Schücking previously, through a process of differentiation in the gender-specific distribution of obligations and was closely bound up with the transformation in the importance of the home. In traditional society, the home had been the multipurpose hub of the family's economy. In the transition to modernity, the economic subsistence of the family is shifted from there into the realms of wage labor outside the home, while the home in turn is transformed into the seemingly private locus of reproduction. The social character of work there evaporated, and female labor in the household was transmuted into a "labor of love." However, concomitant with this shift in meaning was another circumstance: increasing demands were being placed on household work. Rising hygienic standards played a role here; this was coupled with an altered view of the home as the bosom of a warm and emotionally satisfying family life and the medium of social representation to the world without. All this was part of the scroll of duties and obligations delegated to the lady of the house. Women were responsible for the education of their children, which was accorded greater attention and care. And it was also largely women who were active in philanthropy, devoting themselves to the growing problem of social poverty by means of new modalities of welfare. Within the Protestant churches, the status of women was also upgraded through their qualities as homemakers and educators and their activities in the social arena.

Pietistic biographies imbued the role of the mother with an almost mystical veneration. In his book on the Pietist Friedrich August Weihe, Ludwig Tiesmeyer writes: "A mother, especially a pious mother, is the best gift a human being can have in their upbringing."[81] The Pietist Philipp Matthäus Hahn dedicated a eulogy to his mother with the telling title "Beate Paulus née Hahn" (What a Mother Can Do).[82] Scharfe points to the stereotypical image of the parents in Pietistic biographies, where a kind and loving mother is paired with a strict

80. See Friedrich Michael Schiele et al., eds., *Die Religion in Geschichte und Gegenwart. Handwörterbuch in gemeinverständlicher Sprache,* 2 vols. (Tübingen, 1910), article "Ehe"; Erich Beyreuther, *Geschichte des Pietismus* (Stuttgart, 1978), 342f.

81. Ludwig Tiesmeyer, *Friedrich August Weihe. Eine Prophetengestalt aus dem 18. Jahrhundert, zugleich ein Trostbühlein in schwerer Zeit* (Gütersloh, 1921), 1.

82. Quoted in Scharfe, *Die Religion des Volkes,* 37.

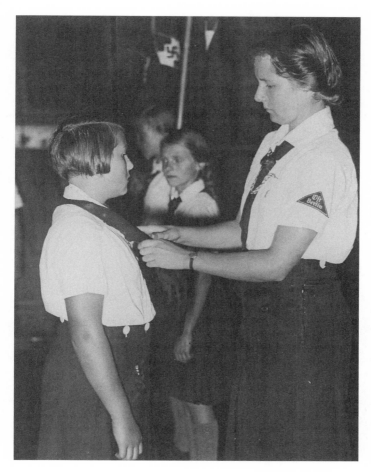

Jungmädelprobe. A young girl gets her neckerchief and leather knot and is formally admitted to the League of German Girls. Berlin, 1939. (Photographer unknown; reprinted with permission from the Bildarchiv Preußischer Kulturbesitz.)

Jungmädel marching. Weimar, 1939. (Photograph by Lala Aufsberg; reprinted with permission from the Bildarchiv Preußischer Kulturbesitz.)

Sports students within the League of German Girls practicing small-caliber shooting, 1936. (Photographer unknown; reprinted with permission from the Bildarchiv Preußischer Kulturbesitz.)

Girls of the BDM. Berlin, 1937. (Photograph by Arthur Grimm;
reprinted with permission from the Bildarchiv Preußischer Kulturbesitz.)

Four leaders of the League of German Girls on a park bench. Lüneburg, 1939. (Photograph by Lisolotte Purper; reprinted with permission from the Bildarchiv Preußischer Kulturbesitz.)

Female anti-aircraft helper at Anhalter railroad station in Berlin, February 1945. (Photograph by Arthur Grimm; reprinted with permission from the Bildarchiv Preußischer Kulturbesitz.)

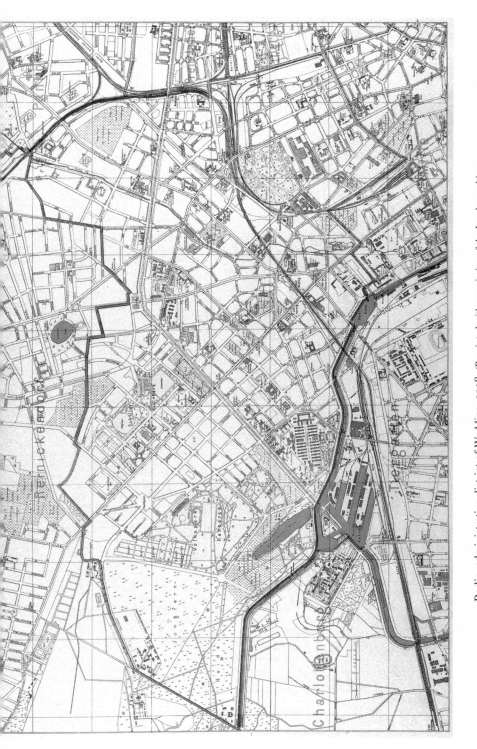

Berlin, administrative district of Wedding, 1938. (Reprinted with permission of the Landes archive Berlin.)

Minden, 1937. (Map reprinted with permission of the Mindener Museum für Geschichte, Landes- und Volkskunde.)

and exacting father.[83] Education took the course described then by Fromm and Horkheimer as departure from the warm, protective lap of the mother and reconciliation with the stern father.[84] However, important for us here are the specifics of configuration: the high value placed on the woman is specifically hinged to her role as housewife and mother. Characteristic for the Protestant-Pietistic family was a pronounced polarity between the genders. It assured the woman in the family a high status as housewife and mother, while presupposing a gender-specific division of labor that left the web of power relations between the spouses untouched, in fact maintaining the power of the man.

After these general remarks that have tried to sketch a historical canvas, let us turn to the special realities on the ground in the families in Minden in the 1920s and 1930s.

M 3: Yes, well, how did we live? Lunch was exactly at a quarter after one every afternoon. See, my dad was a civil servant and had to leave again at 2:45. . . . he'd lie down for a nap on the sofa in the kitchen after lunch, I can still see that, and he usually would fall asleep.

I: And all of you had to stay very quiet then?

M 3: Oh, of course. No, but mom, she'd do the dishes and tidy up the kitchen, that didn't bother him. I mean, he was used to the noise, so she would regularly go about cleaning up. And he would even snore merrily away while she was working. OK, and then I'd do my homework, naturally sitting at the kitchen table, and sometimes my sis would too. In the beginning anyhow, first few years. But then we often got upset when we didn't feel like doing any homework. And like we'd have some popular novel hidden under our school notebook, see. And sometimes I told about it, I sure did, I was a real tattletale.

It is easy to determine that the social background of this vivid sketch is a lower-middle-class milieu. There is a definite sense of the warm comfort of material security. At the same time, there was a lack of any luxury. A sense of quiet and a recurrent rhythm stamped the atmosphere, creating a space for the formation of habits that were etched

---

83. Quoted in Scharfe, *Die Religion des Volkes,* 57.
84. Fromm et al., *Studien über Autorität und Familie,* vol. 1, 57f., 88ff.

into the child's memory. If you focus here less on the individual specifics and more on the structural features underlying the specific manifestation, then the sketch provides an ideal-typical portrait of the internal space of a family in Minden in the early afternoon. In comparison with life in Wedding, the most important distinctive feature was the largely secure economic situation of the family, the presence of a certain number of possessions, however modest. Almost all the women I interviewed grew up in a house that the family had inherited or built, often involving huge effort on their part and much material sacrifice. Having your own house meant a certain abundance of living space, maybe even one's own room, which as a rule was used only as a bedroom, not a place to play or stay in during the day. The family house generally also had a garden, which was never just full of flowers or used for decorative purposes but normally served to supplement the family's dinner table with vegetables and fruits. In the old center of town, where the poorest families lived, buildings were packed so densely together that there was no space for gardens, and this lack of a vegetable garden was at the same time a sure indicator of destitution. By contrast, in the villages close to Minden, there were still agricultural arrangements reminiscent of tenant farming.[85] Not only did the families there cultivate small gardens, but they also planted larger fields. Since they had no draft animals, these fields were plowed in the spring by a wealthier farmer. In return, the women were obliged to work for this farmer at harvest time.

> M 19: And then my mom would always, uh, 'cause we had a big field outside of town, and the farmer had plowed it for us, or put down fertilizer. So my mom had to go to work for the farmer, whenever they'd call her to come. Like then they'd say, it's time to harvest the hay, sun's shining, the hay's got to be mowed and gathered. So they'd call her in the morning, she had to go over. Practically speaking, she had to be on call and ready at any time, like whenever they might need her. Or at harvest time for . . . And you had to gather it all in by hand, see, and then bale the hay, like afterwards for the threshing.
> I: Did your mom find that was a burden?
> M 19: Well, sometimes she did get to complaining, saying it was too much for her, and that at home she also had all the . . . And then

---

85. However, the land was no longer leased but had passed into the possession of the family.

when we were remodeling the house, the farmer helped with all
the transport, he arranged to bring the stones, the sand and stuff.
My mother would help them very often.

I: But was that regulated and organized in some way?

M 19: Yes, well they wrote down the hours. Like the farmer got so
much money for his work for us, and then that was recalculated
in hours that we owed him.

It is quite evident that the household economy in these more rural-
like circumstances was based on work by both spouses. The family
supported itself in part from the wages the father received for his labor.
But a significant part of its daily maintenance also came from the more
or less extensive work in the garden. That was labor performed in the
main by the woman of the house, though as a rule her husband and the
children, depending on age, also lent a helping hand.

We didn't have any horses and cows, see, but we did have pigs, and
a goat too, rabbits, chickens. . . . Earlier on, all the people in the village had a garden, and we had a couple of acres, my dad had inherited that from his family. And we always planted rye and potatoes,
and a big meadow for hay, see, for the goat and the rabbits. (M 14)

Wilms has determined that already in the nineteenth century the
women bore the greater burden for agricultural labor in the tenant
farmer families.[86] During the period we focus on here they also were
involved in a quite extensive amount of work. Along with taking care
of the household and the family, they had to tend to the small animals
as well as planting, sowing, and picking the fruit and vegetables, which
then had to be harvested and prepared. Nor was their labor limited to
their own small plot of land; it also included helping out on a bigger
farm. Even if the barterlike character of the labor obligations incurred
by the women deriving from the conditions of tenancy was very evident, it was basically unpaid work that the women did, part of a
"shadow" economy, manifest solely in the internal economy of the
family. The women's work provided a second source of funds, which
the family could rely on in hard times. The shadow work of women was
thus not only labor—it also constituted an increment in economic
security and prosperity.

What had developed naturally from the ownership of land and the

86. Wilms, *Großbauerntum und Kleingrundbesitz,* 47.

system of tenancy and labor barter in rural areas was consciously exploited in the city as an option for improving one's own material situation. In urban households as well, the expansion of shadow labor offered an opportunity for a family to finance the building of a house, for example. This was always inevitably at the expense of the women.

> Basically she was just overburdened, too much work. We had a garden behind the house, and then we had another kind of field, it was half an hour on foot, and there was no other transport, except maybe if you took a bike. Well, we had this open, uh, today they'd call it a garden plot. But no, it was more like an open field, where we planted potatoes and did all of that ourselves. On top of it she had the two kids, and then all the sewing for the family. So mom just had too darn much work. (M 3)

Except for women in very poor families, who lived in crowded, densely populated streets in the oldest part of town and whose meager income was not even sufficient for leasing a small plot of land for a garden, naturally all women had to take care of the garden. In Minden, a town of the military and civil administration, luxury was rare. Instead, there was a comfortable lower-middle-class milieu that set the dominant tone. It had little direct experience of economic distress but was well acquainted with the necessities of economizing at home. The following quote provides a revealing window into the internal economy and prevailing atmosphere in such families.

> In a moderately hungry Prussian civil servant household, great thrift is the basic rule. Like what you see here, where I have a candle burning, and then a floor lamp on over there, another one over there— well, when I was growing up, in my parental home, that would have been impossible. Like my mom said, we had this ceiling lamp, a fixture that came down over the table, with two 15 watt bulbs in it, and my mom said: look, we can all do what we're doing right under this lamp here. And then you had to move and sit down there. And of course you did, see, because the parents, well, they were an example for kids in their behavior, and for this kind of frugality too. (M 22)

So the women's work in the garden was always an economic necessity, but it was not consciously perceived as such, since it was not factored into the family's household accounting. Instead there was a gender-specific division of roles quite in keeping with the Lutheran ideal of marriage: "In marriage, each should fulfill his assigned office. The man should earn a livelihood, the woman should be thrifty."[87] Each of the spouses had their clearly demarcated space, and a harmonious family life unfolded above a well-calibrated balance of power.

> We had a very intensive family life at home. Like all our meals were in common. And we'd spend the weekends together too, doing things in keeping with my age. Like going on small walks, later bicycling trips, hiking. And during the evening in the summer we would all go swimming together. (M 4)

A well-calibrated power balance also meant a strict maintenance of authority: children were subject to the will of their parents, and the whole family was subject to the authority of the father.

> I was brought up in a really old-fashioned way, as they say nowadays. I would never sit down at the table until my parents had. And I never went on ahead of my parents through a door. I always would make a little curtsy, I think til I was 14, 15 years old. (M 4)

Within this relation of authority inside the family, mothers functioned as the allies of their children, with the knowledge of and by agreement with their father. Their mother shared their secrets and worries, she tolerated small "infractions of the law," and supported personal plans, mitigating in this way the stern patriarchal power of the father. "And my mom, well, I have to tell you, honestly, she really spoiled us a lot. And daddy thought that was just fine, it was OK with him, like, she's the mom" (M 18).

The father remained the chief authority in the family. He was rarely on very intimate terms with the family members. Rather, he always maintained a certain distance. That did not mean in any way that he was less loved than the mother, but love for him was of another kind, infused more with respect and esteem. His power was based on this. It was not violent, not manifested in an authoritarian way, but rather was effective—precisely because it remained unquestioned and was never discussed.

> M 20: We had to be at home on time. That was his rule and wish. And none of us kids would ever have dared to go against it. We

---

87. "Tischreden," *Luther Deutsch,* vol. 9, 277.

exception to that rule: he allowed her to attend an evening course in stenography and typing, taking his daughter there and picking her up. Where parents were not concerned about some professional qualification for their daughter, due to traditional views, their own financial inability, or simply indifference, such as in rural areas or very poor families, sharp conflicts between the generations could erupt, because the girls felt very strongly that they were at an evident disadvantage.

> M 11: Back then, well, we had a real battle, see. When I really wanted to stay on down in Südhemmern. And they said: if you're not back here by Oct. 1, you're no longer welcome in this house. I couldn't afford any commentary in that situation. I didn't know where else I might go. I had no relatives or anybody [M 11 had been adopted at the age of two]. . . . That was the first really big confrontation. I still remember. I really wanted to have that and stay on down there. Oh, I made a big scene. I'd always been such a good girl, and then I . . .
>
> I: What did you like so much in Südhemmern? That you had finally gotten out from under the authority of your mom and dad?
>
> M 11: No, it was that finally I was able there to do something where I'd get a certificate, see, written recognition. I mean, I would have left with a qualification as a household apprentice. And based on that I could have gone on to something more, a little better.

It was not just that girls without vocational training could not stand on their own two feet and be independent—their chances for a marriage also had begun to depend more on what they were and could do and less on their specific social background. "A profession was a better point of departure, was supposed to be a better basis. That was back then, and in many respects still is the case today" (M 18).

Yet especially during puberty and in its wake, many girls no longer thought just of marriage but rather developed ideas and desires for shaping an independent life of their own.

> I: Did you imagine that you'd get married some day?
>
> M 10: Back at that time I had this strong need not to get married but to become independent, to learn a lot and be professionally independent. Like not to have to subordinate myself so much like my mom had done, but more to go my own way.

Here was a nascent tendency toward individualization, toward breaking free and separating from their parental homes. This was a trend that necessarily was on a collision course with customary conceptions of the family. On the one hand, based on the Protestant-patriarchal heritage, families took great pains to equip and prepare their girls as best they could for the future. Yet on the other hand, they had to fear that these very attempts to help turn their daughters into more independent human beings acted to break open the unity and self-contained character of the family's matrix.

The tight weave of the family had begun to unravel. The patriarchal system showed first fissures in which the National Socialists succeeded in gaining a foothold, bringing it eventually to rupture.

League of German Girls

According to National Socialist documentation, a local group of the NSDAP had existed in Minden since 1923.[88] But it must have been very small if not minuscule, because official police observations do not mention the establishment of a Nazi group in Minden until the early summer of 1930.[89] By then, the NSDAP had already chalked up its first great electoral success in the city: in the election to the municipal council, it was able to boast an increase of more than tenfold the number of votes cast for its list in 1928.[90] The growth of the movement is based primarily on the sense of dissatisfaction in the population due to the unfavorable economic situation. This situation is being successfully exploited at the present time by the NSDAP.[91]

People voted for a party they did not know, one that was at diametric odds with the solid social structures in the city.

I was surprised when the mother of one of my friends started talking about the Nazis. I thought this was a family by the name of Nazi. That's how little I knew at the time. (M 1)[92]

88. Nordsiek, *"Fackelzüge überall . . . ,"* 18.
89. See St. A. Detmold, M 4/13. Lagebericht des Pol. Präs. Bielefeld (Situation Report of the Bielefeld Police Chief), July 30, 1930.
90. From 310 (1928) to 3,821; see *Mindener Tageblatt,* Sept. 15, 1930.
91. St. A. Detmold, M 4/13. Lagebericht des Pol. Präs. Bielefeld, Apr. 22, 1930.
92. See also William Sheridan Allen, *The Nazi Seizure of Power: The Experience of a Single German Town, 1930–1965* (Chicago, 1965), 25: "But who were the Nazis? Most Thalburgers would have found it difficult to answer this question in 1930, for individual Nazis were rarely in the public eye."

But it was impossible not to notice this party. It was squarely in the public eye; its political activity was of huge proportions, exceeding even what was the customary fare from the workers' parties, the Socialists and Communists, which middle-class circles in Minden had always observed with vigilant mistrust.[93] Even in the preferred forms of agitation, such as promotional excursions that the party organized by bicycle or truck into surrounding villages, the NSDAP resembled more the tactics of the Socialists or Communists than the middle-class parties whose strength had been evident in Minden up until that time, such as the German People's Party (DVP) or the German National People's Party (DNVP). Yet the party's aims, its aggressive national-ism, its vehement struggle against the hated Weimar Republic, and its elite racism were shared to a substantial degree by the electorate in middle-class Minden. Before 1933, the NSDAP in Minden hardly expressed any antireligious leanings, holding its meetings, for example, in the Protestant Meeting Hall, one of the large middle-class venues for meetings.[94] Seen against this background, the nascent enthusiasm in middle-class circles in Minden for the NSDAP and the rapid turn away from support for the established parties and toward the National Socialists become understandable. Along with consensus about their basic platform, there was the feeling that the NSDAP offered the elec-torate a powerful and effective political organization with which to confront the workers' parties on an equal footing. Yet one thing was abundantly clear: coming from a good middle-class Minden family, one might well cast one's ballot for such a party. But it was hardly pos-sible to support that party actively in its political work, in any case not in any modality beyond attendance at one of its meetings. For that rea-son, it is not surprising that throughout 1930, when the National Socialists already dominated the headlines of the daily press, the Hitler Youth remained invisible, not rearing its head publicly in the town.[95]

It was not until the summer of 1931 that we find any mention of its existence: the Hitler Youth in Bielefeld registered a truck journey to the Hitler Youth in Minden with the police.[96] On August 22, 1931, there

---

93. Of the 176 political meetings and functions held in Minden from July 1, 1930, to Sept. 30, 1930, 59 were by the NSDAP (33.5 percent), 24 by the SPD, 25 by the Communist Party, and 20 by the State Party. See St. A. Detmold, M 4/13. Lagebericht des Pol. Präs. Bielefeld, Oct. 25, 1930.

94. For example, this occurred around New Year's 1929–30; see St. A. Detmold, M 4/72.

95. See, for example, Situation Reports of the Bielefeld Police Chief for the entire year of 1930, Lagebericht des Pol. Präs. Bielefeld. St. A. Detmold, M 4/13, M 4/14.

96. See St. A. Detmold, M 2 Minden C 87, Aug. 16, 1931.

was a district meeting of the Hitler Youth in Herford. The Hitler Youth in Minden wished to take part in this meeting, sending sixty boys, as indicated in a letter from the local group dated August 19, 1931.[97] Since the function was obligatory for all Hitler Youth members, the number of participants is most likely close to the total membership of the Minden Hitler Youth at the time. In the early summer of 1931, there was still no group for girls.[98] There is a related call in early September for a youth gathering from the Hitler Youth in nearby Bad Oeynhausen, stating: "We expect that German-minded parents will prevail on their children to attend this youth meeting. Heil!"[99] The modest extent of interest is evident from the fact that the Hitler Youth in Bad Oeynhausen, only a few kilometers from Minden, felt consciously obliged to resort to using the authority of the parents to fill its meeting hall. Most likely the situation was little different in Minden itself. The degree of the Nazification of middle-class Minden and the huge electoral successes of the Nazis easily mislead an observer when it comes to the actual continuities in social life at the time.

But to vote for the NSDAP was in no way reflective of a fundamental political reorientation. It was easy to combine that with continued membership in the Jahn Athletic Club or the Singing Society Harmony. Even if many young people felt attracted to National Socialism, for most it seemed a more reasonable option to join one of the Protestant youth groups (in any event influenced by the National Socialists) than to enter the ranks of the Hitler Youth.[100] Was it not perhaps simpler to espouse one's political convictions moving from a familiar social context? And maybe young people felt in some way socially and

97. See St. A. Detmold, M 2 Minden C 87.

98. St. A. Detmold, M 4/14.

99. St. A. Detmold, M 2 Minden C 87, Sept. 6, 1931.

100. According to Priepke, the membership in the Reich Union of Protestant Young Men's Associations (Reichsverband evangelischer Jungmännerbünde Deutschlands) in Germany rose from 185,000 in 1932 to 200,000 in 1933. In the Union of German Bible Circles (Bund Deutscher Bibelkreise), the rise was from 18,000 in 1932 to 20,000 in 1933; see Manfred Priepke, *Die evangelische Jugend im Dritten Reich 1933–1936* (Hannover and Frankfurt a.M., 1960), 237. Priepke quotes a declaration according to which some 80 percent of the membership in the Bible Circles in 1932 was Nazi oriented, 17f. See also Johannes Jürgensen, *Die bittere Lektion: Evangelische Jugend 1933* (Stuttgart, 1984), 13. In Minden in 1928, 1,391 male and 1,452 female pupils were members of associations linked with the Local Committee for Youth Welfare; see St. A. Detmold, M 1 I Ju Rep. 40. The relatively high proportion of girls is due to the influence of the church. Thus, for example, the Reich Union of Protestant Female Youth (Reichsverband evangelischer weiblicher Jugend) had 226,238 members in 1932, larger than the Young Men's Union (Jungmännerverband) with 185,000; see Priepke, *Die evangelische Jugend,* 237.

intellectually superior to the Hitler Youth, even if they shared certain programmatic aims or organizational forms.

The history of the Bible Circles (Bibelkreise) points in that specific direction. These groups had a membership largely recruited from among the high school population, with teenage girls organized in the Girls' Bible Circles (Mädchenbibelkreise, or MBK). The Bible Circles were more influenced by the general youth movement than by the Young Men's Union or the Reich Association of Protestant Girls. After 1919, they developed into a group that was increasingly more nationalistic, with ties to the DNVP, the ultra-conservative Stahlhelm, and later to the NSDAP, toward which the Bible Circles oriented their ideological bearings ever more in the early 1930s. Nonetheless, these circles were emphatically opposed to being incorporated into the "folk community of national youth." Together with the other Protestant organizations, they called for a corporative link with Hitler Youth that would allow them to retain their difference and distinctive insignia. Ultimately, they disbanded in order to avoid being incorporated into the Hitler Youth, which they perceived as a form of humiliation.[101] "Defenseless, yes. Without honor, never."[102]

From all this it can be concluded that the Hitler Youth, which before 1933 in Minden was quite insignificant, was largely recruited from the ranks of young people who did not stem from the middle-class strata of Minden. They came from homes that not only voted for the National Socialists but actively supported the work of the party. This is also true for the league, though a compounding factor was the traditional conservatism of Minden in this connection: it precluded any political activity on the part of girls. Moreover, the NSDAP before 1933 was part of a movement of struggle, a so-called *Kampfpartei* involving street violence and electoral contests. Even if a girl felt attracted by National Socialism, it was virtually inconceivable that her parents would allow her to join any organization of that party.

M 2: The BDM came in, and in the beginning, well, I was not allowed to go, because of my parents. They were always very worried, I was the only girl in the family, the boys were permitted to go, but the girl, well, she had to stay at home.

I: When did you want to attend the BDM?

101. Priepke, *Die evangelische Jugend,* 85.
102. This was the slogan of the Bible Circles, which Udo Schmidt, national chair of the Bible Circle groups, recalls in a commentary on the incorporation agreement of Protestant youth, signed by Ludwig Müller; see Priepke, *Die evangelische Jugend,* 76.

M 2: Well, right after they came to power, in '33, when the whole thing got going, when everyone started to join the BDM.
I: Did you want to before that?
M 2: I wasn't allowed to, my parents wouldn't hear of that. I was not allowed to go.
I: But you already knew before that the organization existed?
M 2: Oh yes, I knew there was such an organization, right.

The fact that the Hitler Youth and the League of German Girls in Minden were numerically small before 1933 was due to the specific social structure of the town. What prevented the growth of membership in the National Socialist organizations there was not insufficient interest on the part of young people or a divergent political view. Rather, it was the sheer weight of the pronounced conservatism in this Protestant-patriarchal milieu and the strong class consciousness in the city.

Contrary to initial expectations, this changed even after 1933 only at a relatively slow pace. In a commentary dated April 4, 1934, on the church dispute, the Gau inspector Homann noted:

One should bear in mind that eastern Westphalia is arch-conservative in its attitudes. This is a God-fearing people, thank God, a God-fearing people. The members of parishes are attached to their pastors, still regard them as persons they can trust and confide in. The pastors are also for the most part closely allied with the members of the parish. In eastern Westphalia, the Socialist Party has not pursued policies hostile to the church. . . . If Social Democrats and even Communists were faithful churchgoers, that is all the more true when it comes to the rural population in eastern Westphalia.[103]

An "arch-conservative" attitude meant that the place of a girl was in the family. If she became involved in something external to its confines, then this was in a clear and controlled framework, such as a middle-class sports association, a circle of young girls at the church, or a choir. There had to be an iron-clad guarantee that nothing could penetrate the girl's thoughts and way of life that contradicted the attitude of the family. That was not the case in the League of German Girls for two principal reasons. First, the "protected child" was under the direction of a leader who was barely older than herself and was then integrated into an array of activities whose purpose and utility were anything but

103. St. A. Detmold M 1 I P 656.

clear. Moreover, as underscored by the age of the leader, such activities held out no particular gain for an education befitting their social class. In addition, the girls were exposed to incalculable dangers, since in the view of the parents moral control could in no way be guaranteed in a group made up solely of youngsters. But the most serious objections derived from the fact that membership in the league appeared to be fundamentally at odds with religious convictions. There was an irrevocable gap, a view strengthened by the very vehement church struggle then being waged in the Minden-Ravensberg area.

> The church struggle is to an appreciable extent a struggle for the hearts and minds of youth. On one side you have the churches. They do not want to and cannot give up their work with youth without being cut off from a substantial part of the best and most talented in the younger generation. On the other side, you have the Hitler Youth, which is consciously employed by the system, in the church struggle and elsewhere, as a radical vanguard. For this branch, the party organization finds it easiest to deny responsibility to the outside and can, if need be, recall it from the fray without any loss of prestige.[104]

The pastors, most of whom in the Minden district were members of the Confessional Church,[105] were upset about the fact that the Hitler Youth had come in and supplanted them, taking away their basis for working with Protestant youth.[106] They were afraid that the National Socialist youth organization could undermine and destroy their confession, since the influence of the ideas of Rosenberg that they so vehemently opposed was especially manifest here, espoused with singular ardor by von Schirach.[107] Their public pronouncements from the pul-

104. *Sopade* 2 (1935): 1305.

105. A letter by the mayor of Minden dated November 12, 1934, indicates that some 90 percent of the pastors of congregations in the province of Westphalia belonged to the Confessional Church; see St. A. Detmold, M 2 Minden C 155. The strong influence of the Confessional Church here was also due to the fact that Bethel (Bodelschwingh), an institution for the disabled, was nearby; another factor was the influence of the Oeynhausen presbyter Koch.

106. In a letter dated June 3, 1933, Pastor Pless protested that six of the fifteen members of the Jugendausschuß (Communal Youth Committee) in the town of Minden were members of the NSDAP. Since three seats were occupied by municipal representatives, this meant that there were just six seats remaining to be divided among all the associations; of these, two were reserved for the Protestant church; see St. A. Detmold, M 1 I Ju 18.

107. In a speech given to BDM leaders on February 25, 1933, von Schirach commented on the religious views of the League of German Girls: "The BDM has a religious attitude, there can be no doubt about that. And if you read the church newspapers today, or receive

pit against the "new heathenism"[108] had a certain impact. The community of the faithful was so deeply dismayed and uncertain that subsequent to the installation of bishop Ludwig Müller, a supporter of the German Christians, on September 27, 1933, there were rumors in 1934 to the effect that the population would be compelled to become Roman Catholic and that there were plans afoot for church holidays to be abolished.[109] Viewed against the background of the historical development of Minden, that had to be perceived as an existential threat. At a local level, however, there was something else lurking behind the struggle for political control of youth and the content of their religious faith:[110] the fear of the erosion of traditional Protestant authority, manifested as the loss of the personal authority of the pastor in the eyes of the young.

Along with the teacher, the pastor was one of the inviolable personalities in social life in Minden-Ravensberg. Yet now his religion was publicly reviled, they were being arrested, their newspapers confiscated. In the countryside, there was a close meld, historically evolved, between the school and church: the women's relief association met in the rooms of the school, as did church youth groups, and when there was a funeral people left their overcoats at the school.[111] Now the doors of the school and its facilities were closed to the church. The teachers no longer worked hand in hand with the pastors. Some even sought to oppose them.

Even if now we didn't have to go to classes in religion until later, we had to be back at school at 8:00 a.m. So we had to go over there beforehand. We walked off to the church, and then returned on foot. And God forbid if you weren't back in time. Because back

---

representatives of the church and listen to their complaints, then you know that a clash is inevitable. It will be fateful, and necessarily determined by the course of developments. . . . For us, the nation is an expression of the divine. In our eyes, to be for or against the nation expresses a religious attitude, just as much as if a person cherishes a belief in something else"; see BA Koblenz, NS 26/336. It was precisely this link between the nation—that is, politics—and faith that the Confessional Church branded as a new heathenism and idolatry.

108. See St. A. Detmold, M 1 I P 653 and M 2 Minden C 154.

109. See St. A. Detmold, M 1 I P 652.

110. Scholder distinguishes between the Bekennende Kirche (Confessional Church), which regarded itself as a church, and the Bekenntnisfront (Confessional Front), the alliance of all those church leaders, district churches, and congregations that did not belong to the "Deutsche Christen" (German Christians); see Klaus Scholder, *Die Kirchen und das Dritte Reich,* vol. 1, *Vorgeschichte und Zeit der Illusionen 1918–1934* (Frankfurt a.M., Berlin, and Vienna, 1977), 718.

111. See St. A. Detmold, M 1 36/37.

then, well, the church was sort of out of favor. And the teachers had that same opinion too, I mean it was required from them. (M 11)

This evident loss of power and prestige by the church provided young people in particular with a new latitude for action that they gladly put to use, based on their oppositional attitude as adolescents. They would cut classes for confirmation without giving it much thought or worry. Or they would have some fun by challenging the pastor, who could be easily ruffled or even seriously threatened by a vigorous "Heil Hitler."

I: But practically speaking, all of you would go to the classes for confirmation, right?

M 11: Yeah, but they were a little more cheeky at that time, because they'd been stirred up a bit. I mean by the boys, not the girls. The boys, where maybe their parents were also a little against the church, didn't like it. Because their parents were younger, well, they were more open to those ideas, I mean some of them. And you could see that, like the boys would toss some firecrackers, that kind of stuff.

There were conflicts over authority that erupted between pastors and young people. These conflicts might even go so far that a pastor was arrested because a young person had denounced him to the police. For example, "improper behavior" was the reason for a conflict between a pastor of the Confessional Church from Bad Lippspringe and the Hitler Youth. Instead of voicing his fundamental opposition to the politics of the National Socialists, the pastor, a former member of the DNVP, assured the police after he had been called down to the station: "If you ask me how I see the National Socialist government today, then I can only reply that in accordance with the teaching of the Holy Bible, I am happy to be subservient to the authorities, and am contributing my share to the advancement of the folk."[112]

What might appear contradictory at first glance becomes comprehensible against the backdrop of Lutheranism. Based on the same Christian conviction that undergirded subservience to the state and its authority was the demand for obedience from youth. And then something happened that was incomprehensible to the pastors, triggering

112. St. A. Detmold, M 1 I P 655.

their resolute opposition. By appealing to the state, that is, utilizing their relation to authority, the young people succeeded in undermining the authority of the pastors. But this action challenged moral commandments that were irrevocable and absolute in Lutheranism. Based on traditional convictions, many parents remained faithful to the pastors. There was a sense that more was at stake here than just the personal reputation of an individual. A geometry of solid and transparent relations of authority was replaced by the authoritarian present, and in this process young people became the willing lieutenants of the state, doing its dirty work.

For these reasons, it is understandable that initially some circles had reservations about the Hitler Youth. This was especially the case for families from the urban upper classes and farming families in the nearby countryside. A woman from a solid, middle-class family reports about the league membership among her classmates:

M 4: Well, it was very restrained in our case. I mean maybe from our class, we were 28 pupils, like maybe there were ten in the organization from the start. The others were all kept back from joining by their parents.

I: What were the reasons, what arguments did they use? What arguments against it did your own dad have?

M 4: My dad was a civil servant, so he had to be very careful about what he said. Now he said to me first: "You know, I think, if you join then you won't do as well at school and your grades will go down." And afterward he said: "Well, listen, then you'll be so busy in the afternoons, you won't be able to play with your friends any more." And so he always had some kind of argument, which I somehow just didn't recognize as valid. But actually we were living in a patriarchal household. When dad thought something was no good, then that opinion was actually accepted, leastwise in the first few years. So I only asked. We were always being asked by older pupils at school who already had some kind of position: "Look, why don't you just ask at home whether you can come?" And then my dad made me this offer: "Listen, wouldn't you rather go to the sports association, but you can only do one thing." Or later on: "Hey, you always wanted to go rowing. But we can't pay for two memberships, so you've got to decide." Or he said: "So just think about it carefully." And somehow, well, I was a little manipulated by him.

However, here is already an intimation of the sensitive point: the civil servants, as a municipal elite, were characterized by the fact that they were very dependent on the state, to which as pious Lutherans they in any case felt a duty of loyalty. For that reason, compulsory measures, especially when they were laminated by legality, had to prove especially effective.

In intensifying these measures, the Hitler Youth made use of an especially effective accomplice: the schools. The teachers became the decisive fulcrum for organizing and controlling membership in the Hitler Youth. In Minden, they made use of the teachers quite openly. For example, a letter by the district superintendent dated April 20, 1934, states:

> Bearing in full mind the paramount national and social pedagogical value of educating the Hitler Youth for the new state, we must attempt to unite all of German youth from the appropriate age on within the organization. For that reason, I am making it an obligation for school directors and teachers to vigorously support publicity for the Hitler Youth. In particular, one class hour will be set aside each month and put at the disposal of the Hitler Youth for a promotional presentation in which all pupils must participate.[113]

As early as the end of 1933, the superintendent of the province of Westphalia had made it obligatory for all schools of secondary education (*höhere Schulen*) to submit figures every three months on the membership of pupils in the various youth associations.[114] A report of the municipal girls' *Mittelschule* in Minden dated August 14, 1934, indicates that 63 percent of the female pupils between the ages of ten and fourteen were members of the Jungmädelbund, with the number of girls who were members rising in proportion to their age.[115] If one bears in mind that the Jungmädelbund was then already the larger organization inside the League of German Girls and that the pressure to join rose as girls moved into secondary schools, these figures are not especially impressive.

113. St. A. Detmold, M 1 II B 4420.
114. St. A. Detmold, M 1 II B 4420, letter, Dec. 23, 1933. At the end of 1933, four of the diverse youth organizations were still in operation: Quickborn, Bund Christdeutscher Jugend, Bund Artam, and Neudeutschland; see Bernhard Schneider, *Daten zur Geschichte der Jugendbewegung* (Bad Godesberg, 1965), 120.
115. Some 14 percent of the ten-year-olds, 62 percent of the eleven-year-olds, 78 percent of the twelve-year-olds, and 79 percent of those who had reached the age of thirteen; see St. A. Detmold, M 1 II B 4420.

The Staatsjugendtag (Day of State Youth) introduced in June 1934 and abolished in 1937 became the decisive instrument for forcing youngsters to become Hitler Youth members; here, too, the teachers played a central role. According to official pronouncements, the Staatsjugendtag was supposed to be dedicated to sports in the Hitler Youth. An instruction was issued that all pupils who were not members of the Hitler Youth had to attend school on that day. That alone was enough to persuade many that joining the National Socialist youth organization made sense.

Basically, it was just plain laziness, pure downright laziness. On Saturdays, you didn't have to go to school if you had BDM. And we had to go to school. And then we thought, that should be, I mean, after all, what the heck. I think it was in my last year at school, and then I took part in the cultural unit. It was choir, a mixed choir, amateur theater, folk dancing. And, though I didn't play in it, there was orchestra too. (M 18)

Since members of the Hitler Youth were not supposed to be put at any disadvantage at school as a result of their activities in the Hitler Youth, it was decided that there would no longer be regular classes on Saturdays. So those who were not members of the Hitler Youth and therefore had to attend school were now to visit classes in what was termed "national-political instruction." Teachers worked out detailed lesson plans.[116] As a result, while the Hitler Youth members were out roughhousing on the sports field, those kids who for some reason did not want to or could not become members were at their desks in school, getting pumped full with National Socialist ideology.

For a long time, I used to go to school Saturdays, and then they decided that those of us who went to school on Saturdays would have two hours of national-political instruction. I can remember

116. For example, a lesson plan for ten-year-olds at a school in Bielefeld addressed the following topics: 1. Meaning of the Day of State Youth. 2. Day of German Labor. The Labor Service. 3. NS People's Welfare. The Red Cross. 4. German youth hostels. 5. Germanic mythology, harvest festival, solstice festival. 6. Arnim (Hermann the Cheruscan), leader of the first national freedom movement. 7. German peasantry. 8. Family, folk, race, genetic heritage and racial health. 9. Frederick the Great. 10. Men in the Wars of Liberation, 1813–1815. 11. The bard of freedom, Theodor Körner. 12. Luise, queen of Prussia. 13. Heroes in the World War, on land, in the air, at sea. 14. Battles in the Baltic region and Upper Silesia. 15. The disgrace of Versailles. Each Saturday was devoted to one of these themes; see St. A. Detmold, M 1 II B 4420.

that the teacher would come to school in a uniform, and then he taught the class in uniform. But that guy didn't last long, and vanished from the scene pretty quickly. . . . Saturdays, no academic subjects were supposed to be taught, so that those who went to the service did not miss anything. I mean, that was the rule. So we had needlework classes, an hour of gym and then two hours of national-political instruction. Maybe, when I think back about it, what we had was a much more organized indoctrination, because the teacher was on the ball, he knew exactly what he wanted and what he had to say. While in the BDM and the Jungmädel, well, those were girls more or less still wet behind the ears, the so-called leaders. Usually they had a big mouth but nothing much upstairs. (M 4)

The sweeping success of the introduction of Staatsjugendtag can be judged by the measures that accompanied it: for example, in disciplinary infractions in Herford, Hitler Youth leaders excluded Jungvolk members from service, forcing them instead to take part in the national-political classes at school.[117] With the aid of the school, not only did it prove possible to finally fill the ranks of the Hitler Youth, but the school also continued to function as an institutional source of control to keep the members in line. Reduced to powerlessness, the school could do nothing to counter this reality aside from impotent protest. The hand-in-glove cooperation between the school and the Hitler Youth, the very obvious role of the teachers as accomplices of the party, and the patent ideological content of instruction all resulted in an erosion of the authority of the teachers over the pupils. That was especially true in the case of those pupils who had leadership functions in the Hitler Youth, who were well aware of these processes and in some cases were themselves directly involved. Right from the beginning, conflicts arose, and there was repeated need for the party and state to exercise a moderating influence on the Hitler Youth.[118] While the pastors could counter the onslaught of the National Socialist state with their own credibility, this was far more difficult for the teachers. Their dependency on the state significantly narrowed their latitude for action, placing them personally in an unfavorable light.

117. St. A. Detmold, M 1 II B 4420, letter, Sept. 15, 1934. The district school superintendent objected to this, arguing that the school could not be viewed as a kind of penal institution.
118. See St. A. Detmold, M 1 II B 4420; see also Wilfried Breyvogel and Thomas Lohmann, "Schulalltag im Nationalsozialismus," in Peukert and Reulecke, *Die Reihen fast geschlossen,* 199–221.

The forced or voluntary support by teachers for the ends and aims of the Hitler Youth continued throughout 1935. Initiatives such as the "campaign for the hoisting of the Hitler Youth banner"[119] between the end of 1935 and the middle of 1936 provided a welcome occasion for action. On December 1, 1935, of the 197 girls in the Minden Mittelschule, 179 were members of the Jungmädelbund, a total of 91 percent.[120] In Volksschulen, the percentage for membership ranged between 49 and 73 percent, averaging around 62 percent.[121]

In the course of the large promotion campaign for the Jungvolk in the spring of 1936, the teachers were once more called on to pitch in. In Minden, the Jungvolk asked the teachers, in writing and in no uncertain terms, to "dictate a short announcement into the children's notebooks instructing them that new members have to report, and telling them where."[122]

Finally, when the Hitler Youth Law of 1936 was brought into effect, service in the Jungmädelbund became a matter-of-course obligation for girls ages ten to fourteen in Minden. The legalistic framework now nipped all possible opposition in the bud. Blanket recruitment into the ranks became the rule; control in this easily monitored small-town milieu was absolute. The girls' service in the League of German Girls became part of everyday life.

Right, let me think back to how it was then. Gee, why it was exactly like, well, like you started school at a certain age, and then at the age of 10 you went to the Jungmädel. And when you reached 14, the BDM. I think that you were ordered to, I mean when you reached the age for it. It was really obligatory. (M 17)

And just as the school experience was different for girls, some liked it, some did not, some found service in the league stimulating, some thought it was boring, some found it a source of enrichment, and some resented that their free time was being restricted. What importance the league had in the life of a girl was significantly dependent on the type of leader they had. But it was also dependent on what other options a girl had in her free time. Especially in the villages in the nearby countryside, girls were grateful for the welcome diversion and variety the

119. The banner could be hoisted if 90 percent of the pupils were members of the National Socialist youth.
120. See St. A. Detmold, M 1 II B 4420, letter, Dec. 12, 1935.
121. St. A. Detmold, M 1 II B 4420, letter, Jan. 9, 1936.
122. St. A. Detmold, M 1 II B 4420, letter, Mar. 13, 1936.

league offered in their hard-working lives that held so little in the way of new experience.

In Minden the League of German Girls was the everyday reality for all "Aryan" German girls ages ten to fourteen between 1936 and 1943. After 1936, there was systematic registration of all girls. They were sent formal written instructions ordering them to register, or lists were posted at school, designed to ensure the flow of information and at the same time to serve for controlling the girls. The girls were grouped according to residence area, which meant that personal friendship or preference for a particular leader was no longer taken into account, though earlier that had been possible.

> Well, I must tell you, when I think back to the time I was a Jung-mädel, or later in the BDM, for me that was, well, I don't want to say that it was a nuisance, like having to do some obligation. It was simply part of your everyday routine. I mean, that on Wednesdays and Saturday afternoons, you'd go there. But I can't say that I was ever enthusiastic about it, even back then. (M 17)

The fuller the scope of total registration was realized, the more the initial enthusiasm of the young people waned. The mood of excitement, a new beginning, faded, the revolutionary pathos ebbed away, and service in the League of German Girls became a part of the girls' everyday life just like school. This was disappointing especially for those girls who had been very enthusiastic and committed members before and who after 1936 were generally active as leaders. Obligatory youth service had been their heartfelt desire. Now they had to look on as the huge bureaucratic bubble began to decompose from within.

> M 3: You know, it was after all voluntary down to '36. . . . So any-how, by then the old volunteers had, for all practical purposes, left the organization or had gotten married. Anyhow, the ones who'd joined up out of enthusiasm had gotten older and were no longer around, they'd become leaders or were gone. And then when it came to the younger girls, well . . . I mean, I don't know if I'd have joined up myself if I hadn't become a leader. I just don't know. Oh, something I remember, my sister was never in that bunch, she's four years older, was born 1916. Why she never had a thing to do with the league, nothing. The fact is, she wasn't among those girls who were registered and taken into it in '36. I mean the girls born in a certain year, they were actually con-

scripted into it. I mean, people went out with these lists and summoned them to report.

I: Were you working together with the registration office for municipal residents on this?

M 3: Yes, that's where we had the lists from.

The "movement," which in any case had always been dependent on the concerted cooperation of the party, a legalistic external framework, flowed directly into the state youth. This ensured it a higher degree of support on the part of the public authorities, while removing it from direct competition with other organizations. Instead, the efforts that previously had been directed to the outside now shifted and were focused internally. It was necessary to ensure the active involvement of the girls, their cooperation maintained. Otherwise the waning enthusiasm might take a political turn, changing into resistance. Although the legally anchored obligation for youth service prevented any open rebellion, the league was powerless when it came to the cunning of the girls who refused to serve behind their backs.

And when there were some get-togethers, free-time activities on weekends, I would never go along. I don't want to rule out that this existed. But like I already told you, I was sick pretty often. I was quite sickly as a kid. And I'd always get a slip from the doctor. And when I didn't feel like going, I'd get one too. So I always was irregular in my attendance. I'd always cut something now and then. Then I'd go there again, then stay away for a couple of days, then go back again. (M 10)

Although as in school, the leaders were authorized to demand an excuse in the case of absences, they could nonetheless not prevent resistance to this; occasionally, their authority was even totally questioned.

I remember, I really used to hate it when we had to do gymnastics with the Hitler Youth. But that was because I just didn't enjoy doing gymnastics. And another reason was that we'd use the municipal gym, where there was no regular floor, just sawdust, that stuff used to stink like hell. So I thought it was incredibly unaesthetic to have to do somersaults when you'd rub your hair in this smelly sawdust. Because of that, I was very much inclined to say I can't participate in gymnastics, which you certainly could put forward as an excuse, for physical reasons. So I really made use of that. I remember one incident, that once one of the kids—and I was really impressed by that, I mean, I myself would never have been able to do that [M 6 had one Jewish grandmother but was nonetheless accepted to join the league]—well, this girl had to bring an excuse from her mom, because she'd been absent. And she said: "My mom says she won't write an excuse for children." And by "children," she meant the leader. So she had to swallow that, and I thought it was great. I mean, she herself felt a bit insecure, because after all, they were only two or three years older than us. (M 6)

Consequently, the question of the internal content of the service of the league became ever more urgent after 1936. Basically, there was no general answer possible. Different solutions had to be worked out depending on the age, social background, and the level and type of education of the girls. In fact, the first two or three years of service in the Jungmädel seemed to go very smoothly. In 1935, a report of the *Sopade* commented: "In its current state, the HJ is something for pupils aged 13, 14."[123] The special ceremonies of induction into the "association of national youth," the new uniforms, the feeling that you were no longer just a "child" (in the sense of von Schirach) spurred motivation and commitment. In addition, the content of activities was in keeping with the needs of their age, giving priority to physical movement, song, and handicrafts over intellectual discussion and debate.

Yes, I certainly can tell you why I liked it. I mean, when you're in a group where there's so much singing, which you enjoy doing anyhow, and then the sports and games. Maybe there, sure there definitely was something political too in the thing, but we didn't see it that way. (M 1)

Well, we used to do handicrafts and stuff. But a real kind of instruction, I mean if you think we really had classes, where something was really dictated to us to learn, no, there was nothing like that at all. All I can remember was games, that kind of activity, all the stuff we did, playing around. That's how I recall it. (M 16)

Yes, well, we read a lot, did sports, we used to do knitting, somebody always read aloud. And then we did things for the Winter

123. *Sopade* 2 (1935): 214.

Relief. I don't know, I mean, we knitted tons of triangular cotton pants, all of us, and then socks, some also crocheted little caps, stuff like that. But I wasn't very good at it, so I always stuck to those little pants, that's what I kept knitting. (M 21)

However, as puberty set in, interest in the league service began to wane as other interests entered the picture. The way this process unfolded in terms of time was largely dependent on factors such as the leader, the other leisure time options a girl might have, and what she normally expected from her free-time activities. To illustrate this, I will contrast comments from an interview with a girl who attended the girls' high school in Minden and had strong intellectual interests with two other quotes from girls who lived in the nearby countryside and had grown up under conditions one of them described in no uncertain terms: "It was simply, well, nothing was happening. I mean, you could just forget it. There was nothing doing, zilch" (M 11).

People would sit down, bring along their little fretsaw. First you'd sing some song, the leader would say a few words, and then you started in on some handicrafts. Afterwards we packed our stuff, and when that was finished, then it was put in the big cabinet for charitable purposes. So we went on home, we'd done our duty. For me, it was always a kind of obligation that I had to fulfill. (M 4)

When I was serving my *Pflichtjahr* [obligatory year], there was a kind of, well, through this whole BDM and the HJ, there was a kind of community there, and you could feel a part of it right away. I thought back then, I thought, well, it was very nice. I mean, nowadays there's not so much available for young people. Then these sorts of things were very well organized. And people were not so fanatic in the rural areas, it was more just the fun of it, the fact that you were all together. People did gymnastics, folk dancing, there was singing and . . . I thought that was very nice at the time, a lot of fun. (M 11)

M 12: Participate in what I could, and in your free time. Because as a kid, like doing something on your own initiative from your own home, I mean, we didn't go anywhere. So we simply had to join in, something like that.

I: And so you had the feeling that you were getting out and around a bit, right?

M 12: Right, we also used to do things, like we'd take bike trips, we'd borrow these bikes and then you could . . .

I: Who'd lend you the bike?

M 12: Oh, we'd borrow the bikes from the neighborhood, when there were bike trips. And we'd hike on foot, out up into the mountains, and that was really beautiful. Afterwards, after I'd left school, we also did that, went out there hiking with a group of young people.

While the girl who was at the girls' high school found going to the Jungmädelbund a burden, a duty that it was incumbent on her to fulfill, for the two other girls, service in the organization had a clear plus point: here was a community in whose framework they could find desirable options for using their free time. So while the first girl went to the activities willy-nilly, so as to protect her social status as a girl at a prestigious school, in the two other instances it was membership in the Jungmädelbund that opened up possibilities for the girls to gain certain social advantages in the first place. Yet in all three instances, politics played no role whatsoever in their evaluation of the Mädelbund.

The attraction the girls' organization held out for these adolescents began to fade at the latest when they reached puberty, and generally the transition from the Jungmädelbund to the BDM formed a kind of natural caesura. In any case, this juncture marked the beginning of a new stage in life for many girls, as they left school and started an apprenticeship or a job. This meant that their free time virtually disappeared. Mewes calculated the average working day for a young female employee in the garment industry in 1929 at 10.5 hours, in office work even 11.5 hours.[124] And working time in smaller towns was on average one hour more than in large urban areas.[125] Many girls did not return home from a hard day on the job until seven or eight o'clock in the evening. They were exhausted and physically so tired out that they were hardly able to take proactive part in the life of the Mädelbund. A report in the *Sopade* in February 1936 commented:

The Jungvolk and Jungmädel take in school kids and have a very simple arena for doing promotional work in the schools. Yet in this ambit, the Hitler Youth and BDM can only rely on young people in

124. Bernhard Mewes, "Der durchschnittliche Arbeitstag der erwerbstätigen Jugend," *Das junge Deutschland* 23, no. 6 (1929): 257.

125. Mewes, "Der durchschnittliche Arbeitstag," 256.

high school. Most of the adolescents in the age bracket 14 to 18 have already left school and are on the job, either as young workers or apprentices. So they are subject to other influences and no longer have enough time to devote themselves to the romanticism of the HJ like those youngsters still at school.[126]

For many girls, then, departure from the Hitler Youth was almost a natural, matter-of-course concomitant of graduation from school: "I think I was only there until graduation, I can't recall that we continued in the organization after that. In general it wasn't that way, you went until you finished school" (M 14).

If the girls nonetheless moved on from the Jungmädelbund to the BDM, they often found that, due to vocational reasons, it was difficult to continue in the service.

> M 13: BDM was once a week, and sports was also once a week, and of course I had less free time then since I was doing the courses. So I had to organize my time, I mean, you can't be in Minden one evening and then do sports out here on another. So I had to reduce my participation, because I had to go to training courses at least two and sometimes three times a week. I can remember that I didn't participate in all the activities any more, since I was so busy with the other stuff.
> I: Was that accepted, OK?
> M 13: Oh yes, your occupation had top priority, even back in those days.

I must say that I didn't participate much any longer in the BDM, I mean I really didn't have the time, since I was going to vocational school. (M 19)

So when teenagers reached the age of fourteen or fifteen, the ranks of the Hitler Youth started to thin out. Only a few exceptions, as a rule those who were politically motivated and die-hard members, continued to take part in the organization despite their jobs or training courses. The others who stayed were for the most part high school girls. In order not to endanger their place at high school, they were forced to remain in the BDM. But they made quite high intellectual demands on the organizations. The following interview excerpts illus-

126. *Sopade* 3 (1936): 173.

trate some of the difficulties the Mädelbund had to grapple with in this process.

I: What was the difference between service in the BDM and the Jungmädelbund?

M 4: I really can't say now, I had very little interest in it. . . . I don't have any recollection whatsoever of the content of these political instruction sessions in the evening or activities in the afternoon, since actually, that didn't interest me in the slightest, I mean due to my education and my family background.

I: So what changed when you became a BDM member?

M 10: Well, you went there even less than before, nothing at all was happening. . . . I remember this incredibly authoritarian BDM leader, she was notorious throughout Minden, since she used to shout/scream at us terribly, and was almost vicious. So people tried their darndest to avoid her. And were careful not to pick a fight with her. You steered clear of her and tried to be more or less on time, otherwise she'd start yelling something awful.

These comments point up that, especially when it came to the older girls, it seemed imperative to make activities in the BDM more interesting; after all, these activities differed from the contents in the Jungmädelbund only, if indeed at all, in respect to what topics were covered in political instruction classes.[127] In Minden, there were two available options for this: a girl could advance to the level of leader or work in the so-called cultural unit. The Kultureinheit Minden, whose groups gradually formed at the end of the 1930s, was not an actual institution of the League of German Girls or Hitler Youth. The groups were dependent on the initiative and talent of interested individuals. Thus, a teacher directed a choir, a musically gifted pupil led an orchestra, a girl who was interested ran a handicrafts group. The following report by a teacher on the genesis of a choir that existed between 1940 and 1943 typifies the process by which such groups came about.

And with the boys at school . . . I made some real nice music together with them. And the *Bann* (battalion) heard about that. Are

127. Jutta Rüdiger is somewhat vague in her remarks about the difference between the Jungmädelbund and the BDM: "Just as the demand for education of character was paramount in the Jungmädelbund, guiding the BDM was the principle of achievement: motivating a girl to do her best." Rüdiger, *Die Hitler-Jugend,* 22.

you aware what a Bann is? That was a higher level unit in the Hitler Youth, this one was the Hitler Youth Bann Minden. Well, they got to know about me, since I did all kinds of musical stuff with the guys. So they asked me whether I wanted to create a choir. That's how I made contact with the BDM. And then I took it on my own initiative, I said, hey, let's make a choir. Wow, that would be great. So then we had, uh, those were largely girls from the senior high schools in Minden. They used to come, and liked it too, because I could offer something special, namely, guys. That attracted the girls, of course. And since I was very active and full of pep in working with the guys, they enjoyed coming to us. They'd come over to our school, we did music, and I set up a choir. (M 5)

There were also other groups, such as an amateur drama ensemble, a group for handicrafts, an orchestra, and a folk dancing group. These groups were made up largely, though not exclusively, of high school girls.

> M 4: So I think, if I recall rightly, these were interest groups. And I was in one for handicrafts. We made a lot of things for families with many kids. And I remember that my [future] husband was director of the Bann orchestra here in Minden. He was very musical; there were various categories and you could decide what you wanted to do.
> I: Was it the same in the Jungmädelbund too?
> M 4: No, no, we all did some political instruction there and then played games, sometimes marched through town, learned songs, that kind of stuff.

As a rule, these groups were organized in addition to the normal activities in the BDM, but naturally there was a certain amount of overlapping as a result of practice sessions, rehearsals, and performances. These allowed the girls a chance to avoid the regular fare of BDM activities.

> I'll tell you something interesting. They'd often come over and say: "Listen, [name]—they always said —— to me, didn't address me using my Hitler Youth title—we've got sports scheduled again for this afternoon. Can't you arrange a practice session for music?" And so I often did that. Then they'd go over to the Bann and say: "—— said it's urgent, we have to give a performance in a couple of places.

So we can't go to sports today." We usually were successful with
that. So this is the way I became so popular with them, and it was
also a reason why they liked to come to me. (M 5)

Sports was not the only reason to prefer the groups of the cultural
unit over normal BDM activities. By choosing an interest area, it was
also possible to decide on being with a particular leader. This was an
aspect that had played a role right from the outset when it came to a
girl's cooperation and level of involvement and had been neglected by
the state youth.

And this handicrafts group, it was directed by the daughter of a vet-
erinarian, and I always had the impression that she didn't think
much of these ideas. I mean, we did handicrafts more, political
instruction was actually rare. (M 4)

The unity of the old social elites was thus reproduced through these
interest groups. This is already echoed in the previous quotation. The
special groups consisted almost exclusively of pupils in higher-level
secondary schools, especially from the girls' Lyzeum.

I already told you last time that in our class, a relatively large number of girls tried to get around this service. There was a whole group
of kids who lived on the left bank of the Weser, they were all in the
amateur theater group. (M 4)

By contrast, the girls in elementary school either were too young or
did not have the necessary larger amount of free time required for participating in these special groups. In addition to these external selection
mechanisms, there were also some factors that lay much deeper, as
reflected in the following comments.

M 5: There were also a few kids from elementary school in the
    choir, but most of them were too young, they were only fourteen.
    . . . And when they came, they didn't feel comfortable there, and
    sometimes they were forced out again by internal pressure. Or
    they were put in the folk dancing group, which I also had in our
    school. I'd started a folk dance group, and many girls came to
    that, from elementary school, like from Hausberge, places like
    that. . . . They didn't have to perform at a high level, I mean it was
    simple, they had pleasure in the sheer movement of their bodies.

... Sometimes at such celebrations we'd make a joint appearance with them, but they weren't as good as my musicians.

I: You said they were too young. But afterwards, when they were working, they could also be in the BDM, right?

M 5: That's right, but then they didn't come. And it was pretty obvious they didn't feel comfortable in that circle. It was too, well, in today's terms, it was too middle class for them. I mean, the whole setup. I don't want to say too hoity-toity or something pretentious. No, it wasn't that, that'd be wrong.

It is quite obvious that the ambiguous "successes" of the state youth were in some way revoked by the reality of what these cultural groups were. They were no longer composed solely according to external criteria, subject to a fixed and rigid program that was not open to discussion. Rather, they were shaped by the interests of the participants and at the same time constituted a framework in which the personal relations and friendships of the girls from their everyday lives were preserved. The attractiveness of these groups was based precisely on the fact that they did not insist on the folk community as the compulsory reference point. Rather, they gave scope to individual needs, allowing at the same time for social mechanisms to gain traction and to operate. This development was not driven by intentional educational ideas but rather sprang from the compulsion to guarantee that BDM service would be accepted by the girls. The fear was that otherwise the legally anchored state youth might, by a massive circumvention of service, turn into a kind of boomerang that would reveal how little youth actually identified with the goals of the National Socialist state. On this level, the BDM was forced to deal with and address individual and social needs and in effect face competition. That became especially manifest in the confrontation between the BDM and the women's organization over the older girls. To a certain extent, the cultural groups in Minden in fact anticipated the more topic-oriented approach in the working groups of the BDM section "Faith and Beauty," which was geared to girls' specific interests. The following quotation provides eloquent comment on how these groups came into being, extracted from an interview with a woman who served as a full-time BDM leader in the 1940s.

M 3: That ["Faith and Beauty"] came into being in '37 or '38. It was a competitor for the women's organization. The youth groups of the women's organization, well. It was relative, different depending on the locality, or very active depending on the leader. And basically they wanted these girls who were over sixteen. Suddenly, they had a different orientation, different interests.

I: And they were leaving the organization?

M 3: Exactly, and we wanted to catch hold of them again, and so we offered study groups. Let me add that I think the name was pretty stupid, I mean "Faith and Beauty."

I: That certainly must have provided occasion for a lot of ridicule, right?

M 3: Oh yeah, a lot. Like "do you believe in beauty?" [*Glaubst du an Schönheit?*]. Gosh almighty, sometimes I'd just be so peeved at the soldiers, and then when my [future] husband would, uh, I mean, we weren't engaged then, but were going steady. Well, I visited him once in the field hospital, and my old man, he was such a mutton-head, and so he made a story of this "beauty" thing. Then maybe they started up with me, see, and I was so naive and wanted to explain it to them. But then, thank God, I noticed in time, saw that they were only joshing, or maybe really ribbing me. So then I just kept my mouth shut.

As these remarks reflect, the foundation of the BDM section "Faith and Beauty" as an independent institution was the most visible result of a series of experiences the Hitler Youth had undergone in the wake of the introduction of the Hitler Youth Law. This venture was the most manifest response to the impact of the state youth, yet it remained marginal within the league, a small institution in which only one of my interviewees indicated that she had been a member.

I: What motivated you to go into "Faith and Beauty"?

M 18: My age. That was actually, well, the thing was finished when you reached 18, I think. So then there was this. And then the interest in that kind of faded, yeah, and then they set up these groups for sports, they were a product of "Faith and Beauty."

I: Sports?

M 18: There was rowing, I did a bit of gymnastics. Then that gradually fell apart too. The older girls got married, so as time passed, a lot of girls left, went somewhere else. And then of course they started with this thing, assisting the flak batteries, they were called flak helpers. And then, I don't know, gee, there were all kinds of things, like helping in the navy. So "Faith and Beauty" also sort of fell apart on account of this. And there was also nobody here who was really in charge of it. It was no longer the way it had been. And of course the war was also in full swing.

These comments also point up the passing and peripheral character of the venture, which left few traces. Most girls simply were aware that it existed but did not participate.

M 19: I can still recall very clearly, they'd do gymnastics exercises, with rubber tires, Indian clubs and rings.
I: And did you think that was pretty neat?
M 19: Oh, yeah, right. I though it was great, liked it.
I: Although actually as a girl you liked the games, like *Völkerball,* games like that and not gymnastics, you didn't think the gym exercises organized by your teacher were really all that terrific, right?
M 19: Right, I didn't. But just the sight of it was so, I mean, when they'd march on into a stadium, with music, that was really great. . . . I'd have loved to have been a part of it, but there simply was no, uh, as I already said, down at work we were getting a lot of extra on-the-job training. You know, stenography, typing, a course in German, in math. So that was a big load.

The BDM section "Faith and Beauty," whose ranks the Hitler Youth found it virtually impossible to fill by external pressure, remained basically a peripheral institution of the league, though it enjoyed a strong public image as a result of its rhythmic gymnastics. This venture of the league, which absorbed the experiences of the state youth in a positive way and gave them a productive expression, served to illustrate an underlying dilemma: the league was both unable to exist within a framework imposed by external force and unable to go it alone without that framework. Instead, the idea of an all-encompassing girls' organization could only be made a reality if other needs of youth, outside the level of political consciousness, were addressed. This helps to explain both the content of the league's activities and the fact that its membership ranks remained more or less restricted to a specific age. As explored earlier, as an institution for political socialization, the League of German Girls did not find its concrete expression in the inculcation of political ideology but rather in the mass implementation of specific forms and content that were appropriate for youth and thus at the same time in tune with the times.

I can remember, we always had to memorize that stuff, Adolf Hitler
was born on April 20, 1889, in Braunau am Inn, we'd rattle all that
off. But it didn't go any further, actually it didn't extend beyond
that. Our political world, I mean, to repeat Hitler's biography, that
actually was enough, then you more or less had your high school
diploma. So it wasn't so awful, since we also did very beautiful
things, the activities in these special groups, that was loads of fun.
And you know, the odd thing was that after '45, almost all these
same people reappeared and got together again. They'd suddenly
lost their jobs; all of the HJ leaders showed up at the Youth Red
Cross. The orchestra was there again, the amateur drama group
reconstituted itself. Somehow that was quite a joke, see, they felt
they had to continue working with young people. Actually it was a
quite brown affair, I mean, they only dropped Hitler and National
Socialist stuff. But I'm sure that we were still singing Hans Baumann songs. And didn't even notice that sometimes we were singing
absolute nonsense. The songs were in the songbooks. OK, we no
longer had that Nazi favorite *"Die Fahne hoch."* But we had a music
teacher at school; right down 'til he retired he used to play Baumann
songs. He played them for 20, 30 years of his life, see. And he never
paid attention to the lyrics. So some of the people did not go
through this critical about-face until much later. Or they never went
through it. (M 6)

The cultural groups, then, were an attempt to answer young people's needs by means of activities, whereas the opportunity of a "career
as leader" was a way to transform the interests of the league into those
of the girls themselves. I have dealt elsewhere in detail with the path,
content, and consequences of a career as leader. Here I am interested
only in the impact such a trajectory had on girls against the background of the specific historical and social milieu in Minden. As previously shown, it was mainly girls in the upper social strata who were targeted as potential leaders. As pupils in senior high schools, they were
the only ones older than fourteen who had enough free time for such
involvement, and because they were still at school, they were required
to stay in the league. For these girls, the function of a leader in the
league provided an arena for power and influence that expanded as
they advanced up the ladder. This ambit and function were difficult to
reconcile with the compliance and obedience still demanded of them in
the family.

M 9: Yes, naturally, this led to conflict, sure. With my dad less, because he was very, very quiet, even-tempered. But my mom was another story.

I: What did you have friction about?

M 9: Well, like when I had to do something. I recall, for example, that we used to stay and go on talking for hours after leaders' meetings. So that I used not to get home maybe until midnight, as a girl 16, 17. Now there was nothing with guys, anything like that. Well, my mom was really in a state, she was all worked up and sent my dad out to look for me. And then all us girls were doing was standing out there at the corner of Königsstrasse talking away, no guys in sight! So that would lead to conflict, mainly with my mom.

The expanded latitude they enjoyed and the amplified scope for authority that the parents were no longer able to influence enhanced the self-confidence and self-esteem of the girls.

I recall that I used to get these feelings, like of power. After all, I was . . . leader [rank of her leadership] and had those many circles at the time. . . . So that was a huge area, and sometimes I used to think, well, I mean it wasn't admiration for myself, but like: "Man, you sure as heck have got a lot to say!" So, right, OK, I sometimes had these thoughts, I really had quite a lot of power. (M 3)

The enhanced sense of self was coupled with a feeling of distance from the parental family. Precisely because the girls felt more and more independent and on their own, it became possible for them to criticize their parents and to distance themselves from home.

When I was older, very early on I developed, uh, how should I put it, a certain distance from home. At a very early point. I kind of split with home. Actually, well, my parents gave me a negative example. I mean, I thought to myself: don't be like them! No way! Like with marriage and a family. (M 3)

The ideology of femininity the girls espoused was in striking contrast with their personal advancement as leaders. But precisely in dealing with that ideology, in objectively separating oneself from the content of what they were supposed to represent, it becomes clearer here than elsewhere that the girls had stepped out from under the shadow of the patriarchal family into the middle-class, capitalist world.

> I: So to what extent was that compatible with Nazi ideology? I mean, now you were supposed to be a faithful housewife and mother, basically very modest and virtuous.
> M 9: Yes, well, to what extent was that compatible? On the other hand, these leaders were somehow trained personnel. And so sure, naturally, they'd talk about being a housewife and mother. But for me, well, actually, it never personally meant much to me. . . . For me, the interests I had in a whole slew of things, well, that's what was important. And in part that was satisfied by the league!
> I: Yes, of course, I mean you made a quite nice career in the league, didn't you?
> M 9: Oh, I sure did! [laughter]

Especially when you look at the girls who became full-time leaders in the league, you can see that primary in their minds was the sense that they had a job to do.

> First I was appointed as a so-called executive manager there. I had to learn the job. So I also had to type and write the letters too, that kind of stuff. And I didn't like it much. I had this stupid guy who handled the accounts, I couldn't stand him. But then they disappeared, they were conscripted into service. So afterwards we actually were just a kind of girls' boarding school down there in the Bann office, there were just women working. (M3)

Ideology was overshadowed by the vocational aspect; in any case, the ideology provided nothing more than the frame for their activity. Corresponding to this objective and no-nonsense approach of the girls was the position of the National Socialist bureaucracy, which was likewise quite functional in dealing with them. And by not taking sexual matters into account in any way, it made it abundantly clear that the ideology of womanhood propagated was nothing but an empty shell. That shell barely concealed the fact that the new way of dealing with women was value free and purely purposeful.

I: And so you left the organization when you got married?

M 3: No, not all! After all, I had my service obligation! I mean, honey, listen, we were at total war. And me with my big tummy in the sixth month, I was still running around in a league's uniform, and I thought that was disgusting. I felt I no longer really belonged in any way, let me tell you.

CHAPTER 5

A Study in Local History: Wedding

Red Wedding, Poor Wedding

> Unfortunately, Wedding is still today for
> many an unknown part of town. Or what is
> even more regrettable, it's an area of question-
> able repute, and consequently a place people
> fear and avoid.[1]

On October 1, 1920, the Law on the Creation of the Unitary Community of Greater Berlin became effective; it spliced together eight cities,
fifty-nine rural communities, and twenty-seven estate districts.[2] Wedding was the third administrative district in Berlin. It included the
neighborhoods of Wedding, Gesundbrunnen, the northern section of
Voigtland, and the eastern part of Plötzensee. Its total area covered
1,304 hectares; in 1925, only a third of this was built up.[3] From the
Stettin train station to Seestraße, the *Mietskasernen* (tenement barracks), typical of Berlin built in a construction frenzy around the turn
of the century, dominated the cityscape. In 1925, Wedding's population was 337,193.[4] The district was crowded, extremely dense, with one
building right on top of the next, for the most part five-storied apartment houses, with two or three courtyards in back. The few areas of
green parkland amounted to no more than 60 hectares,[5] most of which
was in Humboldthain Park. The townscape had a distinctive physiognomy, crisscrossed by cavernous gray streets. Especially at night, in the
dim light of the few gas lanterns, there was a thick ubiquitous gloom.[6]

1. Franz Gottwald, ed., *Heimatbuch vom Wedding* (Berlin, 1924), 4.
2. The law was passed on April 27, 1940; see *Preußische Gesetzessammlung,* no. 19, no. 11,882 (1920): 123–50.
3. See *Statistisches Taschenbuch der Stadt Berlin,* New Edition, 2 (1926): 3.
4. This was equivalent to a density of 726 people per hectare of built-up area; see *Statis-tisches Taschenbuch der Stadt Berlin,* New Edition 2 (1926): xii.
5. *Statistisches Jahrbuch der Stadt Berlin,* New Edition 3 (1927): 3.
6. In 1951, on the occasion of the celebration of seven hundred years of Wedding, the first electric street lamps were installed; see Bezirksamt Wedding, ed., *Der Wedding gestern und heute* (Berlin, 1958).

The struggle to survive eradicated all that was superfluous, and poverty was pervasive.

The historical locality of Wedding extends south of Seestraße, around Nettelbeckplatz and Weddingplatz and the old streets of Wedding: Wiesenstraße, Triftstraße, Fennstraße, Gerichtstraße, and Schulstraße. The Gesundbrunnen lies to the east of this. The elegant houses on Badstraße and Brunnenstraße or Prinzenallee are the final testimony to the bygone grandeur of a former spa. In between stretches the Humboldthain, the only larger green park area in the district below Seestraße. In the far south, on the boundary to the Central District, around Hussitenstraße, Ackerstraße, and Gartenstraße, the northern part of the former Voigtland protrudes into Wedding.

The core of dense concentration of population in the Wedding district lay between Triftstraße, Müllerstraße, Seestraße, Osloerstraße, and the Wedding district boundary. Three large stations of the Berlin S-Bahn[7] were located here: Wedding (at Nettelbeckplatz), Gesundbrunnen (on Brunnenstraße), and Humboldthain (on Wiesenstraße). Every evening, the great river of workers from the large industrial areas in the north and west of the city would pour home to Wedding. Unlike Kreuzberg, for example, Wedding was a mass tenement district housing the Berlin working class.[8]

> Well, Wedding back then was a quite poor district. . . . Someone like my aunt, the wife of a civil servant, like that was very rare in Wedding. Most people were storekeepers who had their shops, folks who also lived in the same building. Generally they were residents there. And some actually were just workers, employed all round about here in the factories. Brunnenstraße, AEG, all these factories, Osram and so forth, and Telefunken came along later. (B 12)

In 1925, some 57 percent of the population of Wedding were workers,[9] while another 20 percent were classifiable as white-collar workers (office personnel, civil servants, minor government workers, and lower-level office staff), whose income was only slightly above that of a

7. While the U-Bahn in Berlin is an underground railway system, the S-Bahn—Stadtbahn—is elevated and runs largely aboveground.

8. See Ilse Balg, "Berlin—eine Stadt im Werden," in Karl Schwarz, ed., *Berlin: Von der Residenzstadt zur Industriemetropole Ein Beitrag der Technischen Universität Berlin zum Preußen-Jahr 1981* (Berlin, 1981), 161.

9. See *Statistisches Jahrbuch der Stadt Berlin,* New Edition 3 (1927): 9. This social composition remained basically intact as a constant in Wedding until 1939. In statistics after 1945, there is no breakdown of the population by social class according to districts.

worker. The facade and layout of the housing blocks were geared to these social strata. Most buildings were functional and plain; few could boast large apartments and the comfort of central heating or a bathroom. Wedding also lacked the middle-size industrial plants typical of Kreuzberg. Modest little handicraft workshops dotted the back courtyards, but the typical industrial sites were the large factories between the residential complexes, such as the Bergmann AG in Seestraße; the AEG on Brunnenstraße, Ackerstraße, and Gerichtstraße; Schering on Müllerstraße; Schwartzkopf on Scheringstraße; the gas works flanking Sellerstraße; the north harbor; Löwen breweries on Badstraße; and Schulzendorf breweries on Schulzendorfer Straße.

The streets of Wedding were teeming with life. The big department stores Held and Tietz beckoned on Müllerstraße and Brunnenstraße, while smaller businesses abounded.[10] On the side streets, there was shop next to shop, each with some special items on sale, serving the daily needs of the locals. The stores were a key social locus: women would meet here, there was an air of familiarity, regular customers would buy on credit if they were short on cash. Between the shops were snack bars, small fast bakeries, ice cream parlors, cafes, and countless taverns (*Kneipen*),[11] some with an additional meeting room. There political parties held meetings, teenagers were prepared for *Jugendweihe*, political courses were taught,[12] and demonstrations and

10. Some 12 percent of the population in Wedding was self-employed in 1925; see *Statistisches Jahrbuch der Stadt Berlin,* New Edition 3 (1927): 9.

11. According to B 7, just in Kösliner Straße alone, with a total of twenty-four buildings, there were four taverns.

12. Jugendweihe (consecration of youth) is a lay ceremony that marks the transition from childhood to youth and takes place when a child reaches the age of fourteen. The Jugendweihe had its origin in free religious and freethinker circles. Jugendweihe is celebrated by those who no longer are part of any religious community and can be compared to confirmation in the Protestant context or *Firmung* in the Catholic church. It was introduced in Berlin in 1859 by Bruno Wille as a free religious practice. With the founding in Kassel in 1922 of the Gemeinschaft proletarischer Freidenker/Verband für Freidenkertum und Feuerbestattung (Society of Proletarian Freethinkers/Association for Free Thought and Cremation), the consecration of youth became a ceremony to mark graduation, in which schoolchildren leaving school after the obligatory eight years of Volkschule were then inducted in a solemn ceremony into the community of proletarian society; see *Brockhaus Enzyklopädie* (Wiesbaden 1955 and 1970); *Die Religion in Geschichte und Gegenwart. Handwörterbuch für Theologie und Religionswissenschaft* (Tübingen, 1929), article "*Jugendweihe.*" Jugendweihe became part of the cultural heritage in the political left during the nineteenth century and was customary in the traditional workers parties, SPD and KPD. It played an important part in the former GDR, where it was able to outnumber the religious ceremonies, and is popular in the new Länder even today. The equivalent during the Nazi time was *Verpflichtung der Jugend,* which marked the transition from Jungvolk and Jungmädelbund to HJ and BDM. For an anthropological account of Jugendweihe festivities in the former territory of the

other actions were prepared and launched. In the major thoroughfares, heavy traffic ruled the pavement, but the quieter side streets still belonged to the children and their games. There, the kids spun their tops and tires, played ball, jump rope, and hopscotch.

Northwest of Seestraße, the built-up area thinned out. In the far eastern section of Wedding, above Plötzensee, was the Jungfernheide, covered with small fir trees and thick undergrowth; well down into the 1920s, it was at points still extremely dense and hard to penetrate.[13] This area intersected Müllerstraße. On the southwest side was the African Quarter, which ran down to the boundary with Reinickendorf and the Rehberge. In 1926, in a special emergency program for urban renewal, work had begun on Rehberge Park.[14] The former exercise grounds with its huge sand dunes was transformed into a park with a pool, toboggan course, and large playing field for sports competitions.[15] In the middle of the neighborhood north of Müllerstraße lay Schiller Park, like the Rehberge a mass of trees planted on former sand dunes, previously known as the Wurzelberge. Between Müllerstraße and Schiller Park was the English Quarter, south of it the densely built-up area centering on Ofenerstraße, Türkenstraße, Barfußstraße, and Schöningstraße.

Wedding was the district in old Berlin with the largest surface area that was not built up, yet there was little building activity in the 1920s. As in all of Berlin, construction stagnated to about 1925. Between 1925 and 1930, 3,099 new buildings were constructed with the help of public funds.[16] The problem facing those who were politically responsible was that they wished to create new forms of housing,[17] while the social

---

GDR, see Barbara Wolbert, "Jugendweihe nach der Wende. Form und Transformation einer sozialistischen Initiationszeremonie," in *Zeitschrift für Volkskunde* 94, no. 2 (1998): 195–207.

13. Until 1918, this was used primarily for military purposes.

14. See Franz Affeld, *Der Volkspark Rehberge. Seine Geschichte, Pflanzen und Tiere* (Berlin, 1961), 13.

15. See Franz Rück, *Der Wedding in Wort und Bild* (Berlin, ca. 1930), 13f.

16. See Rück, *Der Wedding in Wort und Bild,* 70. In 1927, residential cubes designed by Mies von der Rohe were built on Afrikanische Straße; in 1931, the Friedrich Ebert Housing Estate was built at the northern end of Müllerstraße by the architects Taut, Emmerich, and Mebes. Both complexes were in the Bauhaus-influenced style of the *neue Sachlichkeit* (New Objectivity). The Schiller Park Estate was a spaciously laid out complex surrounded by new buildings, constructed between 1924 and 1928 between Schiller Park and the edge of Reinickendorf. See Bernd Schimmler, *Der Wedding anno dunnemals* (Berlin-Wedding, 1980), 32f.

17. The government had a clear idea of the nexus between poor living conditions and the politicization it could lead to; see Gustav Böß, *Berlin von heute. Stadtverwaltung und Wirtschaft* (Berlin, 1929), 40. Gustav Böß (1873–1946) was mayor of Berlin from 1921 to 1929.

strata whose housing problems they wanted to upgrade were unable to pay the higher rents for the new apartments. Many new apartments simply stood empty, especially in the working-class neighborhoods.[18] So at first glance, housing policy in Wedding seemed flawed, yet the record shows that it did produce long-term results. The social homogeneity of the working-class district of Wedding dissolved on its periphery. An observer writing in the early 1930s noted: "Up here it seems as if a new district is springing up: the old Wedding intersects here with the new."[19] Housing blocks with lots of space in between were laid out here among park areas of rolling green. The apartments had inside toilets and even a bathroom; they were sunny, without a murky back courtyard, and free from the noise and clatter of some nearby factory. But no worker could afford the high rent. Residents here came from the stratum of lower-level office and government workers, a kind of "white-collar proletariat." New social and political influences percolated into Wedding from this periphery.[20] The old workers' neighborhood of Wedding had little in common with these new housing projects. Historically, the structure of its population was connected with the process of industrialization and the distinctive specific history of Wedding as a residential district.

The chronicle of Wedding goes back to the thirteenth century, but settlement remained sparse well into the nineteenth century.[21] In contrast

18. See K. Wild, "Die Bedeutung der mit öffentlichen Mitteln errichteten Neubauten für die Berliner Wohnungswirtschaft," in Jakob Schallenberger and Erwin Gutkind, eds., *Berliner Wohnbauten der letzten Jahre* (Berlin, 1931), 9. At the end of the Weimar Republic, the very evident social tensions bound up with housing policy led to the idea of doing without central heating and central hot water so as to make the apartments more affordable for a broader cross-section of the population. See Groß-Berliner Verein für das Kleinwohnungswesen, ed., *Wohnungspolitik von Gestern und Morgen* (Berlin, 1931), 16. The National Socialists evidently tapped this fund of experience. In the so-called Brown Housing Estate located on Nachtigall Square, few apartments could boast a balcony and most had no bathroom; see Bruno Stephan, *700 Jahre Wedding. Geschichte eines Berliner Bezirks* (Berlin, 1951), 81f.

19. Rück, *Der Wedding in Wort und Bild,* 10.

20. Already as early as the mid-1920s, the paper *Rote Fahne* commented that fascism had struck roots here "in the far north around Seestraße" (*Rote Fahne,* June 30, 1926). In the framework of the present research, I was unable to verify this claim. Yet it is intriguing that the celebration for the founding of the Wedding Hitler Youth took place in the Experimental and Training Brewery on Seestraße and not in the heart of Wedding; see comments by Artur Axmann, *Der Deutsche Sturmtrupp* 1, no. 7 (1933). In numerical terms, however, the influence of these new housing estates was marginal.

21. A document from 1251 mentions a village, founded in 1210, that had a manor and several smaller farms and was called "Weddinge" after a family of knights. In 1245, the village was abandoned, and its residents relocated to nearby Berlin. The same document speaks

with the fertile land to the south and west of the city, the north was mainly sandy soil. In 1640, a thick forest still covered the entire area, which was then cut down within a century.[22] A sandy desert began to spread, and it seemed ever more imperative to introduce cultivation there, since storms carried its sand aloft, swirling far down into the city. The area had few charms and little allure for which a person might have been inclined to leave the security and comfort of the city. But the discovery and development of a mineral spring transformed the Gesundbrunnen for a time into a popular summer resort for the wealthier social classes in Berlin. In 1782, a broad avenue was constructed, the present-day Brunnenstraße, so as to make this spot readily accessible.[23]

Under Frederick the Great, a concerted effort was begun to settle the barren land to the west of the Gesundbrunnen. In 1751–52, Frederick II had 120 houses built between Brunnenstraße and Invalidenstraße, with two families to each tiny dwelling. The new residents, masons and carpenters from Voigtland, were given the plot on the condition that they cultivate the garden around the house. In 1770 and 1772, additional houses were built in the vicinity of present-day Gartenstraße and were placed at the disposal of ten gardener families from Neuenburg and Valengin. The stipulation was also that they clear and plant the attached land, about four acres. Colonists from Bohemia settled in Koloniestraße; in 1784 there were already twenty-one families. Thirteen houses located in Wedding's core were given to families

---

of a mill, located roughly on present-day Badstraße, that Friedrich von Kave sold for twenty-one silver marks to the nunnery of the sacred Jungfrauenkirche (Church of the Virgin) in Spandau, which then owned it for three hundred years (Jungfernheide). On the history of Wedding, see Gottwald, *Heimatbuch vom Wedding;* Rück, *Der Wedding in Wort und Bild;* Schimmler, *Der Wedding anno dunnemals;* Bernd Schimmler, *Der Wedding. Ein Bezirk zwischen Tradition und Fortschritt* [= Schriftenreihe des Berliner Heimatvereins "Verein für Weddinger Geschichte," vol. 1] (Berlin, 1985).

22. Eduard Kuntze, *Das Jubiläum von Voigtland oder Geschichte der Gründung und Entwicklung der Rosenthaler Vorstadt bei Berlin von 1755–1855* (Berlin, 1855), 3f. See also Johann Friedrich Geist and Klaus Kürvers, *Das Berliner Mietshaus, Band 1: 1740–1862. Eine dokumentarische Geschichte der "von Wülcknitzschen Familienhäuser" vor dem Hamburger Tor, der Proletarisierung des Nordens und der Stadt im Übergang von der Residenz zur Metropole* (Munich, 1980), 30.

23. According to legend, Frederick I, returning from a hunting jaunt in 1701, is said to have stopped at the mill near the Gesundbrunnen and asked for a drink of water. The miller's wife handed him a mug of mineral water, which he found strangely and wondrously refreshing. The water was tested and deemed similar to that of a weak Eger Fountain (at the famous Eger spring in Bohemia). The druggist Dr. Heinrich Behm then set up a bath and pump room that was given the name Friedrichs-Gesundbrunnen (Frederick's Fountain of Health). In 1799, Queen Luise visited the spring. With her permission, it came to be called Luisenbad.

from Ansbach-Bayreuth. They also received a large plot of land, along with a cow and 240 fruit trees. But it soon became clear that the gardeners could not live off the orchards alone. So they opened up saloons, beer joints, and gin mills on their property. The crowds flocked in, and drinks were cheap, since there were no taxes beyond the city gates.[24] Complaints about the immoral lowlife carousing outside the northern gates were soon commonplace. Since the food and rent were cheaper there than inside the city walls, those who settled in the area were mainly the poor. New houses were built helter-skelter and without any plan. There were no streets, no lights, no drainage.

Economically speaking, Berlin into the nineteenth century was a town of smallholders. Industry developed at a snail's pace. Its beginnings were in Wedding, at a grinding mill at the Panke, a small stream, where the Royal Iron Foundry was established in 1804.[25] In 1815, the Cockerill brothers opened a factory for tool machines nearby, and in the same year Freund established a factory for steam-driven engines. In 1828, F. A. Egells set up the New Berlin Iron Foundry, followed in 1837 by the foundry Borsig and Wöhlert. The so-called Machinists' Quarter (Maschinenbauerviertel) came into being, a dense congeries of factories that were to provide thousands with a livelihood.[26]

Catalyzed by this expansion in production, the population in Wedding grew.[27] Housing speculation was soon rife. Between 1820 and 1824, the apartment buildings of Heinrich Otto von Wülcknitz went up on Gartenstraße, the predecessors of the later tenement blocks. These buildings, with up to five stories, contained a total of 426 rooms, some fitted with a cooking niche, others only with a small oven. In April 1827, there were 2,108 persons living in this complex, in some cases crammed in 12 to a room.[28]

Following on the heels of the incorporation of Wedding into the city of Berlin in 1860, there was a renewed economic upswing and a con-

24. Geist and Kürvers, *Das Berliner Mietshaus, Band 1,* 56f.
25. See Geist and Kürvers, *Das Berliner Mietshaus, Band 1,* 62ff.
26. In 1837, Borsig had fifty workers; in 1844 the workforce soared to eleven hundred. The first locomotive was built there in 1841; in 1854, locomotive number 500 rolled off the production line. See Verein Berliner Kaufleute und Industrieller, ed., *Berlins Aufstieg zur Weltstadt.* A memorial. On the occasion of its fiftieth birthday. With contributions from Max Osborn, Adolph Donath, and Franz M. Feldhaus (Berlin, 1929), 42.
27. In 1801, there were 150 residents, which more than doubled over the decade to 356 in 1810. By 1827, the population had risen to 2,217; in 1852, the Nazareth parish alone had 3,281 inhabitants. See Hermannn Neubauer, *Geschichte der Nazareth-Gemeinde 1835–1925* (Berlin, 1926), 9; Ludwig Diestelkampf, *Geschichte der Nazareth-Gemeinde auf dem Wedding zu Berlin von 1835–1885* (Berlin, 1885), 8, 11.
28. See Geist and Kürvers, *Das Berliner Mietshaus, Band 1,* 98 f., 134.

comitant surge in population.[29] In 1850, Wedding could count some 3,000 residents, soaring by 1866 more than fivefold to 16,840. The population in 1890 was around 100,000, climbing by 1910 to some 348,000.[30] In the span of a few short years, Wedding's character was transformed. The plight of its inhabitants was manifest: a grinding poverty, reflected most starkly in the housing shortage and miserable living conditions. New buildings, streets, and whole blocks sprang up like mushrooms. Characteristic for Wedding, the "primordial cell of big industry in Berlin," was the tenement block, a stark and unadorned functional structure with five or six stories surrounding three or four back courtyards. In 1920, such a building housed 75 residents on average.[31] A virtual emblem of the slum conditions in Wedding was Meyer's Court (Meyers Hof), praised by William I at its dedication in 1874 as a shining "example of social policy."[32] Here, living on an area 40 by 150 meters, there were at times as many as 2,000 persons crowded together, for whom a police officer had to be appointed in order to "guarantee public safety and order."[33] In 1889, a chronicler commented:

How much misery and sorrow, suffering and worry is hidden behind these plain, whitewashed walls, how many imploring prayers for help resound from this wretchedness! When the socialist specter begins to take on flesh and blood, then it will draw ample nourishment from this Berlin district.[34]

29. The incorporation was decided on January 28, 1860, by order of the cabinet. Berlin had long resisted its incorporation, due principally to the anticipated high costs of providing care for the indigent; see Stephan, *700 Jahre Wedding,* 58; Schimmler, *Der Wedding anno dunnemals,* 15f.

30. See Carl Matthes, *Der Wedding, wie er war und wurde* (Berlin-Schöneberg, 1935), 68.

31. See Werner Hegemann, *1930. Das steinerne Berlin* (Braunschweig and Wiesbaden, 1979), 333.

32. Ilse Balg, "Die Sozialstruktur als städtebauliches Element—Ein historischer Aufriß am Beispiel des Wedding in Berlin," Zentralinstitut für Städtebau, Technische Universität Berlin, lecture series, winter semester, 1958–59, no. 6:21. Balg correctly points out that for the young people migrating to Berlin from the countryside, who were accustomed to difficult rural living conditions, these apartments were a step up and represented a decided improvement.

33. Schimmler, *Der Wedding anno dunnemals,* 28f. For a detailed history of Meyer's Court, see Friedrich Johann Geist and Klaus Kürvers, *Das Berliner Miethaus 1862–1945. Eine dokumentarische Geschichte von 'Meyers Hof' in der Ackerstraße 132–133, der Entstehung der Berliner Mietshausquartiere und der Reichshauptstadt zwischen Gründung und Untergang* (Munich, 1984).

34. Lindenberg, quoted in Stephan, *700 Jahre Wedding,* 65.

Poverty runs through the history of Wedding like a red thread. That distress was accompanied by the constant complaints of the burghers regarding crime and immorality. The building of the massive city wall around 1800, designed to replace the wooden palisades, not only served as a customs barrier but was also a social boundary meant to keep the "less savory" residents of the Rosenthal suburb far from the inhabitants of Berlin proper.[35] But the forcible exclusion of poverty was just as futile a bid to "solve the social question" as was the venture to ensure social peace by laying on religious instruction. In 1832, the burghers of Berlin sought to counter the deepening destitution and slack morals of the proto-industrial society of the time by building four churches before the northern entrances to the city, the Oranienburg Gate, the Hamburg Gate, and the Rosenthal Gate.[36] In a tone of resignation, the head of a commission for the poor reported in 1837 on the dismal "success" of the churches in Moabit and Wedding.

> By the way, it can often happen that there are only 12 to 14 people in these churches aside from the church personnel. Yes, there have even been Sundays where the number in church did not exceed six worshippers. And on the last two days of Christmas, that number was only four. By contrast, the tobacco shops, dancing halls and liquor shops are bustling with customers.[37]

Instead, the deepening social plight fused with a growing class consciousness, discharging for the first time in the unrest of March 1848. In Wedding, this was especially associated with the "Rehbergers," who had been hired on in a social employment scheme to drain the swampland in the Wedding Rehberge area.[38] The famous Socialist leader Eduard Bernstein characterized these poor souls as the most desperate and destitute of the workers.[39]

> In their adventurous outfits, bright straw hats and with bunches of flowers on their heads, the Rehbergers were inclined to dancing,

35. See Geist and Kürvers, *Das Berliner Mietshaus, Band 1,* 59.
36. The four churches were St. Elisabeth's (Voigtland), St. Paul's (Gesundbrunnen), St. John's (Moabit), and Nazareth (Wedding).
37. Report, head of the Commission for the Poor, No. 56, I and II, Jan. 2, 1837, quoted in Geist and Kürvers, *Das Berliner Mietshaus, Band 1,* 384.
38. Affeld, *Der Volkspark Rehberge,* 6f.
39. Eduard Bernstein, *Die Geschichte der Berliner Arbeiterbewegung,* vol. 1 (Berlin, 1907), 38ff.

music and engaging in every manner of mischief. The irrepressible robust Berlin sense of humor was also in full flower on the Rehberge. After long discussion, a black signboard with a warning from the authorities to work harder was ceremoniously placed in a coffin, over it a marker reading: "Here lies the Berlin City Council. May it rest in peace."[40]

In the wake of the crushing of the revolution, there was the "peace of the graveyard" in the workers' movement,[41] but the burghers in Wedding instituted a whole array of philanthropic measures in the struggle against poverty, establishing an array of diverse associations. The association Dienst am Arbeitslosen (Serving the Jobless) opened the Schrippenkirche in 1899,[42] a church where religious edification was garnished with the good deed of a warm cup of soup and a roll (*Schrippe*). Other associations viewed the main evil in the appalling housing conditions, where a "proper and ordered family life" appeared all but impossible. They tried to remedy this situation by establishing building societies. Yet against this veritable sea of poverty, all these initiatives were little more than a drop in the proverbial bucket. And since little could be done to improve their hardship and misery, the "Socialist specter" took on ever more sinewy form.

Ever since 1877, when the SPD had won the elections in the Machinenbauerviertel for the first time, Wedding had been a bastion of social democracy.[43] Famous Social Democrats such as Wilhelm Hasenclever, Wilhelm Pfannkuch, Wilhelm Liebknecht, and Georg Ledebour came from the ranks of the Wedding SPD.[44] At the same time Adolf Stoecker had been put forward here as a candidate for the Christlich Soziale Arbeiterpartei (Christian Social Workers' Party), a right-wing party he had founded in 1878. Stoecker, however, suffered a crushing

40. Ernst Kaeber, *Berlin 1848* (Berlin, 1948), 140f. The Rehbergers included workers, unemployed artisans, as well as teachers. They found their political leader in Gustav Adolph Schlöffel, the son of a Silesian estate owner who had been expelled from Heidelberg University as a revolutionary and had come to Berlin in March 1848. There he edited a paper called the *Volksfreund* (named after Marat's *Ami du Peuple*), which he distributed free of charge to the Rehbergers. He was later arrested for attempted incitement to rebellion and sentenced to prison. Schlöffel fled, went initially to Hungary, and then to Baden, where he was killed in June 1849 in a duel near Waghäusel; see Kaeber, *Berlin 1848*, 142ff.

41. Bernstein, *Die Geschichte der Berliner Arbeiterbewegung*, 92.

42. *Schrippe* is the Berlin slang term for a roll.

43. Bernstein, *Die Geschichte der Berliner Arbeiterbewegung*, 319ff.

44. Or they came from the sixth Berlin electoral precinct, which comprised the northern part of the center of the city.

defeat at the polls.[45] When on November 9, 1918, the revolution broke out, naturally the revolt's first sparks flared among the workers in the large Wedding factories. But it soon became clear that the population in Wedding did not feel represented by the new republic that had been proclaimed and the party at its helm, the SPD.[46] This was already evident in the poll for the National Assembly on January 19, 1919, which *Spartakus* had called on workers to boycott. The turnout in Wedding was 81.6 percent, higher than the Berlin average, yet the SPD tallied far fewer votes.[47] By contrast, with 46.4 percent in Wedding, the Independent Social Democracy (USPD) could point to its largest electoral success in all of Berlin.[48] A year later, this tendency had spread across the city. On June 6, 1920, three months after the Kapp Putsch, the SPD plummeted to 17.5 percent of the vote in the new Reichstag elections, a loss of more than half, while the USPD emerged as the strongest party with 42.7 percent.[49] In Wedding, this result was even more striking. The SPD polled 15.7 percent there, while the USPD won a whopping 57.3 percent of the votes cast. With that success it established a veritable record at the polls, one that the Kommunistische Partei Deutschlands (Communist Party of Germany, or KPD), in Wedding the obvious successor to the USPD, was never able to match.[50]

From 1928 on, the KPD was the strongest party in Wedding.[51] It remained the number one party down to the elections for the city council in March 1933, that is, after the burning of the Reichstag and the first massive clampdown on the left-wing specter by the National Socialist regime.[52] Though the KPD was never able to gain a majority

45. In the Reichstag election of July 30, 1878, Stoecker received 818 of the 38,000 votes cast in the sixth precinct; he called the evening of July 30 the most "shocking moment" of his life; see Bernstein, *Die Geschichte der Berliner Arbeiterbewegung,* 388, 393.

46. Space does not permit me to sketch the struggles over the foundation of the republic and developments in the immediate postwar period. As Rosenhaft points out, the political factions were based on social differences, in particular the emergence of a stratum of skilled workers, which after 1917 played an ever more important role. See Eve Rosenhaft, *Beating the Fascists! The German Communist and Political Violence, 1929–1933* (Cambridge, 1983), 5.

47. It polled 32.5 percent, falling far below the 36.4 percent average for all of Berlin; see *Statistisches Jahrbuch der Stadt Berlin* 34 (1920): 884.

48. *Statistisches Jahrbuch der Stadt Berlin* 34 (1920): 884.

49. *Statistisches Jahrbuch der Stadt Berlin* 34 (1920): 885.

50. *Statistisches Jahrbuch der Stadt Berlin* 34 (1920): 885.

51. In the Reichstag poll on May 20, 1928, it garnered 40 percent; see *Statistisches Jahrbuch der Stadt Berlin,* New Edition, 4 (1928): 308.

52. In this last poll the KPD was permitted to participate in, the party won 33 percent of the vote; see *Statistisches Jahrbuch der Stadt Berlin,* New Edition, 9 (1933): 268f.

of votes even in Wedding, it came quite close in the November 1932 Reichstag election, tallying an impressive 47 percent.[53] The term "red Wedding" and its associated repute became a household word after the May 1929 revolts, if not earlier.[54] In the political ambience at the beginning of the 1930s, for the KPD Wedding now stood as a firm bulwark against fascism, symbolizing the dawn of a new Socialist world.[55] While the image of Wedding in the respectable middle-class paper *Berliner Tageblatt* was tainted, associated with the large Moabit prison and a shady milieu of poverty and crime, in the Communist paper *Rote Fahne* the district was projected as a suppressed giant now beginning to rise up, shaking its fist in defiance.

Residents in Wedding had a more finely calibrated differentiation of their home place.

Wedding in general doesn't exist. I mean, there's the district of Wedding, OK, then there's the Wedding neighborhood, then there's Gesundbrunnen as a section. And we lived in Gesundbrunnen or Plumpe or whatever, that somehow was the better quarter. (B 17)

Hidden behind this spatial differentiation was a structure of social class, making it clear that the external perception of Wedding was also adopted by residents and in circulation there.

Sure, we were part of the Wedding district . . . but we were from Gesundbrunnen, not Wedding. Because Wedding was always "red Wedding," and my dad didn't want to be associated with that. So it

53. *Statistisches Jahrbuch der Stadt Berlin,* New Edition, 9 (1933): 264f.
54. During these events termed *Blutmai* (Bloody May), the police—headed by a Social Democrat—killed twenty-four people, all of them innocent bystanders. The tragic toll was exploited by the Communist Party for their new political orientation against the Social Democracy and had the support of many left-wing intellectuals. Johannes R. Becher and Erich Weinert both wrote poems about the events. The Weinert poem was later transformed into a popular song, "Roter Wedding," composed by Hanns Eisler. Klaus Neukrantz wrote a novel, which appeared in 1930 as part of an affordable book series, called *Der—Rote—Eine Mark—Roman* (The Red 1 Mark Novel), geared to a working-class readership. Klaus Neukrantz, *Barrikaden am Wedding. Der Roman einer Straße aus den Berliner Maitagen 1929* (1931; reprint, Berlin, 1970). See Thomas Kurz, *"Blutmai." Sozialdemokraten und Kommunisten im Brennpunkt der Berliner Ereignisse von 1929* (Berlin and Bonn, 1988), 33ff., 128ff.
55. Rosenhaft has calculated that contrary to hasty assumptions, Wedding was only seventh among the Berlin districts in terms of the frequency of violent clashes. She suspects, and is probably correct, that the reason for this was that Wedding was both more proletarian than all other Berlin districts, and more Communist; see Rosenhaft, *Beating the Fascists!* 22.

was always important for him to say that he lived in Gesundbrunnen, not in Wedding. I mean, maybe it was sort of conceited on his part, puttin' on airs. (B1)

In a district that was both discriminated and stereotyped, people felt it was important to differentiate internally, dissociating themselves from certain negative images. Here the distancing had a political character, referencing "red" Communist Wedding. But who were "the Communists"?

What should I say, how should I put it? I mean, those were people, they were all, uh, there were some who said that Communists have to be poor or the other way around, that poor people had to be communists. (B 1)

Thus, behind the metaphor of "red Wedding" there was nothing but poverty. And it was true that the quality of the residential housing in the historical section of Wedding, the streets around Wedding Square and Nettelbeck Square, was appalling. It was hard to overlook the fact that an underclass lived here, the poorest of the poor, in the most wretched housing, the most dreary and depressing streets. Their down-and-out misery, living on the edge, appeared to constitute a potential threat, especially in a district like Wedding, where shortages and deficiencies abounded and it was easy to slip beneath the poverty level.

I: What was the relation between Kösliner Straße and the other streets? I mean, like when you told people you lived on Kösliner Straße?

B 7: They just gave you one of those looks. We were, uh, today you'd say we were disreputable, not respectable. When someone today says: "On that street? You lived on Kösliner?!" Then I'd say, "OK, right, and what of it?!" I had a wonderful childhood, I don't give a darn about anything else. Maybe some of the people livin' there then were sort of lowlife, a certain shady element, or something . . . and then they used to say, the commies, say they're commies.[56]

56. Kösliner Straße was the street where in May 1929 barricades had been erected.

Internal Family Structures and the Ballot Box

Just, as I said, at home we were always dirt poor. (B 6)

At the end of the 1920s, Karl Freudenberg calculated the social index for all Berlin districts.[57] Wedding came in last.[58] In 1930, it had the lowest percentage of *Kleinrentner* anywhere in Berlin but was number one when it came to *Sozialrentner*.[59] Wedding ranked fifth in Berlin for tuberculosis mortality rates.[60] It had the second highest number of stillborn babies,[61] and 12.5 percent of all children in Wedding were getting free meals at school.[62] Expenditures usually exceeded the district budget for general and youth welfare, so that the district felt the need to press for a "hardship factor" to supplement their strapped funds.[63] Even if only a small portion of the inhabitants of Wedding were on social welfare, most lived on the edge, between a rock and a hard place, barely making ends meet.

Mom came at six. We picked her up at the train station. I remember that. We often went there to get her, specially on pay days. That's when there'd be the weekly wages. It was always on Friday. We all went down there, and then went shopping together from the station. (B 12)

57. The social index took into account four criteria in the social structure of the administrative district: (1) the average number of rooms in an apartment; (2) the number of domestics per one hundred inhabitants; (3) the number of high school pupils per one hundred pupils; (4) the number of unemployed on the dole. See Karl Freudenberg, "Fruchtbarkeit und Sterblichkeit in den Berliner Verwaltungsbezirken in Beziehung zu deren sozialer Struktur," in Alfred Grotjahn, Leo Langstein, and Fritz Rott, eds., *Ergebnisse der sozialen Hygiene und Gesundheitsfürsorge*, vol. 1 (Leipzig, 1929), 5.

58. Freudenberg, "Fruchtbarkeit und Sterblichkeit," 11.

59. See Rück, *Der Wedding in Wort und Bild*, 54f. According to Young-Sun Hong, Kleinrentner were "rentiers whose financial assets had been devastated by the inflation" (91), while Sozialrentner "were recipients of disability and old-age pensions who had seen the value of the accumulated capital held by the social insurance fund evaporate—and with it their ability to pay these pensions," personal communication, Hong to the author. For further information, see Young-Sun Hong, *Welfare, Modernity, and the Weimar State, 1919–1933* (Princeton, 1998), esp. chaps. 3 and 4.

60. *Statistisches Jahrbuch der Stadt Berlin*, New Edition, 8 (1932): 23.

61. *Statistisches Jahrbuch der Stadt Berlin*, New Edition, 8 (1932): 18.

62. Rück, *Der Wedding in Wort und Bild*, 44f.

63. That factor was to be based on four criteria: (1) the number of small apartments; (2) the number of persons on charity; (3) the number of individuals on a social security pension; (4) the number of jobless; see Rück, *Der Wedding in Wort und Bild*, 19ff.

The poorest got by with a little help from their friends and hoped for better times. In most cases this was an inescapable circle.

The merchants, they had a lot of customers buyin' on the cuff. They had a number of such regulars, and most important, we'd known each other for a long time, had lived there for ages. So when Friday came, pay day or the dole, then I had to go and pay something. (B 7)

The extent of the poverty can best be gauged by comparison with the lifestyle of a well-to-do family.

My dad was director of a company. My mom had been a secretary, but then she stopped working, was just a housewife. I was the only child in our family. . . . Why, I even had a governess, and my mom just ran the household, she also had a woman who came in for the washing. We were very well off—why we had a car back in '32—I mean, financially we had no worries. (B 11)

Class differences ran sharp and deep, but the upper class was a very thin crust, at least in Wedding. For the great majority of Wedding residents, the affluence in a few corners of their neighborhood was hard to fathom. It stood in stark contrast with their own lives, marked by a constant lack of basic necessities, if not by destitution and hunger. There was hardly a family where women could make it to the end of the month; even in the better-off families, it was necessary to carefully plan the budget, cutting to the bone.

They really had to tighten their belt. I mean, in contrast with things today, our situation was very modest, we had to pinch pennies. Like to take a big vacation trip, that was absolutely out of the question. . . . to visit grandma in Silesia, even that was a big trip when we had the money for the fare. (B 10)

People scrimped and saved for any larger purchase or bought items on the installment plan. Unexpected emergencies, such as an illness, would devour all of one's savings and in the worst-case scenario brought financial ruin. Yet under this surface of general scarcity, there were clear differences. If they watched their budget, the better-off families of skilled or white-collar workers could make some small special wishes come true. But in families of unskilled laborers, they scraped the bottom of the barrel, living hand to mouth. Their meager wages or dole money sufficed solely for the most basic needs. There was no money for most purchases beyond food. That poverty was painfully visible, especially in the shabby clothing families had to make do with.

> I know we didn't have any dough because I got a lot of hand-me-downs, always! All the time just hand-me-down clothes! But what was bad, and I'll never forget that, never, long as I live, I didn't have a dress for confirmation, I didn't have any shoes for my confirmation. I could cry today when I think about it, all just used stuff, hand-me-downs. (B 7)

People cut corners, but food was the last thing they skimped on. Food, immediate consumption, the short-term simple pleasure of eating, took on a paramount importance. The pervasive privation in their lives stirred the inner man.

> And on holidays, they'd bake lots and lots of cake. Like we had a bakery right next door. I mean, if you could have seen how much cake the people would haul up from there, like on Christmas and Easter. So the people would make their cakes, prepare them at home and then bring them down to the bakery for the final baking. So the bakery was busy all day long with this. What I remember is that there used to be a whole lot of baking, like some families used up 10 pounds of flour, and they'd eat it all too. The kids out on the street, why Christmas, all they'd eat would be cake. So like I said, in some families that was really rare for kids to, uh, like I used to get these nice buns. But some kids, well, their parents didn't even have enough money to buy any, even though they only cost three for ten cents. (B 1)

> What mother could do, she did do. (B 7)

The boundaries between privation, poverty, and destitution were fluid. But the extent of women's work makes abundantly clear just how close even better-off families were to having the wolf at the door. The mothers of most of my interviewees were forced at times to take a job outside the home to bring in a bit of cash. Only in four families did the women do "nothing" but take care of the household. However, three of these four families were financially far better placed than all the other families.

One of the most drastic consequences of the war was the changed role of women in production. The situation of women after the war was quite different than before 1914. The impact was far deeper and more powerful on them than even on the men who had fought four years in the trenches at the front.[64]

In 1907, women made up 32.57 percent of the workforce, rising to 34.34 percent in 1925. The comparatively small increase can be explained by the fact that the workforce itself had expanded. If we look only at women in gainful employment, we find that, in 1925, 35.12 percent more women were employed than in 1907, while the increase among men was 24.76 percent.[65] Nonetheless, one can speak of a stagnation in women in the workforce for over a century,[66] because the increased percentage of females working outside the home was due primarily to better statistics on family members helping out in the family business.[67] For this reason, Bajohr believes there was only a slight rise in female employment but an increase in duration of occupation.[68] This meant at the same time that the proportion of married women in the workforce climbed.[69] Yet as a consequence of increased measures of rationalization beginning in the mid-1920s, the structure of women's employment outside the home also changed.

In industry, rationalization and mechanization of labor went hand in hand. The upshot of this was that in many cases, the skilled worker was replaced by the semi-skilled and unskilled worker, and especially semi-skilled and unskilled female labor.[70]

Thus, for example, at Siemens the percentage of women in the workforce rose from 48.1 percent in 1929 to 51 percent in 1930, despite

64. *Illustrierte Geschichte der deutschen Revolution* (Berlin, 1929), 125.

65. See E. E. Schulz, "Die Frau im Erwerbsleben Preußens," *Jugend und Beruf* 5, no. 11 (1930): 253.

66. See Gisela Brandt, Johanna Kootz, and Gisela Steppke, *Zur Frauenfrage im Kapitalismus* (Frankfurt a.M., 1973), 60; Renate Bridenthal and Claudia Koonz, "Beyond Kinder, Küche, Kirche: Weimar Women in Politics and Work," in Renate Bridenthal, Atina Grossmann, and Marion Kaplan, eds., *When Biology Became Destiny. Women in Weimar and Nazi Germany* (New York, 1984), 44ff.; Mason, "Zur Lage der Frauen in Deutschland," 121ff.

67. See Bajohr, *Die Hälfte der Fabrik,* 18; Bridenthal and Koonz, "Beyond Kinder, Küche, Kirche," 45.

68. Bajohr, *Die Hälfte der Fabrik,* 27.

69. Annemarie Niemeyer, *Zur Struktur der Familie. Statistische Daten* [= Forschungen über "Bestand und Erschütterung der Familie in der Gegenwart," vol. 2] (Berlin, 1931), 114.

70. Schulz, "Die Frau im Erwerbsleben Preußens," 253.

ongoing downsizing.[71] As plant operations in industry were rational-
ized and revamped, the need rose for better administration, manifested
in the growing number of women employed in office jobs.[72] Compounding the external conditions that shaped the structure and scope
of female employment was the palpable deterioration of the economic
situation in many families following the war.

In summary, we can note that mechanization of the economy is creating greater opportunities in the job market for women, while the
economic situation is forcing women to enter that market in greater
numbers than before.[73]

About one-third of the working women were married,[74] and two-
thirds were employed as relatives working for family businesses of
some kind.[75] In Berlin, married women made up 40 percent of those
independently employed, while they accounted for only 7.9 percent of
women working in offices and shops; 21.4 percent of women employed
in industry were married.[76] Only a small proportion worked out of a
"love" for their job or profession.

There can be no doubt that in the case of married women in the
workforce, in most instances they are working because of economic
necessity. There is thus no justification in terming them part of a
double-income family.[77]

The close nexus between the economic pinch in the families and the
jobs the mothers were compelled to seek to alleviate the hardship is
also clearly reflected in the interviews.

71. Hans-Jürgen Arendt, "Der Kampf der Kommunistischen Partei Deutschlands um
die Einbeziehung der werktätigen Frauen in die revolutionäre deutsche Arbeiterbewegung in
der Periode der Weltwirtschaftskrise 1929–1932," PhD diss., Leipzig, 1970, 28.
72. See Winkler, *Frauenarbeit im "Dritten Reich,"* 20; Mathilde Kelchner, *Die weibliche
werktätige Jugend der Großstadt* [= Sonderdruck aus dem *Handbuch der pädagogischen
Milieukunde,* ed. Adolf Busemann] (Halle [Saale], 1932), 250f.
73. Schulz, "Die Frau im Erwerbsleben Preußens," 254; see also Niemeyer, *Zur Struktur
der Familie,* 118.
74. Niemeyer, *Zur Struktur der Familie,* 109.
75. These workers were so-called *mithelfende Familienangehörige;* see Luise Walbrodt,
"Die Ehefrau im Erwerbsleben," *Jugend und Beruf* 6, no. 2 (1931): 31.
76. Walbrodt, "Die Ehefrau im Erwerbsleben," 31.
77. Walbrodt, "Die Ehefrau im Erwerbsleben," 32.

I'd say, we weren't exactly wealthy. But we weren't among the poorest either. Anyhow, like I told you, my mother really had to work her fingers to the bone. (B 1)

Another factor in the equation enabling married women to more easily enter the job market was the drastic decline in the number of children in working-class families. This decline in the birth rate began toward the end of the nineteenth century and quickly became a topic for heated political controversy, as in the "pregnancy strike" debate in the Socialist Party in 1913. In 1875, the fertility rate in the Reich stood at 42.3 per thousand, in Berlin the rate was 46.1, while in Wedding it was 64.1. Yet between 1900 and 1914 it sank in Wedding to 29.2 per thousand, still above the Berlin citywide average (22.3) but slightly under that for the country as a whole (30.7).[78] In his study on fertility and mortality in the administrative districts of Berlin in relation to social structure, Freudenberg concluded in 1929 that "social structure in the individual Berlin districts no longer leads to any difference in fertility in marriage."[79] In a study on the declining birth rate, Burgdörfer goes further: "In Berlin, the process of leveling is so far advanced that today it is the working class neighborhoods which have the lowest birth rate, not the wealthy neighborhoods in the west of the city."[80] While there was an average of 3.7 persons in Berlin households in 1910, by 1925 that number had dropped in Wedding to 3.2; in 1933, it dipped to 2.8 and in 1939 to 2.6 persons.[81] Reduction in the number of children spread slowly as a tendency in the working classes, but it was irrevocable and pervasive, driven by unconscious decisions rooted on the one hand in social privation and its hardships and on the other in a new conception of the family and a changing identity among women. Only two of my interviewees had more than two siblings,[82] while the others had one or none. Most interviewees were an only child. Yet even if households had as a rule no

78. Balg, "Die Sozialstruktur als städtebauliches Element," 26.

79. Freudenberg, "Fruchtbarkeit und Sterblichkeit," 21. Yet there were substantial differences among large urban areas, small towns, and the countryside. In 1925, the number of new births in Berlin was 12.2 per thousand; in all Prussian urban areas, 19 per thousand; and in rural Prussia, 24.8 per thousand; see Freudenberg, "Fruchtbarkeit und Sterblichkeit," 20.

80. Friedrich Burgdörfer, "Der Geburtenrückgang mit besonderer Berücksichtigung der verschiedenen Bevölkerungsschichten." *Freie Wohlfahrtspflege* 4, no. 10 (1930): 446.

81. *Statistisches Jahrbuch der Stadt Berlin* 33 (1916): 4, 289; 3 (1927): 4; 11 (1935): 15; 15 (1939): 14.

82. One of these women is from a wealthy background, and the other is from a very impoverished family.

more than three or four in the family, the amount of work was substantial, demanding considerable physical strength and mental stamina. Though household appliances were available, working-class families found they could not afford to buy them.

Yet to work outside the home constituted a huge sacrifice. It was an open admission that the family was hard strapped for funds. Consequently, only a small segment of women with children were in permanent jobs, most helping out in the family business. Others who entered the labor market in the longer term were generally compelled to do so by some unforeseen external event, such as the death or illness of their spouse. Low wages and exhausting extra demands on women's energy justified that decision only if dictated by dire necessity and as a temporary source of secondary income. So the greater proportion of mothers who worked did so only occasionally. Generally, this was accomplished by taking in work at home in order to tide the family over when their spouse was temporarily unemployed, to help finance the purchase of some more costly item, or to pay for a move to another apartment. Sometimes, the extra marks were only used to supplement their meager diet. Or they provided a bit of pocket money of their own. The close link between economic distress and female employment is the principal reason why my interviewees found it difficult to speak about working mothers.

> B 20: Sure, my mom did take a job outside. I think they wanted to buy some new furniture, and then I was supposed to be confirmed. Let me think . . . Well, one day mom said: "I'm going to take a job for a couple of years so we can buy ourselves some new furniture." That was awful.
> I: What was so awful?
> B 20: Well, I mean, that they didn't have enough money, from what dad earned, it wasn't enough to buy new furniture.

It is important to understand the primary motivation here. The wish that their father was better paid so their mother could stay home was nourished less by the ideology of a middle-class family and more by the simple desire to have a bit more money, to be free from the grinding burden of poverty. For the same reason and as a general rule, great value was placed on a strict division of labor between the man and his wife. To be "just a housewife" was a small patch of happiness most women were grateful for.

We considered Dad to be a little, like, the way they say today, "his nibs," you know, kind of self-important. Though he was not like that at all. But my mom thought it was her duty, since she didn't have to work. Which she liked very much, because what would she have . . . uh, as I said, some poorly paid work that she could have done at home, or a job working as a domestic somewhere. And that would have been really terrible for her. So she always used to say that this was the very least she could do, it was her duty to see to it that dad got up for work, that his breakfast was ready, that he had dinner on time. Mom was basically just a housewife. (B 10)

"A candle burning at both ends." This is the image Gertrud Hermes uses to describe the dilemma of women caught between work in the home and employment outside.[83] They quickly exhausted themselves in the effort to harmonize the two.

Mom was at home by noon, she used to work just five hours. Like she'd leave at four in the morning, start work at 5 a.m., and then when I'd get back from school, there she was, waiting for me at home. (B 14)

Ultimately, the survival of a family and its level of prosperity depended on the strength of the mother, the energies she could tap and bring to bear.[84] That became clear in times of economic crisis.

The capacity of individual families to resist the psychological consequences of unemployment is not only dependent on external living conditions, material resources, political and religious convictions. Rather, it depends in large measure on the mental fortitude of the wife of the jobless man.[85]

While women worked outside the home whenever it was necessary and possible, it was extremely rare for a man to pitch in with the housework.

83. Quoted in Franzen-Hellersberg, "Die Frau und die Jugendbewegung," 21.

84. See also Alice Salomon and Marie Baum, *Das Familienleben in der Gegenwart* [= Forschungen über Bestand und Erschütterung der Familie in der Gegenwart, vol. 1] (Berlin, 1930), 149.

85. Ruth Weiland, *Die Kinder der Arbeitslosen* [= Schriftenreihe des deutschen Archivs für Jugendwohlfahrt, no. 11] (Berlin, 1933), 36f.; see also Silvia Kontos, *Die Partei kämpft wie ein Mann. Frauenpolitik der KPD in der Weimarer Republik* (Frankfurt a.M., 1979), 30f.

The man went to work. And when you'd be out visiting your friends, when their father came home from work in the evening, well, he'd plunk himself down on the coach, open a beer. And his wife had to take care of the household. In between she would go out to some job of her own, that was already the situation in these other families, I mean, the wives had to go out to work. They had the obligation to do everything. (B 17)

The unequal distribution of work, the unreasonable double burden placed on the mother's shoulders, and the behavior of the father were, as detailed previously, almost always justified as the "way things were." Just as the women sought to repress the memory of the actual job their mothers had outside the home, they defended the household as a female domain.

I: And your mom, she never complained that your dad didn't help with the housework?

B 7: Nope, that's the way it was then.

I: Yes, but, I mean, you could say that someone who's a real Communist should want to help share some of the burden. . . .

B 7: Oh, what are you talking about? Like I can't remember a single time a man ever pitched in and helped out.

I: Even when they were out of work?

B 7: Nope, then they'd have a meeting, because they'd go out on a demo, or there was something else and, like, they were always busy. Nope, no, not at all, they didn't do any work at home, nothing like that.

I: And the idea that some day this is what you would do for a man, did that sort of frighten you, I mean that prospect?

B 7: No, it didn't. Let me tell you honestly, my big dream was to have a good marriage. Like a husband who goes to work, is hardworking, faithful, that was my dream. And in my dream, I'm the faithful loving missus, with two or three kids, and I'd have coddled them, showered them with love and kisses. So how does that strike you, what do you say to that? I mean, you don't hear that kind of talk nowadays! Like they say: "Old lady's off her rocker!"

At the time, Lisbeth Franzen-Hellersberg bemoaned the fact that "the place of women was nowhere so little respected as among the proletariat."[86] Exploited to the very limits of her mental and physical

86. Franzen-Hellersberg, *Die jugendliche Arbeiterin*, 46.

capacity, and subject to the arbitrary will and violence of her husband, the working-class woman was the "beast of burden" in her family. Yet this does not adequately describe the actual state of affairs in Europe in the interwar period. A study on family marriage relations, household money, and domestic violence among port workers in Liverpool in the interwar era points up the contradictions in the position of working-class women, looking especially at how the budget for the household was handled.[87] The men bragged that they let their wives have a free hand in dealing with the money and did not interfere with expenses for the household. In so doing, they tacitly left it to their spouses to administer the hardship of their lives, the trying task of making ends meet on wages that were never enough. On the other hand, their wives were also able to derive a certain gratification and prestige from this burden of "economic autonomy." This ambivalence, as reflected in the example of managing the budget, was also true of the position of the working-class woman more generally.

> How family life is organized in these circles is easy to imagine. Father leaves home early in the morning and returns at dusk. The 12-hour-shift that has been reintroduced in most plants removes him totally from the ambit of family life.[88]

> B 20: My dad, well, I hardly used to see him. He'd leave real early in the morning and come home late at night.
> I: Which means you were mostly with your mom?
> B 20: Always.

The mother stood at the very hub of life in the family. As a result of long wearying hours on the job, fathers not only were unable to take part in family life but also eluded this responsibility, sometimes limiting themselves to demonstrating their authority by physical violence.

> My dad, when he was off work and could rouse himself to do something, well, he'd take us kids for a walk. That was the only thing, otherwise it was always my mom, she was the driving and sustaining force in the family; that was her personality when it came to educating us too. (B 2)

87. Pat Ayers and Jan Lambertz, "Marriage Relations, Money, and Domestic Violence in Working-Class Liverpool, 1919–1939," manuscript.
88. Jüngst, *Die jugendliche Fabrikarbeiterin,* 51f.

When he heard we'd gotten a D– in a test, then he would wake up. Then we'd get a whacking. But otherwise, well, mom handled everything, just like me. (B 5)

In virtually all families, mothers played the central role in the life of their children. While in better-off households the father as provider bore all the accoutrements of external power and respect, in proletarian families this was often precisely where he failed. His effort and toil notwithstanding, the pay envelope was at best meager, the loss of one's job a permanent threat. As a result of working for a wage themselves, the women, and to a certain extent their children as well, had better insight into what working life was all about and thus had a far better appreciation of the father's success or failure. Against this background, the overbearing patriarchal airs of many proletarian fathers took on another meaning. In particular, the self-important, violent gestures so frequently associated with poverty appeared coarse and humiliating.

I: So your dad was the domineering person in the family?
B 6: Yeah, right. He [laughter], nobody could say anything, not even mom. He was pretty physical. I mean, he was a good man, but sometimes he'd get very rough, for nothing, some trifle, and I'd get my bottom smacked pretty hard. Anything was possible.
I: And your mom?
B 6: Oh, she was a very dear person, very loving.

The close bonds in working-class families were generally between the mother and her children.[89] Especially in poor families, the children had a clear sense of the contribution their mothers made, responding to it with tenderness and gratitude.

---

89. Alcohol played an important role in the alienation between fathers and children, as pointed out, for example, by Günther Krolzig, *Der Jugendliche in der Großstadtfamilie. Auf Grund von Niederschriften Berliner Berufsschüler und Schülerinnen* [= Forschungen über "Bestand und Erschütterung der Familie in der Gegenwart," vol. 4] (Berlin, 1930), 68ff.; and Kelchner, *Kummer und Trost jugendlicher Arbeiterinnen,* 24ff. Yet in the interviews, the problem of alcohol was seldom raised and was evidently a taboo topic. Two women mentioned in passing that their fathers drank. Interviewee B 7 was most open in broaching the problem, from which characteristically she was quick to exclude herself. Asked about the taverns on their street, she replied: "I know there used to be some. We had one, two, three, four taverns on our street. Just think about that, 24 apartment buildings and four taverns. I mean, poor people, they drink, you know that!" (B 7).

In a patriarchally structured society, the working-class family thus appeared to be "mother-centered."[90] The deeper the economic crisis, the poorer the family, the more uncertain and insignificant the contribution of the father to the family funds, the stronger the authority of the mother, whose gainful employment became the mainstay for survival, particularly when it came to the children. In their remembrances and feelings, the children associate the survival of the family "internally," the factual and material dimension, with their mother.[91] Representations of the family "externally," its pride and dignity, are associated with the father. In this role, fathers represented the level of politics.

My dad was actually a sort of romantic. He was a person who believed in ideals, he had a soft spot for communism, because from the time he was a teenager he'd been brought up with it. (B 12)

I also know that from my uncle, he had the same views. This was the be-all and end-all for these small families. They believed it was something useful, I mean, to help poorer people, like so many are. Back then, there used to be idealists too, the Communists included. (B 6)

In Wedding, to talk about politics means to talk about communism, about the Soviet Union, about disappointed dreams. Even if my interviewees did not come from homes where communism was the domi-

90. This idea is confirmed by a number of authors; see Salomon and Baum, *Das Familienleben in der Gegenwart,* 14; and Weiland, *Die Kinder der Arbeitslosen,* 36f. Dinse, *Das Freizeitleben der Großstadtjugend,* 20, reports that children of both sexes tried in every way possible to help their mother and take some of the load off her back. Franzen-Hellersberg, "Die Frau und die Jugendbewegung," 21, comments that one of the reasons girls went out to work at an early age was to assist their mother. Kelchner, *Kummer und Trost jugendlicher Arbeiterinnen,* 12ff., notes that girls had a positive relation with their mother, while their father remained a vague and fading presence in their lives (20f.). Krolzig, *Der Jugendliche in der Großstadtfamilie,* 82ff., observes something similar, mentioning Eduard Spranger in this connection, who wrote in his classic *The Psychology of Youth:* "The stronger the distance from one's father, the greater the tendency to maintain the close bond with one's mother"; Eduard Spranger, quoted in Krolzig, *Der Jugendliche in der Großstadtfamilie,* 85.

91. On the historical causes of the "cult of the mother" in the "fatherless society" of the Weimar Republic, see Karin Hausen, "Mothers, Sons, and the Sale of Symbols and Goods: The German 'Mother's Day'," in Hans Medick and David W. Sabean, eds., *Interest and Emotion: Essays on the Study of Family and Kinship* (London and New York, 1988), 371–413. Detlev J. K. Peukert, *The Weimar Republic: The Crisis of Classical Modernity* (New York, 1997), chap. 3.4.

nant conviction, they nonetheless had grown up in an atmosphere impregnated with and stamped by that movement, in a form and intensity unique for Germany at the time. Rebellion, struggle, and hope for a better world shaped this milieu. Their great hope was symbolized by the Soviet Union, an enigmatic giant wrapped in mystery.[92] The National Socialist seizure of power in January 1933, Stalinism,[93] the war, direct contact with Soviet citizens for the first time, the experience of the postwar Soviet occupation, and the reality of the German Democratic Republic all led to a stepwise dismantling of their dreams for a Socialist world. Great expectations gave way to disillusionment, disappointment, and for some even a feeling of betrayal.[94]

Most of my interviewees are diffident when they talk about the membership of their parents in the Communist Party or their Communist sympathies. The narratives are accompanied by an embarrassed smile or an apologetic objection. To admit that their parents were Communists is not only the acknowledgment of a battle lost. It also discloses the social class to which a family belonged. For the non-Communists, the link between economic hardship and communism looms large in their memory, as already mentioned before. By contrast, membership in the SPD also represented a sort of social advancement.[95]

My maternal grandparents, they were workers too, but workers with a special kind of consciousness. My grandpa was a lathe operator, a skilled worker. And when he used to talk about his family, well, there's something that has stuck in my mind. He'd say: my six kids all learned a trade. He had six, and then he'd mentioned each one. And people were proud about this. I mean, this was a certain source of pride for us. Actually, we had nothing in common with all

92. It was precisely the contradictory reporting about the Soviet Union in the media of the day that sparked and spurred their imagination. Only a small number of workers were able to form an opinion based on firsthand observation. Yet how important that was for them is reflected in the fact that on July 10, 1925, the first delegation of workers from Wedding left for a visit to the Soviet Union. It was sent off with much ceremony the day before in a large meeting in Friedrichshain; *Rote Fahne,* July 11, 1925.

93. *Sopade* points to the deep sense of insecurity among the workers in response to the Moscow trials; *Sopade* 3 (1936): 1108f.

94. On working through one's attitudes toward communism in Berlin after 1945, see the extensive study by Harold Hurwitz, *Demokratie und Antikommunismus in Berlin nach 1945,* 3 vols. (Cologne, 1983–84).

95. In the context of the present study, the question of what social strata were organized in the KPD and what strata were organized in the SPD can only be treated from the per-

those who were scraping the bottom somewhere. Sure, we were workers, but we had a very special consciousness as workers. That was also very much the case with my other grandparents too. Their apartment was clean as a whistle, and my grammy, well, she was a perfect housewife. And they had their little garden, my grandpa had his club. See, and they never tried to hide that he was in this party. Even later on, it was general knowledge that he was a Social Democrat, but he was different from the so-called *Lumpenproletariat.* (B 17)

In the interviews, only in a small number of cases did the wives share the political convictions of their spouses; rarely did they have their own clearly differing views on party politics. Most interviewees recalled their mothers as being "nonpolitical."[96] And even where the mothers had definite political leanings, they generally did not become actively

---

spective of the people involved, not in a broader analytical frame. Rosenhaft views the difference between KPD and SPD membership as historically sited in the watershed between 1917 and 1919, calling it the difference between the employed and unemployed, highly skilled and underskilled fluctuating industrial workforce. For the jobless and poorly skilled, trade unions, the traditional base of the SPD, had lost some of their importance. Taking a different tack, Wunderer argues that it is difficult to draw "lines of demarcation between the KPD and SPD rank and file according to criteria such as the level of skills, (potential) opportunities for advancement and consciousness of class and status," thus seconding the thesis of Ossip Flechtheim. Weber puts forward a similar argument, pointing out that from 1929 on, the KPD recruited primarily jobless workers to its ranks. The findings of Peukert point in the same direction; he notes that only one-fifth to one-tenth of all new members recruited to the KPD in 1931 in the Rhineland and the Ruhr district were employed. Important in this connection are also the findings of Fromm, who established the existence of a pronounced left wing inside the Social Democrats. Overall, then, as von Plato indicates, there was probably a more permeable boundary between the KPD and SPD rank and file than one might expect, given the hardened political positions of the two parties, especially toward the end of the Weimar Republic. See Rosenhaft, *Beating the Fascists!* 5; Hartmann Wunderer, "Materialien zur Soziologie der Mitgliedschaft und Wählerschaft der KPD zur Zeit der Weimarer Republik," *Gesellschaft. Beiträge zur Marxschen Theorie,* vol. 5 (Frankfurt a.M., 1975), 270; Hermann Weber, *Die Wandlung des deutschen Kommunnisus. Die Stalinisierung der KPD in der Weimarer Republik* (Frankfurt a.M., 1969), 283f.; Detlev Peukert, *Die KPD im Widerstand. Verfolgung und Untergrundarbeit an Rhein und Ruhr 1933 bis 1945* (Wuppertal, 1980), 51ff.; Erich Fromm, *Arbeiter und Angestellte am Vorabend des Dritten Reiches. Eine sozialpsychologische Untersuchung* (Munich, 1983), 86; Alexander von Plato, "'Ich bin mit allen gut ausgekommen'. Oder: war die Ruhrarbeiterschaft vor 1933 in politische Lager gespalten?" in Lutz Niethammer, ed., *"Die Jahre weiß man nicht, wo man die heute hinsetzen soll." Faschismuserfahrungen im Ruhrgebiet. Lebensgeschichte und Sozialkultur im Ruhrgebiet 1930 bis 1960,* vol. 1 (Bonn, 1983), 31–65.

　96. This included, for example, B 12 and B 10.

involved.[97] For my interviewees, politics was largely bound up with the person of their father and was always synonymous with party politics. Yet it is clear from the interviews that their mothers also had opinions of their own.

My mom had no interest in politics whatsoever. That didn't start until much later, toward the end of the war, when she saw the worsening plight people were in. She started to talk against the Hitler government, and often endangered herself because of this. Once she was even down on Alexanderplatz, and they took her into custody. They took her in for questioning but then released her. (B 12)

I: Tell me about shopping? Did you used to go to the Konsum [food co-op organized by the unions]?"

B 10: Yeah, my dad was in the union and he wanted us to shop there, so he said to my mom: "Listen, I want you to shop at Konsum." And my mother went down there like she'd been told. But then she discovered that some items were a little more expensive. So then she was adamant: "No way, I'm not going to shop there anymore."

The KPD in particular complained about the "conservative" women, especially housewives, who were less politically active.[98] There were two reasons behind these complaints: first, the proportion of female members and voters in the Communist Party was unusually low;[99] and second, the KPD expected far more from the women than the Social Democrats. After 1918, the aim of political work with women in the SPD had been primarily to win them over as voters, and the party focused increasingly on proactive work in the parliament to

97. This was in part also due to the hard facts of economic life: the family often could not afford party dues for two members. See also Karen Hagemann and Brigitte Söllner, "'Denn der Mann hat gesagt: Es genügt, wenn ich in der Partei bin'. Die sozialdemokratische Frauenbewegung Hamburgs in der Weimarer Republik," in Jörg Berlin, ed., *Das andere Hamburg. Freiheitliche Bestrebungen in der Hansestadt seit dem Spätmittelalter* (Cologne, 1981), 237.

98. See Michael Rohrwasser, *Saubere Mädel, starke Genossen* (Frankfurt a.M., 1975), 67ff.; Kontos, *Die Partei kämpft wie ein Mann*, 131ff.

99. According to Wunderer's calculations, 16.5 percent of KPD members were female, contrasted with 20 percent of the SPD membership; see Wunderer, "Materialien zur Soziologie," 262.

advance women's interests.[100] At the same time, the Social Democrats increasingly excluded "prepolitical" female needs and ways of behaving that were hard to integrate directly into party work. In so doing, they abandoned a portion of their emancipatory politics in favor of winning over the masses to their cause.[101] By contrast, the KPD tried to take control of these aspects, to unmask them as ideology and struggle against them. Many women in particular (though not exclusively) were affected by these differing tacks taken by the two workers' parties.

That can be illustrated by the practice and institution of confirmation. Among all my interviewees, only one Roman Catholic family had a strong inner bond with religion. In many families, the parents had formally left the church,[102] though generally economic factors were cited as the main reason, and only in rare cases anything political or religious.[103]

100. See Christl Wickert, *Unsere Erwählten. Sozialdemokratische Frauen im Deutschen Reichstag und im preußischen Landtag 1919 bis 1933* (Göttigen, 1986), 226ff. On Social Democratic women's policy in the Weimar Republic, see Renate Pore, *A Conflict of Interest: Women in German Social Democracy, 1919–1933* (Westport, CT, 1981).

101. Hagemann and Söllner mention Hamburg as a place where the SPD attempted to splice "female interests" with "Social Democratic politics." They quote Mrs. W: "And we had good success in holding on to the women. But we were only able to do that by throwing in a handicrafts evening now and then, or a social get-together with coffee and cake. It was not so easy reaching out to the women and connecting with them on an intellectual level. What they lacked at home when it came to a bit of diversion and stimulation, well, we could give that to them, along with something of our aims, like our views on democracy, through our lectures. That's also why we organized excursions into the heather and handicrafts evenings, even though on principle I was opposed to that. I was very much against that"; Hagemann and Söllner, "Denn der Mann hat gesagt," 237.

102. The first Socialist agitation encouraging people to leave the church began in Berlin in 1878 in connection with the establishment by Stoecker of the Christian-Social Party. After 1906, the movement to break with the church gathered momentum. Between 1919 and 1932, an annual average of 182,180 persons formally left the church. After the alliance between the throne and the altar had been eliminated as a result of the abolishment of the monarchy, the SPD abandoned its hostile position to the church, declaring church membership to be a private matter. Thus, the movements in the Weimar Republic campaigning for people to leave the church stemmed mainly from the KPD and the Independent Socialists. Kaiser regards these movements as poorly organized and driven by differing motives in diverse strata of the population. In Fromm's study, 13 percent of the Social Democrats and 2 percent of the Communists indicated they were church members, while the greater majority referred to themselves as atheists. See Fromm, *Arbeiter und Angestellte*, 88; Jochen-Christoph Kaiser, *Arbeiterbewegung und organisierte Religionskritik. Proletarische Freidenkerverbände in Kaiserreich und Weimarer Republik* (Stuttgart, 1981), 31, 38, 40ff.; see also Hartmann Wunderer, "Freidenkertum und Arbeiterbewegung. Ein Überblick," *Internationale wissenschaftliche Korrespondenz zur Geschichte der deutschen Arbeiterbewegung (IWK)* 16, no. 1 (1980): 1–33.

103. Dehn distinguishes between proletarian motives and the motives of free thinkers; see Günther Dehn, *Die religiöse Gedankenwelt der Proletarierjugend* (Berlin, 1926), 68.

And then we went to school over here, because my dad had some trouble with the church in 1919, a hassle over the church tax. They sent a bailiff down from the court and wanted to take our kitchen furniture, to seize it for non-payment of taxes,. And then he said, the hell with the church, let's get out of the thing. That they wanted to send a bailiff over to confiscate our stuff in the name of piety. Though he had no job and two kids to feed! Wow, he was really angry about that. (B 6)

Although the parents had left the church and were "godless" or "dissidents," as they called themselves, the children were often baptized and confirmed. The desire to have a confirmation often came from the youngsters themselves, a response to a felt need for ritual.[104] The confirmation drew a clear line, a rite of passage between childhood and youth.

In our case, we also finished school at the same time. So that was sort of the beginning of real life, if you want to call it that. It made a kind of beautiful ending to things. (B 21)

Due to their broad conception of politics and its scope in daily life, the decision whether a young person was confirmed in the church or through the ceremony of Jugendweihe led to conflicts, especially in Communist families. Frequently, the wish of the youngsters was shared especially by their mother, who helped them to prevail over the opposition of their fathers.

I: But were you baptized and confirmed?
B 20: Yes, both. That was mom's doing, without much, uh, see, I didn't have much of an interest in the church. I mean, in the church not at all, I was more interested in religion. So there was no connection whatsoever with the church. . . . The children were all confirmed, but I wasn't. And I started to beg and cajole my dad, and then we kind of softened him up and he agreed. So I was baptized on January 30th. This was in order to be confirmed the following March 6th.

For the KPD, confirmation was an annoyance especially because the party understood that the teenagers often did not have much of a

---

104. Mitterauer, *Sozialgeschichte der Jugend,* 62ff.; Dehn, *Die religiöse Gedankenwelt,* 21, 23.

religious motivation. This is clearly reflected in the tone of sarcastic commentary in the *Rote Fahne* from 1927: "Oh, but he's going to be 'confirmed' nonetheless! First of all, it's always been that way, and why should 'our boy not make the grade'? And it's such a wonderful ceremony too. Anyhow, like I said, it certainly doesn't do any 'harm,' does it?!"[105]

With its support for Jugendweihe, the party sought to compete directly with the churches, while attempting to satisfy the need of youngsters for a ceremony to mark the end of childhood, thus draining confirmation of some of its inherent attraction.

> And then later on, at the wish of my dad, who was very left-wing in his thinking, I had to endure Jugendweihe, the consecration of youth ceremony, go through that. Now I had an appointment with the pastor, and dad sad: "Nothing do, kid. You're not going there, what that guy stuffs your head full of is a lot of lies. I'll come down and drag you out of there by your hair." So I wasn't allowed to go, and then I went through the Jugendweihe here on Badstraße. Well, we couldn't celebrate much, there wasn't enough money for that. And like in the case of my brother, I mean his ceremony was a lot better, in the former Mercedes Palace. . . . But I thought I'd have a stroke or something, all the red flags and stuff. I didn't like it at all. I hated it. (B 6)

So the fathers stressed the political dimension for the young people, the obligation for Jugendweihe, and the need to forego any church confirmation, while the mothers supported their youngsters in what they themselves wanted. Politics in Communist-oriented families not only penetrated deeper into the tissue of everyday life, but the relationship with one's father also led a youngster to a differential assessment of this politics, depending on what their father represented and meant to them. In a solid Social Democratic family, the father was a respected figure, someone who had accomplished something, was proud of belonging to the working class, and, embedded in a certain modicum of material security, strove to achieve a better future for himself and his family. For my interviewees, their father was often a fair and broad-minded friend.

> My dad was exceptionally tolerant, he was very interested in equality and equity for people, and had a strong orientation toward the

105. *Rote Fahne*, Aug. 20, 1927.

trade unions. He told me a lot about when he was young, like when they still had to work until ten at night, and there was no vacation whatsoever. And he told me a lot about the unions, how they'd help to make possible a better life for the workers. . . . He was very tolerant toward others, and he loved to discuss things. It was always really great to talk with him, he taught me many things. My dad would never have forced me to learn some profession I didn't want to. Or say: you have to do that. Or when I had a rough time of it at school, he'd always encourage and help me. But there was never any constraint, nothing like that. (B 10)

By contrast, the burden of material hardship beset the Communist families. In many, the dominant tone was authoritarian; their narrow and pinched circumstances were discharged in outbursts of aggression and violence, which often came from the father.

Back then you couldn't take the initiative very much. You were always, uh, if I can speak honestly, it was a kind of hereditary servitude, because you were always under pressure. You always had to obey. You understand what I mean? You couldn't oppose your father. (B 6)

This had far-reaching consequences for the politics embodied principally by the father: far more than in Social Democratic families, in many Communist families the relation of the family members to the party remained ambivalent.

With the founding in 1925 of the Roten Frauen- und Mädchenbund (Alliance of Red Women and Girls, or RFMB), the KPD strengthened its efforts to win over women to the cause.[106] Beginning in 1929, it concentrated its agitation on women in the factories.[107] Although by 1932

---

106. Grossmann, *Reforming Sex*, 108–12. Kontos, *Die Partei kämpft wie ein Mann*, 59ff.

107. Among the 10 percent of female KPD members in Thuringia, less than one-tenth were factory workers; see Wunderer, "Materialien zur Soziologie," 262. Ernst Thälmann commented on this at the Twelfth Party Congress of the KPD in Berlin/Wedding: "The work we have carried out among housewives in recent years should be continued, but the main emphasis must be on women in the factories," quoted in Arendt, "Der Kampf der Kommunistischen Partei Deutschlands," 75. Kontos observes ironically: "Paradoxically, it was the proletarian housewives, whose influence the KPD wished to reduce in its turn toward women in the factories, who initiated and implemented the movement of delegates, a mass movement in the party, which at its high point in 1930/1931 mobilized thousands of women delegates across the nation"; see Kontos, *Die Partei kämpft wie ein Mann*, 71.

the number of women members had been doubled,[108] this cannot be viewed as a resounding success since there was a general rise in the membership ranks at the time.[109] In an essay on street cells, Walter Ulbricht comments on the "very conservative housewives," noting that "frequently the wives of the workers constitute the greatest obstacle to influencing these workers and winning them over as subscribers and party members."[110]

Yet if we examine this criticism against the background of the reality of a working-class household, the conservatism with which the women were labeled soon appears anything but convincing. It becomes evident that, in its party work, the KPD was failing in its attempts to speak to the vital interests of women. Not only did their membership mean that additional party dues would have to be paid from the meager budget that a family scraped by on, but once the men became party members, the families lost their support at home completely. As Detlev Peukert has shown in connection with the economic crisis in the Rhineland and the Ruhr, about half of the new members were enlisted in party work and were distinguished by the intensity with which they were involved in these new tasks.[111] What was a gain for the party was always at the expense of the women, who, in a dire economic situation because most of the newly recruited members were jobless, were then left alone to fend as best they could.

I: And when your dad was out of work, did he contribute anything?

B 7: No, nothing. Like he'd look out, once, down at a stand where this guy sold vegetables at the corner, he stood there one time and made some paper bags. We used to have these paper bags, made out of old newspapers, you rolled them and made these bags. So he made a few pennies doing that, because back then it was a matter of a few cents to be earned. That already made a difference.

I: And your mom never complained that your dad didn't pitch in?

B 7: Nope, that's the way it was then!

108. According to Arendt, there were thirty-five thousand women who were KPD members in 1932; see Arendt, "Der Kampf der Kommunistischen Partei Deutschlands," 252.

109. According to Weber, at the end of 1929 the KPD had 135,160 members, and at the end of 1932 this had soared to 252,000; see Weber, *Die Wandlung des deutschen Kommunnisus,* 363f. Peukert notes, for example, that the proportion of new women members in the KPD region Ruhr in January 1933 was lower than in the previous month; see Peukert, *Die KPD im Widerstand,* 53.

110. Quoted in Neukrantz, *Barrikaden am Wedding,* 144f.

111. Peukert, *Die KPD im Widerstand,* 57; Fromm, *Arbeiter und Angestellte,* 87.

Because poverty buffeted the sexes differentially, the interests of the party collided head-on with those of the women. That can be illustrated by another example. As Eve Rosenhaft established for the group of Communist street fighters, the lack of a female presence in their ranks was not necessarily indicative of their general absence in politics. Rather, she noted that women were active in other ways and in other types of operations.[112] By contrast, what is clear from our interviews is that membership in a party had a gendered connotation; it was a male-only domain from which the women were virtually excluded. This was true of both major workers' parties,[113] but its manifestation was especially drastic in the KPD. In view of the more hopeless economic situation and the growing sense of personal impotence, many young men in particular sought to salvage their personal dignity by flocking to political work. This helps to explain the sexist configuration as manifested in the type of the Bolshevik.[114] The top party echelon was confronted here with an insoluble dilemma, because willy-nilly it became an ally of male chauvinism. There were two reasons it could not have any interest in such a role. On the one hand, this behavior of the predominantly male membership always tended to exclude women from the party's ranks.[115] On the other hand, the party profited not only

112. Rosenhaft, *Beating the Fascists!* 153ff. Both among Communists and National Socialists, stories about women who hid weapons were part of the myth of the street battles. See also the section "Youth Organization and Gender Relations," later in this chapter. The findings of Kontos, who mentions women involved in revolts and street unrest over groceries at the beginning of the Weimar Republic, point in a similar direction; see Kontos, *Die Partei kämpft wie ein Mann,* 208.

113. Dehn reports about a father who was in the SPD and prohibited his daughter from joining the Socialist Workers' Youth, remarking that it would be better for her to stay home and darn socks; see Dehn, *Die religiöse Gedankenwelt,* 50.

114. On the type of the Bolshevik, see Rohrwasser, *Saubere Mädel, starke Genossen;* Peukert, *Die KPD im Widerstand,* 57f.; Oskar Negt and Alexander Kluge, *Öffentlichkeit und Erfahrung. Zur Organisation von bürgerlicher und proletarischer Öffentlichkeit* (Frankfurt a.M., 1972), 404.

115. The question of the age of the women cannot be dealt with here. While in the KPD ranks after 1930 young men predominated, there are only conjectures about the age of the women members. Franzen-Hellersberg estimates there were at the most 20 percent under the age of twenty-five. Arendt contends that figure may have been as high as 60 percent. Yet his calculations appear fanciful and fraught with error. On the one hand, they are based on a small sample of 404 members, including most of the course participants at the Rosa Luxemburg Reich Party School in Fichtenau. How this influences the sample remains unclear. On the other hand, his calculations yield the following figures: 5.7 percent between nineteen and twenty-two years of age, 45.5 percent between twenty-three and thirty-two years of age, and 32.2 percent between thirty-three and forty-two years of age. I am unable to understand how, on the basis of these numbers, Arendt can conclude that over 60 percent of the women members of the KPD were under twenty-five years of age and 45 percent were even younger than twenty years old; see Hans-Jürgen Arendt, "Weibliche Mitglieder der KPD in der Weimarer

from the economic misery but also from the tectonic shifts in the structures of power in the family. But in so doing, it exposed itself to an
internal dynamics that, because the party did not analyze its workings,
was largely removed from its political influence.[116] The "radicalism" its
young male members exposed was thus often found "nonpolitical,"
had not been politically fathomed, and found its precise opposite and
counterimage in the external appearance and impression made by
young female blue- and white-collar workers. In contemporary studies,
these young women were regularly denigrated as "frivolous."[117] They
were accused of having a penchant for diversion; of relishing amusement, movies, dancing, and raucous fun; and of having a highly blink-
ered range of interest, restricted to fashion, consumption, flirtation,
and men. These women generally remained internally alien to the
KPD, which castigated all their passions as morally reprehensible.
With their propensity for hedonism, they were of little practical use for
the work of the party, and they were seldom taken seriously.[118] Their
distinctive feature was their radical earthiness that sprang from the
fleeting moment, opposed to any and all long-term reflection. It is thus
not surprising that a female Reichstag deputy of the KPD and a fore-
man in a factory both summed up the "limited utility" of these young
proletarian women in the same words: "They're all a bit too frivolous
and flighty, their heads filled with other things."[119]
Juxtaposed to the mass of these girls was a small contingent whose
very personality inclined toward communism.

> If you take a closer look at the type of youth communist women, it
> hardly fits in with anything that has been said about the female fac-
> tory worker. With her powerful almost masculine head, her well-
> turned athletic figure, her functional clothing, this girl does not
> make the impression of someone fun-loving, but rather pragmatic

---

Republik—Zahlenmäßige Stärke und soziale Stellung," *Beiträge zur Geschichte der Arbeiter-bewegung* 19, no. 4 (1977): 659f.; Franzen-Hellersberg, "Die Frau und die Jugendbewegung," 90.

116. In a similar way, the party also lacked clarity when it came to the rowdyism of young street fighters. Here, too, the KPD appropriated proletarian ways of behavior without really being able to influence and shape them; see Rosenhaft, *Beating the Fascists!* 146ff.

117. See Erna Barschak, *Die Schüler in der Berufsschule und ihre Umwelt* (Berlin, 1926); Franzen-Hellersberg, *Die jugendliche Arbeiterin;* Jüngst, *Die jugendliche Fabrikarbeiterin.*

118. Rosenhaft, *Beating the Fascists!* 154.

119. Quoted in Franzen-Hellersberg, "Die Frau und die Jugendbewegung," 90.

and streetwise. Every movement exudes an aura of the Amazonian.[120]

These girls corresponded to Communist conceptions that anticipated the woman as a reliable comrade, her life centered around political struggle. Her relation with the opposite sex was to be based on a sense of partnership, permeated by cool-headed functionality. As a result, they abandoned any and all "female" trinkets; and by not tying down the man and confusing him with erotic allurements, they released him for work in and for the party. A striking cameo of this new woman was projected by the poem "Image of a Woman from the New Russia," published by the paper *Rote Fahne* on June 23, 1931.

The dust cloth's gone, the broom's cast aside
Don't call me a woman, to be a comrade is my pride.
Take me as an example, girls, listen and hear
My youngster, an infant, already is pioneer.

We've got full rid of the pastor
Our nuptials performed by a justice of the peace.
Our culture of the body is bringing flush renewal
I wear no make-up, not even a jewel.

Whose hand's still adorned with flashy rings?
Whose face with rouge still clings?
A woman is your partner, don't forget that, young lad
Or remain forever bachelor, unmarried and sad!

[Das Staubtuch ist weg, der Besen ist hin,
Ich heiß nicht mehr Frau, heiße Bürgerin.
O, nehmt euch, ihr Frauen, ein Beispiel an mir,
Mein Jüngster ist Säugling und schon Pionier.

Wir haben den Pfaffen bereits abgebaut.
Uns beide hat nur der Beamte getraut.
Die Körperkultur uns Erneuerung bringt.
Ich geh ungepudert, ich geh ungeschminkt.

120. The number of those who were serious, longer-term members of a Communist youth league has been estimated at 1 to 2 percent at the most; see Franzen-Hellersberg, "Die Frau und die Jugendbewegung," 91.

Wer trägt noch die Hände mit Ringen verziert?
Wer hat noch die Fratze mit Farbe verschmiert?
Ein Mann, der zur Frau als Genossin nicht spricht,
Bleibt Junggeselle, den heiratet nicht!]

This female ideal not only contrasted in many ways with the girls and women from the working-class milieu; it was also older historically, harking back to the bourgeois movements for emancipation of the nineteenth and early twentieth centuries.

Youth Organization and Gender Relations

On August 25, 1926, an article appeared in the *Berliner Tageblatt* by Gabriele Tergit, entitled "The Struggle over the Flag."[121]

Two young women, Schuster and Hundke, stand accused. They make no bones about the fact that the year is 1926. And one wears a short skirt and hair to match. And has more of a liking for boldness than distinction. In addition, the two ladies had learned their German on the pavements in the more northern reaches of Berlin.

It's all about politics. In the beautiful month of May, patriotic associations staged a march. So Fräulein Fülge was quick to hang a black, white, and red flag from her window. Now in a building where all the possible shades and hues of German politics were represented, that was bound to cause some ill feeling. This intensified to the point where an angry crowd gathered before the house. Several men separated from the murmuring mob and tried to make their way to Fräulein Fülge's black, white, and red flag fluttering in the breeze. That was prevented when the doors were slammed loudly shut. But the ladies Schuster and Hundke had better luck. They wanted to remove the flag, and the word "filthy swine" was heard above the crowd's murmur. Two days after this clash, as Fräulein Fülge was returning home accompanied by a lady friend, Madames Schuster and Hundke were waiting in the lurch for her in the vestibule. In the words of her friend, one of the women lunged at Fräulein Fülge, "pushing and beating her." To make a long

---

121. In deliberations on the adoption of the new Weimar constitution, there were long heated arguments about what the flag should be. The compromise finally worked out was that the national colors should be, memorializing the German Revolution of 1848–49, black, red, and gold. The right-wing parties had vehemently] espoused sticking to the colors of the old empire—black, red, and white. The national colors as embodied in the flag also remained a symbol during the Weimar Republic for its acceptance or rejection.

matter short, a real scuffle broke out. Or rather a scratching free-for-all. And all this, the court reporter muses, because of a fight over a flag?! How improbable can you get? How very doubtful, despite women's suffrage. But this drama is nonetheless about the chasms separating two worldviews: Because the witness Fräulein Fülge, with a large blond braid in her hair, and a white cambric dress that hangs down to her flat-heeled shoes is protest incarnate against 1926, and Madames Hundke's and Schuster's more real and shorter-skirted views on life." And then she said I was some sort of creature beneath her," Frau Hundke complains. "I sure ain't beneath the likes of her."[122]

With this triad of Fräulein Fülge, Frau Schuster, and Frau Hundke, Gabriele Tergit attempted to capture two characteristic types of the female generation. How do they differ? Fräulein Fülge with her staid white cambric dress, her blond braid, and flat-heeled shoes can easily be pigeonholed: she is part of the *Jugendbewegung* and the *Lebensreform,* the life reform movement. By marked contrast, Frau Schuster and Frau Hundke embody the "new woman" of the Weimar Republic, whose external emblem was the bobbed hair.

The bobbed hairstyle means far more than some matter of external form. It became something akin to the expression of a view of the world, a philosophy of freedom and life, a characteristic of everything that was progressive—the symbol of being free, at least from a few common prejudices.

Out on the Kurfürstendamm in the heart of Berlin, the snipping of one's braids was "publicly" celebrated as the symbolic act of an open break with tradition, and there are reports of emotional scenes where the women "broke out in tears."[123] Female emancipation acquired its physical emblem in the bobbed hairstyle—*dem Bubenkopf* (boy's head)—a special rather severe and masculine haircut that became something you could buy, a commodity that spelled freedom. For the young female factory and office workers, the shorter hairstyle was the stylish new trend with which they expressed their attitude of being open to life in the present. These women were distinguished by an unsublimated vitality, which also included their relation with the opposite sex. Sporting their bob, the girls demonstrated that they were "children of their times."[124] Their relations with men were not defined by

122. *Berliner Tageblatt,* Oct. 6, 1925.
123. *Berliner Tageblatt,* Oct. 6, 1925.
124. Klaus Mann, *Kind dieser Zeit* (Berlin, 1932).

bourgeois conventions, and they confidently sought to pursue their own sexual wishes and dreams for partnership.

Instead of immediacy, Fräulein Fülge, on the other hand, valued "distinction." Her cambric dress that reached to the ground was a clear farewell to pleasure. Instead of fun, she cherished "higher ideals," such as the black, white, and red flag.

And it was hardly a coincidence that Frau Schuster and Frau Hundke lived in the more northern reaches of the Berlin metropolis—in Wedding. Here in particular you could find many women who in numerous contemporary sociological studies were accused of superficiality, a weakness for consumerism and sexual interests.[125] There were similar descriptions of the young female shop and office workers, the new masses of "typists" and "shop assistants" whose incomes and social background were barely different from that of the factory workers.[126] Characteristic for the tenor of these statements is a quotation from a study by Lisbeth Franzen-Hellersberg on the young female worker: "It is correct to say that in the case of 80 to 90 percent of them [the young female workers], eroticism is a kind of recompense for their unhappy childhood, a compensation for their unsatisfying jobs. Eroticism for them is the fulfillment of a life that is so poor in intellectual content and impressions. It is the natural release for everything else."[127]

As Detlev Peukert stresses, the perception of the young in the field of social research on the young that established itself after World War I was shaped by social and class views.[128] In the case of the female researchers at least, it was not solely bourgeois middle-class origin that shaped the norms of their views on social pedagogy. Even where they had not been active participants themselves, the Jugendbewegung became the measure of ideal of the human being and the pedagogical efforts of this generation of researchers. Precisely when it came to the relation between the sexes, the Jugendbewegung had established new criteria with its ideal of comradeship. The girl in the youth movement had become a comrade by means of the concept of youth that was equally valid for both genders. "The fact that the Youth Movement also included girls as part of youth: with this seemingly obvious

---

125. See Barschak, *Die Schüler in der Berufsschule;* Franzen-Hellersberg, *Die jugendliche Arbeiterin;* Jüngst, *Die jugendliche Fabrikarbeiterin.*

126. See Grossmann, *Reforming Sex.*

127. Franzen-Hellersberg, *Die jugendliche Arbeiterin,* 86.

128. Detlev Peukert, *Grenzen der Sozialdisziplinierung. Aufstieg und Krise der deutschen Jugendfürsorge von 1878 bis 1932* (Cologne, 1986), 164f.

demand it probably broke in the most powerful way with conventional bourgeois notions of girlhood."[129]

Instead of girls being socially pigeonholed as a "future wife and mother," and dependent on the man, the notion of a period of development between childhood and adulthood provided them with an opportunity to develop their own personality. If eroticism was downplayed to an equal extent, this not only was the product of a demand for abstention beholden to bourgeois convention[130] but also sprang from the very nature of this form of education in and for community. In a special issue of the periodical of the Reich Committee of the German Youth Associations *Das junge Deutschland,* entitled "Changes and the Current State of Common Coeducational Education in the Youth Associations," Max-Otto Katz wrote in retrospect in 1930: "Coeducation is an attempt to simplify the question of the sexes. In it, through being naturally together from an early age, the sexual tensions between girls and boys are intended to be reduced to a minimum."[131]

In the youth leagues, the idea of comradeship was not uncontroversial, and especially after the publication of Blüher's book *Bourgeois and Intellectual Antifeminism* in 1916, it was discussed ever more frequently and with increasing vehemence.[132] While for some the demand for a community between the sexes with simultaneous strict sexual abstinence led to an atmosphere of "sterile innocence," others feared boys could become more "effeminate" and girls more "masculine." At the beginning of the 1920s, the debate led on the one hand to a fundamental acceptance of sexual relations and on the other hand to a more pronounced separation of the sexes in conjunction with a more strict organization and "masculinizing" of the youth organizations that was generally observable.[133] Yet this new relation between the sexes could

129. Busse-Wilson, "Liebe und Kameradschaft," 327. On the history of girls in the youth movement, see Andresen, *Mädchen und Frauen in der bürgerlichen Jugendbewegung;* Musial, "Jugendbewegung und Emanzipation der Frau"; Klönne, *"Ich spring in diesem Ringe";* de Ras, *Körper, Eros und weibliche Kultur;* Schade, *Ein weibliches Utopia.*

130. Busse-Wilson, "Liebe und Kameradschaft," 328ff.

131. *Das junge Deutschland* 24, no. 4 (1930): 198. Leonhard Burger argues in a similar way in regard to the *Naturfreunde-Jugend* (188).

132. Hans Blüher, *Der bürgerliche und geistige Antifeminismus* (Berlin, 1918); Elisabeth Busse-Wilson, *Die Frau und die Jugendbewegung. Ein Beitrag zur weiblichen Charakterologie und zur Kritik des Antifeminismus* (Hamburg, 1920). A kind of prelude to this discussion was the short essay by Hans Breuer "Das Teegespräch" in the periodical *Wandervogel* in 1911, as well as Hildegard Wegscheider's response to it. See also Claudia Bruns, "Vom Antifeminismus zum Antisemitismus. Kontroversen um Hans Blüher in der Frauen- und Jugendbewegung," in *Ariadne. Forum für Frauen- und Geschlechtergeschichte* 43 (2003): 46–51.

133. Among the earliest pleas was Alfred Kurella's essay "Körperseele" in the journal *Freideutsche Jugend* in July 1918, which is worth reading today solely for its high-sounding

not be characterized either as progressive or reactionary. Instead, a paradigm had taken hold in all groups and associations: the paragon of comradeship.[134] The new ideal of objectified sexual relations was valid quite apart from whether a common or separate organization was preferred or whether sexual relations were permitted or not.[135] Objectified sexual relations were considered the desired norm both in National Socialist and Communist organizations, even if that sometimes clashed with reality. Two examples can illustrate this.

Let me also say something here about the brides of the men in the SA. When the most dangerous moment arrived, after work, as they walked home, often with their comrades, SA buddies, but often also alone, through these seemingly so quiet streets, then they were there too. They walked on the other side of the street, in order to have their weapon ready if needed. Or to vanish with it if not. And they played an important role in putting up posters. And at home, it was necessary to wash the shirts, carefully sew on their small uniform mirrors, and in many cases also dish out dinner. They were like SA men, these girls. Did they want some thanks? A handshake was enough.[136]

Our slogan is: everything for the proletarian masses. Love too. If it serves in the class struggle, promotes it, gives new strength, then it is good, no matter how the people went about it. But if it gives rise to

pathos. The objective tone of the Weimar Republic is still totally absent in his discourse. See *Freideutsche Jugend* 4, no. 7 (1918): 235–52.

134. Already in 1924, Leopold von Wiese writes in the foreword to his book *Kindheit* (Childhood), in which he worked through and reflected on his memories of his education in Prussian military academies, "Everywhere in Germany we can see more and more signs of a voluntary 'militarization' of education. What I mean by that is not external preparations for war but an internal shaping of young people according to the rules and principles of a spirit of obedience." See Leopold von Wiese, *Kindheit. Erinnerungen aus meinen Kadettenjahren* (Hannover, 1924). The brightly dressed throng of *Wandervögel,* in short pants, checked shirts, and dresses from the Reform back-to-nature movement, wandering through the forests, guitar in hand, became in the course of the 1920s something else: a rigidly organized group according to the model of the scouts, with uniform clothing and a strict code of rules. To become a member often meant passing a test with fixed, rigorously specified conditions. The tendency toward "scoutization" affected all the youth organizations equally, including religious and left-wing youth organizations. It became ever stronger toward the end of the 1920s and the beginning of the 1930s. It is clear that in the eyes of such groups girls were less and less acceptable as members.

135. It should be noted that attempts to objectify relations between the sexes can be traced back to the beginnings of the modern era. See Reese, "Jenseits der 'Ordnung der Geschlechter.'

136. Julek Karl von Engelbrechten, *Eine braune Armee entsteht. Die Geschichte der Berlin-Brandenburgischen SA* (Munich, 1937), 166.

confusion and creates chains, then get rid of it. Then it's petty bourgeois, sentimental, backward. Not until we have a free, socialist
state will we be able to love as we want. In a way that everyone likes.
Then there will be nothing but comradeship and sexuality.[137]

But Max Fürst, who belonged to a leftist group that was not connected to a political party inside the Jewish youth movement, also
writes about a lack of sexual awareness coupled with great physical
openness among the young members.[138] So objectifying gender relations did not flow at all from some specific ideological view. Rather, it
sprang directly from organization itself and was the result of the fact
that the content and goals of the organization came between the sexes
on the one hand, while on the other hand they gathered their interests
together on a new rational level. "Every group formation in youth
achieves its final meaning only after it begins to slow down the individual's personal sexual attachment."[139]

The opposite of the ideal of comradeship predominant in the organizations and propagated by them was the eroticized relation between
the sexes that held sway among young female factory and pink-collar
workers. Researchers on youth culture postulated that the girls had
surrendered to a "culturally destructive" quest for "superficial pleasure."[140] They noted that the greater mass of the girls was trapped in a
kind of "this-worldly mundane universe."[141] Contrasted with them
were the small number of young females who committed themselves to
higher, nonpersonal goals.[142] Quite aside from their social place and
political views, they were considered the desired elite.

How Young People Spent Their Free Time before 1933

Free Time in Wedding before 1933

We used to play a lot out on the street. Marbles, we'd spin tires, play
ball, there was hardly any traffic. We used to play *Völkerball* on the

137. Walter Schönstedt, *Kämpfende Jugend. Roman der arbeitenden Jugend* (1932;
reprint, Berlin, 1971), 88.
138. See Max Fürst, *Talisman Scheherezade. Die schwierigen 20er Jahre* (Munich and
Vienna, 1976), 99ff. *Das junge Deutschland* 24, no. 4 (1930): 173.
139. *Das junge Deutschland* 24, no. 4 (1930): 173.
140. See Elisabeth Knoche, "Die jüngste Mädchengeneration. Versuch einer psycholo-
gischen Überschau und eines pädagogischen Ausblickes," *Das junge Deutschland* 24, no. 9
(1930): 394–99.
141. Knoche, "Die jüngste Mädchengeneration," 395
142. Knoche, "Die jüngste Mädchengeneration," 399.

street, cops and robbers, oh all kinds of games! As I always say, you just gotta feel sorry for kids nowadays. I mean, they've got everything, but they sure don't have a real childhood today. Not like it used to be. We played down in the courtyard, like we'd draw an apartment with chalk, then we laid out blankets and brought down our dolls, kids' chairs and stuff. And we played the whole day. I mean, today you just won't see kids doing that. (B 1)

In the 1920s and 1930s, the working-class neighborhood Wedding had few facilities especially geared to the wants of children or teenagers. The parks were designed for adults in need of recreation, not for children. Children were to be kept out: they were prohibited from trespassing the meadows and had to keep on the pathways, and there was a special guard appointed to see to it that this regulation was enforced. There was a small number of sandboxes for the smallest children (in the Humboldthain, the Rehberge area, in Schiller Park, and at the Gesundbrunnen). In Schiller Park and the Rehberge, the city had also set up a wading pond. There was nothing whatsoever for children who were a little older: nowhere any horizontal bars, nowhere a swing or teeter-totter.

Just as Wedding lacked facilities, there was also not enough time for mothers to devote to their children. Franzen-Hellersberg reports that it was fathers who would take their children out for a walk, strolling in the park on Sunday morning, while their wives were busy at home with the household chores.[143]

The more restricted the amount of time their mothers had at their disposal, the sooner the children integrated into the community of kids out on the street. Gravitating toward the pavements, they removed themselves ever more from the grip of authority: parental control and educational influence. They pursued their games and fun in the courtyards and on the street, gaining great pleasure from the simplest things, like a ball, an old tire, a top to spin, marbles, jumping rope, chalk, dolls, in wintertime a sled. Roller skates or scooters were expensive yet much-desired bits of luxury few could afford.

We were so poor and I wanted so bad to have roller skates. Well, see, I played marbles, and after winning a few games, I'd gotten

143. Franzen-Hellersberg, "Die Frau und die Jugendbewegung," 49. The report of a young man cited by Krolzig points in a similar direction: "Sunday I go out with my dad and sister for a walk, while mom stays home and cooks dinner. Or we visit a museum or take in some other sights"; Krolzig, *Der Jugendliche in der Großstadtfamilie,* 126.

myself some animal on those little wooden wheels, the kind little kids have. I'd been playing a lot, and so I had managed to get some of those things. Well, I took a piece of rope and I sat down on the curb in Glasgower Straße and tied these animals on rollers right to my feet. And I thought: who cares about them, you've got a pair of roller skates now too! Then I stood up and—well, these things just cracked apart under the weight, crunch. (B 5)

In descriptions of the children's games given in most of the interviews, there's a sense of how carefree their play was. Yet the space available to children was clearly restricted. In the courtyards, a "doorman" made sure there was peace and quiet and prevented the kids from engaging in any kind of play. Out on the major thoroughfares, the traffic had already pushed the children off the street. The scant natural open land that remained either was built up, as in the Rehberge area, or its attractiveness for children had been significantly reduced by a recreation park laid out on the site.

For example, we also went to Schönholzer Forest, that was the only wooded area you could really move around in. Because in the park, like Schiller Park and the Rehberge and Humboldthain and all those spots, everything was just paths to walk on. I mean, there was no big grassy area where you could lie down, the way it is today. All that part was sealed off. And then there used to be those guards, why they'd start walloping you right off. For example, once we threw some stones to knock down chestnuts. And the guard ran over and hit us with his walking stick. I was all swollen, let me show you, swollen right here from that. And the Schönholzer Forest, for those of us in Gesundbrunnen, that was the closest spot. It was in Schönholz, over in Pankow. So we used to go over there a lot. We were a few kids from the block, we'd light out and run over there. And we took along a blanket, and I got a bottle to take along too, with raspberry juice drink. Yes, I sure remember that. (B 1)

It was precisely in the poorest social strata that this limitation on space for the children generated destructiveness and aggression.

B 7: Us, the kids on the block, yeah, we all played together. Then we said let's go to the Plumpe [Panke, the small brook running through Wedding], and so we all went there. Or we just continued with our games where we were. Or, what was pretty bad, we'd get

involved in street battles. It was awful, with clubs and stuff, I
didn't like it at all.

I: You used clubs?

B 7: Yeah, they were all tough kids, brutal, but they didn't swing
the clubs so hard, the excitement was much better. Oh, the excitement. Then I went with my girlfriend. I wanted to kind of check
out the place. Oh, we were so interesting, us kids. So we went over
there, and counted, OK, how many of us are there? Then we came
back: OK, now so and so many here! Then we all got together for
a rumble, see, we'd rip into them, and, well, maybe they tore into
us too. But anyhow, what the heck, I mean, nobody was killed.

The atmosphere at home was in stark contrast to their outside
world: there were rarely any games in the small, cramped apartments.
On rainy days, the kids would stay at home with their brothers and sisters; at the most another friend came over as well. Maybe there was a
doll's house or a toy farm; often all they had to while away the time
were a few decals or a small papier-mâché doll that you could dress and
undress. The children resorted to their rich capacity for make-believe.

Then there was this coat lining, the material was delivered in large
boxes. There were always tubes, the lining was wrapped around
these big cardboard tubes. And when the boxes were empty, they'd
be standing up against the wall. And I'd get inside, see, and pretend
that was my train or something. And I'd take off in the thing, I
mean, in my imagination. (B 16)

The free time spent with the family had a quite different character
from the playtime activities with the other children on the block.
Going on vacation was a rarity, among my interviewees almost nonex-
istent. So the rare weekend family excursions ranked among the high
points of their childhood. The trips to the country, out to see the trees
in bloom in Werder, down to Potsdam, Bernau, Tegel, or even just
over to Lake Plötzensee, crystallized into veritable family rituals.

Our aunt, she'd always come along. Once a year it was obligatory to
go to Potsdam. Everybody went to Potsdam, it was a real big excursion, I mean, *the* big family excursion. Or we'd go to Werder, to see
the trees in bloom. Then we'd drink apple cider or something, it was
real cheap. Back then, the only expensive thing was the train ticket.
Like to Potsdam the ticket was 50 or 60 pfennigs, but for us that was

a lot of money at the time, so my aunt always used to pay for that. But it was obligatory, to take the annual trip, once a year we went to the zoo, and once a year to Potsdam. That was obligatory in our family. (B 12)

A special attraction were *Lauben,* very simple wooden summer houses with a small garden, and in rare cases the family even had a small boat.

The grandparents of one of our girlfriends had a summer house, and once we went along with her. Oh, it was terrific, like we went swimming in the fountain, we picked some strawberries to eat, that was something real nice. (B 7)

But in some families there wasn't even enough money for the train fare, and in many cases the stultifying routine of workaday life paralyzed any desire to take some initiative. One interviewee, when asked what she did on weekends, replied: "Oh, we had to stay home and put our stuff in order. Then we had to darn and wash, and tidy up the cabinets" (B 3).

At the age of fourteen most boys and girls in Wedding finished school and began an apprenticeship or work in a factory. The generous free time they had had was now a shrunken image of its former self, reduced to a few hours in the evening, Saturday afternoon, and Sunday. In Dinse's study on leisure time among urban youth, 9 percent complained that they had too little free time. This was a common complaint among the girls, especially the shop clerks.[144] A salesgirl commented: "When I started my apprenticeship, I didn't have much time left. If I was lucky, I got home from work at 8:00 p.m." (B 13).

The working day was long and physically exhausting.[145] There was hardly any energy left for organizing spare time in the evening. Generally people got a quick bite to eat and then met a friend or a group of friends. They strolled through the street, talked, flirted with guys, and maybe took in a movie in the nearby neighborhood movie theater.

B 13: Then I went out, stayed until 10:00 or 11:00, came back and went to sleep, and the next morning . . .

144. Dinse, *Das Freizeitleben der Großstadtjugend,* 7.
145. According to Mewes, the average working day of a young person in an urban area was eleven hours, fifteen minutes; see Bernhard Mewes, *Die erwerbstätige Jugend. Eine statistische Untersuchung* (Berlin and Leipzig, 1929), 68.

I: What did you do outside on the street?

B 13: Well, what did we do? Let's see, uh, we took walks, gabbed. There was a lot of endless talking, it went on and on. And we were in these cliques, like we were together, see, all the same age. Yeah, and actually then we stayed together too, leastwise til the war came. Then one got killed, he was drafted, and then we got bombed out. (B 13)

The young Wedding girls took little advantage of the many opportunities for amusement offered by Berlin, or as Kelchner formulates it: "Most of the girls had little interest in consciously utilizing their free time in any specific direction."[146] The girls spent a substantial proportion of their sparse leisure time helping their mothers with the housework.[147] There was keen interest in sports among the girls, especially in gymnastics, swimming, hiking, and excursions to the country. Some enjoyed handicrafts,[148] while others played parlor games. Due simply to financial reasons alone, musical interests in Wedding were reduced to the passive listening of popular music on the radio and gramophone. But the most popular diversion was going to the movies.

Movie parties. We'd go from one show to the next. There were lots of movie houses around here. Alhambra, the Pharus Halls, then there was the Schiller Theater across the way, and then a little before you got to Wedding, the World Theater. Then, where Aldi supermarket is nowadays, over on the Reinickerdorfer, there was the Holland Theater. So there were these shows all over, lots of movies. (B 6)

There were but few large movie houses in Wedding but a sizable number of small neighborhood theaters.

We always used to call them slipper shows, you could almost go there in your house shoes. . . . nearly on every corner in our neighborhood there was a movie show, small shows, maybe 20 rows of

146. Kelchner, *Die weibliche werktätige Jugend,* 257.
147. Dinse reports that some 56 percent of the semiskilled and nonskilled female workers he surveyed did housework; see Dinse, *Das Freizeitleben der Großstadtjugend,* 17ff. See also Jüngst, *Die jugendliche Fabrikarbeiterin,* 51; Kelchner, *Die weibliche werktätige Jugend,* 258.
148. In Wedding this was some 43 percent; see Dinse, *Das Freizeitleben der Großstadtjugend,* 34.

seats, six to eight across. Like in our immediate vicinity, I was familiar with at least three or four that were real close by. (B 10)[149]

The program was geared to the public's tastes.

Posters in garish yellow, red and green colors invite you to visit
exciting sensational films. Five, six, seven old ones! Luciano Alber-
tini! Harry Piel!—shout the banners. The names of the actors guarantee exciting "adventures" beyond every expectation. Excessively
cheap, sugar-coated shots of some film goddess promise big thrills.
Along with nationalistic propaganda, militaristic nonsense and
Philistine sentimentality in films like "Das deutsche Mutterherz,"
"Die dritte Eskardon," "Die elf Schillschen Offiziere." All tickets 50
pfennigs, or 50 pfennigs for the cheapest seats, 60 for rear stalls and
70 pfennigs for a box seat.[150]

In our small neighborhood shows, naturally they didn't get every
new movie, and we didn't go downtown to take in a film. Nope, we
never did that. (B 10)

According to what Dinse terms a representative survey, 88 percent
of the films mentioned by Wedding girls were R-rated movies,
restricted for young people.[151]

We went to the movies very often, and we always tried to trick them
a little, like we'd lie about our age. Then we heard how the others
did it. "Are you 18?"—"Sure, of course, naturally I'm 18." And then
sometimes we did just the opposite. Like there used to be movies for
kids to the age of 14, tickets were just 40 pfennigs. So we'd pretend
to be young girls, we laughed a lot and acted like kids so as to make
them think we were just 14. (B 19)

Dinse explains the fact that young people preferred the movies to
going to a play or concert by economic constraints: "for most, what
they actually can afford is simply a ticket to see a movie."[152] To con-
tend that notion is, I think, an inaccurate assessment of the actual real-

149. B13 and B 14 report the same information.
150. *Rote Fahne*, Sept. 5, 1926.
151. Dinse, *Das Freizeitleben der Großstadtjugend*, 72.
152. Dinse, *Das Freizeitleben der Großstadtjugend*, 71.

ity. By opting for the movies, young people were at the same time
choosing the medium with the greatest power of suggestion. In a world
of hopelessness, the dreams and wishes of those whose empty lives
denied them any sense of self-actualization were fulfilled vicariously as
they watched these celluloid dreams. Especially for the girls, movies
provided a valued surrogate for real life, because it was so readily
affordable and close at hand.

> If you ask what other interests the girls have, it's pretty spare pick-
> ings. Right at the top is movies! . . . To a certain extent, a knowledge
> of the latest weekly films is part of the general education of the
> working woman.[153]

Echoing through the complaints voiced by the social workers dealing with the young is an abiding elitist sense of superiority about
motion pictures, a form of entertainment that had become part of popular mass culture in the 1920s. That attitude decried the cult of cheap
diversion, the lack of any intellectual and moral challenge to movie-
goers. These educators contrasted the silver screen with the stage, but
unlike the ubiquitous movie houses, the theater remained a sphere
apart, hardly accessible to one and all.[154]

In addition to the price of a theater ticket, you also had to be able to
pay for a wardrobe suitable for going to a theater performance. Girls
in particular found that their meager wages barely sufficed for any such
finery: "I've never been to a theater, no. But I do have a boyfriend, and
I guess later on I'll go there sometime too."[155] Yet the primary reason
behind the scant interest in the theater was that it failed to ignite audi-
ences: "most mediocre stage plays have as much of an obligation to
address the feelings of theatergoers and respond to present-day realities as motion pictures, from which they differ only by the greater boredom they exude."[156]

Aside from the "comedies and tragedies, highbrow revues and
assorted tricks of the director's trade dedicated to the intellectual
(Berlin) bourgeoisie,"[157] the theater targeted a middle-class and lower-

153. Jüngst, *Die jugendliche Fabrikarbeiterin,* 90.
154. "From the workers in the suburban neighborhood movie houses all the way to the
upper classes in the Palasttheater, today all social strata are flocking to the cinema"; Siegfried
Kracauer, "Film 1928," in Kracauer, *Das Ornament der Masse* (Frankfurt a.M., 1977), 295.
155. Quoted in Dinse, *Das Freizeitleben der Großstadtjugend,* 73.
156. Siegfried Kracauer, "Die kleinen Ladenmädchen gehen ins Kino," in Kracauer, *Das
Ornament der Masse,* 282.
157. Kracauer, "Die kleinen Ladenmädchen," 282.

middle-class audience. For these strata, going to the theater was not only food for the mind but also a social event, a status symbol. By becoming a member of a theater community, the upwardly mobile sought entry into "higher circles," while their children in high school were initiated into "better culture" by means of drama in the schools.

My parents had always been members of the *Volksbühne,* and you could always go along as their guest. So they'd regularly get me a ticket, too, and I saw all the plays that were put on. That was always really nice. (B 16)

Light entertainment was the preferred fare, such as stage shows, operettas, and musicals.

Actually, we used to go to the theater quite a lot back in those days. I just can't recall, maybe with my uncle, I went with him or with some girl friends. We went to the Admiralspalast, at the Friedrich-straße Station, then there was the Wintergarten, which was destroyed by bombs later. But in the beginning, it was still there, and we saw a lot of plays. Then, let's see, there was Theater des Volkes, the Friedrichstadtpalast, before it used to be called Theater des Volkes. That place was always jumping, lots going on. Of course, not musicals, I mean, there were real stage plays, operettas, and drama. They performed plays like *Des Meeres und der Liebe Wellen* or *Minna von Barnhelm.* (B 21)[158]

Yet someone who had never had the pleasure of attending a gala performance at the Admiralspalast, the Friedrichstadtpalast, or the Wintergarten did have the chance to go to a "genuine" Wedding theater, such as the one on "red" Kösliner Straße, housed for a few years on the premises of a former movie house.[159]

B 7: That was a pretty big theater, not small by any means. Once they put on the play *Ella, die Seiltänzerin.* And Ella, like she was a real blimp, I mean, just huge, and so we sat there and imagined her tiptoeing up on the tightrope. Well, that was how we amused ourselves.

I: And the players, were they some kind of amateur group?

158. These are plays by Franz Grillparzer and Gotthold Ephraim Lessing from the classical German repertory.
159. The theater was in operation until about 1935–36.

B 7: Well, they were us, we did it. OK, sure, some people were actually employed, regulars in the ensemble, had been for years, they
played all the roles, whether it was a mother or a queen, no matter. And if they needed extras, well, that's where we came in, and
they let us act with them, part of the play.

I: So the whole gang would get involved in the latest performance?

B 7: Yeah, right. And when I went down the street, why, I'd feel so
proud: me, Her Majesty the Queen. I told you the story with the
guy who took my wash and tried to get friendly. I said I didn't
know him. And he says: hey, I know you from the theater. My
God, I was already a married woman then!

If the theater was a socially recognized entertainment, the movie
house a widely accepted diversion, then a visit to the fairgrounds was
considered anything but commendable. Nonetheless, it was quite a
popular spot with young workers.

The booths are usually crammed in somewhere between the tenement buildings, each with its special "attraction." Every evening the
place is jumping, weekdays and Sundays. And every evening the
people pour in, young and old. But only proletarians. And unfortunately, many working-class young people.[160]

Overall, the various forms of diversion in Wedding were inexpensive
and unassuming, primarily a ready source of low-cost distraction.[161]
Leisure time meant whiling away one's free time with something
light and entertaining. Even their reading material reflected the desire
to flee their depressing everyday world and its massive lack of
prospects, seeking refuge in a world of fantasy. Dinse indicates that 69
percent of the unskilled female workers he surveyed said they did some
reading; in the case of store clerks it was even 80 percent. Way up at the
top of the list of their favorite authors was Hedwig Courths-Mahler, a
highly popular writer of tearjerkers and light romantic novels.[162]

160. *Rote Fahne,* June 5, 1926.
161. Especially for the KPD, this was a constant source of annoyance. They tried to
address the problem by appealing to morality, on the one hand, and, on the other, by developing their own cultural program (starting in the late 1920s and early 1930s). By using agit-
prop groups, such as "Roter Wedding," showing Soviet films, and organizing lectures and
musical evenings with singing, they sought to harness the cultural industry to stem the tide of
"stultification" and depoliticization in the working classes. However, these initiatives were
not reflected in any remarks by my interviewees.
162. See Dinse, *Das Freizeitleben der Großstadtjugend,* 46; Dehn, *Die religiöse Gedankenwelt,* 12; Peukert, *Grenzen der Sozialdisziplinierung,* 186ff.

These girls are tormented not only by a hunger for physical movement, but a hunger for intellectual experience. The actual sheer boredom of their lives leaves them parched, with a feverish thirst for impressions of any kind.[163]

What Kracauer noted in reference to film was also applicable to books: "The stupid and unrealistic cinematic fantasies are the daydreams of society: here its actual reality breaks to the surface, its otherwise repressed desires surge."[164] The need for diversion, "the great emotions that stir the heart," was compared with the need for physical movement, the pleasure in dancing. This latter desire was more powerful for the girls than for the boys.

> B 6: I loved to dance but wasn't allowed. I used to go out secretly to dance. When I was 17, I came in first in a competition for best dancer. And then I was afraid to go home with the prize, a ship made of crystal. But I could tell my mom. She said: "So you were out dancing again, kid? Hope your dad doesn't find out!"
> I: You weren't allowed to go dancing?
> B 6: I was 16, like 16 or 17. You weren't allowed at that age!
> I: But there were spots for afternoon dancing then, weren't there, what were called *Tanztees*?
> B 6: Yes, later on I went. When my brother was at the Excelsior Hotel, he got me some free tickets. Then I went with my girlfriend, to the Excelsior or the Esplanade. But earlier on, we used to sneak out and go dancing. Up the street on the corner . . . there used to be a big hall. On Müllerstraße, just before you get to Schumacher Square. You'd climb up these high stairs, and then in the back there was this large hall. But I had to be back home at 10:00. I used to go dancing on the sly, see, because I really loved it.

Hardly any girls went to dancing school; most learned how to dance from their girlfriends or brothers or by attending dances. What dance hall they opted for depended mainly on their social background. Unskilled female blue-collar workers generally had no more than three marks a week in their pocket,[165] so at best the dance floor of choice was one of the many local neighborhood establishments in Wedding.

163. Jüngst, *Die jugendliche Fabrikarbeiterin,* 78.
164. Kracauer, "Die kleinen Ladenmädchen," 280.
165. Dinse, *Das Freizeitleben der Großstadtjugend,* 84.

Very young girls, hardly a few months out of school, press their undernourished body up tight against that of their "partner," and both revel in the frenzied beat of steaming sensuality. . . . There's a break. The bodies, exuding sweat, sit down at the tables. There's smoking, drinking, the occasional flirt. The faces are aglow. "Hey man, is that dude a stupid dancer, he keeps stepping on your feet, the big lug," a young thing tells her girlfriend. This is the tone of the dance floor. Other talk is about bobbed hairdos, clothes, chic shoes you are just dying to buy—if only there were enough money.[166]

Girls with a little self-respect, which meant mainly the young white-collar workers, avoided such dance halls, frequenting instead a dance coffeehouse. There you could avoid the suspicion of immoral sensual excess simply by taking part in a virtuous five o'clock tea, with dancing on the side for entertainment. The high point was a late afternoon spent in one of the large Berlin coffeehouses, such as the Haus Vaterland, the Moka Efti, or Excelsior.

The sojourn between these walls, which signify the world, may be defined as a company outing to paradise for employees. The furnishings of the Moka-Efti-Lokal, whose spatial excesses are scarcely outdone by those of the Haus Vaterland, correspond to this exactly. A moving staircase, whose functions presumably include symbolizing the easy ascent to the higher social strata, conveys ever new crowds from the street directly to the Orient, denoted by columns and harem gratings. . . . Up here, you do not sit, you travel.[167]

Dance, in which the inner meaning of the times finds a symbolic expression, had risen to its most sober embodiment in the 1920s: emphasizing the rhythmic beat, it had become a veritable "cult of movement and motion."[168] Dance was thus an integral component of the battery of diversions for which an expanding cultural industry provided the prerequisites. Consumerism, sport, and the dream machinery of the cinema offered an outlet through which the harried masses could discharge the frustrations that built from their meaningless work and the rapidly shrinking scope for action. Beyond all the partisan lines of

166. *Rote Fahne,* Sept. 5, 1926.
167. Siegfried Kracauer, "Asyle für Obdachlose," in Kracauer, *Schriften,* vol. 1 (Frankfurt a.M., 1971), 188.
168. Siegfried Kracauer, "Die Reise und der Tanz," in Kracauer, *Schriften,* 41.

party politics, working-class youth in particular welcomed the wares of the cultural industry, girls apparently with greater gusto than young men. The more the social environment failed to satisfy their vital needs, the more they sought distraction in a world of illusion. Dinse is resigned in summing up the findings of his research on how urban youth used their leisure time:

> All the art and knowledge the large metropolis offers does not exist for the preponderant majority of our young people, because it is not accessible to them, and they are unprepared to appreciate its value. But the boys and girls are animated by a powerful inner longing for something reaching beyond the confines of their narrow everyday lives, something that holds out excitement and seems to fulfil their fantasies.[169]

Girls in the Youth Organizations

Günther Dehn noted early on that "almost 50 percent of all young people appear to be members in some sort of organization." But he also qualified that by saying that "only a very small percentage are in the hands of regular youth counselors, and far less are in the youth movement."[170] Using data supplied by the local and district committees for youth welfare, official statistics were gathered on how many persons between the ages of fourteen and twenty-one belonged to youth organizations in Prussia for the year 1928. The results indicated that 47 percent of all girls and 52 percent of all boys in this age group in Berlin were on the membership roll in some kind of organization.[171] This surprisingly high figure was discounted by arguing that the data on the total number of young people ages fourteen to twenty-one were inaccurate, thus skewing the findings.[172]

Just several months earlier, this same source had noted that about one-quarter of all young people in Berlin were in organizations, while some 75 percent "went their own way" during their leisure time.[173] Dinse arrived at similar conclusions, indicating that one-third of the

169. Dinse, *Das Freizeitleben der Großstadtjugend,* 72f.

170. Dehn, *Die religiöse Gedankenwelt,* 12f.

171. *Das junge Deutschland* 23, no. 12 (1929): 581.

172. Mewes, *Die erwerbstätige Jugend,* 158, points out that some were members in two organizations.

173. According to these figures, there were 719,432 young people in Berlin in the period 1925–27. Of these, 182,408 were in organizations, including 68,590 girls (37 percent); see *Das junge Deutschland* 23, no. 3 (1929): 126.

boys belonged to an organization but only one-quarter of the girls did so.[174]

All sources agree that a lower percentage of girls than boys were members of organizations. According to Mewes, the percentage of girls and boys in the leagues of the youth movement was roughly the same, but the religious associations had more female than male members and the number of girls in the sports associations was also high.[175]

No official statistics covered the young people who belonged to associations not affiliated with the Reich Committee of the German Youth Associations. These groupings included several leagues but primarily involved the political organizations, the Communist and National Socialist youth, the defense leagues (*Wehrverbände*), and numerous cliques. These latter played a key role particularly in the working class.[176] Yet girls were clearly underrepresented in these associations. So while we can assume that a greater percentage of young males in Wedding belonged to an association than official statistics indicate, the percentage of girls indicated is probably too high. Among my twenty-two interviewees, five were members of organizations before 1933. They belonged to an athletic association or a Communist or Socialist youth association. None before 1933 were members in a league of the youth movement or in the League of German Girls.

Bund deutscher Mädel

In a report over several installments published in 1933 with the telling title "Blutnächte im Wedding" (Nights of Blood in Wedding) Artur

---

174. Dinse, *Das Freizeitleben der Großstadtjugend*, 101f.

175. Mewes, *Die erwerbstätige Jugend*, 158.

176. A former member of a clique estimated the number of such cliques in Berlin at the end of the Weimar Republic at around 250, totaling 3,000 members; see Helmut Lessing and Manfred Liebel, *Wilde Cliquen. Szenen einer anderen Arbeiterjugendbewegung* (Bensheim, 1981), 39. The most profound newer study is Alfons Kenkmann, *Wilde Jugend. Lebenswelt großstädtischer Jugendlicher zwischen Wirtschaftskrise, Nationalsozialismus und Währungsreform* [= Düsseldorfer Schriften zur neueren Landesgeschichte und zur Geschichte Nordrhein-Westfalens, vol. 42] (Essen, 1996); see also Eve Rosenhaft, "Organizing the 'Lumpenproletariat' Cliques and Communists in Berlin during the Weimar Republic," in Richard J. Evans, ed., *The German Working Class, 1888–1933. The Politics of Everyday Life* (London, 1982), 174–219.

Axmann[177] described the development of the Hitler Youth in Wedding during the *Kampfzeit,* as the Nazi movement termed its "period of struggle" during the Weimar Republic:

> If I want to describe events truthfully, I'm forced to admit that the school kids in red Wedding helped initiate the conquest of the hearts and minds of the militant youth in the class struggle. They were also quite solid boys, guys with plenty of the ball. We attended the "6. Oberrealschule" [Senior General High School No. 6]. At the time that was the largest school in Prussia. Most of us paid no tuition fees, social exemption. A lot had parents who were dirt poor. And those parents said to themselves: look, we worked like mules all our life. Now we're going to have our son learn something useful, so he'll have a better deal than we ever did. What mother, what father, in their healthy wish to get ahead in life, has not had similar thoughts? . . . The seed soon started to grow, yielding first fruit. Our class became a Nazi class, our school a Nazi school.[178]

As Axmann stresses, the process of Nazification was sluggish, faltering.

> I can still recall the first meeting of pupils in Wedding. It was down at the "Kajüte" on Müllerstraße. The "Rummel" [fairgrounds] is close by. The street is brightly lit. Locals in Wedding have nicknamed it the "marriage market." You can hear hurdy-gurdy music and the calls of the hawkers. A swirl of people coming and going. This is where the "Kommune" [the Communists] decided to have its little rendezvous. We had to pass the "Rummel." I realized one thing early on: that I'd have to run the gauntlet there many more

---

177. Axmann, a member of the Hitler Youth since 1928, himself came from Wedding. In 1932 he was appointed head of the Organization for Nazi Youth in Factory Cells and later headed the Social Office of the Hitler Youth. In mid-1940, he was appointed Reich youth leader and thus successor to Baldur von Schirach, who was promoted to Gauleiter of Vienna. Axmann remained in this capacity until the end of the war.

178. *Der deutsche Sturmtrupp* 1, no. 6 (1933). Axmann's assertion that the "6. Oberrealschule" was Prussia's biggest is incorrect. According to the *Statistisches Jahrbuch der Stadt Berlin* 9 (1933): 148, the school had 664 pupils. That certainly made it one of the larger schools in Berlin but by no means the largest. The school was a reformed high school stressing math and modern languages.

times to come. Already on the way to the first meeting, that dawned on me. Suddenly someone lunged at us, a fist from the crowd. Bang, a couple of slaps right in my face. Even today I don't know who hit me. Now that was not what you'd call a favorable omen. I got to the hall. Stuck around, waiting there two hours. Nobody showed up. Then I went out into the street and stopped some fellow pupils I knew. I made five snapshots. I was very proud of that.[179]

The league of Nazi pupils began to unravel. Soon it existed only on paper.[180] But Axmann did not give up.[181]

There were plans to establish the Hitler Youth in Wedding. A *Gefolgschaftsführer,* a high-ranking Hitler Youth leader, contacted us. First we were supposed to motivate all the pupils to take part in the founding meeting. Each one of us had to bring along a young worker.[182]

By selling used paper and rags, they scrapped together enough money to print leaflets. The founding meeting of the Wedding Hitler Youth took place in a venue on the edge of the actual workers' quarter, in the *Versuchs- und Lehrbrauerei* (Experimental and Apprentice Brewery) located on Seestraße. Forty young men declared they would become members. But setting up the organization was not enough, just a start. Axmann goes on to describe the difficulties of the early period when the movement's "banner" shriveled rather than grew. Axmann also is careful to add that the "defectors" were mainly "cowards," idle "goldbrickers" whose sole motive was fear of the dangers of the "strug-

179. *Der deutsche Sturmtrupp* 1, no. 6 (1933). The "Kommune" most certainly did not decide to "have a rendezvous" at the Rummel fairgrounds. In the eyes of the KPD, such fairgrounds, especially the one in Wedding, were a degrading place of distraction and amusement for the working classes. This was a source of cheap diversion that distracted them from the class struggle. Numerous articles in the *Rote Fahne* warned people again and again to stay away from the fairgrounds, the haunt as a rule of the most destitute and the young.

180. *Der deutsche Sturmtrupp* 1, no. 6 (1933).

181. In practical terms, it was also impossible for Axmann to throw in the towel, so to speak, since, as he describes in the first installment of his "Nights of Blood," he himself had failed his high school leaving exam (Abitur). Naturally he blamed his political activities for his scholastic misfortune. Yet it seems logical that in the period of economic crisis in the early 1930s, marked by high unemployment, the Hitler Youth was for Axmann the only realistic alternative.

182. *Der deutsche Sturmtrupp* 1, no. 7 (1933).

gle" and the violence of the "commune." As Axmann would have it, the "wheat was separated from the chaff."[183]

In the later installments of Axmann's narrative, the "Nights of Blood in Wedding" were reduced to a march through the red "Fischer-kiez," a neighborhood not actually in Wedding;[184] Axmann's personal participation in a discussion with Communist youth at Sparrplatz;[185] a description of his own unlawful activity in a safe house somewhere in Brandenburg;[186] along with a few basic thoughts sandwiched in between—as well as a street battle with Communist boy scouts near the Post Stadium, a political rumble in which the Communists, as one might "expect," ended up slugging it out with each other.[187]

Like many National Socialist descriptions of the Kampfzeit, this one is also characterized by temporal inaccuracies and a dearth of facts, even if Axmann must have had a strong interest in painting as militant and active a picture of the Hitler Youth as possible on the turf of "red" Wedding, a classic workers' neighborhood hostile to National Socialism.

The simplest conclusion is the most illuminating. If we strip Axmann's narrative of its heroic pathos and look soberly at what lies beneath, then we can surmise that the stimulus for establishing a National Socialist youth organization in Wedding in the late 1920s came from those high schools that, as a result of their progressive character, were attempting to provide a ladder for "getting ahead through education" precisely to children from the lower middle classes. Yet down to the end of 1931, membership remained scant. After that the Hitler Youth did increase in terms of numbers, but one thing is clear from the few activities that Axmann mentions: in fact, down until the Nazis took over, the Hitler Youth in Wedding remained an insignificant element in the political landscape. Its strength in Berlin lay elsewhere, namely, in Wilmersdorf,[188] Steglitz, and quite evidently also in Neukölln.[189] Wedding evidently lacked that specific social stra-

183. *Der deutsche Sturmtrupp* 1, no. 7 (1933).
184. *Der deutsche Sturmtrupp* 1, no. 9 (1933).
185. *Der deutsche Sturmtrupp* 1, no. 13 (1933).
186. *Der deutsche Sturmtrupp* 1, no. 14 (1933).
187. *Der deutsche Sturmtrupp* 1, no. 15 (1933).
188. There were numerous meetings of the Hitler Youth there before 1933.
189. This was possibly due to the work of Robert Gadewoltz, the first Gau leader of the Hitler Youth, who was then replaced by Elmar Warning at the end of 1931 or beginning of 1932.

tum from which the Hitler Youth recruited amounting membership in other more middle-class districts of the city.[190]

Even if we lack analogous stories for the League of German Girls and its ambience in Wedding, the conclusions drawn from Axmann's narrative are nonetheless applicable, even in a heightened form, to the girls. If membership of the Hitler Youth in Wedding consisted primarily of children drawn from the lower middle classes who were secondary school pupils, at least up to their Mittlere Reife, it is evident that this included more boys than girls.[191] This was not only a question of class background. It was also the result of access patterns to leisure: young workers hardly had the necessary free time at their disposal to become members of the Hitler Youth. Consequently, one of the strongest girls' organizations before 1933 was the Nationalsozialistischer Schülerinnenbund (National Socialist League of Female Pupils, or NSSi).[192] Yet in Wedding, most girls were already working by the age of fourteen. Even the small number of girls who went to high school seldom graduated with the Abitur but rather left school after completing the tenth grade. On the other hand, before 1933 the League of German Girls had hardly any members who were younger than fourteen. That means that, before 1933 in Wedding, only very few young men and hardly any young girls existed that came from those social strata that members of the Nazi youth recruited their members from; neither the Hitler Youth nor the League of German Girls, therefore, could score any inroads into the youth sector in the working-class district of Wedding.

190. This contradicts Stachura's thesis that the Hitler Youth concentrated in the main on organizing working-class youth; see Stachura, *Nazi Youth in the Weimar Republic,* 57–62, and Stachura, "Das Dritte Reich und die Jugenderziehung. Die Rolle der Hitlerjugend 1933–1939," in Karl Dietrich Bracher, Manfred Funke, and Hans-Adolf Jacobsen, eds., *Nationalsozialistische Diktatur 1933–1945. Eine Bilanz* [= Schriftenreihe der Bundeszentrale für politische Bildung, Bonn, vol. 192] (Düsseldorf, 1983), 237. Interesting in this connection is an article by Hubertus Prinz zu Löwenstein in the *Berliner Tageblatt* (Jan. 8, 1931) entitled "Youth and National Socialism." He writes: "The swastika, through its honest espousal of socialism, has also gained followers among working-class youth, some of whom have been recruited from the ranks of the communists, because they feel disgruntled or disregarded there. National Socialism promised them a far more rapid transformation of the social order. . . . Yet despite their active propaganda among proletarian youth, the main contingent of National Socialism continues to consist of young men drawn from the lower-middle and middle classes."

191. In 1931 in Wedding, there was a municipal junior high school with 485 female pupils and two municipal girls' high schools with a total enrollment of 960 pupils. The total number of all high school pupils in Wedding at the time was 2,130, distributed among four schools; see *Statistisches Jahrbuch der Stadt Berlin* 9 (1933): 156, 154.

192. Stephenson, *Nazi Organization of Women,* 83.

The Nazi seizure of power in January 1933 constituted a turning point for the League of German Girls. A woman from Wedding recalls this watershed.

> B 1: Well, first of all, it was something we all expected. I mean, I'd already heard at home from my dad that the NSDAP would make it. It was January 30, and we were, well, let me tell you, we were all pretty enthusiastic, I mean we young people.
>
> I: What were your expectations?
>
> B 1: Well, nothing, actually. Basically, nothing at all. But there were a lot of us, I also left school in '32, I hadn't found an apprenticeship. And in '33, at the time, I was still unemployed. Then there were also some who were one or two years older than me, and they were all out of work. All of them used to hang out on the streets. And so they were enthusiastic. They said: now things are going to change. And then we simply decided, those of us from the block: OK, we're going to join the BDM.

These young people were swept up by a sense of enthusiasm for the national revolution, seized by a powerful mood of change, new departures, mixed with the hope that now everything would be different. It is not hard to reconstruct that popular sentiment. The young people, largely left to fend for themselves on the pavements of Wedding, decided to join the Hitler Youth and went in large cliques with their friends to their first evening gathering, the *Heimabend*. The economic situation they found themselves in at the end of the Weimar Republic also weighed heavily in that decision. Unemployment brought home to many the sense that they were superfluous, not needed, a kind of social flotsam.[193] Initially, substantive or ideological elements were scarcely a factor among reasons for joining up. Most of the girls were unfamiliar with the league's political aims or its concrete program. Rather, the decisive factor was the desire to be "in on the action," to "get involved"

---

193. Detlev Peukert's essay on youth unemployment during the Great Depression in Germany concludes that joblessness was the plight particularly of trained young males between the ages of eighteen and twenty-five, while the younger male workers and the female workers were still in demand as cheap labor in the job market. For this and other reasons, I have not dealt in greater depth in this study with the question of unemployment. Moreover, in my own sample, joblessness played a role at the most among the older generation of women, born around 1920, while the younger girls, the actual BDM generation, hardly had any experience of being unemployed. See Detlev Peukert, "Die Erwerbslosigkeit junger Arbeiter in der Weltwirtschaftskrise in Deutschland 1929–1933," *Vierteljahresschrift für Sozial- und Wirtschaftsgeschichte* 72, no. 3 (1985): 305–28.

and to "do something"—the urge to pitch in and help bring about some change. Let us contrast the initial quotation from Axmann with comments by Lisbeth Franzen-Hellersberg, in which she describes why young girls joined the Communist youth association, if only for a short time.

> Propaganda trips in red-bedecked cars out to the next neighborhood, all the bustle and ballyhoo that went with it, the marching songs. For a brief moment, all this anticipates the longed-for dream of a real revolution, it helps you to forget the dull misery of humdrum existence.[194]

Here a similar dynamic is at play: programmatic content gives way to the need for change in direct proportion to how oppressive the social situation had become. It was precisely the hopelessness of their economic plight that acted as a damper on continuous political work among the young. Instead they looked for the quick fix, immediate action. And young people found that immediacy in equal measure at both antipodes: on the red-emblazoned trucks of the Communist youth and in the snappy marches of the Hitler Youth and the League of German Girls. But the caesura in their change of behavior was 1933.

If Wedding up to this point in time had appeared to be socially homogeneous and politically stable—a district in which the National Socialists had been hard put, despite massive efforts, to make any headway[195]—the violent and almost total destruction of Communist Party cadres after 1933 led here to a serious power vacuum.[196] By consciously creating an atmosphere of fear and violence, the National Socialists catalyzed a sense of political paralysis among the residents of the working-class neighborhoods.[197] The swift clampdown on the Communist Party, the evident lack of adequate preparation for illegal underground activity, and the sheer brutality of the new regime can help to explain the surprisingly low level of Communist resistance,

194. Franzen-Hellersberg, "Die Frau und die Jugendbewegung," 92.

195. Rosenhaft, *Beating the Fascists!* 22.

196. On February 27, 1933, 4,000 arrest warrants for KPD members were prepared. According to KPD reports, down to the end of 1933, 130,000 party members were interned in concentration camps and 2,500 were murdered. See Siegfried Bahne, *Die KPD und das Ende von Weimar. Das Scheitern einer Politik 1932–1935* (Frankfurt a.M., 1976), 42, 44.

197. Peukert reports that in the city of Bochum leading Communists were brutally beaten by the SA, pummeled through the streets and left lying at a street corner. This event led to an "atmosphere of paralysis" among the workers. See Peukert, *Die KPD im Widerstand,* 88.

given the impressive strength of the party before 1933. But they do not explain why people about-faced, turning to a National Socialist organization. There was another factor operative here. As I have attempted to show, Wedding's political coherence was due to its social homogeneity. Yet it also became clear that the same poverty that guaranteed the party a certain number of recruits was at the same time a kind of whirlpool that eluded the party's grasp and influence. As pointed out earlier, that was evident not only in the relation to sexism and violence[198] but also in the entire proletarian lifestyle that the KPD tried in various ways to shape and change.[199] All these efforts pointed up a striking fact: the party did not represent the destitute masses in the economic crisis—rather, in the main it symbolized their hopes, a kind of emblem of their dreaming. There was a huge gap between the party cadres, their supporters and electoral constituency. After 1933, that gap appears to shift, cracking open into a general lack of orientation. To the same extent as Communists were now forced onto the defensive, the National Socialists scored victory after victory, in effect storming the barricades.

It is quite understandable why especially the young people were able to muster little resistance to the organizing work of the NSDAP. On the contrary, precisely because they were itching for action, a program like that of the National Socialist youth groups could seem attractive to them, its political content imparted in modes basically devoid of ideology.[200] Only against this background can we account for the kind of almost seamless switch over from a Socialist to a National Socialist organization, the volte-face described in the following comments.[201]

> I was also a member of the BDM, 'cause I quit the Falcons, see. And then I was in the Club der Auslandsdeutschen. I can't remember whether that was from school or. . . . Right, I think it was organized at school. So they said again and again: listen, there's this Association for Ethnic Germans abroad. And so I decided to join the thing. They had evening activities twice a week, once for gymnastics and once for a get-together, a Heimabend. But that wasn't much of any-

198. See section "Youth Organization and Gender Relations," this chapter.

199. It offered alternative cultural events and leisure time activities.

200. See chap. 3, section "Between Tradition and Progress," this study.

201. Franzen-Hellersberg describes a similar smooth switch over from a Communist to a Protestant group in the period before 1933. The girl indicated her reason for the change: "my aunt wanted me to, and besides, there was nice folk dancing there." See Franzen-Hellersberg, "Die Frau und die Jugendbewegung," 92.

thing and then it kind of fell apart. So, in any case, afterwards I went over to the BDM and joined up. (B 14)[202]

The parents of this interviewee were both working; she was their only child. When she was young her grandmother, who also lived with them, cared for her. She describes the consequences this had for her.

I still recall, grandma had responsibility for me. She used to sit there all day on the bridge with the old people, and she'd hold my hand all day long. That was terrible. But she said: well, if something happens to you, I'm the one responsible. So when my mom came, then I'd finally have some free time for myself. Except when there were wagons full of apples that'd rumble cross the bridge. Like when an apple fell off, I was allowed to go down over the embankment and get it. (B 14)

As she grew up, she turned into a genuine Wedding "street brat," out on the pavement from morning to evening, involved in every kind of deal, a tomboy as "wild as five guys." To get her off the street and teach her to "obey a little" and stop mucking about, her parents sent her to a youth organization.

To get me off the street, I found myself in the Red Falcons. Back then there was only Fichte [Spruce], that was Communist or from the Socialist Party. So I was put in the Red Falcons, so as to get me off the streets leastwise twice a week. (B 14)

Even the choice of this youth organization was not guided mainly by questions of programmatic substance. Of the many and diverse youth organizations in the Weimar Republic, only two were coming into the minds of these Wedding parents, namely, the Communist and Social Democratic groups. The decision as to which one to choose was made beyond the perimeter of strict political categories. The crucial factor was the evident superiority of the Social Democratic youth groups

---

202. The Falcons are the SPD youth organization still today. The Verein für das Deutschtum im Ausland (VDA) was renamed Volksbund für das Deutschtum im Ausland in 1933. It had started out in 1881 as Allgemeiner Deutscher Schulverein. The VDA exists still today. The National Socialists used the association for their own political aims and racist propaganda. The VDA was especially active in schools. See Rudolf Luther, *Braun oder Blau. Der Volksbund für das Deutschtum im Ausland (VDA) im NS-Staat 1933–1937* (Neumünster, 1999). Interesting in this interview is the seamless change from a left-wing to a right-wing organization. The VDA is a mediator in this transition.

when it came to organizing. "It was snappier, see, no drill, I wouldn't want to say that" (B 14). This interviewee had been a member of the Red Falcons since the age of eight. At the same time, she was a pupil at a secular school on Wiesenstraße, at the corner of Pankstraße, deep in the heart of Wedding. Consequently, much of her everyday life was spent in a politically conscious milieu. Yet she hardly resisted National Socialism in any substantive way as it gained ground around her. Though she initially hesitated to join the League of German Girls, she became a member of the VDA, going over to the league half a year later.

One might of course reason that this political abstinence was something typically feminine, and it is true that the interviewee does describe her fellow pupils as being more political and more resistant.

> I can recall one thing. Once our boys were in class, see, and the SA came in. Well, these guys started shouting. And let me tell you, we had this principal, wow, he was one big Nazi. . . . anyhow, I can remember that these guys started shouting *"Rot Front!"*[203] And we also had some kids of parents who were Communists. Well, so then this principal storms in and makes a huge scene. Let me tell you, that guy blew his top, see, was absolutely furious. (B 14)

The behavior of young workers during the Great Depression in Germany clearly showed an array of diverse features. While most of the girls sought refuge in the dream world of cinema and the desires and pleasures of consumerism, the militant political formations were largely the reserve of young men. There was an internal structural affinity of sorts between these groups of young men, quite apart from their politics. For example, macho sexism was a veritable defining feature of all the radical groupings, along with their penchant for violence. This points to a stratum of fundamental underlying social needs sited beyond all ideological differences. Driven by dissatisfaction and the frustrations of their daily lives, these young men were itching for political action. They compensated their own impotence by taking such action, enhancing its value via a gender-specific stylization. By contrast, due to the barriers thrown up by male chauvinism, the girls remained excluded, dependent on the surrogate satisfactions held out by a world of illusions. But even if the behavior of the young men had a political edge and thrust, like the behavior of the girls, it ultimately

203. *"Rot Front"* (red front) is a main slogan of the Communist movement.

eluded political control. This is demonstrated by the uncommon though possible shift from one political antipode to the other.[204] It is also manifest in the surprisingly low degree of Communist resistance after the Nazi takeover, given the formidable strength of the party before January 1933.

The attraction the NSDAP had after 1933 for young people in Wedding ran up against the resistance of their politically more conscious parents. But the parents were not always present on the scene. For most of the day, young people were mainly among themselves and left to their own wits. And at an early age, many were already largely independent and free when it came to decisions.

> Well, the thing was, see, actually I had joined the BDM without first discussing it with my mom and dad. And the rule was, first you had to be in it for a certain specified time, and then we got a form to fill out, a membership application. And so when I got that form, my dad had to sign it, see, so then I had to tell them I wanted to join the BDM. Like before, well, I'd never discussed it with them at all. So I told my dad I was in the BDM, and he, well, at first he was a little shocked. But, OK, it had happened, I was a member, and I think the dues per month were like 20 pfennigs. But all the girls used to wear blue skirts, and those white blouses, and then the tie with the special knot. And I thought that was very fashionable, I mean, I wanted to have that too. But my dad, well, it took one heck of a long time 'til he roused himself to say something about this. And though he always gave me whatever I wanted, this time he kept stressing that we couldn't afford it, we didn't have the money. Well, anyhow, then he finally did come up with the dough after all. (B 1)

The younger the girls, the more subject they were to parental authority. Generally it was the father who was opposed to the daughter's wish to join the league. Even in retrospect, the following narrator is hardly aware of the strength of her feelings of aggression triggered by her father's resistance to her joining the league, manifested as latent content in her dream that her dad was arrested by the Gestapo.

> Then I wasn't so small any more, I was 13. And at school, I guess I let the other girls sweep me up in their excitement about this new

---

204. Rosenhaft calls this switch over "exceptional, but commonplace," referring principally to the groupings among the street fighters. See Rosenhaft, *Beating the Fascists!* 164f.

thing. I guess it was when I got to school after the torchlight parade on January 30. I hadn't heard anything about it. And they said: yesterday there was this terrific torchlight parade, now Hitler's in power. So they kind of infected me with their enthusiasm. And there was always this contradiction for me between my life at home and school. Right, and then there was this dream I had. I dreamt that they came and arrested my dad. Because he was against it, and had wanted to convince me too, but the school was stronger, and all my fellow pupils, see. Anyhow, I was not allowed to join the BDM. That made me very sad at the time. He just forbade me to join. (B 8)

In the case of most girls, the allure the League of German Girls had for them was evident. Yet it was not always manifested directly. Precisely when being involved was impossible for ideological reasons, that attraction appeared in a more covert way. Yet, all the girls were fascinated by the uniforms. It elevated the wish for becoming a member to a symbolic plane while also appealing to the young girls' susceptibility to the allures of consumerism. The following quote is from an interviewee whose parents were staunchly Communist. Her father had been active in the Rotfrontkämpferbund (Red Front Fighters' League), was arrested during the Nazi period, and had spent some time in the Oranienburg concentration camp north of Berlin. The narrator never had any desire to join a Nazi organization. Nonetheless, she found it hard to resist the beguiling charm of the uniform.

For a time I said to myself, wow, they all look so beautiful. They have such beautiful strong and durable shoes. I mean, I really thought they were attractive. And they wore these short jackets, which for a time I thought was very snazzy. But maybe that was also just a passing fashion. (B 7)

Significant here is that this commentary does not foreground the attractions of a political program but rather points to a felt need for a sense of social belonging. It sprang from and was reproduced by the social misery in which the inhabitants of Wedding eked out their lives. Thus, tensions surrounding membership in the league had a social undertone, not a political one. The young people resisted the possible onus of social exclusion that the political convictions of their parents placed on them. Whether this generated open conflict was dependent on the authority their parents' political views had for the girls. On the other hand, confrontations at home exacerbated the level of individual consciousness of a girl and were bound up with how self-evident it was for her to prioritize, articulate, and implement her own needs and desires. This is instantiated in the following examples.

Some girls yielded submissively to the will of their parents, especially their father, seemingly without any feelings of loss or rage and without attempting in any way to resist or rebel.

> I: And why weren't you in the BDM?
> B 3: Well, like, my parents were against it, see. And we didn't discuss it either. I didn't ask them, and I knew darn well they didn't want me to join. So then I didn't ask them about it either. And maybe I didn't have the least gumption to say to them: hey, listen, I want to be a member, something like that. And no one said anything to me about it. So that's how it remained. Today, right, I mean I'm happy that's how it was. But back then, well, maybe, just a little, sometimes, when you'd see them in their uniforms walking along, you used to think: they can do that, and they're allowed, but you simply aren't.

Others at least ventured on occasion to assert themselves.

> I can recall I came home once and said: "I want to join the BDM too. They're always doing so many things." I remember that quite well. And my dad, well, he almost, uh, well he must have been at home that time. (B 20)

What often remained were feelings of anger and sadness.

> I had a girlfriend whose daddy was in the SA, and she was also in the BDM. And she'd always be wearing this beautiful uniform, with the monkey jacket and the special knot and the white blouse. Well, I thought that was very classy. And they used to always go out on these excursions, see. So when I said I wanted to join up too, my dad was very categorical, he said "no." He didn't explain to me why, just said he was against me joining. That it was out of the question. So naturally that got me upset. (B 9)

For some girls, being a member of the League of German Girls was more than just a symbolic representation of a sense of relatedness, belonging. Not being a member was bound up quite concretely with social exclusion or disadvantages in one's personal career.

B 17: Actually the problems all started when I wanted to go to high school. I wasn't allowed to because my parents were considered politically unreliable.[205] That was the reason I joined the Jungmädel.

I: Yet that didn't do any good?

B 17: No, none at that point. It was too late. The first kids transferred to these high schools or these *Realschulen* (secondary modern schools), as they were called at the time, when they reached the age of 10. And then there was the possibility of a junior high, what they called *Aufbauschule*. That was a kind of experiment back then, you'd transfer there from primary school at the age of 12, like today from the comprehensive school. But when I was 10 my parents didn't think about it. And I myself wasn't able at that age to say what I wanted. But I had girlfriends and knew kids who were at the high schools or secondary modern schools, like from neighbors' families, and I was still in primary school. And as I got older I started to think: you can do what they can do. And I also started to think about a vocation for myself. So I said: I want to transfer to a secondary school, and not just stay on in primary school until I finish the 8th grade. And my parents said: OK, we'll have to check into that. So I went to this exam, and I can remember that they were kind of talking among themselves. And then they, uh, well, I was turned down because my parents were considered "politically unreliable," and also because I wasn't a member of the BDM or anything else. So then, even against the will of my parents—I didn't even bother to ask—I upped and went off to join the Jungmädel. Simply because the teacher also intimated: if you were at least a member there, then maybe it might have worked, and they might have seen your good intentions.

And then there were a smaller number of girls who associated their membership in the league with a feeling of independence of mind: that they were consciously countering the adult world with something of their own, something individual.

When I look back on it now, I think it was as important for me as when I went to the children's service at church against my parents'

---

205. B 17 is the granddaughter of a well-known Social Democrat who was forced to emigrate after 1933.

will. They carried on, there were the same nasty remarks about that. (B 15)

In contrast with plausible expectations, deriving from the history of the district and its political voting profile, the interviews showed that after 1933 young people in Wedding were most certainly attracted by the League of German Girls. But the turn toward the Nazi youth organizations ran up against the opposition of the parents, whose influence on their children, though less in the working-class milieu, was still a factor when it came to the girls. This is substantiated by the interviews. In order to fill the ranks of the youth organizations, the National Socialists in Wedding, as in Minden, thus had to resort to ways and means of compulsion.

Like in Minden, the schools in Wedding were the natural arena in which to implement such pressure. But initially here the main priority was to scrap the reforms in educational practice that had been introduced during the Weimar Republic. Interest came to center on a principal bastion of those reforms: Berlin *Sammelschulen* (collective schools). These schools, popularly dubbed "secular schools," went back to the November 1918 revolution.

Already in the first weeks of the revolution, a movement was launched in Berlin among parents and teachers against educating children in the spirit of the parochial primary school. The decree of the Ministry of Science, Art and Public Education on "Revocation of the Obligation for Religious Instruction in the Schools" of November 29, 1918 and later art. 149, para. 2 of the Constitution made it possible for parents to have their children exempted from classes in religion. This assumed larger proportions only in a few districts. This movement involved revolutionary demands for the schools, wishes and calls for comprehensive educational reform and the creation in general of a new type of free school.[206]

On April 1, 1923, in Wedding, eight collective schools were opened, for a total of 126 classes.[207] On November 1, 1926, the collective

206. Jens Nydahl, ed., *Das Berliner Schulwesen* (Berlin, 1928), 46f.
207. Wedding thus had the largest number of school classes of any district in Berlin. A total of forty-two schools with three branches and 556 classes were opened. See Nydahl, *Das Berliner Schulwesen,* 47.

schools had an enrollment of 15,099 children, which surged by May 1, 1927, to 18,858 pupils.[208]

> Since right from the start, the socialist working classes and libertarian-minded teachers pinned high hope on these schools, associating them with support for a general restructuring of the school and education more broadly, these schools have developed beyond the perimeters of their initially conceived framework. They are not mere "schools of subtraction" (i.e., where religious instruction has been eliminated from the curriculum), though otherwise also obligated to observe the syllabus, timetable and regulations binding on all schools in Berlin. . . . Parents and teachers seriously desired a new type of school, a new education: "away from rote learning and the old authoritarian education toward a practically oriented school, a school of true education, a school of and for life."[209]

Religion as a subject was replaced by *Lebenskunde* (knowledge of life). Shop and handicraft studies were given special promotion. Many schools set up workshops and school gardens. The attempt was made to introduce a modern curriculum whose learning objectives were defined in terms of children's interests. Instead of a mere accumulation of isolated facts, schools attempted to impart knowledge about processes at work. Folk dancing, rhythmical gymnastics, and swimming were stressed. Excursions, trips to museums and other historical sights, and stays at school country hostels were prioritized in these schools. Corporal punishment was abolished, and the classes were coeducational at almost all such schools. The collective schools were obliged to adhere to the syllabus and timetable binding on all Berlin primary schools. But the six *Lebensgemeinschaftsschulen* (experimental and life-community schools), approved by the progressive school superintendent Wilhelm Paulsen in the spring of 1923 after long disputes and quarrels, had their own guidelines. These provided the new educational initiatives with a legally anchored framework. Like the collective schools, the Lebensgemeinschaftsschulen were largely located in proletarian districts. The most famous was the Karl Marx School headed by Fritz Karsen in Neukölln. In Wedding there was no real life-community school of this type, but many of the collective

208. Nydahl, *Das Berliner Schulwesen*, 48.
209. Nydahl, *Das Berliner Schulwesen*, 48f.

schools drew on the concept of Lebensgemeinschaftsschule in their work.[210] Throughout the entire Weimar period, the collective and life-community schools remained controversial, especially among teachers. Since many staunch Social Democratic and Communist parents sent their children to collective schools, they acquired the reputation of being "Communist schools."[211]

> I: So your father did not want to send you to a secular school?
>
> B 10: Oh no, he really did want me to go!! But my mom, although she always let my dad have the say in everything, remained a bit determined when it came to this. And since my dad was very good-natured in everything, he said: well, if that's the way you want it, I guess it makes no difference. . . . No, the school I went to was not a secular school, although there was one just a few houses away down the street from my school.
>
> I: Why was your mother so against your going to such a school?
>
> B 10: Well, like she said, it was too Communist, too red, and she didn't like Communists very much. Though actually she was totally apolitical.

> Yeah, in the secular schools, like over on Gotenburger [Straße], there was one there. And we used to call it the Communist school. The kids there were the ones who had no classes in religion. (B 1)

Shortly after the seizure of power, in February 1933, Bernhard Rust issued an order for the stepwise dismantling of the collective schools.[212] That same year, Hans Meinshausen, the newly appointed National Socialist head of the Berlin school administration, ordered the collective schools dissolved.[213]

Conjunct with these decrees were the elimination of coeducation

210. In Wedding, that was especially true of the school on Leopoldplatz headed by Kreuziger and School No. 244 at Pankstraße 20, whose principal was Mr. Hädike. See Nydahl, *Das Berliner Schulwesen*, 58.

211. On January 27, 1931, in the wake of an intensified dispute between the KPD and SPD, the *Rote Fahne* called on parents not to send their children to secular schools but rather to send them to the neighborhood school closest to their home and then to have them taken out of classes in religion. The argument here was that the secular schools were not educating children for class struggle properly.

212. Bernhard Rust, 1883–1945, minister of education since 1934, was appointed minister of education in Prussia in February 1933.

213. See Hans-Norbert Burkert, Klaus Matußek, and Wolfgang Wippermann, *"Machtergreifung" Berlin 1933* [= Stätten der Geschichte Berlins, vol. 2] (Berlin, 1982), 228.

and the reintroduction of religion as a subject in the former *Sammel-und Lebensgemeinschaftsschulen* (collective and life-community schools). Many teachers were dismissed; principals were fired and replaced by new National Socialist principals. Pupils at the collective schools were "integrated" into the new order by the "quiet compulsion" of obligatory participation in classes on religion.

> B 2: I was the only one in class who was allowed not to take religion. That wasn't very nice, for a kid that's no good. Of course, one nice thing was that I could come to school an hour later, because religion was always the first class. But later on when I got older and the teachers would always say—"what, you're not taking any religion?! You're going to be dismissed from school for that"—then it wasn't very nice.
> I: But the other kids, they didn't tease you about this?
> B 2: No, I can't recall that.

> B 7: So after 1933 they introduced religion as a subject, even in the secular schools, in spite of the fact that Hitler was against the church. Then they asked us who wasn't going to take part in religious instruction. It was almost half the class. And it didn't take very long, soon only a few girls would stand up when they asked. And later on, I was the only one who would stand up. And then I could go home from school earlier than the other kids.
> I: So you weren't required to go to the religion class?
> B 7: No, but it's ugly, I mean the remarks you'd hear.

The children were subject to enormous pressure. Just in 1933 alone, more than thirty special celebrations, memorial hours, and consecration ceremonies were held in the recalcitrant Karl Marx School, a stronghold of opposition.[214] These functions were always accompanied by the singing of the "Horst Wessel Song," and the authorities were meticulous in making sure that all pupils participated in the singing. This brought the children into serious conflict. In a number of cases, the state authorities were able to seize parents who were at political odds with them as a result of the lack of caution showed by their children.

> But I had one experience where I nearly got my dad in serious trouble. There was a May 1st celebration at school, and initially I didn't

---

214. Burkert, Matußek, and Wippermann, *"Machtergreifung" Berlin 1933,* 229f.

feel like going. "C'mon," my dad said, "just go. Go on." So then there was the "Horst Wessel Song," that kind of stuff. And there was this one girl, Tutti was her name, she went down front and said: S. wasn't singing with the rest. Then the principal asked me why and I said, like an idiot: "My dad can't stand that song." Like I mean, wow, you know, I ask myself today: how could a big grown-up girl say something stupid like that? But I always used to tell my mom everything. Anyhow, I got home, and it didn't take long: two Nazis arrived and they asked to see Dad. "Sorry," said my mom, "he's not here." So they said: "he should report tonight to the SA, along with you and your daughter." Oh, my God, for the love of Mike! I thought. So mom looked out the window. These guys went down and my dad was coming up along the street. So she signaled to him to be careful. Then mom went downstairs. Afterwards she told me: "OK, your dad says we should go there." Dad came home, we sat down and had dinner. Then Dad says to me: look, you stay at home. So they didn't take me along. And Dad worked it out, he told them I was a bit under the weather. And that I'd told him I had to sing, but I had a throat ache. Something like that. And he said he told me: so don't sing at school if you're sick. Then they gave him a beautiful king-size cigar, and let him go. So that's the story. I mean, I almost got him in a real jam. (B 7)

The Nazi Party drove its wedge between the parents and the children. Not only did the parents have to fear that their unsuspecting children might betray themselves, but as a result of the ever more massive blanket of propaganda, parents were not always successful in convincing their children of their own political views. B 18 came from a staunch Social Democratic family yet wanted, based on her own political convictions, to join the VDA.

That's simply what they told us at school. They talked about the poor Germans suffering abroad, who were being harassed and needed our support. So then I came home and my mom was hard-pressed to explain to me that this was propaganda. And she wasn't able to convince me. So then she said: OK, then I simply forbid you to join. No way. (B 18)[215]

The NSDAP very consciously pursued the aim of rupturing the relationship between parents and children. For example, surveys were

215. The *Sopade* (February 1935) carried a report by a teacher stating that most of the kids at school were in the VDA; see *Sopade* 2 (1935): 210.

done in which children were asked about what party their parents belonged to or whether they themselves were members in a National Socialist organization.[216] Precisely because pressure on the children intensified, though no direct coercive measures were taken, the confrontations were shifted into the arena of the families: "I also told mom at home, I said mommy, please let me [take part in religion class]. And she said: no, no, no. So what could you do?" (B 7).

In this situation, some parents sought a remedy by changing the school that their children attended. B 20 switched from a collective school to a normal school and then officially dropped religious instruction. B 12 went from a normal school to the Waldschule, a Berlin school were she was able to elude the rising pressure of joining the League of German Girls. Yet in other families where the parents were unable to deflect the pressure on their children, the question of membership in a National Socialist organization could become a crucial test between parents and children.

But this other thing, the fact that I wasn't allowed to join, that naturally was incredibly bad for me. And I must tell you, I also criticized my parents, reproached them for this back then. Because of you I'm not allowed, and because of you my future's . . . I've got to do something and can't do what I really want to. (B 17)

None of my interviewees can recall a concrete case of being denounced to the police, but some mention the possibility.[217] However, the degree of confrontation and intensity of the tug-of-war within the family was quite evidently associated with the sense of a loss. Divergent interests of parents and children had to be at stake. These were always social interests. Yet if social pressure was to be effective, a potential loss of social status had to be possible in principle. Thus, it was primarily (though not exclusively) better-off families that were affected, more from the Social Democratic than the Communist camp.

I joined the BDM later after my apprenticeship, then stopped in '39 and wanted to start working in the postal service. Then they said to me: are you in BDM, or connected with the party, or something? No, no one, like not a single person in my family. Well, then you have to join the BDM. OK, fine, so I joined up. (B 13)

216. *Sopade* 2 (1935): 690. Reference to such surveys in a Berlin collective school; see also BHSA, Sec. 1, MK 14.858.
217. For example, B 2 and B 18.

Especially those girls who, based on their social background, aspired to a good high school education planned right from the start on being a BDM member.

> B 11: The situation was that many things were made a condition, a prerequisite, see, so that you had to be in some organization. It could have been the scouts, they were still in existence back then, but the main tendency was to join the Jungmädelbund, nothing else than that.
>
> I: So people told you this when you were enrolled at school?
>
> B 11: They asked: is your daughter in the Jungmädelbund? My mom was along with me. Is your daughter in the . . . ? And I already was a member, right, like I already belonged. And I'd joined up earlier, see, because I was interested in continuing at school. So all that worked out OK.

As B 11 recalls, all the girls in her high school were members of the League of German Girls. By contrast, education for most kids in Wedding meant completion of the eighth grade of primary school. That was even more the general case during the Third Reich than in the Weimar Republic. In 1925, 87 percent of the children attended a primary school.[218] In 1938, that figure rose to 90 percent.[219] Yet few children, especially few girls, finished secondary school, and their number was in drastic decline in absolute terms in the 1930s—though only slightly when seen in relation to the dropping numbers of available children.[220] Of the two schools for girls among the six high schools in 1928, only one was still in existence in 1938.[221] This was also true of the junior

218. This amounted to some 30,319 out of 35,958 pupils; see *Statistisches Jahrbuch der Stadt Berlin* 3 (1927): 82.

219. This amounted to a total of 21,152 out of 23,425 pupils; see *Statistisches Jahrbuch der Stadt Berlin* 15 (1939): 149f. The statistical data can no longer be readily compared from 1939 on, since students in special education were classified in separate categories, such as disabled children and children with visual handicaps, and were not included in figures for the total number of pupils.

220. In 1927, 36.5 percent of all pupils in higher education were female; in 1937, the overall number of children in higher education had dropped by one-fourth, from 80,296 to 60,565 children, of whom 37 percent were female. The declining number of children in higher education was due to declining numbers of births—the number of births never reached those before the Great War—and the loss of Jewish children within higher education. The proportion of Jewish children within higher education was especially high among girls. In 1927 it amounted to 9.5 percent, while the boys had only 7.1 percent Jewish children. In 1937, for both boys and girls the numbers of "Israeliten," as the Jewish children were then named, dropped to a level of insignificance (1.1 percent for the boys, 1.3 percent for the girls).

221. See *Statistisches Jahrbuch der Stadt Berlin,* New Edition, 6 (1930): 189; 15 (1939): 155.

high schools in 1925 attended exclusively by girls.[222] There was a drastic decline in the number of girls with high school education between 1925 and 1938. In junior high schools, the drop in numbers was from 855 in 1925 to 261 in 1938, a plunge in absolute terms of 69.3 percent,[223] in relative terms of 1.3 percent. In May 1928, there were 932 girls attending the high school. By 1938, that figure had plummeted to 389 girls, 58.3 percent less in absolute terms and 1 percent less in relative terms.[224] The proportion of female pupils at junior high schools dropped off markedly between 1925 and 1928,[225] while their numbers at high schools remained stable during the economic crisis, dropping only after 1934. Consequently, only a small number of girls in Wedding were forced to join the league due to scholastic ambitions. This is also true in the case of most parents. Rarely did the position of the father provide any opportunity for exerting pressure on the party-affiliated organizations his children joined.

And then there comes a very sad chapter in my story. When the Nazis came to power, my dad was a Social Democrat, people of course knew that. And so naturally in the beginning he had big problems and was terribly worried that he might lose his job. By then he was in his late 40s, his health was not the best and he had nothing to fall back on. . . . My dad was a middle-level civil servant, the superiors were all old Nazis. The higher the position, the more rigorously they, the old Social Democrats, were purged from municipal service. So this guy, my dad's superior, comes up to him and says: "Hey, I hear you were in the SPD too." And my dad, he was very exact, see, so he said: "Yes, that's right."—"Until when, how long?"—"Well, right down to the present, until it's banned." Then this guy says to him: "Congratulations, you have my respect. You're actually the only one who admits it. All the others claim they weren't, say they were old Nazis." This impressed the man, my dad's candor. And then he inquired a bit about our family: "You've got a daughter? At the high school? A member of the BDM?"—"No."—"But, well that would be very appropriate if she were. After all, we'd

222. See *Statistisches Jahrbuch der Stadt Berlin,* New Edition, 3 (1927): 174; 15 (1939): 156.

223. See *Statistisches Jahrbuch der Stadt Berlin,* New Edition, 3 (1927): 174; 15 (1939): 156.

224. See *Statistisches Jahrbuch der Stadt Berlin,* New Edition, (1930): 92; New Edition, 15 (1939): 155.

225. By 48 percent; see *Statistisches Jahrbuch der Stadt Berlin,* New Edition, 3 (1927): 174; New Edition, 6 (1930): 194.

really like, uh, you're a good worker, and you were also a soldier in the war, something that Hitler admires, or you were wounded. I see from your file that you're ill. And I don't wish to fire you. But actually, I mean, you should join the party, and your daughter the BDM." Anyhow, then my dad kind of maneuvered his way on through down to '36, and about in '35 I myself, uh, now I don't want to tell you a lie, it was the end of '34 or the beginning of '35 if I recollect, well, my dad said: "I don't know any more what I should do. Either now I've got to take the consequences or . . . I have to tell him now: yes, OK, my daughter's joined the BDM." And so I joined the BDM. (B 10)

Although it is certainly correct that the pressure on children intensified between 1933 and 1936, in Wedding it ran up against limits that derived from the social prerequisites of the working-class milieu. Whoever was set on avoiding membership in a Nazi organization found ways and means. That was even clear to those who submitted to this pressure: "You know, the pressure actually consisted in the fact that you were always a little afraid you might have some disadvantages" (B 10). The Hitler Youth Law of 1936 provided for the legal basis of the league membership. In actuality, at this juncture all school-girls (not all girls) in Minden between the ages of ten and eighteen were in the league, without a single exception. In Wedding the picture looked different.

Naturally, here too many girls were members of the league, especially, if not almost exclusively, when it came to girls attending high school. In contrast with practice in Minden, however, the league in Wedding never became an integral component of feminine "education," a self-evident obligation accepted by every girl, analogous to going to school. Instead, faced with heightened pressure, some girls resorted to cunning.

My last teacher whom I had during the final years at school was in the party. He was no longer a young man, was already in his mid-50s when I left school. And this teacher was a strict supporter of the party. So that he always wanted to urge us to join the youth organization. And my teacher for needlework, whom I remember very well, Miss —— she lived alone, unmarried, with her sister on —— Street, I can still recall. And these two teachers were so closely linked to the party, he with the NSDAP, she with the Women's Organization, so ardent, that it was pretty bad. I mean, we were repeatedly admonished to join, even in the lower classes. And the other teachers would always say we ought after all to join up, become members. Now since my dad had a very low opinion of that government, he arranged for me to be transferred to the Wald-schule. (B 12)

Even where evident compulsion was exercised, a sense remained that there was room to maneuver. The girls did what was demanded of them but not a step further beyond what was required.

It was exactly the same thing in my sister's class: "OK, who's not in the BDM?" Until the only one left was my sister. And then she had to join too. And I was obliged to as well. But I can't recall what the thing was then. They wanted to give Hitler something special for his birthday. And then I had to sign on some dotted line that I was voluntarily entering the BDM or something. Like it couldn't have been the Women's League, I mean, I was still a girl. Anyhow, some such organization. But I never went to the evening meetings or anything like that. (B 7)

B 7 entered the league on Easter in 1936, during the last big recruitment drive before promulgation of the Hitler Youth Law. At a point where her refusal to join would have become open resistance, her joining the organization became unavoidable. At the same time, however, this act remained little more than a signature on a piece of paper, with no further consequences. The interviews indicate that political pressure alone was not enough to ensure the allegiance of the young—it had to correspond to and resonate with a social milieu that was susceptible. Where the social milieu had not capitulated right from the start out of fear of threatened sanctions, urban anonymity assured youngsters in large cities sufficient space for maneuver that could be utilized to avoid being pulled into the Nazi organizations. And use was certainly made of such space.

Yet I have no intention here of invoking the misleading image of a Wedding solidly bent on resistance. Instead I only wish to show that alternatives existed within the Wedding social milieu. This, of course, also means that some girls there were eager members of the league and took an active part in its activities.

That was over on Afrikanische Straße, at Goethe Park, a house standing alone at the corner, it still exists. Well, there was a ground-floor apartment, and that's where you had to sign up. And then they told you about the activities. Like every Monday from 3:00 to 5:00 there was a gathering, and Thursdays there'd be something else. And then they met at the dancing circle, that was in Goethe Park, like a small outdoor stage. And they had games there, played ball or did gymnastics and that stuff. You know, like along the lines of "Faith and Beauty." And I thought that was neat, I liked it. (B 21)

But analogous to the situation in Minden, activities in the league in Wedding likewise were hardly political. They proved attractive to the girls because they responded to their social, physical, artistic, and even erotic needs and were able to satisfy them.

Actually, the political lectures that were also a part of these get-togethers didn't bother me. Rather, I have to say, I found the other things really nice. Like the group, the sense of community, that we got together as a group and performed in a movie theater, singing. It was a request concert of some sort. If I think about it today, well, I suppose it was not very good, but I thought this situation of practicing and performing was great. We also had an opportunity, maybe that was an exception, but anyhow we got together with this group of boys. And that's terribly important at that age, because we performed as a mixed choir. And I mean, that was not so common at the time. So I thought that was pretty neat, it was very important we had an opportunity to get together with other boys. (B 17)

Yet the fact that the focus of service in the league was on content and activities specific to youth, not political content and ideology, at the same time restricted its sphere of influence. The upshot was that in Wedding, too, interest in the league declined, waning as puberty budded.

I mean, initially I was even full of enthusiasm. In the beginning I really liked to go down there, but later on it wasn't so much fun. Because they wanted us to, uh. You know, it's like this: when you're still a kid, OK, fine. But when you've finished school, then it's good to, uh, you want to have a break from all that stuff. And so to go down there, at three o'clock sharp, that's what I liked less than the things we did there. (B 21)

However, unlike in Minden, the league in Wedding was forced to compete with an array of urban leisure-time activities oriented to cultural consumerism. Specifically within the working-class milieu in Wedding, as girls became older it was increasingly harder for the league to maintain its position. In order to get a job at the post office, B 13 joined the BDM. At the time, she was sixteen or seventeen, a bright, young, cheeky Wedding teenager with a sense for stylish clothes, makeup, pop songs, and everything the urban environment offered. Since she valued her appearance, she was jokingly dubbed "Fräulein Potsdam" by her friends. So this saucy Fräulein joined the BDM, not voluntarily but most certainly without putting up much resistance.

> Once or twice that year, some girls talked to me and said I ought to come on down. So, OK, I went. I mean so that they couldn't later on tell me I was against it even though I had no idea what it was, see. So I went once, and wow, it was really stupid. Then they started singing, but not some popular hits, nothing like that. And then they painted something or pasted stuff, some kind of handicrafts or needlework. In any case, I thought it was pretty darn stupid. And then, when they started to talk about things, like, it wasn't a normal conversation. They didn't have a clue. I mean, you couldn't have a normal conversation with them! . . . I don't know, I think they only had talk about politics, somehow. I mean, really, the way they sometimes present the BDM today, these faithful German girls. All a bit silly and stupid. (B 13)[226]

It is evident that the league forfeited its attractiveness more quickly in the larger urban areas. A compounding factor was that the girls whose interest in the league began to flag first and strongest were those from Wedding working-class families. In Minden, the organization had succeeded in binding the ambitious—and thus more "problematic"—group of high school girls to the league by holding out the possibility of a career as leader. This option was lacking in Wedding. The upper class there was a very thin stratum, and there were only a small number of girls attending secondary schools. Moreover, girls in that category who were from SPD families also had to be excluded: though they had joined the league, by no means were they prepared to make a career there.[227] Yet the other girls were not suited either by dint of their

---

226. B13 has a working-class background. It is interesting to see that Kenkmann found that "Edelweisspiraten," cliques in the Ruhr area, sang *Schlager,* popular hits broadcasted by radio. Kenkmann, *Wilde Jugend,* 210.

227. This was the case for B 10, for example.

social background or their schooling. They hardly had the necessary time available and were, the older they became, increasingly more occupied with other matters. Ultimately, the league had little more to offer them than a questionable modicum of augmented power and the development of organizing skills that they would hardly ever be able to put to use in real life. Only two of my interviewees from Wedding became leaders. They both were in high school and came from well-to-do families. I have described earlier in some detail just how critical the problem of leaders became, especially shortly after 1933, at the time of the first great spurt in growth for the league, specifically in Wedding.[228] As the organization ballooned into gigantic proportions, leaders were in great demand and were sought everywhere. While the social milieu in Minden produced a large number of girls who could be taken into consideration, the selection in Wedding was sparse pickings, so that the organization even had to resort to considering ten-year-olds, like B 15. Precisely those middle-class qualities—reliability, promptness, discipline—essential for leading a group were rare among the girls in Wedding. In Minden, the politically resistive social strata had been made amenable, their resistivity broken, by driving a wedge between parents and children through the harnessing of the qualities of the children for useful service, thus cementing their allegiance. In Wedding, that was difficult to achieve. Instead, the obstacle in Wedding proved to be the same social prerequisites that initially had generated an unexpected interest in the league: given the history of Wedding, the attraction of the league was astonishing. Yet, after 1933, the same social conditions were the reason why the league failed here. Never did they manage to acquire the same level of support than in Minden, because they did not have an alternative to offer to this social milieu and held out no prospect of fundamental social changes.

The girls in Wedding reacted just like those in Minden to the waning attractiveness of the League of German Girls: they didn't come to meetings.

Shortly before confirmation I didn't much feel like continuing to go down there. And when they sent me repeated notes saying: "You missed the evening get-together again," stuff like that, well, so I thought, OK, maybe I'll . . . Then —— said: "Eva, why don't you go one time?" So I went with her, this girl [shows a school photo], she

228. See chap. 3, section "Making Careers: Leaders in the League of German Girls," this study.

used to go down there just as little as I did, Eva P. And she lived nearby, see, so I said to her: "Hey kid, how about you and me going down there again?" Or maybe she said to me: "Hey, they've written a note again, should we drop by?" Then they also asked us stuff: like where have you been keeping yourselves, just look at your fingernails, are they clean? Stuff like that, lots of questions. And then we said: "Our fingernails, what business is it of yours?!" (B 21)

Girls would cut the meetings and activities more or less frequently, depending on their personal temperament and their social position. The bolder ones were certainly not those who were politically most opposed but rather those who had the least to lose—and thus were hardest to convince. Since it was the leader's responsibility to ensure that girls came regularly, she was also obliged to deal with slackers. The simplest and cheapest method was to pay a visit to the offending girl and warn her that she had better come to meetings. But that led to unexpected problems. As sketched earlier, despite all apparent social homogeneity, Wedding certainly had diverse social strata and divisions. There were poor and less poor areas. Outsiders perhaps did not even perceive these social differences. But a Wedding resident who went from Gesundbrunnen to Kösliner Straße did not simply move from one part of the district to another; she also crossed a social boundary. Even for local residents, Wedding was terra incognita where it was "reddest," that is, where it was poorest.

> I: But now, when you say that sometimes you would go down to Wedding and look around, what was that all about?
> B 17: I went with girlfriends. It was suffocating!
> I: How come?
> B 17: Stifling, 'cause everything was so cramped, the houses so small, and then there was also this darkness. I mean it was dismal, gloomy. It was kind of eerie, and there was also a bit of the itch for adventure if you went down with some girlfriends to take a peek, look around the place.

It should be clear from what has been stated that girls specifically from the most poverty-stricken areas of Wedding hardly had any qualifications for being able to become leaders in the League of German Girls. The leaders, to which there was always a certain social distance, tended instead to come to Wedding mostly from outside and had to learn to cope and prevail in a social milieu that was alien and unfamiliar to them. This generated considerable social anxiety. B 15 became a leader at a very young age. Her job was to collect unpaid membership dues from the parents of the girls in her Jungmädel group.

> Normally they used to bring the money with them, and then I had to write it down. These amounts were just pfennigs, and when I'd accumulated a bit of money, I don't know, like maybe 10 times 5 pfennigs, and then I had to add it up and finish the account. I can't recall now how often. Anyhow, I needed these 50 pfennigs, and then I had to go to their house. It had to be in the evening, because the father had to be there, the mothers couldn't give me the money. They only had the money for food, and sometimes they'd only get enough for a single day. So I always had to drop by in the evening. And now and then my dad would go along and wait downstairs for me. And I used to go in, trembling. (B 15)

It is obvious that a father only rarely was able or even willing to support the activities of his daughter to such an extent. And in this instance, the father's assistance was not at all due to his politics but purely for human reasons: a parent trying to aid his daughter in a situation that was daunting for her. Similar conflicts were avoided when warnings were delivered in written form, but this engendered new problems. The leaders—young girls who were certainly not especially keen on administrative paperwork—had to keep a careful account of who had missed meetings; had to write out and send warning notes; and had to take care of all this along with their schoolwork, job, and preparations for meetings and activities of the league. On the other hand, a letter like the following probably had little real resonance in a proletarian household: "Dear Grete, You've missed your Jungmädel afternoon meeting twice already. If you are absent a third time without proper excuse, I will have to report it. Cordially, your Lotte."

It becomes clear again at this point that where coercive measures were ordered there also had to be effective threats of possible penalties for the system to work. Since 1939, both the Hitler Youth and league had legal means at their disposal to force youngsters to join and attend meetings, but they lacked the administrative machinery to implement them. Instead, the league remained to a high degree dependent on tacit acceptance. It relied on fears about possible material disadvantages that might accrue from infractions, control by the social milieu, the ambition and apprehensions of the teachers, the resentment of neighbors, and the garrulous character of the streets and their rumor mills. Consequently, the league developed its special strength in the more circumscribed social space of the small town and its ambience, while in the anonymity of the urban areas it lost its binding character. This was especially true for a social milieu like Wedding, where social dreams came to an early end, smashing against the hard rocks of reality. Yet if the compulsory youth service was openly undermined, resistivity might morph into open opposition. If sanctions proved ineffective due to the bureaucratic machinery they required, defensive forms of dealing with this had to be found. In Wedding they evidently consisted in the maintenance of appearances, a semblance of order. Thus, for example, in the official diction and discourse of the league, resignations from the organization were "unknown," as this high-ranking leader claims.

> B 22: You also asked me once about formal resignations. And I inquired among a few of my former comrades about that. And they said: well, resignations as such no, anybody we didn't want was pushed out. But otherwise everybody was trying hard to get into the organization, not exit from it.
> I: I also know young people though who simply left the thing, and how was that handled?
> B 22: Well, like how old were they when they left the organization?
> I: Different ages, like some were . . .
> B 22: Maybe because they were engaged or had gotten married.
> I: No, no, that's not what I mean now.
> B 22: The Jungmädel? There were no resignations there!
> I: And if some girl simply stopped coming?
> B 22: Well, as I see it, and I've also asked the others, they confirmed it, they simply all came. No one stayed away.
> I: Even later on, after 1936?
> B 22: Oh, come on, what are you talking about? They came on in droves after 1936.
> I: But the last time you said that girls also showed up then who didn't want to.
> B 22: Gee, my God, the older girls, well, I can't really tell you.
> I: So you don't know at all how that was handled formally . . .
> B 22: Well, I mean we didn't cooperate together with the police on that.

However, in Wedding there were resignations, and open as well as flimsy arguments for this wish of the girls were quietly accepted.

I: So how did you resign, how did you do it?"
B 1: Well, I just didn't go there any more. And then I got a letter and had to report there. So I told them I didn't have the time, and also that I was planning to get married. I was lying, I had no idea whatsoever to get married. My husband then was much too young, and he hadn't yet even finished his labor service. OK, well, so they said then that I would have to fill out a declaration of resignation, and that then I'd have to hand in my ID. Back then that was all still very easy. Afterwards though it got hard to resign.
I: How do you know that?
B 1: Well, I heard about it, I heard then that it had become very very hard to resign. Then you really had to have a good reason.[229]

And then after a year I resigned, it was possible to. Not the way they say today that you couldn't. That's not right, you could. In 1940, I resigned from the BDM. I went down there and said I wasn't interested, and I didn't have the time. That I liked doing what I wanted to do, not what I had to do. So here's my resignation, I said. And they accepted it. (B 13)[230]

Instead of pulling the girls in for compulsory service using an extensive bureaucracy, they were isolated by maintaining a semblance of participation. Although almost half of my interviewees were never members in the League of German Girls, the prevailing feeling was that they stood alone in that.[231] Yet those like B 2 who belonged to the league certainly did not feel that they were part of a majority.[232] By preserving the semblance of a reality, the league nipped all resistance in the bud and prevented solidarity on this issue from emerging. The following two commentaries show that people were also quite prepared to resort to lying.

B 21: Margot here [she shows a photo], the one who's with me in the class photo, she never ever went. I mean I know that for sure.
I: And she never had any hassles about that?

229. She resigned in 1936.
230. Compare also the description given by Ingeborg Drewitz of her resignation; see Ingeborg Drewitz, *Gestern war heute. Hundert Jahre Gegenwart* (Düsseldorf, 1978), 97f.
231. This was the case for B 3, B 5, B 6, B 8, B 20, B 12, B 16, and B 18. B 7 was a registered member of the BDM but never took part in an evening get-together and did not receive any letter to report. B 19 had a Jewish grandparent, which exempted her from the service. By contrast, M 6, likewise with a Jewish grandparent, was recruited into the league.
232. B 11 felt the same way.

B 21: Nope, never. And Hannelore K., this one here, she even said
she wasn't a member at all, and I really never saw her there ever,
not once. But after a year had passed, you were given the special
knot. And I also got one, they gave it as a special gift to us. Then
they started calling the roll, and Hannelore's name was also
called. Although she'd told me she had never joined up. And I'd
like to believe her. Maybe I wasn't there a whole lot, but I never
saw her there a single time. And if she'd been there, well, like we'd
have met or seen each other or something. She really never ever
went there. And I think her dad would have been furious had she
gone.

B 9: Basically I wasn't in the BDM. In any case, I didn't join up voluntarily. Before I went into the Labor Service, we were more or
less drafted into it. It was called obligatory BDM [Pflicht-BDM].
And I was supposed to do my service there, I can't remember if it
was every Sunday or every other Sunday, I had to go to some
school. We were all sitting there together, and then she told us
some story or something. And that was at the time when I was
already working, see. I had to leave very early in the morning and
had to be out in Borsigwalde at 7:00 a.m. And Sunday I was able
to sleep in, have a good rest, 'cause Saturdays we worked. And
then I had to go to the BDM at 9 o'clock, or maybe 8, just can't
remember.
I: How were you accepted there?
B 9: They sent us a letter.
I: How old were you at the time?
B 9: I must have been 17. Because afterwards, then I went to the
Labor Service, I was 18. And my mom sent me this letter: You
have faithfully served a year in the obligatory BDM—which
wasn't even true, see, because I was already in the Labor Service,
and whenever I could manage I didn't go, because simply
enough, I just didn't want to. I mean, early in the morning, on a
Sunday! And this indoctrination we had there, I didn't find that
very interesting—and now you can be accepted into the Stamm-
HJ [core Hitler Youth].

Only where belief in the totalitarian nature of the system could be
maintained was the pressure able to have any real impact, which consisted in "the fact that you were always a little afraid you might have
some disadvantages" (B 10). Where the social milieu did not function

right from the start as a multiplier of the political will, the plan of a comprehensive National Socialist girls' organization was doomed to failure.

> I: How about when it came to your sister?
> B 1: She wasn't a member.
> I: Yes, but didn't she have to?
> B 1: Nope, not at all. Strangely enough, here it wasn't that way. In Berlin it wasn't "obligatory." That probably was more like in smaller towns. Here in Berlin, I never heard that anybody was forced to join. I know for example that my cousins, like there were 10 kids, see, they lived here on Malplaquetstraße, not a single one was a member. And they often got a letter from school saying they had better join. And my aunt, she even had the special medal, the Mother's Cross, because she'd given birth to 10 kids.

In a 1977 interview published in the mid-1980s, Peter Brückner attempted to sum up his experiences with the National Socialist state.

> Today almost everybody who deals in some way with fascism knows this. But earlier on I never believed it either when people would say: but we were so afraid, there was such perfect control. That's all a lot of baloney: control was perfect because people thought it was. That was really anticipatory obedience. They themselves were the prescient control mechanism of the state.[233]

How he succeeded in surviving in Dresden between 1933 and 1945 without letting his interests become dominated by those of an authoritarian state was described by Brückner in his book *Das Abseits als sicherer Ort.*[234] His experiences showing that "resistivity"[235] was possible in the social milieu of the metropolis are also substantiated by the present study. It is quite obvious that the net to catch youthful prey

233. Peter Brückner, "'Wie die Leute vom Krieg reden hat für mich immer eine gewisse Bedeutung.' Ein Gespräch mit Peter Brückner," *Psychosozial* 9, no. 28 (1986): 13.
234. Peter Brückner, *Das Abseits als sicherer Ort. Kindheit und Jugend zwischen 1933 und 1945* (Berlin, 1980).
235. The concept of "resistivity" (*Resistenz*) was first systematically developed by Martin Broszat in connection with his large-scale study on Bavaria in the National Socialist period; see Martin Broszat, "Resistenz und Widerstand. Eine Zwischenbilanz des Forschungsprojektes," in Martin Broszat, Elke Fröhlich, and Anton Großmann, eds., *Bayern in der NS-Zeit*, vol. 4: *Herrschaft und Gesellschaft im Konflikt. Part C*, 691–709.

was far more loosely knit in Wedding than in a small town like Minden. Whoever so desired as a rule also largely succeeded in eluding the grasp of the League of German Girls. In our sample, this amounted to a quite substantial proportion. The reasons they had were in many cases analogous to those that even in Minden had generated a lack of interest and enthusiasm. Consequently, Brückner's statements hold only conditionally for a large urban milieu.

In noting that in Wedding many girls succeeded in eluding the league, I certainly do not intend to style "red Wedding" as a tradition-rich locus of resistance against the regime. The resistivity as presented in the interviews was rooted in the social structure. As sketched earlier in its historical description, Wedding was characterized by the poverty of its residents. Continuing hardship and misery imbued the district with a social homogeneity to the outside. Yet within there were certainly gradations in the economic situation of the families, manifested, for instance, in the political vote. The interviews suggest that it was primarily the poorest social strata that supported the Communist Party. Their economic plight was linked with a certain social structure whose essential characteristic I have described as "radical secularity." Among the strongly hedonistic features that characterized these social strata, eroticism was a key dimension. As became clear in examining the situation in the family, the importance of the mother rose as poverty and destitution deepened. The men, especially the younger ones, salvaged the remnants of their dwindling authority by devoting themselves to party work. This work, almost always a male domain, increasingly acquired sexist forms and features. For the Communist Party, the dilemma was basic: they wished to utilize the radicalism of these strata in political terms but proved unable to exercise much influence on them. That became especially manifest in their failure to enlist women and girls in the organization and in the continuing ideological struggles, imbued with the strong moralism of the party. It would appear that this social structure was sustained right on down into National Socialism. It was precisely the distance of proletarian strata from ideology, the complement of their political radicalism, that made it possible for them at an early juncture to turn toward a National Socialist organization. This was true especially for young people, while numerous parents evidently sought to prevent their children from joining a National Socialist youth organization. On the other hand, membership in a Nazi youth organization did not necessarily mean identification with Nazi ideology. The young people quickly abandoned these organizations if they found that their desires and needs were not satisfied there and could scarcely be prevented from doing so. Consequently, there are many indications that this social milieu in Berlin was far more resistive to National Socialist claims to power than was the case in Minden. In any case, the type of young girl who was bemoaned already before 1933 in Wedding—namely, frivolous, happy-go-lucky, and oriented to consumerism—also turned up after 1933 in the League of German Girls. That is clear from the following comments.

I: And the other girls, did you have any friends among them?

B 10: No, no friends.

I: And you had no relation to them?

B 10: Nope, like none at all. Maybe I'd say that intellectually, I was on the best terms with that platoon leader, but with the other girls, no, they were simply too primitive. They just did everything without thinking. And thought it was great to stroll along traipsing through the heather on Sundays. Far away from their mothers out somewhere. And if in the distance they would catch a glimpse of a group of Hitler Youth, then they were in seventh heaven. So I mean, I hated it, you can believe me, oh yeah, I really did.

The woman narrating here was forced to join the league. She came from an SPD family and was at the girls' high school. Despite her political opposition, she had more in common with her league leader than with the other girls in her unit. What she criticized in these girls was their lack of a critical edge, their gross pleasure in the most silly undertakings, and their openly manifest erotic interests. These girls were separated by differences in social structure that ran deeper than political ideology. Many Wedding girls even after 1933 embodied a type of young woman who was unreflective, oriented to having fun in the present, though tempered by a certain element of freedom and independence.

The social milieu of the metropolis rendered resistivity possible, and Wedding's social milieu formed the reservoir for a broad sense of social refusal. It is necessary to investigate in greater depth why so little opposition sprouted from the soil of that milieu and so little conscious political action against National Socialism. The interview material shows that the state, instead of seeking confrontation and trying to implement its interest "at any cost," sought to defuse the conflict. At the same time, it endeavored to maintain the semblance of its power. If that was indeed the case, then Brückner's "prescient obedience" was based not just on illusion—it was underpinned by a deception that was consciously and systematically constructed.

Conclusion

The point of departure for this study was to try to grasp the attempt between 1933 and 1945 to forcibly organize girls within a National Socialist organization external to the schools. The general question was broken down into several aspects:

To what extent were girls in fact encompassed in and by these structures?

What needs and motives underlay the desire of a girl to become a member of the League of German Girls? And for what reasons did she or her parents oppose her membership there?

What impact did being in the league have on the respective social milieu of a member?

I will try to address these questions in summary form based on the findings of the present investigation.

Both in Minden and Wedding, the League of German Girls was insignificant before 1933, though for different reasons. In Protestant Minden, the high turnout for the Nazis at the polls was hinged to the hope that National Socialism might help in trying to salvage the social milieu of Protestant life that had been unraveling since 1918. Among its main buttresses was the family, marked by a high degree of gender polarity. Central to its compass was the idea that a woman's place (and thus girl's place) was in the home. For that overriding reason, even in families that had supported the National Socialists by their vote, it was considered improper for girls and teenagers to become involved in activities external to the home. In Wedding before 1933, the league likewise had made few inroads among youth. The Hitler Youth there was established by high school pupils, which means it was recruited from social strata numerically in the decided minority in the Wedding district.

The League of German Girls became a mass organization after the National Socialists acceded to state power in January 1933. The

National Socialist girls' organization recruited from several sources. On the one hand, many young people had little choice but to switch to the National Socialist youth organization after the forcible destruction and Gleichschaltung of the youth organizations that had existed prior to 1933 and that they belonged to. On the other hand, young people were compelled to join the ranks of the Hitler Youth and the League of German Girls by measures of the party and regime, culminating in the Hitler Youth Law of 1936 and the implementation decrees on this law of 1939. However, a sizable segment of the huge growth in membership in the league after 1933 can only be explained by the desire on the part of many girls to become an active member.

Yet those who joined up were not necessarily dedicated National Socialists. Most entered the organization's ranks because they felt attracted by the array of leisure-time activities it offered, ranging from sports to singing and handicrafts, and it was quite similar to the fare familiar to them from other youth organizations. This was complemented by the desire to be part of the action and integrated into the ranks of German youth. In comparison, "ideological schooling" was far less significant a motive in most girls' minds. The fact that the league appealed to girls through the range of activities it offered—and not through a specific ideology—helps explain the marked and broad power of attraction it enjoyed. On the other hand, this was likewise the reason why the organization's influence was basically limited to those age groups where its profile of activities resonated most strongly, namely, girls ages ten to fourteen. After they reached the age of fourteen, many girls lost interest in the league and were also able, based on their new vocational involvement, to increasingly withdraw from the ambit of the organization's influence.

The extent of its reach was by no means identical with the wish of the National Socialist state to have every Aryan German girl between the ages of ten and eighteen in the active ranks of the league. Though this policy was massively communicated to the young, a bureaucratic network was required to implement it in a comprehensive manner. Where that network was missing, the system relied on voluntary enlistment as a member. This is why the extent of its coverage remained dependent on the respective social milieu. Initially, both in Minden and Wedding, the schools provided a relatively simple channel for recruitment. Yet a comparison between these two localities indicates that pressure through the schools was not alone sufficient unless simultaneous control and supervision could be guaranteed. Thus, for example, in the urban milieu of Wedding, there were enough ruses and stratagems to avoid obligatory service without any serious consequences. Indeed, one's absence was simply not noticed or registered. In Minden, by marked contrast, from 1936 on if not before, 100 percent of all schoolgirls were members in the organization. This also means that the greater majority of girls in the league were between the ages of ten and fourteen. Once they became apprentices or started working, they had little time, and as a result precious little desire, to fulfill the requirements of service in the League of German Girls. In Wedding, where the extent of inclusion of girls in the organization's ranks was generally less encompassing, girls were pressed into continuing to serve in the league despite their vocational commitments (B 9, B 13). In Minden, on the other hand, it seems to have been accepted for a girl to leave the BDM for reasons of her new job.

As a rule, those who never joined the league had parents who attempted, for fundamental reasons, to prevent their participation. In Minden, these were usually parents with a conservative outlook who rejected any state interference in their daughter's life as unjustified. In Wedding, by contrast, parental resistivity against the National Socialist youth organization derived primarily from their basic political opposition. A sizable number of families in Wedding also succeeded in keeping their daughters out of the league, aided in part by the anonymity of the metropolis. In Minden, resistance by parents largely foundered on the rocks of legislation by which service in the youth organization was implemented. This was a judicial and social bulwark that most Minden families were scarcely able to actively oppose. In this town marked by the military and the large number of civil servants, that can be explained by reference to their stalwart Protestant heritage and long-standing obedience to the state.

Fundamental reservations regarding a girl's participation in the league, expressed primarily by parents but also shared by their daughters as they grew older, were compounded by objections from the girls themselves. Some of these derived from their age, while others were specific to the social background. As already mentioned, interest in the league flagged among many girls after a certain amount of time spent in its ranks. With the onset of puberty, if not before, most could muster little enthusiasm for its activities. The beginning of an apprenticeship or entry into a vocation thus often provided a welcome opportunity to terminate one's membership in the league.

Those who continued on in the organization did so in most instances due to compulsion. In Minden, the group affected here was primarily high school girls. Since these girls, given their social back-

ground and mental capacities, often were quite demanding and dis-
criminating, a solution had to be found for them, lest their lack of
interest blossom into open resistance. For that reason, special groups
were established in Minden, in their scope anticipating the later study
groups of the BDM section "Faith and Beauty." By providing more
latitude for the girls' own interests and allowing them to take better
advantage of their own networks of friends and social relations, their
nascent resistivity was nipped in the bud. An additional factor was
that, specifically in Minden, it proved possible to recruit many high
schools girls as leaders in the League of German Girls, integrating
them in this way into the movement. In Wedding the situation differed
markedly. Naturally here, too, there were high school girls who had
been forced to join the league, but that was a minuscule number. More
problematic here were the girls who felt drawn, as genuine Wedding
proletarian youngsters, by the magnetic pull of the urban culture
industry and its multiple allurements. These young women, who even
before 1933 had been little prone to longer-term membership in any
youth organization, were likewise little attracted by membership in the
league. For them, the prospect of a career as a leader or even the
diverse array of free-time activities, such as sports, choir, amateur theater, and folk dancing, held out minimal allure. So while in Minden
ways and means were found to win over even the "difficult" girls to the
ranks of the league, this proved impossible in Wedding.

If we look at the consequences of compulsory recruitment to the
league outside the schools, they appear to have been more marked in
Minden than in Wedding. The fact that the envelope was successfully
extended to encompass a full 100 percent of all schoolgirls in Minden
meant that parental rights were correspondingly curtailed. This constituted direct interference in the closed and intimate circle of the Protestant family. That process of drawing girls out of the grip and bosom of
their families was continued in the multiple "careers" as leaders to
which girls were enticed. This involved girls primarily in the higher
grades of secondary school, affecting in particular the tradition-
minded families of the Minden upper middle class. This release of girls
from the ambit of their family circle led to a deepening trend toward
individualism that many girls regarded as a positive turn. Specifically
with the aid and by dint of the Nazi youth organizations, girls were
increasingly empowered in effect to go their own ways. But as they
rejected their father's authority, they at the same time overstepped the
protective perimeter of the family, subjecting themselves to the grasp
and interference of the state. Whereas in Minden the social conse-

quences of this cracking of the shell of the Protestant family are quite evident, in Wedding it would seem that the compulsory recruitment to the league led to few profound social changes. One initially astounding aspect is that girls seem to have flocked earlier on into the ranks of the league despite the high turnout before 1933 for the Social Democrats and Communists at the Wedding polls. However, this lack of serious reservation about joining a National Socialist organization was in keeping with general social behavior in the district, which was little shaped by ideology. The program of the league was in basic tune with that dimension.

In Wedding, however, the desire that many girls had to join the league was often effectively stymied by parental wishes. Moreover, interest in staying on in the organization tended to flag more in Berlin than in Minden, especially when it became clear after the girls passed through puberty that the activities offered by the league did little to satisfy the urbanized needs and desires of proletarian female youth. They initially began to cut meetings and ultimately just stopped attending. Consequently, there was never 100 percent inclusion of all youngsters in Wedding in these organizations. Instead, the example of the girls demonstrates that a social structure already dominant prior to 1933 was able to persist under National Socialism.

The Structure of the Hitler Youth

Reich Youth Leadership (salaried leadership corps)
(within the Reich there were about thirty-five *Gebiete* or *Obergaue*)

Obergau	region
Gau	district
Untergau	subdistrict
Ring	battalion
Gruppe	company
Schar	platoon
Schaft	squad

Hitler Youth	**League of German Girls**
Gebiet	Obergau
(encompassing around twenty Banne)	(encompassing around twenty Untergaue)
Bann	Untergau
(four to six Stämme and four to six Jungstämme)	(four to six Mädelringe and four to six Jungmädelringe)

HJ	**DJ**	**BDM**	**JM**
Stamm	Jungstamm	Mädelring	Jungmädelring
Gefolgschaft	Fähnlein	Mädelgruppe	Jungmädelgruppe
Schar	Jungzug	Mädelschar	Jungmädelschar
Kameradschaft	Jungenschaft	Mädelschaft	Jungmädelschaft

(Every unit included four of the lower units. For example, every Mädelring had four Mädelgruppen, every Mädelgruppe had four Mädelscharen, every Mädelschar had four Mädelschaften, and every Mädelschaft had between ten and fifteen members.)

DJ: boys ages ten to fourteen
HJ: boys ages fourteen to eighteen
JM: girls ages ten to fourteen
BDM: girls ages fourteen to eighteen (and up to twenty-one)

The Path of the German Girl

Children entered the Hitler Youth on April 20 (Hitler's birthday) of the year in which they reached their tenth birthday. A youngster was admitted to the Deutsches Jungvolk in the case of the boys and to the Jungmädelbund in the case of the girls. Members then proceeded on from the Jungmädelbund or Deutsches Jungvolk to the BDM or HJ. For girls, there was an additional special organization: the BDM-Werk "Glaube und Schönheit," which they could start joining from age seventeen.

Jungmädelbund
Jungmädelschar 4: ten-year-olds
Jungmädelschar 3: eleven-year-olds
Jungmädelschar 2: twelve-year-olds
Jungmädelschar 1: thirteen-year-olds

The Jungmädelbund is followed by the Verpflichtung der Jugend (ceremony of commitment for youth).

BDM
Mädelschar 3: fourteen-year-olds
Mädelschar 2: fifteen-year-olds
Mädelschar 1: sixteen-year-olds
Pflichtjahr (obligatory year of service)

BDM-Werk "Glaube und Schönheit" (BDM section "Faith and Beauty")
At age eighteen a Hitler Youth member could enter the NSDAP. At age twenty-one girls could be transferred to become members in the NS-Frauenschaft.

Interview Partners

For interviews not identified as an expert interview, they are cataloged according to the following:

- date of birth
- religious affiliation (p = protestant; c = catholic; wc = without confession)
- profession of the father
- political affiliation of the father/mother if politically active
- number of siblings
- education (E = elementary school; MR = Mittlere Reife; A = Abitur)
- member within the League of German Girls (M)
- leader within the League of German Girls (F)
- paid leader within the League of German Girls (hF)

Minden
1. expert interview (League of German Girls and protestant church)
2. 1919, c, artisan (loss of economic independence after 1918), 5, E, M, hF
3. 1920, p, lower civil servant, 1, MR, M, hF
4. 1924, p, civil servant, DNVP, A, M
5. expert interview (League of German Girls and cultural unit)
6. 1930, p (one Jewish grandparent), employee in public service, 1, A, M
7. expert interview (League of German Girls and youth welfare)
8. 1919, p, artisan (after 1918 employee in the public service), SPD, 2, E
9. 1920, p, civil servant, 1, A, M, F
10. 1930, p, civil servant, SPD on mother's side, A, M
11. 1927, p, worker with small farm, E, M
12. 1927, p, mother widow (father worker), 5, E, M
13. 1926, p, worker with small farm, SPD, E, M
14. 1926, p, lower employee within the public service with small farm, 3, E, M
15. 1919, p, worker, SPD, 1, E
16. 1932, p, lower employee, 1, MR, M
17. 1927, p, higher civil servant, 1, A, M, F
18. 1921, c, worker, 2, MR, M
19. 1926, p, artisan with small farm, E, M, F
20. 1920, p, civil servant, DNVP, 2, E (no more schooling because of depression), M

21. 1922, self-employed (business went bankrupt during depression, then employee in the public service), 2, M, F
22. 1917, p, civil servant, 2, M, F
23. expert interview (Minden and KPD)
24. 1914, wc, artisan, KPD, E
25. expert interview (NSDAP and youth welfare)

Wedding
1. 1917, p, self-employed, 3, E, M
2. 1930, p, artisan (several jobs after 1918 as an unskilled worker), E, M
3. 1924, wc, self-employed (haulage contracting firm went bankrupt during the war), KPD, 1, E
4. 1927, c, employee, 1, E, M
5. 1930, wc, unskilled worker (often unemployed, mother works as an unskilled worker), 6, E
6. 1911, unskilled worker, mother partially works as home-worker, KPD, 1, E
7. 1923, wc, unskilled worker (mother works partially), KPD, 1, E, registers with the League, but never goes there
8. 1920, wc, artisan (often unemployed, mother partially works as a home-worker), KPD, MR
9. 1920, civil servant, 1, A, M, F
10. 1919, p, lower employee in the public service, SPD, MR, M
11. 1926, p, manager, MR, M, F
12. 1926, wc, father ill, mother works as an unskilled worker, KPD, E
13. 1921, wc, lower employee in the public service, 1, E, M (in order to get a job at the post office)
14. 1920, wc, both parents work as unskilled workers, E, M
15. 1923, p, well-off pensioner (war disabled, blind), 3, A, M, F
16. 1919, wc, both parents work as skilled workers, both self-employed, SPD, MR
17. 1929, wc, artisan, works as an unskilled worker (loss of job after 1933 out of political reasons, mother works as an unskilled worker), SPD, schooling handicapped because of political affiliation, E
18. 1922, wc, lower employee in the public service, SPD, 1, MR
19. 1922, p, employee (lost job after 1933 as a Jew, mother works as an unskilled worker), MR (schooling was paid for by a friend of the parents)
20. 1924, wc, self-employed (mother partially works as an unskilled worker), KPD, E
21. 1929, wc, artisan (mother works as a white collar worker), 1, E, M
22. expert interview (League of German Girls)

Glossary and Abbreviations

Abitur	examination qualifying for the entrance into the university
Akademie für Jugendführung Braunschweig	Academy for Youth Leadership. Academy located in Braunschweig instructing and training the most high-ranking leaders within the Hitler Youth
Arbeitsgemeinschaft	working group
Arbeitsgemeinschaft nationalsozialistischer Studentinnen (ANSt)	National Socialist female students
Arbeiter Turn- und Sportbund (ATUS)	worker's gymnastics and sports league
Aufbauschulen	comparable to junior high school
Bundesarchiv (BA)	national archives
Berufsschulen	vocational schools
BDM	organization within the League of German Girls. Girls ages fourteen to eighteen/twenty-one
BDM Haushaltsschulen	BDM household schools introduced in 1938
BDM-Werk "Glaube und Schönheit"	BDM section "Faith and Beauty." Organization of girls ages seventeen to twenty-one within the League of German Girls, founded 1938
Bayrisches Hauptstaatsarchiv (BHSA)	Bavarian main archives
Bund Deutscher Mädel	League of German Girls
Bundesführerin	National leader of the League of German Girls, later called "Reichsreferentin des Bundes Deutscher Mädel"
Deutsche Arbeitsfront (DAF)	National Socialist Labor Organization
Deutscher Frauen Orden "Rotes Hackenkreuz" (DFO)	German Women's order "Red Swastika"
Deutsches Jungvolk (DJ)	organization of boys ages ten to fourteen within the Hitler Youth

257

Frauenarbeitsgemeinschaften	Association for National Socialist Women
Führercorps	leader corps; high-ranking employed leaders of the Hitler Youth
Führerinnenring	leaders' circle; high-ranking leaders of the League of German Girls
Gauleiter	regional leader
Gleichschaltung	streamlining; euphemism describing the process of surrendering all German institutions to Nazi policies
Gymnasium	classical secondary school
Heimabend/Heimnachmittag	home afternoon or evening that was obligatory once a week for all members of the Hitler Youth
Hilfseinsatz des Bundes Deutscher Mädel	War Service of the League of German Girls
Jugendbewegung	Youth movement
Jugendführer des deutschen Reiches	Youth Leader of the German Reich; official state title accorded to von Schirach in 1933
Jugendweihe	consecration of youth; secular rite of passage comparable to confirmation that was customary within the working population, especially with members of the Communist party
Jungmädel	member of the JMB
Jungmädelbund (JMB)	organization within the League of German Girls; for girls ages ten to fourteen
Jungmädelprobe	Test introduced in 1935, in which a passing student was awarded a neckerchief and the leather knot; necessary to become a full-fledged member of the League of German Girls
Küken	chick; name for the youngest members of the League of German girls before 1933
Kultureinheit	cultural units within the League of German Girls, such as a theatre group, an orchestra, or a choir
Lebensgemeinschaftsschulen	experimental and life-community schools; reform schools during the Weimar Republic
Lebensreform	life reform; movement started at the end of the nineteenth century in Germany

Lyzeum	secondary school for girls
Mädel	member of the BDM, ages fourteen to eighteeen
Mädelbund	synonym for League of German Girls
Mädelgruppe	girls' company
Mädelring	girls' battalion
Mädelschaft	girls' squad
Mädelschar	girls' platoon
Mittlere Reife	intermediate high school certificate, comparable to the British O-levels
NS-Frauenschaft	National Socialist Women's Association
NS Mädchenschaften	National Socialist girls groups before 1933
NS Schülerbund	National Socialist league of school children
NS Schülerinnenbund	National Socialist league of female school children
Nationalsozialistischer Deutscher Studentenbund (NSDStB)	National Socialist German Students' League
NSV	National Socialist welfare organization
Pflichtjahr	obligatory year introduced in 1938
Pimpfe	boys age ten to fourteen within the DJ
Realschulen	six-form high school leading to Mittlere Reife
Reichsausschuss deutscher Jugendvereine	Committee of the German Youth Reich Associations
Reichsjugendführung	leadership of the Hitler Youth
Reichsleiter	Reich leader; one of the highest positions within the Nazi leadership
Reichsnährstand	Reich Ministry for Nutrition
Reichsreferentin des Bundes Deutscher Mädel	female head of the League of German Girls
Reichssportführer	Reich sports leader
Reichsstatthalter	Reich governor
Rotfrontkämpferbund	Red Front Fighters League
Sammelschulen	collective schools
Schwesternschaften	sisterhoods
Sondereinheiten	special units
Sonderscharen	special groups
Staatsarchiv München (StA München)	State Archive in Munich
Staatsjugendtag	State Youth Day, introduced in 1934
Untergau	district
Obergau	region

Verein für das Deutschtum im
   Ausland (VDA)

Volksschulen
Weltanschauliche Schulung

founded at the end of the nineteenth
   century and still existing today for
   the purpose and welfare of Germans
   abroad; huge increase in membership after 1933 and nazified
elementary schools
ideological schooling

Bibliography

Unpublished Sources
Bundesarchiv (Federal Archive), Berlin and Koblenz (BA)

NS 26   Main archive of the NSDAP, 1935–45
NS 28   Reich Youth Leadership Office
NS 22   Reich organizational leaders of the NSDAP
NS 12   Main Office for Education / Reich Administration of the National
         Socialist Teachers' Association (NS-Lehrerbund, NSLB), 1929–45
R 11   Reich Chamber of Commerce
R 43   Reich Chancellery, 1878–1945
Sammlung Schumacher (Collection Schumacher)

Bayrisches Hauptstaatsarchiv Munich (Bavarian Central State Archive Munich)
    (BHSA)
MK 14858   Ministry of Culture

Institut für Zeitgeschichte, Munich and Berlin (Institute for Contemporary
    History)
Various documents

Staatsarchiv Munich (State Archive Munich)
Pol. Dir.   Police Head Office Munich

Staatsarchiv Detmold (State Archive Detmold) (St.A. Detmold)

M 1 II B   school
M 1 Ju   youth
M 2   Minden holdings
M 4   Head of Police Bielefeld (Polizeipräsident)
M 18   Security Service (SD), in part the series *Meldungen aus dem Reich*
D 2 A   Head of Police Bielefeld (Polizeipräsident)
M 1 I S   social affairs

Municipal Archive Minden
Various documents

Contemporary Periodicals and Newspapers

Amtliches Nachrichtenblatt. Newsletter of the Youth Leader of the German Reich and the Reich Youth Leadership Office of the NSDAP, 1937–40.

Angriff. Evening newspaper in Berlin, 1927–33.

Arbeiter-Illustrierte Zeitung (AIZ). Tabloid, 1933–36.

Der Aufmarsch. Newspaper of the National Socialist Pupils' Association, 1929–32.

Aufruf. Periodical for human rights, 1933–34.

Berichte über die Lage in Deutschland. Die Lagemeldungen der Gruppe Neu-Beginnen aus dem Reich 1933–36. Reports of the socialist resistance group Neu- Beginnen.

Berliner Tageblatt und Handelszeitung. Berlin daily, 1925–33.

Die Fanfare. Agitational periodical against fascism, 1930–33.

Die Frau. Monthly magazine of the Union of German Women's Associations, 1925–33.

Das deutsche Mädel. Newsletter of the League of German Girls in the Hitler Youth, 1933.

Das deutsche Mädel. Paper of the League of German Girls in the Hitler Youth, 1937–40.

Der deutsche Sturmtrupp. National Socialist paper of working youth in Greater Germany, 1933–34.

Die deutsche Zukunft. Monthly for National Socialist youth, 1931–33.

Internationale sozialistische Jugendkorrepondenz. Edited by the head office of Youth International, 1928–33.

Jugend und Beruf. Monthly for promoting occupation consultation and training of young people on the basis of youth psychology, education, and economics, 1926–34.

Jugend und Presse. Newsletter of the press office of the Reich Youth Leadership Office of the NSDAP and German Youth Publishing House, 1933.

Jugend heraus. Central monthly for the youth movement and athletics, 1925–31.

Das junge Deutschland. Edited by the Committee of the German Youth Associations, 1925–33.

Das junge Deutschland. Official periodical of the youth leader of the German Reich, 1933–44.

Der junge Nationalsozialist. National periodical of the Hitler Youth, 1932.

Der junge Sturmstrupp. Agitational paper of the working youth of Berlin, 1931–32.

Jungvolk. 1932. Paper for German boys.

Die Kommenden. Paper of the German youth movement, 1926–32.

Mädelschaft. Paper for organizing home evening sessions in the BDM, edited by the Reich Youth Leadership Office of the NSDAP, Section for Ideological Indoctrination, 1933–37.

Mindener Tageblatt. 1925–33. Minden daily.

Der Reichsbefehl der Reichsjugendführung der NSDAP. Orders and communications for the leaders of the Hitler Youth, 1936–44.

Rote Fahne. Central periodical of the German Communist Party, 1925–33.

Sturmjugend: Hitler Youth Paper. Central periodical of the Hitler Youth for Greater Germany, 1929–30.

Verordnungsblatt der Reichsjugendführung. Official decrees of Reich Youth Leadership Office, 1933–37.

Weserwarte. 1925–33. Minden daily.

Essays and Books

Adorno, Theodor W. *Minima Moralia. Reflexionen aus einem beschädigten Leben.* Frankfurt a.M., 1986.

Affeld, Franz. *Der Volkspark Rehberge. Seine Geschichte, Pflanzen und Tiere.* Berlin, 1961.

Allen, Ann Taylor. "The Holocaust and the Modernization of Gender: A Historiographical Essay." *Central European History* 30 (1997): 349–64.

Allen, William Sharidan. *The Nazi Seizure of Power: The Experience of a Single German Town, 1930–1935.* Chicago, 1965.

Anderson, Benedict. *Imagined Communities: Reflections on the Origin and Spread of Nationalism.* London and New York, 1996.

Andresen, Sabine. *Mädchen und Frauen in der bürgerlichen Jugendbewegung. Soziale Konstruktion von Mädchenjugend.* Stuttgart, 2003.

Arendt, Hannah. "Besuch in Deutschland 1950. Die Nachwirkungen des Naziregimes." In Arendt, *Zur Zeit. Politische Essays,* 43–70. Berlin, 1986.

Arendt, Hans-Jürgen. "Der Kampf der Kommunistischen Partei Deutschlands um die Einbeziehung der werktätigen Frauen in die revolutionäre deutsche Arbeiterbewegung in der Periode der Weltwirtschaftskrise 1929–1932." PhD diss., Leipzig, 1970.

———. "Weibliche Mitglieder der KPD in der Weimarer Republik—Zahlenmäßige Stärke und soziale Stellung." *Beiträge zur Geschichte der Arbeiterbewegung* 19, no. 4 (1977): 652–60.

Ariès, Phillippe. *Centuries of Childhood: A Social History of Family Life.* Trans. Robert Baldick. New York, 1962.

Assmann, Helmuth. "Beiträge zur Geschichte des Kreises Minden von 1816 bis 1945." *Mitteilungen des Mindener Geschichts- und Museumsvereins* 40 (1968): 79–121.

Axmann, Artur. *"Das kann doch nicht das Ende sein." Hitlers letzter Reichsjugendführer erinnert sich.* Dortmund, 1995.

Bahne, Siegfried. *Die KPD und das Ende von Weimar. Das Scheitern einer Politik 1932–1935.* Frankfurt a.M. and New York, 1976.

Bajohr, Stefan. *Die Hälfte der Fabrik. Geschichte der Frauenarbeit in Deutschland 1914–1945.* Marburg, 1979.

———. "Oral History—Forschungen zum Arbeiteralltag." *Das Argument* 123 (1980): 667–76.

Balg, Ilse. "Berlin—eine Stadt immer im Werden." In Karl Schwarz, ed., *Berlin: Von der Residenzstadt zur Industriemetropole. Ein Beitrag der Technischen Universität Berlin zum Preußen-Jahr 1981.* Vol. 1, 151–69. Berlin, 1981.

———. "Die Sozialstruktur als städtebauliches Element—Ein historischer Aufriss am Beispiel des Wedding in Berlin." Zentralinstitut für Städtebau. Technische Universität Berlin. Lecture series, winter semester 1958–59, No. 6.

Barschak, Erna. *Die Schüler in der Berufsschule und ihre Umwelt.* Berlin, 1926.

Bayern in der NS-Zeit [= Publications of the project "Widerstand und Verfolgung in Bayern 1933–1945" commissioned by the Bavarian State Ministry of Education and Culture, handled by the Institut für Zeitgeschichte in cooperation with the Bavarian State Archives. Martin Broszat, et al., eds.]. Bd. 1: Soziale Lage und politisches Verhalten der Bevölkerung im Spiegel vertraulicher Berichte; Bd. 2: Herrschaft und Gesellschaft im Konflikt, Teil A; Bd. 3: . . . Teil B; Bd. 4: . . . Teil C; Bd. 5: Die Parteien KPD, SPD, BVP in Verfolgung und Widerstand; Bd. 6: Die Herausforderung des Einzelnen. Geschichten über Widerstand und Verfolgung, Munich, 1977–83.

Beck, Ulrich. *Risikogesellschaft. Auf dem Weg in eine andere Moderne.* Frankfurt a.M., 1986.

Beck-Gernsheim, Elisabeth. "Vom 'Dasein für andere' zum Anspruch auf ein Stück 'eigenes Leben': Individualisierungsprozesse im weiblichen Lebenszusammenhang." *Soziale Welt* 34 (1983): 307–40.

Becker, Howard. *German Youth: Bond or Free.* New York, 1946.

Bellermann, Christian Friedrich. Part 1: *Die St. Paulsgemeinde vor Berlin. Kurze Geschichte und Beschreibung derselben undd ihres Grundes und Bodens bei Gelegenheit der ersten Jahresfeier ihrer Kirchweih am 17.7.1836.* Berlin, 1836. Part 2: *Zweites Stück. Fortgesetzter Bericht zur 3. Jahresfeier am 15.7.1838.* Berlin, 1838. Part 3: *Drittes Stück. Von 1838–1848.* Berlin, 1848. Part 4: *Viertes Stück. Von Pfarrer Buttmann. Zur Jubelfeier des 50jährigen Bestehens.* Berlin, 1885.

Benjamin, Walter. "Malerei, Jugendstil, Neuheit." In Benjamin, *Das Passagenwerk* [= Gesammelte Schriften Bd. V.2.], 674–97. Frankfurt a.M., 1982.

Bergmann, Anneliese. "Frauen, Männer, Sexualität und Geburtenkontrolle. Die Gebärstreikdebatte der SPD im Jahre 1913." In Karin Hausen, ed., *Frauen suchen ihre Geschichte. Historische Studien zum 19. und 20. Jahrhundert,* 81–108. Munich, 1983.

Bernett, Hajo. *Nationalsozialistische Leibeserziehung. Eine Dokumentation ihrer Theorie und Organisation* [= Theorie der Leibeserziehung—Texte—Quellen—Dokumente—1]. Schorndorf, 1966.

Bernstein, Eduard. *Die Geschichte der Berliner Arbeiterbewegung.* Vols. 1, 2. Berlin, 1907.

Beyreuther, Erich. *Geschichte des Pietismus.* Stuttgart, 1978.

Bezirksamt Wedding, ed. *Der Wedding gestern und heute.* Berlin, 1958.

Blüher, Hans. *Der bürgerliche und der geistige Antifeminismus.* Berlin, 1918.

Boberach, Heinz. *Meldungen aus dem Reich. Auswahl aus den geheimen Lageberichten des Sicherheitsdienstes der SS 1939–1944.* Neuwied, 1965.

———. *Berichte des SD und der Gestapo über Kirche und Kirchenvolk in Deutschland 1934–1944.* Mainz, 1971.

———. "Die schriftliche Überlieferung der Behörden des Deutschen Reiches 1871–1945. Sicherung, Rückführung, Ersatzdokumentation." In Heinz Boberach and Hans Booms, eds., *Aus der Arbeit des Bundesarchivs. Beiträge zum Archivwesen, zur Quellenkunde und Zeitgeschichte* [= Schriften des Bundesarchivs 25], 50–61. Boppard, 1977.

———. *Meldungen aus dem Reich 1938–1945. Die geheimen Lageberichte des Sicherheitsdienstes der SS.* 17 vols. Herrsching, 1984.

Bock, Gisela. "'Zum Wohle des Volkskörpers . . .' Abtreibung und Sterilisation im Nationalsozialismus." *Journal für Geschichte* 2, no. 6 (1980): 58–65.

———. "Racism and Sexism in Nazi Germany: Motherhood, Compulsory Sterilization, and the State." *Signs: Journal of Women in Culture and Society* 8, no. 3 (1983): 400–421.

———. *Zwangssterilisation im Nationalsozialismus. Studien zur Rassenpolitik und Frauenpolitik* [= Schriften des Zentralinstituts für sozialwissenschaftliche Forschung der Freien Universität Berlin Bd. 48]. Opladen, 1986.

———. "Die Frauen und der Nationalsozialismus. Bemerkungen zu einem Buch von Claudia Koonz." *Geschichte und Gesellschaft* 15 (1989): 563–79.

———. "Ein Hiustorikerinnenstreit?" *Geschichte und Gesellschaft* 18 (1992): 400–404.

———. "Antinatalism, Maternity, and Paternity in National Socialist Racism." In David Crew, ed., *Nazism and German Society, 1933–1945,* 110–40. London and New York, 1994.

———. "Ganz normale Frauen. Täter, Opfer, Mitläufer und Zuschauer im Nationalsozialismus." In Kirsten Heinsohn, Barbara Vogel, and Ulrike Weckel, eds., *Zwischen Karriere und Verfolgung. Handlungsräume von Frauen im nationalsozialistischen Deutschland,* 245–77. Frankfurt a.M., 1997.

Bock, Gisela, and Barbara Duden. "Arbeit aus Liebe—Liebe als Arbeit. Zur Entstehung der Hausarbeit im Kapitalismus." In Berliner Dozentinnen, eds., *Frauen und Wissenschaft. Beiträge zur Berliner Sommeruniversität für Frauen im Juli 1976,* 118–99. Berlin, 1977.

Böltken, Andrea. *Führerinnen im "Führerstaat": Gertrud Scholz-Klink, Trude Mohr, Jutta Rüdiger und Inge Viermetz.* Pfaffenweiler, 1995.

Boll, Friedhelm. "Jugend im Umbruch vom Nationalsozialismus zur Nachkriegsdemokratie." *Archiv für Sozialgeschichte* 37 (1997): 482–520.

Böß, Gustav. *Berlin von heute. Stadtverwaltung und Wirtschaft.* Berlin, 1929.

Bourdieu, Pierre. *Entwurf einer Theorie der Praxis.* Frankfurt a.M., 1976. Translated as *Outline of a Theory of Practice.* Cambridge: Cambridge University Press, 1977.

———. "Historische und soziale Voraussetzungen modernen Sports." *Merkur* 39, no. 7 (1985): 575–90.

Brandenburg, Hans-Christian. *Die Geschichte der HJ. Wege und Irrwege einer Generation.* Cologne, 1968.

Brandt, Gisela, Johanna Kootz, and Gisela Steppke. *Zur Frauenfrage im Kapitalismus.* Frankfurt a.M., 1973.

Braun, Helga. "Der Bund Deutscher Mädel (BDM)—Faschistische Projektionen von der 'neuen deutschen Frau.'" In Harald Focke, Uwe Reimer, and Horst Krull, eds., *Sozialistische Erziehung contra Nazi-Verführung* [= Ergebnisse 15], 92–124. Hamburg o.J., 1981.

Breyvogel, Wilfried, and Thomas Lohmann. "Schulalltag im Nationalsozialismus." In Detlev Peukert and Jürgen Reulecke, eds., *Die Reihen fast geschlossen. Beiträge zur Geschichte des Alltags unterm Nationalsozialismus,* 199–221. Wuppertal, 1981.

Bridenthal, Renate, and Claudia Koonz. "Beyond Kinder, Küche, Kirche:

Weimar Women in Politics and Work." In Renate Bridenthal, Atina Gross-
    mann, and Marion Kaplan, eds., *When Biology Became Destiny: Women in
    Weimar and Nazi Germany.* New York, 1984.
Broszat, Martin. *Der Staat Hitlers. Grundlagen und Entwicklung seiner inneren
    Verfassung.* Munich, 1969.
————. "Resistenz und Widerstand. Eine Zwischenbilanz des Forschungsprojek-
    tes." In Martin Broszat, Elke Fröhlich, and Anton Großmann, eds., *Bayern in
    der NS-Zeit.* Vol. 4, *Herrschaft und Gesellschaft in Konflikt, Part C.* Munich
    and Vienna, 1981.
Bruchmann, Marlies, and Ruth Gurny. "Wenn Subjektivität zum Subjektivismus
    wird . . . Methodische Probleme der neueren soziologischen Biogra-
    phieforschung." *Kölner Zeitschrift für Soziologie und Sozialpsychologie* 36, no.
    4 (1984): 773–82.
Brückner, Peter. *Das Abseits als sicherer Ort. Kindheit und Jugend zwischen 1933
    und 1945.* Berlin, 1980.
————. "'Wie die Leute vom Krieg reden, hat für mich immer eine gewisse Bedeu-
    tung.' Ein Gespräch mit Peter Brückner." *Psychosozial* 9, no. 28 (1986): 7–26.
Bruns, Claudia. "Vom Antifeminismus zum Antisemitismus. Kontroversen um
    Hans Blüher in der Frauen- und Jugendbewegung." *Ariadne. Forum für Frauen-
    und Geschlechtergeschichte* 43 (2003): 46–51.
Budde, Gunilla-Friederike, ed. *Frauen arbeiten. Weibliche Erwerbstätigkeit in Ost-
    und Westdeutschland nach 1945.* Göttingen, 1997.
Buddrus, Michael. *Totale Erziehung für den totalen Krieg. Hitlerjugend und nation-
    sozialistische Jugendpolitik, Teil 1 und 2.* Munich, 2003.
Bude, Heinz. *Deutsche Karrieren. Lebenskonstruktionen sozialer Aufsteiger aus der
    Flakhelfer-Generation.* Frankfurt a.M., 1987.
Burgdörfer, Friedrich. "Der Geburtenrückgang mit besonderer Berücksichtigung
    der verschiedenen Bevölkerungsschichten." *Freie Wohlfahrtspflege* 4, no. 10
    (1930): 438–52.
Burgdorff, Stephan, and Christian Habbe, eds. *Als Feuer vom Himmer fiel. Der
    Bombenkrieg in Deutschland.* Munich, 2003.
Burkert, Hans-Norbert, Klaus Matußek, and Wolfgang Wippermann. *"Machter-
    greifung." Berlin 1933"* [= Stätten der Geschichte Berlins, Bd. 2]. Berlin, 1982.
Bürkner, Trude. *Der Bund Deutscher Mädel in der Hitlerjugend.* Berlin, 1937.
Busse-Wilson, Elisabeth. *Die Frau und die Jugendbewegung. Ein Beitrag zur weib-
    lichen Charakterologie und zur Kritik des Antifeminismus.* Hamburg, 1920.
————. "Liebe und Kameradschaft." In Werner Kindt, ed., *Grundschriften der
    deutschen Jugendbewegung,* [= Gemeinschafts werk Dokumentation der
    Jugendbewegung] 327–34. Cologne and Düsseldorf, 1963.
Czarnowski, Gabriele. *Das kontrollierte Paar. Ehe- und Sexualpolitik im National-
    sozialismus.* Ergebnisse der Frauenforschung, Bd. 24. Weinheim, 1981.
————. "Frauen—Staat—Medizin. Aspekte der Körperpolitik im Nationalsozial-
    ismus." *Beiträge zur feministischen Theorie und Praxis* 8, no. 14 (1985): 79–98.
Dammer, Susanna. *Versuche der Vergesellschaftung "weiblicher Fähigkeiten"
    durch eine Dienstverpflichtung (Deutschland 1890–1918).* Dissertation at the
    department of education and instruction at the Technical University Berlin,
    1987.

Dehn, Günther. *Die religiöse Gedankenwelt der Proletarierjugend.* Berlin, 1926.

Deutsches Archiv für Jugendwohlfahrt, ed. *Kleines Handbuch der Jugendverbände.* Berlin, 1931.

Deutschland-Berichte der Sozialdemokratischen Partei (Sopade). Vols. 1–7 (1934–40). Reprint, Salzhausen, Frankfurt a.M., 1980.

Diestelkamp, Ludwig. *Geschichte der Nazareth-Gemeinde auf dem Wedding zu Berlin von 1835–1885. Festgabe zur 50jährigen Feier des Einweihungstages der Nazarethgemeinde am 5.7.1885.* Berlin, 1885.

Dinse, Robert. *Das Freizeitleben der Großstadtjugend. 5000 Jungen uund Mädchen berichten* [= Schriftenreihe des Deutschen Archivs für Jugendwohlfahrt 10]. Eberswalde, 1932.

Donzelot, Jaques. *Die Ordnung der Familie.* Frankfurt a.M., 1980.

Drewitz, Ingeborg. *Gestern war heute. Hundert Jahre Gegenwart.* Düsseldorf, 1978.

Duden, Barbara. "Die Berliner Salons um 1800 —Zur Emanzipation der Frauen. Schriftliche Hausarbeit für das Fach Geschichte." Technische Universität Berlin, 1970. Manuscript.

———. "Das schöne Eigentum. Zur Herausbildung des bürgerlichen Frauenbildes an der Wende vom 18. zum 19. Jahrhundert." *Kursbuch* 74 (1977): 125–40.

Elias, Norbert. *The Civilizing Process.* Trans. Edmund Jephcott. New York, 1978.

Elias, Norbert, and Eric Dunning. "Zur Dynamik von Sportgruppen." In Günther Lüschen, ed., *Kleingruppenforschung und Gruppe im Sport* [= Sonderheft 10 der Kölner Zeitschrift für Soziologie und Sozialpsychologie], 118–34. Opladen, 1966.

———. *Sport im Zivilisationsprozeß. Studien zur Figurationssoziologie.* Ed. Wilhelm Hopf. Münster o.J., 1985.

Engel, Gustav. *Politische Geschichte Westfalens.* Cologne and Berlin, 1968.

Engelbrechten, Julek Karl von. *Eine braune Armee entsteht. Die Geschichte der Berlin-Brandenburgischen SA.* Munich, 1937.

Feilzer, Heinrich. *Jugend in der mittelalterlichen Ständegesellschaft. Ein Beitrag zum Problem der Generationen* [= Wiener Beiträge zur Theologie Bd. 36]. Vienna, 1971.

Finck, Renate. *"Mit uns zieht die neue Zeit."* Baden-Baden, 1979.

Franzen-Hellersberg, Lisbeth. "Die Frau und die Jugendbewegung." In Richard Thurnwald, ed., *Die neue Jugend* [= Forschungen zur Völkerpsychologie und Soziologie, vol. 4], 129–44. Leipzig, 1927.

———. *Die jugendliche Arbeiterin, ihre Arbeitsweise und Lebensform. Versuch sozialpsychologischer Forschung zum Zweck der Umwertung proletarischer Tatbestände.* Tübingen, 1932.

Freudenberg, Karl. "Fruchtbarkeit und Sterblichkeit in den Berliner Verwaltungs-bezirken in Beziehung zu deren sozialer Struktur." In Alfred Grotjahn, Leo Langstein, and Fritz Rott, eds., *Ergebnisse der sozialen Hygiene und Gesund-heitsfürsorge,* vol. 1. Leipzig, 1929.

Frevert, Ute. *Women in German History: From Bourgeois Emancipation to Sexual Liberation.* Oxford, Hamburg, and New York, 1981.

Friedrich, Jörg. *Der Brand. Deutschland im Bombenkrieg, 1940–1945.* Munich, 2002.

Fromm, Erich. *Arbeiter und Angestellte am Vorabend des Dritten Reiches. Eine sozialpsychologische Untersuchung.* Munich, 1983.

Fromm, Erich, Max Horkheimer, Hans Mayer, and Herbert Marcuse, eds. *Studien über Autorität und Familie. Forschungsberichte aus dem Institut für Sozialforschung.* Paris, 1936.

Fürst, Max. *Talismann Scheherezade. Die schwierigen 20ger Jahre.* Munich and Vienna, 1976.

Gallwitz, Esther. *Feiheit 35 oder wir Mädel singen falsch.* Freiburg, 1964.

Gamm, Hans-Jochen. *Führung und Verführung. Pädagogik des Nationalsozialismus.* Munich, 1964.

Gehmacher, Johanna. *Jugend ohne Zukunft. Hitler-Jugend und Bund Deutscher Mädel in Österreich vor 1938.* Vienna, 1994.

Geist, Johann Friedrich, and Klaus Kürvers. *Das Berliner Mietshaus.* Vol. 1: *1740–1862. Eine dokumentarische Geschichte der "von Wülcknitzschen Familienhäuser" vor dem Hamburger Tor, der Proletarisierung des Nordens und der Stadt im Übergang von der Residenz zur Metropole,* Munich, 1980.

———. *Das Berliner Mietshaus.* Vol. 2: *1862–1945. Eine dokumentarische Geschichte von "Meyers Hof" in der Ackerstraße 132–133, der Entstehung der Berliner Mietshausquartiere und der Reichshauptstadt zwischen Gründung und Untergang.* Munich, 1984.

Gerhard, Ute. *Verhältnisse und Verhinderungen. Frauenarbeit, Familie und Recht der Frauen im 19. Jahrhundert.* Frankfurt a.M., 1981.

Gottwald, Franz. *Heimatbuch vom Wedding.* Berlin, 1924.

Gravenhorst, Lerke, and Carmen Tatschmurat, eds. *TöchterFragen. NS-Frauen-Geschichte* [= Forum Frauenforschung, Bd. 5]. Freiburg i.Br., 1990.

Greifenhagen, Martin. *Jahrgang 1928. Aus einem unruhigen Leben.* Munich and Zürich, 1988.

Groß-Berliner Verein für das Kleinwohnungswesen, ed. *Wohnungspolitik von Gestern und Morgen.* Berlin, 1931.

Grossmann, Atina. "Feminist Debates about Women and National Socialism." *Gender and History* 3 (1991): 350–58.

———. *Reforming Sex: The German Movement for Birth Control and Abortion Reform, 1920–1950.* New York, 1995.

Gruchmann, Lothar. "Jugendposition und Justiz im Dritten Reich. Die Probleme bei der Verfolgung der 'Leipziger Meuten' durch die Gerichte." In Wolfgang Benz, ed., *Miscellanea. Festschrift für Helmut Krausnick,* 103–30. Stuttgart, 1980.

Grüttner, Michael. *Studenten im Dritten Reich.* Paderborn, 1995.

Habermas, Rebekka. *Frauen und Männer des Bürgertums: eine Familiengeschichte.* Göttingen, 2000.

Hagemann, Karen. "Of 'Old' Men and 'New' Housewives: Everyday Housework and the Limits of Household Rationalization in the Urban Working-Class Milieu of the Weimar Republic." *International Review of Social History* 41 (1996): 305–30.

Hagemann, Karen, and Brigitte Söllner. "'Denn der Mann hat gesagt: Es genügt, wenn ich in der Partei bin.' Die sozialdemokratische Frauenbewegung Hamburgs in der Weimarer Republik." In Jörg Berlin, ed., *Das andere Hamburg. Freiheitliche Bestrebungen in der Hansestadt seit dem Spätmittelalter,* 235–62. Cologne, 1981.

Hahn, Barbara. "Die Salons der Rahel Levin Varnhagen." In Hannelore Gärtner and Annette Purfürst, eds., *Berliner Romantik. Orte, Spuren und Begegnungen,* 105–22. Berlin, 1992.

Hannsmann, Margarete. *Der helle Tag bricht an. Ein Kind wird Nazi.* Hamburg, 1982.

Harig, Ludwig. *Weh dem, der aus der Reihe tanzt.* München, 1990.

Harvey, Elizabeth. "'Die deutsche Frau im Osten': 'Rasse', Geschlecht und öffentlicher Raum im besetzten Polen 1940–1944." *Archiv für Sozialgeschichte* 38 (1998): 191–214.

———. *Women and the Nazi East: Agents and Witnesses of Germanization.* New Haven and London, 2003.

Hausen, Karin. "Die Polarisierung der 'Geschlechtscharakter'.—Eine Dissoziation von Erwerbs- und Familienleben." In Werner Conze, ed., *Sozialgeschichte der Familie in der Neuzeit Europas. Neue Forschungen,* 363–93. Stuttgart, 1977.

———. "Mütter, Söhne und der Markt der Symbole und Waren: Der deutsche Muttertag 1923–1933." In Hans Medick and David Sabean, eds., *Emotionen und materielle Interessen. Sozialanthropologische und historische Beiträge zur Familienforschung,* 473–523. Göttingen, 1984.

———. "'. . . eine Ulme für das schwache Efeu.' Ehepaare im deutschen Bildungsbürgertum. Ideale und Wirklichkeiten im späten 18. und 19. Jahrhundert." In Ute Frevert, ed., *Bürgerinnen und Bürger,* 85–117. Göttingen, 1988.

Hegemann, Werner. *1930. Das steinerne Berlin.* Braunschweig and Wiesbaden, 1979.

Heine, Heinrich. *Germany: A Winter's Tale.* Published in German, 1844. Trans. Herman Salinger. New York: L. B. Fischer, 1944.

Heineman, Elizabeth D. *What Difference Does a Husband Make? Women and Marital Status in Nazi and Postwar Germany.* Berkeley, Los Angeles, and London, 1999.

Heinsohn, Kirsten, Barbara Vogel, and Ulrike Weckel, eds. *Zwischen Karriere und Verfolgung. Handlungsräume von Frauen im nationalsozialistischen Deutschland.* Frankfurt a.M., 1997.

Heise, Rosemarie. "Aufbruch in die Illusion? Eine Jugend in der SBZ/DDR." In Franz-Werner Kersting, ed., *Jugend vor einer Welt in Trümmern. Erfahrungen und Verhältnisse der Jugend zwischen Hitler- und Nachkriegsdeutschland,* 191–211. Weinheim and München, 1998.

Hellfeld, Matthias von. *Edelweißpiraten in Köln. Jugendrebellion gegen das 3. Reich. Das Beispiel Köln-Ehrenfeld.* Cologne, 1981.

Henke, Josef. "Das Schicksal deutscher zeitgeschichtlicher Quellen in Kriegs- und Nachkriegszeit. Beschlagnahme—Rückführung—Verbleib." *Vierteljahreshefte für Zeitgeschichte* 30, no. 4 (1982): 557–620.

Hering, Sabine, and Klaus Schilde. *Das BDM-Werk "Glaube und Schönheit." Die Organisation junger Frauen im Nationalsozialismus.* Opladen, 1994; reprint, 2004.

Hermand, Jost. *A Hitler Youth in Poland: The Nazi Program for Evacuating Children during World War II.* Evanston, 1997.

Hertz, Deborah. *Jewish High Culture in Old Regime Berlin.* New Haven and London, 1988.

Herzig, Arno. *Judentum und Emanzipation in Westfalen* [= Veröffentlichungen des Provinzialinstitutes für Westfälische Landes- und Volkskunde, Reihe 1, H. 17]. Münster, 1973.

———. *"In unserem Herzen glüht der Freiheit Schein." Die Entstehungsphase der bürgerlichen und sozialen Demokratie in Minden (1848–1878)* [= Mindener Beiträge 19]. Minden, 1981.

Hitler, Adolf. *Mein Kampf.* The First Complete and Unexpurgated Edition Published in the English Language. New York, 1939.

Höhn, Maria. "Frau im Haus und Girl im Spiegel: Discourse on Women in the Interregnum Period of 1945–1949 and the Question of German Identity." *Central European History* 26 (1993): 57–90.

Hong, Young-Sun. *Welfare, Modernity, and the Weimar State, 1919–1933.* Princeton, 1998.

Horkheimer, Max. "Autorität und Familie in der Gegenwart." In Alfred Schmidt, ed., *Zur Kritik der instrumentellen Vernunft. Aus den Vorträgen und Aufzeichnungen seit Kriegsende,* 269–87. Frankfurt a.M., 1967. First appeared under the title *Eclipse of Reason,* New York, 1947.

Horn, Daniel. "Youth Resistence in the Third Reich: A Social Portrait." *Journal of Social History* 7 (1973): 26–50.

Horwarth, Ödön von. *Jugend ohne Gott.* 7th ed. Frankfurt a.M., 1977.

Huerkamp, Claudia. *Bildungsbürgerinnen. Frauen im Studium und in akademischen Berufen, 1900–1945.* Göttingen, 1996.

Hurwitz, Harold. *Demokratie und Antikommunismus in Berlin nach 1945.* 3 vols. Cologne, 1983–84.

Illich, Ivan. *Genus. Zu einer historischen Kritik der Gleichheit.* Reinbek bei Hamburg, 1983.

Illustrierte Geschichte der deutschen Revolution. Berlin, 1929.

Jacobs, Manfred. "Kirche, Weltanschauung, Politik. Die evangelischen Kirchen und die Option zwischen dem Zweiten und Dritten Reich." *Vierteljahreshefte für Zeitgeschichte* 31, no. 1 (1983): 108–35.

Jaspers, Karl. *Die geistige Situation der Zeit.* Berlin and New York, 1979.

Jüngst, Hildegard. *Die jugendliche Fabrikarbeiterin. Ein Beitrag zur Industriepädagogik* [= Neue Beiträge zur Erziehungswissenschaft 5]. Paderborn, 1929.

Jürgens, Birgit. *Zur Geschichte des BDM (Bund Deutscher Mädel) von 1923 bis 1939.* Frankfurt a.M., 1994.

Jürgensen, Johannes. *Die bittere Lektion: Evangelische Jugend 1933* [= aej—Studienband 7]. Stuttgart, 1984.

Kaeber, Ernst. *Berlin 1848.* Berlin, 1948.

Kaeller, Reinhard. *Die konservative Partei in Minden Ravensburg, ihre Grundlagen, Entstehung und Entwicklung bis zum Jahre 1866* [= 26. Jahresbericht des Historischen Vereins für die Grafschaft Ravensberg in Bielefeld]. Bielefeld, 1912.

Kaiser, Jochen-Christoph. *Arbeiterbewegung und organisierte Religionskritik. Proletarische Freidenkerverbände in Kaiserreich und Weimarer Republik.* Stuttgart, 1981.

Kandel, Liliane, ed. *Feminismes et Nazisme* [= Cahiers des C. E.D.R.E.F.]. Paris, 1997.

Kardorff, Ursula von. *Berliner Aufzeichnungen aus dem Jahre 1942 bis 1945.* Munich, 1962.

Kater, Michael H. "Bürgerliche Jugendbewegung und Hitlerjugend in Deutschland von 1926 bis 1939." *Archiv für Sozialgeschichte* 17 (1977): 125–74.

———. "Die Sozialgeschichte und das Dritte Reich. Überlegungen zu neuen Büchern." *Archiv für Sozialgeschichte* 22 (1982): 661–82.

———. *Hitler Youth.* Cambridge, 2004.

Kaufmann, Doris. "Vom Vaterland zum Mutterland. Frauen im Katholischen Milieu der Weimarer Republik." In Karin Hausen, ed., *Frauen suchen ihre Geschichte. Historische Studien zum 19. und 20. Jahrhundert,* 250–75. Munich, 1983.

Kaufmann, Günter. *Das kommende Deutschland.* Berlin, 1940.

———. *Baldur von Schirach. Ein Jugendführer in Deutschland. Richtigstellung und Vermächtnis.* Selbstverlag, 1993.

Kelchner, Mathilde. *Kummer und Trost jugendlicher Arbeiterinnen. Eine sozialpsychologische Untersuchung an Aufsätzen von Schülerinnen der Berufsschule* [= Forschungen zur Völkerpsychologie und Soziologie, vol. 6]. Leipzig, 1929.

———. *Die weibliche werktätige Jugend der Großstadt* [= Sonderdruck aus dem "Handbuch der pädagogischen Milieukunde," ed. Adolf Busemann]. Halle (Saale), 1932.

Kenkmann, Alfons. *Wilde Jugend. Lebenswelt großstädtischer Jugendlicher zwischen Wirtschaftskrise, Nationalsozialismus und Währungsreform* [= Düsseldorfer Schriften zur neueren Landesgeschichte und zur Geschichte Nordrhein-Westfalens, vol. 42]. Essen, 1996.

Keun, Irmgard. *Gilgi—eine von uns.* Berlin, 1931. Reprint, Bergisch-Gladbach, 1981.

Killius, Rosemarie. *Frauen für die Front. Erinnerungen von Wehrmachtshelferinnen.* Leipzig, 2003.

Kinz, Gabriele. *Der Bund Deutscher Mädel. Ein Beitrag zur ausserschulischen Mädchenerziehung im Nationalsozialismus.* Frankfurt a.M., 1989.

Kirkpatrick, Clifford. *Nazi Germany: Its Women and Family Life.* Indianapolis and New York, 1938.

Klaus, Martin. *Mädchen in der Hitlerjugend. Die Erziehung zur "deutschen Frau."* Cologne, 1980.

———. *Mädchenerziehung zur Zeit der faschistischen Herrschaft in Deutschland—Der Bund Deutscher Mädel.* 2 vols. [= Sozialhistorische Untersuchungen zur Reformpädagogik und Erwachsenenbildung. Vol. 3. W. Fabinan und K.-Ch. Lingelbach, eds.]. Frankfurt a.M., 1983.

Klinksiek, Dorothee. *Die Frau im NS-Staat* [= Schriftenreihe der Vierteljahreshefte für Zeitgeschichte No. 44]. Stuttgart, 1982.

Klönne, Arno. *Hitlerjugend. Die Jugend und ihre Organisation im Dritten Reich.* Hannover and Frankfurt a.M., 1955.

———. *Gegen den Strom. Ein Bericht über die Jugendopposition im Dritten Reich.* Hannover and Frankfurt a.M., 1957.

———. "Jugendprotest und Jugendopposition. Von der HJ-Erziehung zum Cliquenwesen der Kriegszeit." In Martin Broszat, Elke Fröhlich, and Anton Großmann, eds., *Bayern in der NS-Zeit.* Vol. 4, *Herrschaft und Gesellschaft im Konflikt, Part C* [= Veröffentlichung im Rahmen des Projekts "Widerstand und Verfolgung in Bayern 1933–1945" im Auftrag des Bayrischen Staatsministeriums für Unterricht und Kultur bearbeitet vom Institut für Zeitgeschichte in Verbindung mit den staatlichen Archiven Bayern], 527–620. Munich and Vienna, 1981.

Klönne, Irmgard. *"Ich spring in diesem Ringe." Mädchen und Frauen in der deutschen Jugendbewegung.* Pfaffenweiler, 1990.

König, Réné. "Familie und Autorität. Der deutsche Vater im Jahr 1955." In König, *Materialien zur Soziologie der Familie.* 2d ed. Cologne, 1974.

Kontos, Silvia. *Die Partei kämpft wie ein Mann. Frauenpolitik der KPD in der Weimarer Republik.* Frankfurt a.M., 1979.

Koonz, Claudia. "Nazi Women before 1933: Rebels against Emancipation." *Social Science Quarterly* 56, no. 4 (1976): 553–63.

———. *Mothers in the Fatherland: Women, the Family, and Nazi Politics.* London, 1987.

———. "Erwiderung auf Gisela Bocks Rezension von 'Mothers in the Fatherland.'" *Geschichte und Gesellschaft* 8 (1992): 394–99.

Kracauer, Siegfried. *Schriften I.* Frankfurt a.M., 1971.

———. *Das Ornament der Massen.* Frankfurt a.M., 1977.

———. *The Salaried Masses: Duty and Distraction in Weimar Germany.* London and New York, 1998.

Krickau, Katharina. *Die Geschichte des Mindener Oberlyzeums 1826–1926. Zum 100-jährigen Gründungstage.* Minden, 1926.

Krieg, Martin. "Einwohnerzahlen der Stadt Minden. Über die Bevölkerungsbewegung in Minden seit 700 Jahren." *Mindener Tageblatt,* December 1, 1949.

Krockow, Christian, Graf von. *Die Stunde der Frauen. Pommern 1944 bis 1947.* Stuttgart, 1988.

Krolzig, Günther. *Der Jugendliche in der Großstadtfamilie. Auf Grund von Niederschriften Berliner Berufsschüler und Schülerinnen* [= Forschungen über "Bestand und Erschütterung der Familie in der Gegenwart," vol. 4]. Berlin, 1930.

Kulka, Otto Dov, and Eberhard Jäckel, eds. *Die Juden in den geheimen NS-Stimmungsberichten 1933–1945.* Düsseldorf, 2004.

Kulke, Leopold. "Die wirtschaftliche Entwicklung der Stadt Minden nach der Entfestigung 1873." *Mitteilungen des Mindener Geschichts- und Museumsvereins* 45 (1973): 15–80.

Kundrus, Birthe. "Frauen und Nationalsozialismus." *Archiv für Sozialgeschichte* 36 (1996): 481–99.

Kuntze, Eduard. *Das Jubiläum von Voigtland oder Geschichte der Gründung und Entwicklung der Rosenthaler Vorstadt bei Berlin von 1755–1855.* Berlin, 1855.

Kurella, Alfred. "Körperseele." *Freideutsche Jugend* 4, no. 7 (1918): 235–52.

Kurz, Thomas. *"Blutmai." Sozialdemokraten und Kommunisten im Brennpunkt der Berliner Ereignisse von 1929.* Berlin and Bonn, 1988.

Lang, Jochen von. *Der Hitler-Junge. Baldur von Schirach. Der Mann, der Deutschlands Jugend erzog.* Hamburg, 1988.

Lange, Helene, and Gertrud Bäumer. *Handbuch der Frauenbewegung.* Vol. 3: *Der Stand der Frauenbildung in den Kulturländern.* Berlin, 1902.

Lauterer-Pirner, Heidi. "Vom 'Frauenspiegel' zu Luthers Schrift 'Vom ehelichen Leben'. Das Bild der Ehefrau im Spiegel einiger Schriften des 15. und 16. Jahrhunderts." In Annette Kuhn and Jörn Rüsen, eds., *Frauen in der Geschichte III.* Düsseldorf, 1983.

Lessing, Helmut, and Manfred Liebel. *Wilde Cliquen. Szenen einer anderen Arbeiterjugendbewegung.* Bensheim, 1981.

Lippe, Rudolf zur. *Naturbeherrschung am Menschen I. Körpererfahrung und Entfaltung von Sinnen und Beziehungen in der Ära des italienischen Kaufmannskapitals.* Frankfurt a.M., 1974.

Litt, Theodor. *Das Verhältnis der Generationen. Ehedem und heute.* Wiesbaden, 1947.

Loest, Erich. *Durch die Erde ein Riß. Ein Lebenslauf.* Munich, 1990.

Loewenberg, Peter. "The Psychohistorical Origins of the Nazi Cohort." *American Historical Review* 76 (1971): 248–58.

Löwenthal, Richard, and Patrick von Zur Mühlen. *Widerstand und Verweigerung in Deutschland 1933 bis 1945.* Berlin and Bonn, 1982.

Lück, Margret. *Die Frau im Männerstaat. Die gesellschaftliche Stellung der Frau im Nationalsozialismus. Eine Analyse aus pädagogischer Sicht.* Frankfurt a.M., 1979.

Lukas, Gerhard. *Geschichte der Körperkultur in Deutschland.* Vol. 1. Berlin, 1969.

Luther, Martin. *Werke. Kritische Gesamtausgabe.* Weimarer Ausgabe, vols. 1–30. Weimar, 1910. Reprint, Weimar, 1964.

———. *Luther Deutsch. Die Werke Martin Luthers in neuer Auswahl für die Gegenwart.* Ed. Kurt Aland. Vols. 1–11. Stuttgart, 1969–2002 (reprint, Stuttgart, 2005).

Mager, Wolfgang. "Haushalt und Familie in protoindustrieller Gesellschaft. Sprenge (Ravensberg) während der ersten Hälfte des 19. Jahrhunderts. Eine Fallstudie." In Neidhard Bulst, Joseph Goy, and Jochen Hoock, eds., *Familie zwischen Tradition und Moderne* [= Kritische Studie zur Geschichtswissenschaft 48]. Göttingen, 1981.

Mann, Erika. *School for Barbarians: Education under the Nazis.* New York, 1938.

Mann, Klaus. *Kind dieser Zeit.* Berlin, 1932.

Mann, Thomas. *Reflections of a Nonpolitical Man.* Trans. and with an introduction by Walter D. Morris. New York, 1983.

Matthes, Carl. *Der Wedding, wie er war und wurde.* Berlin-Schöneberg, 1935.

Maschmann, Melitta. *Fazit. Kein Rechtfertigungsversuch.* Stuttgart, 1963.

Mason, Timothy. "Zur Lage der Frauen in Deutschland 1930–1940. Wohlfahrt, Arbeit und Familie." In *Gesellschaft. Beiträge zur Marxschen Theorie,* 6:118–93. Frankfurt a.M., 1976.

Mewes, Bernhard. *Die erwerbstätige Jugend. Eine statistische Untersuchung.* Berlin and Leipzig, 1929.

Meyer-Renschhausen, Elisabeth. "Das radikal traditionelle Selbstbild." *Geschichtsdidaktik* 10, no. 2 (1985): 129–48.

Miller-Kipp, Gisela. "Der Bund Deutscher Mädel in der Hitler-Jugend. Erziehung zwischen Ideologie und Herrschaftsprozeß." *Pädagogische Rundschau* 36 (1982): 71–105.

Mitterauer, Michael. *Sozialgeschichte der Jugend.* Frankfurt a.M., 1986.

Moeller, Robert. *Protecting Motherhood: Women and the Family in the Politics of Postwar West Germany.* Berkeley, 1993.

Mooser, Josef. "Familie, Heirat, Berufswahl. Zur Verfassung der ländlichen Gesellschaft im 19. Jahrhundert." In Heinz Reif, ed., *Die Familie in der Geschichte,* 137–62. Göttingen, 1982.

Morgan, Dagmar G. "Weiblicher Arbeitsdienst in Deutschland." PhD diss., Darmstadt, 1978.

Musial, Magdalena. "Jugendbewegung und Emanzipation der Frau. Ein Beitrag zur Rolle der weiblichen Jugend in der Jugendbewegung bis 1933." PhD diss., Essen, 1982.

Negt, Oskar, and Alexander Kluge. *Öffentlichkeit und Erfahrung. Zur Organisationsanalyse von bürgerlicher und proletarischer Öffentlichkeit.* Frankfurt a.M., 1972.

Neubauer, Hermann. *Geschichte der Nazareth-Gemeinde 1835–1925.* Berlin, 1926.

Neukrantz, Klaus. *Barrikaden am Wedding. Der Roman einer Straße aus den Berliner Maitagen 1929.* 1931; reprint, Berlin, 1970.

Niemeyer, Annemarie. *Zur Struktur der Familie. Statistische Materialien* [= Forschungen über "Bestand und Erschütterung der Familie in der Gegenwart," vol. 2]. Berlin, 1931.

Niethammer, Lutz, ed. *"Die Jahre weiß man nicht, wo man die heute hinsetzen soll." Faschismuserfahrungen im Ruhrgebiet. Lebensgeschichte und Sozialkultur im Ruhrgebiet 1930 bis 1960.* Vol. 1. Berlin and Bonn, 1983.

Noakes, Jeffrey, and Geoffrey Pridham. *Nazism, 1914–1945.* Vols. 1–4. Exeter, 1995; reprint, 1998.

Nolan, Mary. *Imagining America, Modernizing Germany: Fordism and Economic Reform in the Weimar Republic.* New York, 1994.

Nordsiek, Hans. *Der totale Krieg und seine Folgen. Minden 1944–1946.* Exhibition catalog of the Municipal Archive Minden, October 5–30, 1975. Minden, 1975.

Nordsiek, Marianne. *"Fackelzüge überall . . .". Das Jahr 1933 in den Kreisen Minden und Lübbecke.* Bielefeld, Dortmund, and Münster, 1983.

Nydahl, Jens, ed. *Das Berliner Schulwesen.* Berlin, 1928.

Orland, Barbara. "Emanzipation durch Rationalisierung? Der 'rationelle Haushalt' als Konzept institutioneller Frauenpolitik in der Weimarer Republik." In Dagmar Reese et al., eds., *Rationale Beziehungen. Geschlechterverhältnisse im Rationalisierungsprozess,* 222–50. Frankfurt a.M., 1993.

Orland, Barbara, and Arbeitsgemeinschaft Hauswirtschaft e.V. und Stiftung Verbraucherinstitut, eds. *Haushaltsträume: Ein Jahrhundert Technisierung und Rationalisierung im Haushalt,* exhibition catalog. Königstein, 1990.

Owings, Alison. *Frauen: German Women Recall the Third Reich.* New Brunswick: Rutgers, 1993.

Peters, Dietlinde. *Mütterlichkeit im Kaiserreich.* Bielefeld, 1984.

Peukert, Detlev. *Die KPD im Widerstand. Verfolgung und Untergrundarbeit an Rhein und Ruhr 1933 bis 1945.* Wuppertal, 1980.

———. *Die Edelweißpiraten. Protestbewegungen jugendlicher Arbeiter im Dritten Reich.* Cologne, 1980.

———. "Protest und Widerstand von Jugendlichen im Dritten Reich." In Richard

Löwenthal and Patrick von zur Mühlen, eds., *Widerstand und Verweigerung in Deutschland 1933 bis 1945,* 177–201. Berlin and Bonn, 1982.

———. "Erwerbslosigkeit junger Arbeiter in der Weltwirtschaftskrise im Deutschland 1929–1933." *Vierteljahreshefte für Sozial- und Wirtschaftsgeschichte* 72, no. 3 (1985): 305–28.

———. *Grenzen der Sozialdisziplinierung. Aufstieg und Krise der deutschen Jugendfürsorge von 1878 bis 1932.* Cologne, 1986.

———. "Youth in the Third Reich." In Richard Bessel, ed., *Life in the Third Reich,* 25–40. Oxford, 1987.

Peukert, Detlev, and Jürgen Reulecke, eds. *Die Reihen fast geschlossen. Beiträge zur Geschichte des Alltags unterm Nationalsozialismus.* Wuppertal, 1981.

Pfister, Gertrud. *Frau und Sport. Frühe Texte.* Frankfurt a.M., 1980.

———. "Körperkultur und Weiblichkeit. Ein historischer Beitrag zur Entwicklung des modernen Sports in Deutschland bis zur Zeit der Weimarer Republik." In Michael Klein, ed., *Sport und Geschlecht,* 35–59. Reinbek bei Hamburg, 1983.

Pine, Lisa. *Nazi Family Policy, 1933–1945.* Oxford and New York, 1997.

Plato, Alexander von. "'Ich bin mit allen gut ausgekommen.' Oder: war die Ruhrarbeiterschaft vor 1933 in politische Lager gespalten?" In Lutz Niethammer, ed., *"Die Jahre weiß man nicht, wo man die heute hinsetzen soll." Faschismuserfahrungen im Ruhrgebiet. Lebensgeschichte und Sozialkultur im Ruhrgebiet 1930 bis 1960,* 1:31–65. Bonn, 1983.

Poiger, Uta. "Rock 'n' Roll, Female Sexuality, and the Cold War Battle over German Identities." *Journal of Modern History* 68 (1996): 577–616.

Pore, Renate. *A Conflict of Interest: Women in German Social Democracy, 1919–1933.* Westport, CT, 1981.

Priepke, Manfred. *Die evangelische Jugend im Dritten Reich (1933–1936).* Hannover and Frankfurt a.M., 1960.

Pross, Harri. *Jugend, Eros, Politik. Die Geschichte der deutschen Jugendverbände.* Bern, Munich, and Vienna, 1964.

Rang, Brita. "Zur Geschichte des dualistischen Denkens über Mann und Frau. Kritische Anmerkungen zu den Thesen von Karin Hausen zur Herausbildung der Geschlechtscharaktere im 18. und 19. Jahrhundert." In Jutta Dahlhoff, Uschi Frey, and Ingrid Schöll, eds., *Frauenmacht in der Geschichte. Beiträge des Historikerinnentreffens 1985 zur Frauengeschichtsforschung,* 194–204. Düsseldorf, 1986.

Ras, Marion de. *Körper, Eros und weibliche Kultur. Mädchen im Wandervogel und in der Bündischen Jugend 1900–1933.* Pfaffenweiler, 1988.

———. *Body, Femininity, and Nationalism: Girls in the German Youth Movement.* London and New York, 2005.

Reekers, Stephanie. *Westfalens Bevölkerung 1818–1955. Die Bevölkerungsentwicklung der Gemeinden und Kreise im Zahlenbild* [= Veröffentlichungen des Provinzialinstitutes für westfälische Landes- und Volkskunde, ed. 1, no. 9). Münster, 1956.

———. "Beiträge zur stat. Darstellung der gewerblichen Wirtschaft Westfalens um 1800. Part 2: Minden-Ravensberg." *Westfälische Forschungen* [= Mitteilungen des Provinzialinstitutes für westfälische Landes- und Volkskunde, vol. 18], 75–129. Münster, 1965.

Reese, Dagmar. "Bund Deutscher Mädel—Zur Geschichte der weiblichen deutschen Jugend im Dritten Reich." In Frauengruppe Faschismusforschung, ed., *Mutterkreuz und Arbeitsbuch. Zur Geschichte der Frauen in der Weimarer Republik und im Nationalsozialismus*, 163–86. Frankfurt a.M., 1981.

———. *Rationale Beziehungen. Geschlechterverhältnisse im Rationalisierungsprozess*. Frankfurt a.M., 1993.

———. "The BDM-Generation: A Female Generation in Transition from Dictatorship to Democracy." In Mark Roseman, ed., *Generations in Conflict: Youth Revolt and Generation Formation in Germany, 1770–1968*, 227–46. Cambridge, 1995.

———. "Mädchen im Bund Deutscher Mädel." In Elke Kleinau and Claudia Opitz, eds., *Geschichte der Mädchen- und Frauenbildung*. Vol. 2: *Vom Vormärz bis zur Gegenwart*, 271–82. Frankfurt a.M., 1996.

———. "Verstrickung und Verantwortung. Weibliche Jugendliche in der Führung des Bundes Deutscher Mädel." In Kirsten Heinsohn, Barbara Vogel, and Ulrike Weckel, eds., *Zwischen Karriere und Verfolgung. Handlungsräume von Frauen im nationalsozialistischen Deutschland*, 206–22. Frankfurt a.M., 1997.

Reese, Dagmar, and Gertrud Pfister. "Gender, Body Culture, and Body Politics in National Socialism." *Sport Science Review* 4, no. 1 (1995): 91–121.

Reese, Dagmar, and Carola Sachse. "Frauenforschung und Nationalsozialismus—Eine Bilanz." In Lerke Gravenhorst and Carmen Tatschmurat, eds., *TöchterFragen. NS-Frauen-Geschichte* [= Forum Frauenforschung, Bd. 5], 73–106. Freiburg i.Br., 1990.

Reese-Nübel, Dagmar. "Kontinuitäten und Brüche in den Weiblichkeitskonstruktionen im Übergang von der Weimarer Republik zum Nationalsozialismus." In Hans-Uwe Otto and Heinz Sünker, eds., *Soziale Arbeit und Faschismus. Volkspflege und Pädagogik im Nationalsozialismus*, 223–41. Bielefeld, 1986.

Rohrwasser, Michael. *Saubere Mädel, starke Genossen*. Frankfurt a.M., 1975.

Rosenbaum, Heidi. *Formen der Familie. Untersuchungen zum Zusammenhang von Familienverhältnissen, Sozialstruktur und sozialem Wandel in der deutschen Gesellschaft des 19. Jahrhunderts*. Frankfurt a.M., 1982.

Rosenhaft, Eve. "Organizing the 'Lumpenproletariat': Cliques and Communists in Berlin during the Weimar Republic." In Richard J. Evans, ed., *The German Working Class, 1888–1933: The Politics of Everyday Life*, 174–219. London, 1982.

———. *Beating the Fascists! The German Communists and Political Violence, 1929–1933*. Cambridge, 1983.

Rosenmayr, Leopold. "Jugend." In Réné König, ed., *Handbuch der empirischen Sozialforschung*. Vol. 6. 2d rev. ed. Stuttgart, 1976.

Rosenthal, Gabriele, et al. *1945—Ende oder Neuanfang? Lebenslaufrekonstruktionen von Angehörigen der "Hitlerjugendgeneration"* [= Institut für Soziologie, Freie Universität Berlin, Mitteilungen aus dem Schwerpunktbereich Methodenlehre, no. 10]. Berlin, 1984.

———. " . . . *wenn alles in Scherben fällt* . . ." *Von Leben und Sinnwelt der Kriegsgeneration*. Opladen, 1987.

Roth, Lutz. *Die Erfindung des Jugendlichen.* Munich, 1983.

Rück, Franz. *Der Wedding in Wort und Bild.* Berlin, ca. 1930.

Rüdiger, Jutta. *Die Hitler-Jugend und ihr Selbstverständnis im Spiegel ihrer Aufgabengebiete.* Lindhorst, 1983.

———. *Ein Leben für die Jugend. Mädelführerin im Dritten Reich.* Preußisch Oldendorf, 1999.

Rupieper, Hermann-Josef, and Alexander Sperk, ed. *Die Lageberichte der Geheimen Staatspolizei zur Provinz Sachsen.* Vol. 1: *Regierungsbezierk Madgeburg.* Halle (Saale), 2003. Vol. 2: *Regierungsbezirk Merseburg.* Halle (Saale), 2004. Vol. 3: *Regierungsbezirk Erfurt.* Halle (Saale), 2004.

Rupp, Leila. *Mobilizing Women for War: German and American Propaganda, 1939–1945.* Princeton, 1978.

Sachse, Carola. *Siemens, der Nationalsozialismus und die moderne Familie. Eine Untersuchung zur sozialen Rationalisierung in Deutschland im 20. Jahrhundert.* Hamburg, 1990.

———. "Frauenforschung zum Natioanalsoziualismus. Debatten, Topoi und Ergebnisse seit 1976." *Mittelweg 36. Zeitschrift des Hamburger Instituts fuer Sozialforschung* 6, April–May (1997): 24–33.

———. *Gerechtigkeit und Gleichberechtigung in Ost und West 1939–1994.* Göttingen, 2002.

Saldern, Adelheid von. "Victims or Perpetrators? Controversies about the Role of Women in the Nazi State." In David Crew, ed., *Nazism and German Society, 1933–1945,* 141–65. London and New York, 1994.

Salomon, Alice, and Marie Baum. *Das Familienleben in der Gegenwart* [= Forschungen über "Bestand und Erschütterung der Familie in der Gegenwart," vol. 1]. Berlin, 1930.

Saurbier, Bruno. *Geschichte der Leibesübungen.* Frankfurt a.M., 1955.

Schade, Rosemarie. *Ein weibliches Utopia. Organisation und Ideologien der Mädchen und Frauen in der bürgerlichen Jugendbewegung 1905–1933.* Witzenhausen, 1996.

Scharfe, Martin. *Die Religion des Volkes. Kleine Kultur- und Sozialgeschichte des Pietismus.* Gütersloh, 1980.

Schiele, Friedrich Michael, and Leopold Zscharnack, eds. *Die Religion in Geschichte und Gegenwart. Handwörterbuch in gemeinverständlicher Sprache.* 2 vols. In cooperation with Hermann Gunkel and Otto Scheel. Tübingen, 1910.

Schimmler, Bernd. *Der Wedding anno dunnemals.* Berlin-Wedding, 1980.

———. *Der Wedding. Ein Bezirk zwischen Tradition und Fortschritt* [= Schriftenreihe des Berliner Heimatvereins "Verein für Weddinger Geschichte," vol. 1]. Berlin, 1985.

Schirach, Baldur von. *Die Hitler-Jugend. Idee und Gestalt.* Leipzig, 1934.

———. *Ich glaubte an Hitler.* Hamburg, 1967.

Schneider, Bernhard. *Daten zur Geschichte der Jugendbewegung.* Bad Godesberg, 1965.

Scholder, Klaus. *Die Kirchen und das Dritte Reich, Bd. 1. Vorgeschichte und Zeit der Illusionen 1918–1934.* Frankfurt, Berlin, and Vienna, 1977.

Schönfeld, Sybil, Gräfin. *Sonderappell. 1945—Ein Mädchen berichtet.* München, 1984.

Schönstedt, Walter. *Kämpfende Jugend. Roman der arbeitenden Jugend.* 1932. Reprint, Berlin, 1971.

———. "Neuere deutsche Geschichte und protestantische Theologie." *Evangelische Theologie* 23 (1963): 510–36.

Schörken, Rolf. *Jugend 45. Politisches Denken und Lebensgeschichte.* Opladen, 1990.

———. "Singen und Marschieren. Erinnerungen an vier Jahre Jungvolk 1939–1943." *Geschichte in Wissenschaft und Unterricht* 49, no. 718 (1998): 447–61.

Schücking, Levin L. *Die Familie im Puritanismus. Studien über Familie und Literatur in England im 16., 17. und 18. Jahrhundert.* Leipzig and Berlin, 1929.

Schulte, Wilhelm. *Volk und Staat. Westfalen im Vormärz und in der Revolution 1848/49.* Münster, 1954.

Schulz, E. E. "Die Frau im Erwerbsleben Preußens." *Jugend und Beruf* 5, no. 11 (1930): 253–58.

Seraphim, Hans-Jürgen. *Das Heuerlingswesen in Nordwestdeutschland* [= Veröffentlichungen des Provinzialinstituts für westfälische Landes- und Volkskunde, ed. 1, no. 5]. Münster, 1948.

Shanahan, William O. *Der deutsche Protestantismus vor der sozialen Frage, 1815–1871.* Munich, 1962.

Simmel, Georg. *Philosophie des Geldes* [= Gesamtausgabe, vol. 6]. Frankfurt a.M., 1989.

Simmel, Monika. *Erziehung zum Weibe. Mädchenbildung im 19. Jahrhundert.* Frankfurt a.M. and New York, 1980.

Soder, Martin. *Hausarbeit und Stammtischsozialismus. Arbeiterfamilie und Alltag im Deutschen Kaiserreich.* Giessen, 1980.

Stephan, Bruno. *700 Jahre Wedding. Geschichte eines Berliner Bezirks.* Berlin, 1951.

Stachura, Peter D. "The Ideology of the Hitler Youth in the Kampfzeit." *Journal of Contemporary History* 8, no. 3 (1973): 155–67.

———. *Nazi Youth in the Weimar Republic.* Santa Barbara and Oxford, 1975.

———. "Das Dritte Reich und die Jugenderziehung. Die Rolle der Hitlerjugend 1933–1939." In Karl Dietrich Bracher, Manfred Funke, and Hans-Adolf Jacobsen, eds., *Nationalsozialistische Diktatur 1933–1945. Eine Bilanz* [= Schriftenreihe der Bundeszentrale für politische Bildung Bonn, vol. 192], 224–44. Düsseldorf, 1983.

Statistisches Amt der Stadt Berlin. *Statistisches Jahrbuch der Stadt Berlin,* vol. 34 (1920).

———. *Statistisches Jahrbuch der Stadt Berlin,* New Edition, vols. 2–15 (1928–1939), Berlin.

———. *Berlin in Zahlen: Taschenbuch der Stadt Berlin,* vols. 1–14 (1926–1945), Berlin.

Stephenson, Jill. *Women in Nazi Society.* London, 1975.

———. *The Nazi Organization of Women.* London, 1981.

———. "Modernization, Emancipation, Mobilization: Nazi Society Reconsidered." In Larry Jones and James Retallack, eds., *Elections, Mass Politics, and Political Change in Germany, 1880–1945,* 223–43. Washington, DC, 1992.

Sternheim-Peters, Eva. *Die Zeit der großen Täuschungen. Mädchenleben im Faschismus.* Bielefeld, 1987.

Stoehr, Irene. " 'Organisierte Mütterlichkeit.' Zur Politik der deutschen Frauenbewegung um 1900." In Karin Hausen, ed., *Frauen suchen ihre Geschichte. Historische Studien zum 19. und 20. Jahrhundert,* 221–49. Munich, 1983.

———. "Neue Frau und alte Bewegung. Zum Generationenkonflikt in der Frauenbewegung der Weimarer Republik." In Jutta Dahlhoff, Uschi Frey, and Ingrid Schöll, eds., *Frauenmacht in der Geschichte. Beiträge des Historikerinnentreffens 1985 zur Frauengeschichtsforschung,* 390–400. Düsseldorf, 1986.

———. "Das Jahrhundert der Mütter? Politik der Mütterlichkeit in der deutschen Frauenbewegung 1900–1950." In Meike Baader, Juliane Jacobi, and Sabine Andresen, eds., *Ellen Keys reformpädagogische Vision. Das Jahrhundert des Kindes und seine Wirkung,* 81–104. Weinheim, 2000.

Theweleit, Klaus. *Männerphantasien.* 2 vols. Frankfurt a.M., 1977–78.

Tiesmeyer, Ludwig. *Friedrich August Weihe. Eine Prophetengestalt aus dem 18. Jahrhundert. Zugleich ein Trostbüchlein in schwerer Zeit.* Gütersloh, 1921.

Timmermann, Heinz. *Geschichte und Struktur der Arbeitersportbewegung 1983–1933.* PhD diss., Marburg/Lahn, 1969.

Tornieporth, Gerda. *Studien zur Frauenbildung. Ein Beitrag zur historischen Analyse lebensweltorientierter Bildungskonzeptionen.* Weinheim and Basel, 1977.

Trepp, Anne-Charlott. *Sanfte Männlichkeit und selbstständige Weiblichkeit. Frauen und Männer im Hamburger Bürgertum zwischen 1779 und 1840.* Göttingen, 1996.

Tröger, Annemarie. "Die Frau im wesensgemäßen Einsatz." In Frauengruppe Faschismusforschung, ed., *Mutterkreuz und Arbeitsbuch. Zur Geschichte der Frauen in der Weimarer Republik und im Nationalsozialismus,* 246–72. Frankfurt a.M., 1981.

Trommler, Frank. "Mission ohne Ziel. Über den Kult der Jugend im modernen Deutschland." In Thomas Koebner, Rolf-Peter Janz, and Frank Trommler, eds., *"Mit uns zieht die neue Zeit." Der Mythos Jugend,* 14–49. Frankfurt a.M., 1985.

Tschap-Bock, Angelika. *Frauensport und Gesellschaft. Der Frauensport in seinen historischen und gegenwärtigen Formen. Eine historische und empirische Untersuchung* [= Sportwissenschaftliche Dissertationen, vol. 20]. Ahrensburg, 1983.

Twellmann-Schepp, Margrit. *Die deutsche Frauenbewegung im Spiegel repräsentativer Frauenzeitschriften 1843–1889.* Meisenheim, 1972.

Ueberhorst, Horst, ed. *Geschichte der Leibesübungen.* Vol. 1. Berlin, Munich, and Frankfurt a.M., 1972.

Usborne, Cornelie. *The Politics of the Body in Weimar Germany: Women's Reproductive Rights and Duties.* Houndsmill, Basingstroke, and Hampshire, 1992.

Verein Berliner Kaufleute und Industrieller, ed. *Berlins Aufstieg zur Weltstadt. A Memorial.* On the Occasion of its Fiftieth Birthday. With contributions from Max Osborn, Adolph Donath, and Franz M. Feldhaus. Berlin, 1929.

Vogel, Angela. *Das Pflichtjahr für Mädchen. Nationalsozialistische Arbeitseinsatzpolitik im Zeichen der Kriegswirtschaft.* Frankfurt a.M., 1997.

Wagner, Leonie. *Nationalsozialistische Frauenansichten. Vorstellungen von Weiblichkeit und Politik führender Frauen im Nationalsozialismus.* Frankfurt a.M., 1996.

Walbrodt, Luise. "Die Ehefrau im Erwerbsleben." *Jugend und Beruf* 6, no. 2 (1931): 31–32.

Walser, Martin. *Ein springender Brunnen.* Frankfurt a.M., 1998.

Watermann, Karl Friedrich. *Politischer Konservativismus und Antisemitismus in Minden- Ravensberg 1879–1914.* Hausarbeit zur ersten Staatsprüfung für das Lehramt an Gymnasien. Teil 1 und 2 (maschinenschriftl.). Münster, 1979.

Weber, Hermann. *Die Wandlung des deutschen Kommunismus. Die Stalinisierung der KPD in der Weimarer Republik.* Frankfurt a.M., 1969.

Weber, Marianne. *Ehefrau und Mutter in der Rechtsentwicklung. Eine Einführung.* Tübingen, 1907.

———. "Vom Typenwandel der studierenden Frau." In Weber, *Frauenfragen und Frauengedanken. Gesammelte Aufsätze,* 179–201. Tübingen, 1919.

Weckel, Ulrike. "A Lost Paradise of a Female Culture? Some Critical Questions Regarding the Scholarship on Late Eighteenth- and Early Nineteenth-Century German Salons." *German History* 18, no. 3 (2000): 310–36.

———. "Was kann und zu welchem Zweck dient das Efeu?" In Barbara Duden, Karen Hagemann, Regina Schulte, and Ulrike Weckel, eds., *Geschichte in Geschichten. Ein historisches Lesebuch,* 78–83. Frankfurt a M., 2003.

Weiland, Ruth. *Die Kinder der Arbeitslosen* [= Schriftenreihe des Deutschen Archivs für Jugendwohlfahrt, H. 11]. Berlin, 1933.

Weinberg, Gerhard L. *A World at Arms: A Global History of World War II.* Cambridge, 1994.

Wellerhoff, Dieter. *Der Ernstfall. Innenansichten des Krieges.* Cologne, 1997.

Wheeler, Robert F. "Organized Sport and Organized Labour: The Workers Sports Movement." *Journal of Contemporary History* 13 (1978): 191–210.

Wickert, Christl. *Unsere Erwählten. Sozialdemokratische Frauen im Deutschen Reichstag und im preußischen Landtag 1919 bis 1933.* Göttingen, 1986.

Wierling, Dorothee. "Gebrochener Aufbruch. Rosemarie Heises Jugenderfahrungen in der SBZ." In Franz-Werner Kersting, ed., *Jugend vor einer Welt in Trümmern. Erfahrungen und Verhältnisse der Jugend zwischen Hitler- und Nachkriegsdeutschland,* 213–20. Weinheim and Munich, 1998.

———. "Von der HJ zur FDJ." *Bios* 6 (1993): 107–18.

Wiese, Leopold von. *Kindheit. Erinnerung aus meinen Kadettenjahren.* Hannover, 1924.

Wild, K. "Die Bedeutung der mit öffentlichen Mitteln errichteten Neubauten für die Berliner Wohnungswirtschaft." In Jakob Schallenberger and Erwin Gutkind, eds., *Berliner Wohnbauten der letzten Jahre,* 5–10. Berlin, 1931.

Willmot, Louise. "National Socialist Youth Organizations for Girls: A Contribution to the Social and Political History of the Third Reich." PhD diss., Oxford, 1980.

Wilms, Wilhelm. *Großbauern und Kleingrundbesitz in Minden-Ravensberg* [= 27. Jahresbericht des Historischen Vereins für die Grafschaft Ravensberg zu Bielefeld]. Bielefeld, 1913.

Winkler, Dörte. *Frauenarbeit im "Dritten Reich."* Hamburg, 1977.

"Wir Schaffen." *Jahrbuch des BDM.* Munich, 1938.

Wisotzky, Klaus. *Das Schriftgut der NSDAP, ihrer Gliederungen und angeschlossenen Verbände. In der Überlieferung staatlicher Behörden im Bereich des heutigen Landes Nordrhein-Westfalen, Part 1–3.* Düsseldorf, 1981.

Wobbe, Theresa. *Nach Osten. Verdeckte Spuren nationalsozialistischer Verbrechen.* Frankfurt a.M., 1992.

Wohnbauten der gemeinnützigen Baugenossenschaft Steglitz. Archiv für Bauten und Entwürfe. *Sonderheft* 8 (1928).

Wolbert, Barbara. "Jugendweihe nach der Wende. Form und Transformation einer sozialistischen Initiationszeremonie." *Zeitschrift für Volkskunde* 94, no. 2 (1998): 195–207.

Wolf, Christa. *Kindheitsmuster.* Darmstadt and Neuwied, 1977.

Wortmann, Michael. *Baldur von Schirach, Hitlers Jugendführer.* Cologne, 1982.

Wunderer, Hartmann. "Materialien zur Soziologie der Mitgliedschaft und Wählerschaft der KPD zur Zeit der Weimarer Republik." *Gesellschaft. Beiträge zur Marxschen Theorie,* 5:257–81. Frankfurt a.M., 1975.

———. "Freidenkertum und Arbeiterbewegung. Ein Überblick." *Internationale wissenschaftliche Korrespondenz zur Geschichte der deutschen Arbeiterbewegung* 16, no. 1 (1980): 1–33.

Wysocki, Gisela von. "Der Aufbruch der Frauen: Verordnete Träume, Bubikopf und 'sachliches Leben.' Ein aktueller Streifzug durch Scherl's Magazin, Jahrgang 1925, Berlin." In Dieter Prokop, ed., *Massenkommunikationsforschung, 3 (Produktionsanalysen):* 295–305. Frankfurt a.M., 1977.

Index

Abitur (high school diploma), 52, 127
Ack-ack girls, 6
Alienation: between fathers and children, caused by alcohol, 181n. 189; of women from own gender, 101; of women from parental authority, caused by National Socialist education, 59; of women from society, 55, 73; of youth from society, 50
Apprenticeship: as form of youth in Middle Ages, 49; of girls, 127, 128; as opportunity to resign from league, 249; and reduction of free time, 83–84, 146–47, 203
Arbeiter-Turn- und Sportbund (Workers' League for Gymnastics and Sports), 67
Arbeitsgemeinschaften (organization of National Socialist female students), 38
Arch-conservative attitude, in Minden, 133
Aßmann, Martha (1895–1941), 28
Axmann, Artur (1913–96), 1n. 2, 60n. 56, 162n. 20, 213–16, 218

Bauer, Anna, 27
Baumann, Hans (1914–88), 92n. 121, 154
BDM, "Faith and Beauty" section of: age bracket of membership, 2; creation of as concession to women's organization, 58; establishment of, 2, 4, 38, 57, 151–52; leadership of, 26; rhythmic gymnastics in, 23, 60n. 55, 153; study groups of, 24, 25, 82, 250
BDM Haushaltsschulen (BDM schools for home economics), 4
Becker, Howard (1899–1960), 2n. 5
Bernstein, Eduard (1850–1932), 166, 167n. 41, 168n. 45
Bible Circles (Bibelkreise), 131n. 100, 132
Blüher, Hans (1888–1955), 197

Bubenkopf (hairstyle), 195

Campe, Johann Heinrich (1746–1818), 53, 64
Ceremony of Commitment for Youth (Verpflichtung der Jugend), 23
Children's play, 96n. 125
Choir: as BDM activity, 139, 148–50, 236, 250; participation in acceptable to conservative families, 133
Cinema: as escapism, 221; free passes for, 95n. 124; as outlet for frustration, 210; in Wedding, 204–6
Coeducation, 197, 227
Communist Party: proportion of female members and voters in, 185; in Wedding, 168–69, 183, 218–19, 245
Community of peers, girls' search for, 93
Comrade/comradeship: Communist conception of female as "reliable comrade," 193; "female comrade" image, influence on girls, 47; ideal of comradeship between sexes, 55, 196–99
Confessional Church, 134, 135, 136
Confirmation, religious, 187–88
Consciousness of youth among girls, 54–55
Cords marking the rank of a leader, 80

DAF (National Socialist Labor Organization), 33
Dance: as DFO activity, 56; as pastime for young female workers, 209–11. See also Folk dancing
Decomposition of Hitler Youth after 1936, 38, 39
Deutscher Mädel Ring, 28
Deutsches Jungvolk (German Young Folk), 1, 22, 35, 36, 255

Relationship of League of German Girls to
Hitler Youth, 30
Religion: in Minden, 109–12, 134–36; in
Wedding, 186–88, 226–27, 228n. 211,
229, 231
Resignation from the league, 241–42
Rhythmic gymnastics, 23, 60n. 55, 153, 227
Richardson, Samuel (1689–1761), 118
Rise in league membership after 1933,
31–33
Rivalry between the sexes, 9, 101
Rosegger, Peter (1843–1918), 84
Rosenberg, Alfred (1893–1946), 134
Roten Frauen- und Mädchenbund (RFMB;
Alliance of Red Women and Girls), 189
Rot Front (red front), 221, 223
Rotfrontkämpferbund (Red Front Fighters'
League), 221, 223
Rüdiger, Jutta (1910–2001), 2n. 4, 24n. 11,
38, 43, 44n. 7, 60, 60n. 57, 62, 73n. 106,
74, 77n. 110, 78n. 111, 148n. 127
Rummel (fairgrounds), 208, 213
Rust, Berhard (1883–1945), 228

Sammelschulen (collective schools), 226
Schirach, Baldur von (1907–74), 1, 26, 29,
30, 32n. 30, 36, 38, 38n. 58, 69, 73, 74,
213n. 177
Scholtz-Klink, Gertrud (1902–99), 38
"Second sex" status of women, 93
Service in the league, 94
Shadow work of women, 123–24
Singing: as activity after 1945, 154; of
"Horst Wessel Song," 229–30; as league
activity, 23, 48, 60, 89, 91, 144, 145, 236,
237, 248; as part of free play, 97
Singing Society Harmony, 131
Sisterhoods, 27, 28, 44, 45
Sonderausbildungen (special courses), 23
Sondereinheiten (special units), 23
Sonderscharen (special groups of the
BDM), 38
SPD: and collective schools, 228; and
Jugendweihe, 160n. 12; meetings in
Minden, July–September 1930, 130n.
93; in Wedding, 167–68, 183; and
women, 185–86. *See also* Red Falcons
Sportwartinnen (sports supervisors), 60n.
57, 86
State youth, 11, 40, 73, 143, 150, 151, 152,
153

State Youth Day (Staatsjugendtag), 33, 86,
139–40
Stoecker, Adolf (1835–1909), 106, 110, 112,
167–68, 186n. 102
Storm, Theodor (1817–88), 84
Street, as locale for free play, 97–99
Subjugation, of children to parental authority, 126; Luther's views on, 116–17
Subjugation, of women: in early Protestant
marriage, 119–20; in marriage, Luther's
views on, 118–19; in sexist society, 73

Teacher(s): and collective schools, 226–29;
hostility of toward Jewish student,
17–18; as Rehbergers, 167n. 40; and
requirement to teach National Socialism
during Saturday classes, 33–34; role in
old-style youth organizations, 73; role in
organizing and controlling Hitler Youth
membership, 138–41; role in pressuring
young people to join Hitler Youth,
34–35, 225, 234–35, 240; and supervision of children in evacuation camps,
39n. 67
Thälmann, Ernst (1886–1944), 189n. 107
Theater, 206–8; amateur, 139, 150, 250;
open air, 95
Töchterschule, 52
Type of girl/type of woman: chosen for
league leadership, 77; promoted by
National Socialism, 62–63

Ulbricht, Walter (1893–1973), 190
Uniform, League of German Girls, 21, 22,
57, 63, 93, 144, 157, 223, 224; for leaders, 26, 80; before 1933, 4, 57
Uniform, worn by teachers, 33–34, 140
Uniform, youth groups, 1920s and early
1930s, 198n. 134
USPD (Independent Social Democrats),
168

Vaterländisches Turnen (patriotic gymnastics, German gymnastics), 61, 64, 67,
71
Verein für das Deutschtum im Ausland
(VDA), 220n. 202, 221, 230
Vieth, Gerhard Ulrich Anton (1763–1836),
64
Vocational training, and independence,
128